Niger Delta Rivalry

IBADAN HISTORY SERIES
General Editor K. O. Dike, Ph.D.

Published by Northwestern University Press

CHRISTIAN MISSIONS IN NIGERIA 1841–1891
By J. F. A. Ajayi
Professor of History, University of Ibadan

THE ZULU AFTERMATH
by J. D. Omer-Cooper

Professor of History, University of Zambia

Published by Humanities Press

THE MISSIONARY IMPACT ON MODERN NIGERIA 1842–1914
by E. A. Ayandele
Department of History, University of Ibadan

BRITAIN AND THE CONGO QUESTION
by S. J. S. Cookey
Department of History, The University, Nsukka

THE SOKOTO CALIPHATE
by Murray Last
Research Fellow, Ahmadu Bello University, Zaria

BENIN AND THE EUROPEANS 1485–1897
by A. F. C. Ryder
Professor of History, University of Ibadan

In preparation: to be published by Humanities Press

POWER AND DIPLOMACY IN NORTHERN NIGERIA 1800–1906
The Sokoto Caliphate and its Enemies
by R. A. Adeleye
Department of History, University of Ibadan

Other titles will follow

IBADAN HISTORY SERIES

Niger Delta Rivalry

Itsẹkiri – Urhobo Relations and the
European Presence 1884–1936

Obaro Ikimẹ Ph.D.
Department of History, University of Ibadan

Humanities Press

First published
in the United States of America 1969
by HUMANITIES PRESS INC.
303 Park Avenue South
New York, N.Y. 10010

Library of Congress Catalog Card No. 68–54522

Printed in Great Britain

Contents

missionary activities in Itsękiriland – Effect of European contact on the Itsękiri – The beginnings of Itsękiri superiority complex – Itsękiri-Urhobo commerce in the nineteenth century – Palm oil replaces slaves as export commodity – Consequences for Itsękiri-Urhobo relations – The internal slave trade in the nineteenth century – Itsękiri-Urhobo relations on the eve of the establishment of British rule.

The age and antecedents of Nana – Itsękiri trade and politics in the age of Olomu, Nana's father – Olomu's rise as a great trader – His commercial organization and spheres of activity in Urhoboland – Friendships and marriage alliances – General relations between Olomu and the Urhobo.

The Governor of the River – His position in the 1850s – European concept of the office – and the Itsękiri concept – The Governor and the question of trade debts – Olomu's last days – his appointment as Governor in 1879 – his death in 1883.

Nana succeeds his father – Brief note on Nana's early days – War against Eku and Abraka – its causes and significance – Nana as Governor of the River (1884) – Difficulties of the office in 1884 – The Itsękiri protection treaty of 1884 – its importance. Nana's inheritance – Nana's trade organization in Urhoboland – Nana's commercial activities and the Urhobo reaction to his wealth and power. Nana and the British – Hewett uses Nana to further British imperial aims – Nana stops trade on account of low prices in 1886 – Reaction of British consul – Dilemma of Governor's position – Royal Niger Company – Treaties and commercial activities along the Forcados River – Effect on Itsękiri trade – Nana's reaction – Macdonald's mission of 1889 – His report a blow to Nana's prestige – British policy towards Itsękiriland – The establishment of the Niger Coast Protectorate – Its implications for Nana – Macdonald's visit to Itsękiriland in 1891 – His views on Nana – The years of commercial unrest, 1891–3 – The question of Nana's monopoly – Nana's relations with the British deteriorate, 1892–4. Prelude to war – Ralph Moor's attitude to Nana – The Urhobo mere pawns in pre-war diplomacy – The Ebrohimi Expedition of 1894 – Pretexts and causes – Nana's fall – his trial and exile – his return and death – Effect of Nana's régime on Itsękiri-Urhobo relations.

By-products of reorganization and their effect on Itsẹkiri-Urhobo relations – Itsẹkiri-Urhobo relations at the end of the period.

Acknowledgements

The publishers are grateful to the following for permission to reproduce photographs:

Shell Photographic Service for plates facing page 42; Ministry of Information, Ibadan, for plates facing pages 250 and 251. Plates 3b and 4b are from photographs owned by the author. Plates 2, 3a and 4a are from *Benin, Lagos and the Surrounding Country, West Africa* by J. Pinnock. We have been unable to discover the publishers of this book and apologise for any possible infringement of copyright.

List of Abbreviations

A.D.O.   Assistant District Officer
Cal. Prof.   Calabar Province
C.M.S.   Church Missionary Society
C.S.O.   Chief Secretary's Office (Nigeria)
C.O.   Colonial Office (British)
D.C.   District Commissioner
D.O.   District Officer
F.O.   Foreign Office (British)
J.H.S.N.   Journal of the Historical Society of Nigeria
N.C.P.   Niger Coast Protectorate
R.N.C.   Royal Niger Company
W.A.I.S.E.R.   West African Institute of Social and Economic Research
War. Prof.   Warri Province

Ibadan History Series
General Editor's Introduction

The 'Ibadan History Series' grew out of the efforts of some members of the Department of History, Ibadan University, Nigeria, to evolve a balanced and scholarly study of the history of African peoples South of the Sahara. In the years before the Second World War, the study of African history was retarded, and to some extent vitiated, by the assumption of many scholars that lack of written records in some areas of Africa meant also the absence of history. Documentary evidence had become so overwhelmingly important for the European scholar that he tended to equate written documents with history, and to take the absence of documents to mean the absence of events worthy of historical study. As a result in the nineteenth century, when Europe occupied Africa, her scholars did not attempt to understand or to build on the historical traditions in existence there; they sought instead to challenge and to supplant them. The history of European traders, missionaries, explorers, conquerors and rulers constituted, in their view, the sum total of African history.

Fortunately for the historian of today, African historical consciousness remained alive throughout the period of colonial rule: that tradition was too much a part of the African way of life to succumb to the attacks of the European scholar. Even in the heyday of white supremacy some educated Africans of the period were sufficiently dominated by their past to feel impelled to commit to writing the laws, customs, proverbs, sayings and historical traditions of their own communities. Notable among these may be mentioned James Africanus Horton of Sierra Leone, Reindorf and Sarbah of Ghana, Otomba Payne and Samuel Johnson of Nigeria, Apolo Kagwa of Uganda, to name but a few. The published works they left behind have become important sources of African history today; but they were swimming against the current of their time and made little impression on contemporaries. Historians continued to write as if Africans were not active participants in the great events that shaped their continent.

The decided change towards a new African historiography came with the movement towards independence. African nationalists rejected the European appraisal of their past. They demanded a new orientation and improved educational facilities to effect this re-appraisal. With the establishment of new universities in Africa, it was inevitable that the teaching of history and the training of African historians would receive a new impetus. For obvious reasons the changeover was slow in coming. Even in the new universities the old theories for a time prevailed: besides European history, there were courses only on 'European activities in Africa' at the under-graduate level, and at the post-graduate level research was generally on British and French policy towards their African territories.

By the late 1940s, however, African research students were insisting that African history must be the history of Africans, not of Europeans *per se* in Africa; that local records and historical traditions must be used to supplement European metropolitan archives; in short, that oral tradition must be accepted as valid material for historical reconstruction. No doubt the validity of non-written sources for historical research had been pointed out before, but it was new for university departments of history to accept it, especially in relation to African oral tradition. Even then not everyone was happy about it. Anthropologists replied cautiously that oral tradition, even when seemingly factual, was not history and could only be interpreted in terms of its functions in society and within the particular culture. But this did not destroy its validity as material for history; it only argued for a return to the link between history and sociology advocated in the fourteenth century by the famous Tunisian historian, Ibn Khaldun.

Even in studies of European impact on African societies and cultures, where European archival material still remains our major source, this source should be checked and supplemented by oral tradition, material artefacts and other sources of history in Africa. The achievement of the present position in the study of African history has been the result of individual and co-operative efforts of many scholars in different parts of the world, but I think it is fair to say that the Universities in Africa, and Ibadan in particular, have played and are playing their part in this pioneering work.

Enugu   K. ONWUKA DIKE
June 1967

Preface

The phenomenon of ethnic loyalty resulting in group conflict is of particular relevance to Nigerian history at the time of writing. Although the subjects of 'tribalism' and inter-group conflicts are freely discussed in academic and other circles, it is a fact that no one has attempted a historical study of the factors which have been operative in creating tension between ethnic groups. The historian may not furnish all the explanations, but the usefulness of a historical analysis of the factors which have produced the tensions with which we are so painfully familiar can hardly be debated. Thus the historian has a very real and urgent role to play in seeking an answer to some of our present problems through a deeper understanding of the factors which have determined the actions and reactions of the various ethnic groups in the country.

This work is concerned with a study of the relations between two peoples of the Delta Province, Midwestern state of Nigeria. These peoples are the Itsẹkiri, fisher-folks and traders, who occupy the coastal belt, and the Urhobo, a hinterland, agricultural people. The respective geographical location of these peoples has been one of the most important determinants of the relationship between them. It was this which dictated their varying occupations and so determined the nature of their commercial and other relations. Geographical location not only determined the nature of Urhobo-Itsẹkiri relations during the period covered by this study, it was also of the most crucial consequence for the relations of each of these groups with Europeans operating in the Western delta of the Niger. The theme of coast versus hinterland is therefore a major one in this work. This theme may well serve to deepen our knowledge of inter-group relations elsewhere in the Federation of Nigeria.

The other major factor which determined Itsẹkiri-Urhobo relations was the imposition of British colonial rule as from 1884. The reactions of these two peoples to this event differed. So also did British attitudes to them. The Itsẹkiri at the coast were naturally the first to come in contact with the British imperial power. After a period of initial resistance, the climax of which was a British military and naval onslaught on Nana Olomu, Itsẹkiriland's un-crowned head, the Itsẹkiri resigned themselves to their fate and soon became trusted friends of the British. By the time, therefore, that the British were seeking to penetrate the Urhobo hinterland, they found in the Itsẹkiri useful allies and tools. The services rendered to the British by the Itsẹkiri during this period of pene-tration decided the British attitude to them during most of the colonial period. The Urhobo for their part not only resented the role played by the Itsẹkiri during the period of 'pacification' but also the favoured position they occupied in the political and judicial institutions introduced by the British. British policy thus became instrumental in deciding Itsẹkiri-Urhobo relations. Indeed that tension between the Itsẹkiri and the Urhobo which has been a noticeable feature of contemporary Nigerian politics has its roots in the colonial period. As the colonial experience is one common to the entire Federation of Nigeria, it will be instructive to discover how this experience has affected relations between other groups in the country. Hence although the present work is essentially a case study, it is hoped that it may serve to inspire work along similar lines which should ultimately be of national significance.

As has already been stated, the colonial experience has been decisive in the development of Itsẹkiri-Urhobo relations. In order that the full impact of British rule on the respective institutions and general pattern of life of the Itsẹkiri and Urhobo may be fully appreciated, the introductory chapter deals with the social and political institutions of these people in the pre-colonial period. There can be no questioning the usefulness of such a survey for a work of this nature. In order, however, to carry through such a survey, a great deal of on-the-spot investigation was necessary. Indeed throughout this work not only has available documentary material been supplemented by oral evidence, but also such docu-mentary material has often been re-assessed and re-interpreted in the light of evidence obtained through field work.

In connexion with my field work I would like to place on record my gratitude to the many chiefs, elders and educated young men who furnished me with much needed information. It will be impossible for me to mention names without producing an extremely long list. Suffice it to say that without the co-operation of my many informants, some of whose names appear in the footnotes, this work would never have been produced in its present form. In this same connexion I wish to thank particularly Mr. & Mrs. G. E. Umukoro, Mr. & Mrs. D. A. Ẹdẹmatie, Mr. & Mrs. E. A. O. Awala, Mr. & Mrs. S. T. Bajah, Mr. & Mrs. S. Egubẹ and Mr. & Mrs. A. Ziregbe for their kindness and hospitality towards me on many an occasion. I am also grateful to my friends Messrs Miller Uloho, William Oshevire, and Johnson Ekpẹrẹ who accompanied me even in the most inclement of weathers on some of my fact-finding tours.

I thank the University of Ibadan for the grant of a research scholarship, and Professor H. F. C. Smith, former Acting Head of the Department of History at the University, for stimulating my interest in historical research. I thank the following people for their help during the preparation of the thesis out of which this book has grown:— Professor J. F. A. Ajayi, Professor A. F. C. Ryder, Dr. (now Professor) A. B. Aderibigbe, Mr. J. D. Omer-Cooper, Dr. P. C. Lloyd and Dr. T. N. Tamunọ, all then of the University of Ibadan, and Dr. I. A. Akinjọgbin of the Department of History, University of Ifẹ. I wish also to record my gratitude to Dr. B. J. Dudley, Department of Political Science, University of Ibadan, for his advice with regard to the introductory chapter of this work; to my friend and colleague, Dr. R. A. Adelẹyẹ, for his constant help and encouragement; and to Mr. L. A. Banjọ, Department of English, University of Ibadan, who kindly read through the entire manuscript and made useful suggestions with regard to style and presentation.

The recorded material for this work was collected largely from the Nigerian National Archives, Ibadan, and the Public Record Office, London. I thank the staff of both institutions for their help and co-operation. I am also grateful to the Librarian and staff of the Commonwealth Society Library, London, for meeting my many demands. I thank the authorities at Salisbury Square, London, for permission to consult the C.M.S. Archives and the firm of Messrs. John Holt & Co Ltd., for making their papers available to me.

While I was working in London Mr. D. H. Jones, School of Oriental and African studies, University of London, looked after my work. I am grateful to him for his concern over the progress of my work, and for his many useful suggestions. I wish to put on record my special gratitude to Rev. & Mrs. Bernard Adeney and Rev. & Mrs. Tony Dines, vicar and curate respectively of Christ Church, Highbury, London, for all they did to sustain my spirits when my research notes were stolen during a journey from Liverpool to London. In this connexion I wish also to thank the parishioners of Highbury for their Christian fellowship during that period; my many friends in London and back home in Nigeria for their visits and letters of sympathy; and my wife who in the most trying period of my research life taught me the meaning of true love and fellowship.

I owe inexpressible thanks to my brother, Isaac, without whose love and concern I would never have received any education and who has always taken the keenest interest in my progress and general welfare.

Department of History,   OBARO IKIM
University of Ibadan.
March, 1968.

Dedication

This book has grown out of my thesis for the degree of Doctor of Philosophy of the University of Ibadan. In preparing that thesis I had to contend with the usual problems of the research worker. But there were many ways in which I had to contend against peculiar problems posed quite often by man's inhumanity to man. There were thus periods of mental and physical torture when the end of the road appeared unattainable. That the goal in view was ultimately attained was due to one whose rare love, devotion and solicitude for my success sustained me through all my trials. I can never repay in sufficient measure that love, that devotion, that solicitude. It is, however, as a little token of my deep gratitude that I dedicate this book to my wife, Hannah.

Chapter 1
Introduction:
Indigenous Antecedents

The Itsẹkiri and the Urhobo are two neighbouring peoples who inhabit part of the Delta Province of Nigeria, the former along the coast and the latter to the hinterland. From about the thirties until the early sixties of the present century, the relations between these two peoples were remarkably uneasy—perhaps more so than between any two other peoples similarly placed anywhere else in the federation of Nigeria. Yet these two peoples had for a long time been socially interrelated and commercially interdependent, and remain very much so even now. This work attempts a historical examination of the factors which determined the relations between these two peoples in the period immediately before and after the establishment of British rule over both the Itsẹkiri and Urhobo peoples.

The Urhobo together with the related Isoko people inhabit the area lying (roughly) between longitude 5° 30' and 6° 25' East, and latitudes 6° and 5° 15' North in the midwestern state of Nigeria.[1] This area is bounded on the north by the River Ethiope (except at the NW. corner where it embraces a strip of land on the right bank of the river); on the south by the Western Ijọ Division; on the east by the 'Aboh' Division; and on the west by the Warri

---

[1] In the period covered by this work, 'Urhobo' was officially used to refer to both the Urhobo-speaking and the Isoko-speaking people of Delta Province. Both groups have similar cultures and a similar language though the Isoko regard themselves as a separate people. Until 1964 when the Isoko were constituted into a separate political division they used to be referred to as 'Eastern Urhobo'. This work is concerned mainly with Itsẹkiri relations with the Urhobo-speaking people. But as the historical development of the Isoko-speaking group has been closely connected with that of their Urhobo-speaking 'brothers' I bring the former into this work whenever I see fit. For convenience I sometimes use the terms 'Urhobo country' or 'Urhoboland' to designate all the area inhabited by both groups. Nothing done here, however, is calculated to prejudice the Isoko claim to be regarded as a distinct people from the Urhobo.

Division. Their neighbours are thus the Bini to the north, the Ịọ to the south, the Aboh to the east and the Itsẹkiri to the west. At this point it is necessary to stress the significance of the geographical location of the Urhobo country. Hemmed in by four other peoples, the Urhobo could not get to the Niger nor the coast—the centres of early European commercial and other activities—without traversing territory which strictly belonged to one or other of their neighbours. The few settlements that had access to the Niger were too small to be of any account during the eighteenth and nineteenth centuries, when European activities were, wittingly or otherwise, shaping the future roles which the various peoples of this section of the Delta were to play. This fact is to be borne in mind when examining the attitude of the Urhobo to their neighbours.

The Urhobo Division falls within the Evergreen Forest belt of Southern Nigeria, the vegetation being dominated by the oil palm tree, the exploitation of which constitutes a major occupation among the people. Vast areas of the Isoko sector are flooded during the rainy season when the floods of the Niger, overflowing into the Ase River, inundate the surrounding area to form the Bethel and Owe swamps. In fact, during the rains, only the area between these two swamps (from Olomoro to Ozọrọ via Oleh) escapes flooding. The rest of the Urhobo Division can be further divided into two zones—north and south. The southern zone, which consists mainly of the territories of the Ewu, Evwreni and Uwherum clans,[1] is flooded during the wet season when the Ewu River overflows its bank both as a result of rains and the Niger floods which flow into it through the Forcads River and surrounding creeks. The northern zone, consisting of the majority of the Urhobo speaking clans, is on comparatively high land and does not suffer from severe flooding.

A look at the map of the area reveals a great number of creeks and rivers. The most important of these are the Ase River in the Isoko section; the Ethiope River which flows past Sapẹlẹ and through parts of Abraka clan; the Warri River which waters land belonging to the Ughiẹnvwe, Agbarho, Agbọn and Abraka clans; a tributary of the Forcados known as the Okpare creek which at the town of Okpare divides into two—the Kakpamrẹ Creek and the Kiagbodo River,

---

1 See map facing p. 10.

2

this latter being the river which flows through Ughelli and waters part of the Isoko clans of Owe and Emevọ.[1] It will thus appear that not only is Urhoboland well supplied with water systems, but that it has always been very accessible from the coast through the streams which flow into its territory from the Forcados and the Ase, the two main branches of the Niger in this area. Such a conclusion about accessibility, however, requires modification. In the first place, it is necessary to point out that some of the creeks which are today big and passable were, within living memory, small and shallow creeks which could scarcely take a flat-bottomed canoe. At Igun and Okpara, for example, it was said that the river (part of the Warri River) which flows through these places was, as late as the closing decades of the last century, a very narrow fordable creek. The story is told that when Olomu, father of the famous Nana, desired to trade to that area he had to set people to work to dredge and widen the creek in that part so that his canoes could get as far as Igun.[2] Perhaps other rivers and creeks (or parts of them) were similarly narrow and shallow. Secondly, the accounts of early travellers in this area indicate that the latter had no direct knowledge of the Urhobo country.[3] The rivers and creeks which abound in Urhobo country, while they served, and still serve, a useful purpose as a means of communication between the clans and between some of these and the neighbouring peoples, did not necessarily serve as a means of bringing Urhoboland into the highways of foreign travellers and traders. Even in the purely Nigerian context, Urhoboland was, for a long time, a backwoods area. It would appear that at no time, till the very recent British era, did outsiders penetrate into the heart of Urhoboland. The Ijọ and the Itsẹkiri, both renowned 'water men', scarcely penetrated beyond the peripheral

---

1 Details of the geography of the Urhobo country are given by J. W. Hubbard: *The Sobo of the Niger Delta*, Zaria, c. 1952, chapter 4, pp. 57–68.
2 Interviews with the *Okaroro* of Igun, AKODO OGHOGHOVWE (aged c. 98 years) on 16th Sept., 1963, and with MR. ORAKA at Okpara Waterside on the same day.
3 Pacheco Pereira who visited the Forcados River area at the close of the fifteenth century had little more to say of the Urhobo than 'farther in the interior is another country called Subou'. See Duarte Pacheco Pereira: *Esmeraldo De Situ Orbis* (c. 1505)—H. T. Kimble's translation, London 1937, p. 129.

areas of Urhoboland before the coming of the British. Even when the British arrived and began signing treaties with the people, it is significant that for the first few years they treated only with the towns along the Ethiope and Warri Rivers. The greater part of Urhobo country remained largely unknown and remote till the opening decade of this century. Even today the Urhobo must be among the least known of Nigerian peoples. Their geographical location and the extent of their country are little known to most Nigerians.

The remoteness and isolation noted above have left their effects on the Urhobo. As 'civilization' in Nigeria tended (until recently) to be measured in terms of contact with Europeans, the Urhobo country, because of its comparatively late contact with Europeans has been regarded as 'uncivilized'. In contrast were the four neighbours of the Urhobo who, because of their geographical advantages, came into contact with Europeans and the other Nigerian peoples much earlier than did the Urhobo. As it was in the commercial interest of these neighbours not to encourage European penetration of Urhoboland, and as the Europeans on their part were not really eager to attempt such penetration until after the establishment of British rule, knowledge of Urhoboland remained extremely scanty until very recent years.

Even now such knowledge as there is, is far from satisfactory. There can be no doubt that inadequate knowledge of the Urhobo people and their country was partly responsible for the superficial, often uncomplimentary, observations of European writers. For instance Major Leonard, an administrative officer of about ten years standing in the Niger Coast Protectorate, in his work on the 'tribes' of the Lower Niger described the Urhobo as 'shy and timid treacherous and rude'.[1] It is not only about the character of the people that mistakes have been made. There was also the tendency to speak of the Urhobo as a people confined to a few settlements along the Ethiope or Warri River. Thus Gallwey, the first British vice-consul at Warri and the pioneer of British penetration of Urhoboland referred to the Urhobo as inhabiting 'the left bank of the Ethiope River'. Mockler-Ferryman, who served as secretary to Major Claude Macdonald when the latter was appointed special

[1] A. G. Leonard: *The Lower Niger and Its Tribes*, London 1906, pp. 18–19.

commissioner to the Oil Rivers in 1889, was even more specific. The Urhobo, he wrote, 'are not a large tribe but occupy several villages' along the banks of the Warri River.[1] Over the years therefore the impression has been given of the Urhobo as being a small, disunited people, with no political organization to speak of, and the providential victims of the slave-raiding escapades of the neighbouring peoples. Yet the Urhobo occupy some 2,000 square miles of land, with a population (in 1952) of some 436,000[2] at a modest estimate, and possessing complex social and political systems.

The nature of the land occupied by the Urhobo is such that although agriculture is a common occupation, it is more intensive in certain areas than in others, while there is a variation in the other occupational pursuits of the people. Farming is more intensively carried on in those areas where floods are not a serious threat. Yam, plantain, cassava, corn, pepper and banana are among the main food crops. In the Ẹrohwa, Umẹ, Igbide and parts of Uzere, Aviara, Ewu and Uwherun clans, fishing is a major seasonal occupation. In fact it will be found that the people of these clans are nearly as competent fishermen as are the Ijọ and Itsẹkiri. The Ẹrohwa also engage in canoe-building. This diversity of occupational pursuits is interesting, as it indicates that mutual inter-dependence was a basic factor in the economic and social relations of the Urhobo clans. Thus the fisherfolk of Igbide attended the Oleh market and there exchanged their fish and other local products for yams, 'starch', 'garri'[3] and other products from the farms of the Oleh, Olomoro and Ozọrọ people, who occupy most of the higher land in the Isoko area. It was this inter-clan and inter-village trading that brought the people together and gave them some awareness of their common problems and needs.

---

1 See H. L. Gallwey: 'Journeys in the Benin country, West Africa', *Geographical Journal*, Vol. I, 1893, p. 127 and A. F. Mockler-Ferryman: *Up the Niger*, London 1892, p. 250.
2 The figure is from the 1952 census Bulletin. The Itsẹkiri were given out to be 33,000. This figure actually represents an undercount which resulted from the fact that the Itsẹkiri were counted as a separate people only in Delta and Benin Provinces, whereas considerable numbers are to be found in most of the large towns in southern Nigeria.
3 'Starch' and 'garri' are two products of the cassava plant and constitute part of the staple food of the Urhobo and Isoko people.

The Urhobo are, however, better known as producers of palm oil and kernels. It is not known exactly at what date the Urhobo first began to engage in this industry, but it is highly probable that the oil which was being exported from the Forcados River area in the sixteenth century was produced by the Urhobo.[1] What the people themselves say is that their forefathers had been producing palm oil for a long time—long before it became the major export product of the nineteenth century. In fact, in certain clans, oil stored in earthenware pots was used for paying bride-wealth. It would appear that in the days before palm oil became a major European demand, most of the oil produced was mainly for local consumption and sale to surrounding peoples. Most of the kernels were destroyed though some were used for the preparation of *ori*, a kind of local pomade. Both before and after the development of European commerce in this commodity, and perhaps until the early thirties, the palm oil industry was to the Urhobo a source of revenue for providing what used to be regarded in those days as luxuries rather than necessities of life. The nature and relative isolation of their land had compelled the Urhobo to rely on their farms and on the creeks and rivers for their everyday requirements. Hence, though bad markets for palm produce at home and abroad could affect their lives in so far as less 'money' would be available for luxuries, such a contingency could never lead to starvation.

Most of the Urhobo people trace their origin back to Benin. The clans which constitute the Urhobo and Isoko Divisions in fact fall into three migratory groups. There are those which trace their migration to their present location directly from Benin; others say that they moved to their present site from what is now Ijoland; and a third group, the latest arrivals, claim Ibo origin. However, some of the clans in the last two categories have vague memories of an even earlier migration from Benin to Ijo or Iboland. Hence the general statement that most of the Urhobo clans claim Benin origin.

Among the clans which claim to have migrated from Benin are Iyede, Uzere, Owe, Emevo, Ozoro, Aviara, Abraka, Olomu

---

1 Over 200 gallons of palm oil were bought by Portuguese in a voyage to the Forcados River area in 1522. See A. F. C. Ryder: 'An Early Portuguese Trading Voyage to the Forcados River', *J.H.S.N.*, Vol. I, No. 4, Dec. 1959, pp. 307–15.

(though here there was a mixture with people of Ibo origin) Okpẹ and Agbọn. Although all these clans claim to have come from Benin, the traditions of their migrations are different and, with the exception of the Iyede, Owe and Emevọ clans, little related. The traditions of origin as remembered today are rather blurred and incoherent. Very often a claim of Benin origin having been made, very few details are forthcoming to fill up the time between the beginning and the end of the migration.

According to one of these traditions, the Abraka clan was founded by a certain Avbẹka.[1] Avbẹka was a son of an Ọba of Benin whose birth it had been necessary to keep secret in order to save his life, because the then Ọba, his father, had given instructions that all male children born to him should be killed so that there would be no obvious heir to the throne who could become the centre of palace plots. Apparently the Ọba, whose name is not now remembered, was forced after some time to heed the constant appeal of his councillors to the effect that he put an end to this cruel practice. Later a son was born to him and was duly proclaimed heir to the throne. On the death of the Ọba, however, Avbẹka put forward his claim but was rejected as heir, while his younger half-brother, whose birth had been publicly announced, was enthroned as Ọba. Avbẹka for his part refused to pay the customary tribute to the new Ọba. As this was tantamount to an act of rebellion, the Ọba raised troops against Avbẹka who was thus forced to flee Benin. It was this flight from the army of the Benin ruler which eventually took Avbẹka and his followers to Otọ-orhoabraka, the traditional headquarters of the Abraka clan today. The last encounter with the Benin army is reputed to have taken place by a river which is really a branch of the Ethiope but which the Abraka people call 'Adakaji'.[2] From Otọ-orhoabraka the clan spread into the various settlements which belong to it today.

Of the Isoko clans, Iyede is regarded as being one of the oldest. The actual cause of the migration is not now well remembered, but is generally attributed to some dissatisfaction arising from maladministration by an Ọba of Benin. Among those who led the migration

---

1 The name 'Abraka' by which the clan is now known is a corruption of the name of the founder, Avbẹka.
2 Meaning—'Benin was stopped here'.

7

was one Iyede who gave his name to the clan. The Iyede people claim that they passed through the present sites of Olomoro and Oleh and that these people had not arrived on the scene at the time of their own migration. The traditions of the Owe and Emevọ clans connect them with Iyede, though these same traditions emphasize that there was no blood relationship between Iyede and the founders of Owe and Emevọ. They claim that when the founders of Owe and Emevọ clans left Benin for various reasons and at different times, they first settled at Iyede and lived with those people for a long time before scarcity of land and increasing population forced them to move out to their respective present day locations.

Another important clan of Benin origin is the Uzere clan. The founder of this clan was one Uze,[1] who was forced to leave Benin because he was accused of having committed adultery with one of the Ọba's wives. Hubbard suggests that Uze must have known of an earlier movement towards Onitsha and decided to follow the same route.[2] He first settled at Isele-Uku, now in the Asaba Division. Apparently, Eni, Uze's god and protecting spirit, accompanied him and as Eni was a water god, Uze had to find a waterside settlement. Accordingly, he sought permission from the Ẹrohwa,[3] who were already settled in their present site, to settle along the Ẹrohwa creek, but his request was not granted. Later, however, he was allowed to settle at Erukẹ on the Ase River, a piece of land which at that time would appear to have belonged to the Ẹrohwa people, since it was they who granted Uze permission to settle there. The Uzere people lived for a considerable period at Erukẹ, but a war

---

1 The Isoko people call the clan Uze till this day. Uzere (sometimes rendered Usere) is the English rendering which, as often happens, has gained currency.

2 Hubbard, op. cit., p. 219. Hubbard gives an account of an Onitsha in chapter XXIII of his book—see p. 198 et seq. Egharevba claims that the Onitsha are emigrants from Benin: see J. Egharevba: *A Short History of Benin*, Ibadan University Press 1960, p. 5.

3 The Ẹrohwa clan is regarded by all the Isoko as the oldest. Their origin is shrouded in mystery. Tucked away in one of the creeks which flow off the Niger near Patani, these people have maintained an identity which singles them out. Today they are scarcely up to 5,000. They speak a 'language' which is exclusively theirs. Asked about their origins they do not, like most clans, say, 'we came from Benin'. They merely assert that they have always been in their present location. A scientific analysis of their 'language' and a study of their relations with other Isoko people might throw some light on their origin.

with the Aboh people forced them to move away to their present site at a time when Uze himself was already dead. Uzere clan is one of the largest of all the Urhobo and Isoko clans. Its importance, from a historical view-point is not, however, in its size but in the fact that it has given rise to another very large and important clan, the Agbọn clan. This clan, which claims Benin origin, is said to have actually moved from Iriwi (Iri in Isoko) near Oleh. Iriwi itself is one of the towns which make up Uzere clan. Oleh which is today regarded as a separate clan, is also an offshoot of Uzere.

The clans of Ijọ origin are Ewu, Ughiẹnvwe and Ughelle. Ewu and Ughiẹnvwe were related by blood. They were brothers who moved out of Ogoibri in the present Rivers state of Nigeria. These two clans do not today attempt to describe how their ancestors got to Ogoibri. They merely state that they lived at Ogoibri with their Ijọ brothers till a quarrel forced Ewu and Ughiẹnvwe to leave. They set out together, following the creeks. It is said that they settled first around the site of present-day Bomadi and left there for the respective areas they now occupy. The two brothers separated somewhere along the Ewu creek.

The Ughelle clan is of Tarakiri (Ijọ) clan origin. The founder of the clan was one Owha who moved out of his clan because of a quarrel with other families. He apparently first settled at a place called Oviri where he died. His sons—Ogele, Ogọ and Agbarha—could not agree on who was to succeed their father as head of the community and so decided to branch out in various directions, giving their names to the sub-clans of Ughelle, Ogọ and Agbarha, as they are now known. There is a tendency to refer to all three as Ughelle clan, Ughelle being the most important of the three since it became the administrative headquarters of the Urhobo Division.

The Uwherun clan tradition of origin, while it shows a connexion with people now called Ijọ, is slightly different. According to this tradition, the father of Uwherun (his name is not remembered) lived at Benin. He had four sons—Uwherun, Amasuomọ, Utuo and Matolo—all of whom were born at Benin. During one of the wars for which Benin was famed, Uwherun's people accidentally killed one of the Benin princes and had to flee from the wrath of the Ọba. By this time, the father of these four brothers had died. The brothers first fled together to Idah. From there they followed the Niger and

9

the creeks. Amasuomọ, accompanied by Utuo and Matolo, branched off and founded the settlement which bears his name in the Ijọ country. It is not clear whether Uwherun stayed with his brothers for some time at Amasuomọ. Eventually, however, he continued his journey and finally settled at the place now called Uwherun after him.

The clans of Ibo origin are Evbreni, which is said to have been founded by Ibo elephant hunters from somewhere near present day Port-Harcourt, as well as Igbide, Ẹnwẹ and Olomu. The Olomu clan story is interesting. The original founder of the clan was one Igboze who had come there direct from Benin. Igboze is said to have been a prince of Benin who was intent on founding an 'empire' of his own. He wandered as far as Orere-Olomu (as it is today) where he settled. After a long time there he received an Ibo visitor by the name of Olomu. Olomu would appear to have travelled with a sizeable retinue. Olomu lived with Igboze for a long time and succeeded in winning the confidence of Igboze to such an extent that the latter declared him his heir. On Igboze's death, Olomu took the title of *Ovie* by which Igboze had been known. This caused a split. Those who would not be ruled by Olomu moved out and founded the Okpẹ clans—the one with Orerokpẹ as headquarters and the other in the Isoko country. Olomu was thus left in control of those who chose to stay with him—and it is his name, and not Igboze's, that has been given to the clan.[1]

A number of significant facts emerge from these obviously simplified narratives. The first is that so far the traditions of origin discussed refer to individual clans moving out of Benin, the Ijọ country, or the Ibo country, and settling at different times in various places which today constitute Urhoboland. The name 'Urhobo' does not at all feature in these traditions, nor does the discarded name 'Sobo', which the neighbouring peoples used to refer to the people today known as Urhobo and Isoko. Nobody seems to know when the word was first used by the people or how it came about

---

1 No claim is made that the traditions of origin given in this chapter are unquestionable historical facts. They are stated as a synthesis of stories told today and similar stories told earlier and now on record. It is the broad conclusions that can be drawn from these traditions that are important for this study.

that these clans were collectively called by the name 'Urhobo'.[1] Hubbard suggests that all or most of the clans met an aboriginal people called Urhobo or a similar name, and though because of the greater number of the immigrants the original stock became absorbed, their name has survived.[2] Perhaps a scientific analysis of the language and its various dialects would help to throw light on this hypothesis. If there were an aboriginal people, virtually nothing is known about them. Hubbard again suggests that in the Isoko sector the Ẹrohwa people constitute the aboriginal stock.[3] Their distinctive language, which has survived till this day, the smallness and remoteness of their territory are perhaps pointers to their comparative antiquity. Here again a great deal more work remains to be done before the hypothesis can be accepted.

Secondly, it is now impossible to fix exact dates for the migration of the various clans. Pereira, who wrote about 1505, referred to the 'Subou' who lived to the hinterland of the Benin River area.[4] Since Pereira did not penetrate the area himself, it is fair to assume that he obtained his information from the coastal peoples, who by this time probably had commercial and other contacts with the people to the hinterland. Pereira's 'Subou' is close enough to the 'Sobo', the name which these coastal peoples called the Urhobo, for it to be assumed that the reference was, in fact, to the forebears of the present Urhobo. If this be accepted, it would mean that some of the Urhobo were already in the area to the hinterland of the Itsẹkiri country by the end of the fifteenth century, about which time Pereira's voyage took place. This would be in line with William Moore's claim that 'the territory now known as the kingdom of Itsekiri or Iwere was inhabited by three tribes, namely, Ijows, Sobos, and the Mahins before the advent of Prince Ginuwa'.[5] As the Ginuwa[6] migration is now ascribed to about 1485, this

---

1 The people claim that they have always called themselves 'Urhobo'. They were officially known as 'Sobo'—the name by which they were called by their neighbours—until 1st October 1938, when the Government formally recognized their being called Urhobo—see Notice No. 1228, *Nigeria Gazette*, No. 49, Vol. 25 of 8.9.38.

2 J. W. Hubbard, op. cit., pp. 145–7.   3 Ibid., p. 96.

4 Pereira, op. cit., p. 129.

5 William Moore: *History of Itsekiri*, Stockwell 1936, p. 13.

6 See pp. 31–3.

would further strengthen the suggestion that there were some Urhobo in the area by the end of the fifteenth century. Concerning the dates of migrations, nothing more certain than possibilities can be stated.

The third fact which emerges is that the migrations took place at different times and in small groups which are now called clans. Apart from Ewu and Ughienvwe and what are now the two Okpe clans, the migrations were largely independent of each other. The people now called Urhobo did not set out as a body from one place, settle in a given area, and establish a common central system of government. Further, at no time in their history has any one of the clans, or any of the neighbouring peoples, been able, through a war of conquest or other means, to establish unified control over all the Urhobo clans. This explains the relative disunity which has been noticeable among the people in recent times, and which even now has not been completely overcome.

It is, however, possible to exaggerate this lack of unity. If at the beginning of their settlement the clans tended to be distinct and isolated from one another, this situation altered with time. As the clans expanded, they came more and more in contact with their neighbours. The various traditions of war between the neighbouring clans typified the conflict which arose from the first meeting of groups of people, each of which had for a considerable period led a life of its own virtually undisturbed by outsiders. Thus Uwherun fought Igbide and Evwreni over land; Ewu fought Olomu; Igbide and Enwe struggled for possession of land; Emevo and Owe fought with the Iyede people, with whom they had first settled, over farm land. These wars over land and later, over runaway women, were usually terminated with an amicable settlement of the land in dispute and a ceremonial bond of friendship which drew the lately contesting clans together. Uwherun and Igbide after their war entered into a pact of perpetual friendship; Erohwa and Ume, a neighbouring clan, though not related by blood, have a strong bond of friendship which has led to their being regarded for administrative purposes as one clan, the Erohwa-Ume clan, while Erohwa, Aviara and Iyede entered into what is known as *Ovo*—a kind of solemn undertaking which insisted on perfect amity between the clans which entered into it, with dire consequences for any clan members who broke it. Thus, paradoxically, while inter-clan wars might be seen as symbolizing, to some extent, the lack of unity among the Urhobo people, they also ultimately brought the various clans closer together, as they sought a way out of their difficulties and differences. Over the years, therefore, they grew to realize some of their common interests and problems.

The need to trade with their immediate neighbours also drew the clans together. As indicated above, local exchange of agricultural and other products was possible because of the variations in occupational pursuits. Traditions of inter-clan trade are many, but in the present stage of our knowledge, it is impossible to say exactly when these commercial relations developed. Territorial expansion further brought neighbouring clans towards one another. Thus by the nineteenth century Udu and Ughiẹnvwe were territorially inseparable; it was difficult (and still is) to know where Evwreni territory ended and Uwherun's began. Such territorial intermingling had the effect of making the clans more aware of their neighbours and so the ties of unity, however tenuous, began to be forged.

The Urhobo traditions of origin are not definite on how strongly the link with Benin was maintained, or when it began to slacken. How independent were the Urhobo clans after they settled in their present locations? Commenting on this issue. Talbot wrote: 'Each town was independent and was ruled by its own headmen, although all were under the Ọba of Benin or the Olu of Jekri'.[1] That Benin exerted some influence over the Urhobo, and that contact with Benin was, in certain respects, maintained, is not denied. The main reason why the Benin connexion was maintained was because Benin was regarded as a repository of power. The Ọba of Benin was a powerful ruler who was regarded with deep veneration as a near-deity. Those Urhobo clans which possessed the office of *Ovie* (a type of priest-king) used to send the prospective candidate for the office to Benin to be confirmed there by the Ọba. This involved presents both before and after the ceremonies which went with the visit. Failure to get the Ọba to confirm the title tended to make the bearer of it less worthy in the eyes of his people. The clans

---

[1] P. Amaury Talbot: *The Peoples of Southern Nigeria*, London 1926, Vol. I, p. 318.

which had such *Ivie* were Ughelle, Agbọn, Ozọrọ and Iyede. A few other clans had 'kings', but did not send them to Benin but to Aboh for confirmation. The Abraka clan was the chief of these. But the Abraka people say that this relationship did not involve payment of tribute as a regular feature. Some of the other titles which exist in Urhoboland are also of Benin origin—like the titled societies of *Ẹhọnvwọnrẹn* and *Ediọ*. But these did not involve frequent trips to Benin. Once one man had gone to Benin to acquire the title, he became the head of the order and was usually responsible for conferring the title on other members of his clan without further reference to Benin. Fixed yearly tributes to the Ọba, if they existed at any period, seemed to have ceased comparatively early after the migrations from Benin. Apart from the above, the Ọba used to send soldiers occasionally into the Urhobo area. It would appear as if these soldiers were sent out as a matter of routine. They did not interfere with the local government, but it was customary to entertain them lavishly or face condign punishment like the burning down of an entire village. It would further appear that the Ọba regarded the conferring of the title of *Ovie* as his prerogative. An Ọba is said, one one occasion, to have sent troops against Ewu because this clan set up an *Ovie* whose office had not been approved by Benin. Ewu was partially burnt down. The soldiers then withdrew and the Ewu people rebuilt their capital without sending their *Ovie* to the Ọba to be confirmed.[1] Oddly enough, the Ọba did not attempt thereafter to force the Ewu people to acknowledge his right to confer the title. Such then was the nature of Urhobo relations with Benin. It is not known when these connexions were finally discontinued. On the whole the Urhobo seemed to have enjoyed a great deal of independence of action. The trips to Benin only occurred on the death of the *Ovie*, where such an office existed.

Talbot also claimed that some Urhobo towns were 'under the Olu of Jekri'.[2] Exactly what Talbot meant by this is not clear, and he adduced no evidence for his claim. The fact that the Itsẹkiri controlled the trade of the Urhobo hinterland was probably responsible for statements such as the above. It is likely, too, that some Urhobo towns, especially those very close to Itsẹkiri territory, did come under

---

1 C.S.O. 26, File 20653: Intelligence Report on Ewu clan, p. 20.
2 Talbot, op. cit., p. 318.

the influence of the Itsẹkiri, even if the relationship which developed did not involve the payment of tribute, nor political overlordship over the Urhobo, like that usually associated with the Ọba of Benin.

As has already been pointed out, Urhoboland is made up of clans. Each of these clans was made up of a group of villages all of which traced their origin to a common ancestor through the male line. The clan possessed certain customs, traditions and institutions which were peculiar to it and which therefore distinguished it from other clans, at the same time as it shared some of the general features of all Urhobo clans. The clan itself was broken up into villages. Villages were usually founded through a hiving-off process from the clan centre or parent village. Thus a man and his immediate kith and kin might decide to found a new settlement in a search for greater farming and other opportunities, or as a result of some quarrel. At its foundation, therefore, the village might be made up of members of a single family group. As it developed other families might seek permission to settle in it. Consequently a village was not necessarily made up of a single lineage segment, though the family of the founder was usually accorded special respect. The village was divided into quarters, each quarter representing yet smaller sections of the lineage segments that made up the village. The quarter was itself made up of a number of extended families.

The social organization of the Urhobo and Isoko is best studied in the context of the village, for the village constituted the most effective social and 'political' unit. The Urhobo and Isoko had a system of age grades or *itu* (singular *Otu*) as they called them. The men were divided into four *itu*.[1] The most junior was the *Otu-imitete*—young boys up to the age of about fifteen. This *otu* had no real organization and little to do, but they were expected to help in keeping village streets clean.

From the age of fifteen to about thirty-five the men belonged to the *Otu* called *Evrawa* or *Uvbie*. This *Otu* constituted the labour corps of the clan: they built roads and bridges, and communal

---

1 The women were similarly divided. The oldest group was called the *Eweyae* and through their spokesman always made their feelings known to the village council. They were particularly interested in matters to do with fertility and would insist on the necessary cleansing ceremonies being performed when anyone contravened any laws governing fertility rites.

houses like village meeting halls, and markets. They had their own head who took his instructions from the *Olotu-ologbo* (head of the *Iletu*) *and from the* *Otota* (the village spokesman). This *Otu*, like the *Otu-Iletu*, had its own internal organization and could discuss, and take decisions on, matters affecting its members. Through its *Otota* (spokesman) it could make its feelings on current village affairs known to the elders in council assembled.

Between the *Evrawa* and the *Ekpako* (village elders—members of the *Otu-ekpako*) was the *Otu-Iletu*, made up of men 35-50 years old. This *Otu* was the executive and military class. It was directly responsible for seeing that the *Evrawa* carried out their duties. All village council decisions which required action passed through the ranks of this *Otu* and, where necessary, down to the *Evrawa*. Their more specialized duty was war. It was the *Iletu* who organized the village (and clan) for war, leading the fighting men into the field. Their head and commander-in-chief was the *Olotu-ologbo* or *Olotu-rode*. Like the *Otu-Evrawa* they had their own council where they discussed matters pertaining to their *Otu*. They also enjoyed the right to try minor cases between individuals in the village, their verdict being reported to the *Ekpako* and any proceeds from fines being sent up to the *Ekpako* for division among these in their customary way. A portion of these proceeds was usually given to the *Iletu*. As the most senior and able-bodied group, this *Otu* enjoyed great freedom of action. The *Olotu-rode* could, for example, order his men to repel an attack on the village or clan without waiting for instructions from the *Ekpako*, if he thought the situation called for swift action. In a similar way he could, after consultation with the *Otota*, send his men to investigate any reported affront to the village or clan, especially where this affront was of the sort that generally led to war.

The *Otu-Ekpako* was the most senior and was made up of men who had reached considerable age (about fifty and above) and could retire from the more vigorous aspects of village life. Members of this *Otu* formed the bulk of the village council and were the deliberative and judicial authorities over their people. The head of this *Otu* was usually the oldest man in the village, called *Okpako-ewo* by the Isoko and *Okpako-orere* or *Okaroro* by the Urhobo-speaking clans.

In addition to these age-grades, there also existed titled societies.

Among the Isoko there was the Ọdiọ society while the Urhobo had the Ọhọnvwọnrẹn society. The Ọdiọ society existed in all the Isoko clans. Among the Urhobo-speaking people, however, the Ọhọnvwọnrẹn order was not common to all the clans. Thus in Ughiẹnvwe and Uwherun clans the *Adẹ* society took the place of the Ọhọnvwọnrẹn, while in the Urhobo clan of Okpẹ there existed the *Ekakuro* society. By whatever names they were called these societies had one thing in common—they were open to all male members of the village (and clan) who could afford to pay the membership fee as well as perform the prescribed ceremonies. As the fees and cost of performance of the prescribed ceremonies were usually high, the societies grew to acquire a status symbol: members of the societies became regarded as a class of wealthy and leisured gentlemen. For this reason all male members of village and clan sought to become members of the various societies. These societies, especially those of *Ọdio* and *Ọhọnvwọnrẹn*, are thought to be of Benin origin.[1] Seniority within these societies was based essentially on length of membership. As the men sought membership as soon as they could afford the cost, it often happened that the most senior members of the society were also the oldest. But this was not always the case. The most senior *Ọdiọ* was called the *Ọdiọ-Ologbo* while the most senior *Ọhọnvwọnrẹn* was called the *Osivie*. The head of the *Adẹ* was known as the *Odede-Adẹ*. These societies had rules which governed the conduct of their members. Among other things these societies insisted or high moral rectitude. Any member found guilty of offences like stealing and adultery was not only subjected to a heavy fine but was also expelled. Refusal to pay such a fine was a signal for the destruction of the property of the offending member. The importance of these various societies among the Isoko and Urhobo will become clear after the discussion of traditional government which follows.

---

1 The Bini have a title, 'Odion'. It is not clear whether this was merely a word meaning 'old man' or a title conferred by the Ọba. Among the 'councillors of state' reputed to have been created by Ọba Eweka I was one called 'Eholo n'Ire'; the Ọba Ewuare is said to have created a council of state called 'Eghaevbo n'ore'; the Urhobo *Ọhọnvwọnrẹn* order probably owes its origin to one of these two institutions. Likewise the Urhobo title of *Ovie* is probably the corruption of the Benin title *'Ogie'*—see Jacob Egharevba, op. cit., pp. 9, 15 and 18.

Certain clans possessed the office of *Ovie*, a kind of priest-king. There were two types of *Ivie* (plural of *Ovie*). The first type, like those of Ughelle, Iyede, Ewu, Ozoro, Okpẹ (here he is called *Orodje*,) and Agbọn, combined in themselves executive and priestly functions and were in a very real sense the heads of their people. The second type were essentially priests charged with responsibility for maintaining the clan shrine and performing various sacrifices and other sacerdotal duties to the clan god and ancestors. This second type did not usually possess executive authority outside their defined sphere. But as the whole life of village and clan depended on the continued goodwill of the gods and ancestors, the man who ministered to these supernatural agencies was obviously a very important personage in the clan. *Ivie* of the second type existed in Ẹrohwa, Uzere, Igbide and *Uvbiẹ* clans. The *Ivie* were usually connected with specific lineages. Very often the *Ivie* (especially of the first type) came from the lineage of the founder of the clan.[1]

As has already been pointed out, the Urhobo village constituted the most effective 'political' unit of government, commanding the loyalty and co-operation of all the villagers. There was, however, a larger unit which in certain respects possessed greater authority than the village government. This was the clan. The 'institutions of government' at this level—never too formalized or uniformly well defined—were regarded as the final authority within the group, with the village institutions constituting extremely virile local government units. Thus, Okpara, Ukhuokori, Ọrọkpọ, Ẹku and Igun, the main component parts of the Agbọn clan, each had its village 'institutions of government'. But for annual festivals and for decisions on matters of great importance like war, they met at Isiokolo, the clan centre of Okpara. To such a meeting delegates were sent from the various villages.

Since the clan, and not the entire group now called Urhobo or Isoko, was the centre of political and social activity (at its highest level), is there any justification for speaking of the government of the

---

1 It is easy to see that the *Ovie* was not likely to be the oldest man in the village or clan. With regard to *Ivie* of the second type, it is said that the clan god sometimes chose who was to be his priest by some kind of peculiar manifestation.

18

Urhobo and Isoko people? The form of government which each clan adopted was, in certain respects, affected by the human and environmental influences to which it was subject early in its history.[1] The clans have therefore developed along slightly different lines, modifying their government and mode of life to suit their particular requirements. Hence there exist sufficient differences in the form of government in the various clans to put one on guard against sweeping generalizations. Yet over the centuries, their culture and customs have become sufficiently assimilated into a pattern that permits of their being treated as a single group.

It has become generally accepted that government among the Urhobo, as well as with other Nigerian people who did not acknowledge a central authority, was a gerontocracy—government by elders. Thus E. R. Chadwick warns against anything which would 'cut across the Sobo traditional organization which places authority in the hands of the aged'.[2] While there is a great deal of truth in this statement, it remains, nevertheless, an oversimplification of a system which was much more complex.

Government among the Urhobo, whether at clan or village level, was essentially conciliar.[3] At the top there existed a council which had powers to legislate for the whole clan. This council concerned itself only with matters of supreme importance—external war and defence, yearly festivals and sacrifices, inter-clan negotiations and the trial of the more serious breaches of clan law and custom. Matters of less importance and the ordinary day-to-day aspects of government were left to the village councils which, understandably, were much more active than the central bodies.

The composition of the council—the pattern was essentially the same whether at village or clan level—while conforming to a certain general pattern, varied from clan to clan. In most of the

---

1 In Uzere clan, for example, the powers of the *Ovie* have been limited to certain spheres only because, so it is said, early in the history of the clan, an *Ovie* who did not belong to the original Uze family was appointed. See Hubbard, op. cit., p. 103.

2 C.S.O. 26, File 29211: Intelligence Report on the Uvbie clan. Mr. E. R. Chadwick was for years a District Officer in the Urhobo and Isoko country.

3 No system of government ever remains static and unchanging. The system here described is to be understood as that which existed in the nineteenth century, immediately before the impact of foreign influences.

villages, however, there was one man who had a right to membership of the council—the *Ọkpako ẹwo* or *Ọkpako-orere* (i.e. the oldest man in the village).

The bulk of the council was made up of the *Ediọ* (plural of *Ọdiọ*) and the *Ẹhọnvwọnrẹn* (plural of *Ọhọnvwọnrẹn*) or members of corresponding societies. It is not known for certain how these societies came to constitute the base for 'political' recruitment. It will be recalled that the vast majority of the male population belonged to the societies; that it required a measure of opulence to gain membership; and that the rules governing members insisted on high moral conduct. Most of these rules were themselves derived from clan laws and customs, and indeed these societies did tend to become regarded as the custodians of clan law and custom. Herein perhaps lies the explanation of the important 'political' role which these societies played at village and clan level. But since most of the male population belonged to these societies, the number of titled men in the village tended to become too large for effective deliberation. The custom therefore grew of dividing these titled men into two categories— *Ediọ-ilogbo* and *Ediọ-itete*; *Ẹhọnvwọnrẹn-ride* and *Ẹhọnvwọnrẹn-itete*[1] The *Ediọ-itete* and the *Ẹhọnvwọnrẹn-itete* were the junior members of the societies who were excluded from active participation in clan and village deliberations until they graduated into the senior group. In some of the Isoko clans the number of *Ediọ-ilogbo* was rigidly fixed: in Aviara, Igbide and Uzere clans there could be only nine such *ediọ*. In most clans, however, the simple differentiation was regarded as sufficient. While it is true that most of those in the senior category of *ediọ* and *ẹhọnvwọnrẹn* might in fact be older than the junior sector, this did not necessarily apply in all cases, for it sometimes happened that the head of the society was younger than some of the other members.

Most of the *Ediọ* and *Ẹhọnvwọnrẹn* were themselves *Ekpako*, that is elderly men; but this was incidental to their having complied with the requirements for membership. The fact that membership of the societies was restricted to those who could afford it meant that there were *Ekpako* who were not *Ediọ* or *Ẹhọnvwọnrẹn*. The

---

1 *Ologbo* and *Orode* (plural—*ilogbo* and *iride*) each means literally 'big'; *otete* (plural *itete*) is the opposite, meaning 'small'.

position and role of such *Ekpako* in village and clan government are not very clear. It has been said that the oldest man in the village was always regarded as a member of the village council. This statement now requires amplification and clarification. In some places such a man had to be titled if he desired to be recognized. For instance in Ukhuokori, the *Okaroro* had to be an *Ohonvwonren*, whereas in Agbarho clan, while a non-titled *Okaroro* could be head of his village council, he could not feature in such a capacity at clan level where the head of the *Ohonvwonren* order, the *Osivie*, was regarded as the most important man and head of the clan council. In most places the man was recognized as the *Okpako-ewo* or *Okaroro* but his duties and importance varied. As for the other *Ekpako* the most generally applicable conclusion is that they could attend council meetings but were regarded and treated as a junior order to the titled men.[1]

Each village and clan council had what in modern terms would be called a president, a functioning 'head'. There was no generally accepted rule as to who was this 'head'. The position varied from clan to clan. There were three 'officers'—three categories of men—who could fill that post. These were the *Ovie* (in those clans where the office existed), the *Odio-ologbo* or *Osivie*, the *Okpako-ewo* or *Okaroro*. In addition to these 'officers' there was sometimes a fourth, the most senior descendant of the original founder of the clan. The easiest situation existed in those clans which possessed an *Ovie* regarded as the executive, judicial and spiritual head of his clan. In these clans the *Ovie* was 'president' of his clan council, and the symbol of clan unity. As the *Ovie* usually had to come from a particular family, it was scarcely the case that the *Ovie* was the oldest man in the clan at the time he assumed office. So, in this instance, age was not the decisive criterion.

In the other clans the position was rather complex. Where there was an *Ovie* who was essentially a clan priest what was his position *vis-à-vis* the *Odio-ologbo* or *Osivie*? It would appear that in those places the *Odio-ologbo*, or his equivalent in the Urhobo-speaking clans, presided at clan council meetings (except where these

---

1 In the Isoko clans the Ekpako who were not *Edio* were referred to as 'Ekpako-igheghe'—ordinary elders—a term of derision.

meetings were convened primarily to discuss sacrifices or similar ceremonies in which case the *Ovie* presided) though because the whole life of the community was so closely linked with the spiritual world of the gods and ancestors, the *Ovie* had to be a member of the council to be ready for consultation as the need arose. Sometimes, as in Ẹrohwa for instance, he had his own separate 'court' where he could be consulted. As for the *Ọkpako-ẹwo*, or *Ọkaroro*, it sometimes happened that he was also the head of the titled order, having joined that order early in life. In such cases, the position resolved itself. When this man was not titled, each clan decided what his role was to be. In Uzere clan the *Ọdiọ-ologbo* took precedence over the *Ọkpako-ẹwo*, as president of the council, but the latter was always consulted as he was the oldest embodiment of clan law and custom. The *Ọkpako-ẹwo's* specific duties in Uzere were connected with cleansing ceremonies. In some other places the oldest man was theoretically still president and his compound would be the venue of village or clan meetings, but in practice, the head of the titled order would officiate. In yet other clans the oldest descendent, unless he had become titled (in which case he took his place within his order) tended to be confined to the offering of sacrifices to the clan ancestors. The set-up was thus very complicated and fluid in theory, though in the actual working of the system, everybody knew who had what rights, as well as who performed specific duties. This was one of the things which baffled British administrative officers who sought to know who was 'head' of a village or clan. The fact was that at the top there existed a dual or tripartite arrangement of officers, all equally vital, and each dependent on the other for the efficient management and discharge of the duties allotted to him.

So far attention has been focused only on those who formed the bulk of the village or clan council. In addition to these men—titled and non-titled—there were other people who sat on the council by virtue of the offices they held within the village or clan. The most important man in the council after the president was the *Ọtota*, the spokesman of the council.

The *Ọtota* was the president's chief lieutenant. He summoned meetings on instructions from the president. He did most of the president's talking at such meetings, and at trials, voiced the verdict of the clan or village council. He directed the work of the *Iko*, the messengers of the council, who were usually chosen from the *Otu-Evrawa*. He was ultimately responsible for seeing that the edicts of the council were properly disseminated. All representation to the clan 'Head' had to pass through him. He represented, or was at the head of representatives of, his clan at inter-clan negotiations whether these involved matters of peace or war, acting on instructions from the council, instructions which he could not overlook or exceed in essentials.

From the duties of his office it is clear that the *Otota* had to be a man well versed in the traditions, laws and customs of his clan. He was, in fact, chosen because he possessed these qualities, as well as a good speaking voice and a commanding person. In nearly all the Isoko clans the *Otota* was invariably an *Odio*. In Uzere and Owe clans the *Otota* was usually the *Odio* immediately next in seniority to the *Odiö-ologbo*, and succeeded the latter on his death. In certain Urhobo clans (Agbon and Agbarho for example) the *Otota* was the most senior *Ohonvworen* after the *Okaroro*. More generally, however, the *Otota* was selected because he possessed the necessary qualities.

The *Etota* usually had assistants in council. Some clans had permanent officers appointed, like in Olomu and Ughienvwe, where the assistant *Otota* was called *Akpile*, and in Ewu where he was called *Akpoho*. Most clans preferred to call on anyone they thought fit to deputize for the *Otota*, and in this way train future *Etota*. Another officer who sat in council was the *Olotu-Ologbo* or *Olotu-rode*. He was the war leader and head of the clan *Iletu*—the military commanders of the clan. He was chosen for his stature and proven valour in war and similar trials.

As has been indicated, the composition of the village councils was similar to that of clan councils. It was well known who, among those who sat in the respective village councils, had a right to sit on the clan council, the supreme governing body for the clan. At the meeting of the clan council, it was again known who occupied what position. One of the most fascinating things to watch is the gathering of the clan council. As each member arrives so there is a general shuffling among those already present to leave his place vacant. Precedence was observed to a surprising degree.

In addition to clan and village councils, there existed quarter councils—a gathering of the heads of the families which made up the quarter. This gathering was also the lowest 'court' for trying 'cases' which arose between members of the quarter. At this level the oldest *Okpako* was always the head, and presided at quarter meetings.

However complicated the system described above may appear, it was in practice very simple from the point of view of the people who lived under it. The people virtually lived their government. In the first place, when vital issues affecting the village or clan were being discussed, it was usual to allow all villagers and clansmen who cared to watch to occupy the open courtyard which was a feature of all meeting places in Urhoboland. But even more important was the system of *Itu*, each with a definite organization and specific duties to perform.

These duties were ultimately directed from the village or clan council. From the description of the *Itu* and their duties, it is clear that government was very much an affair of the people. The village or clan council met and took decisions. By the time these decisions were implemented, virtually all the age-grades would have participated in the implementation. The duties were shared out from the oldest man to the adolescent. Everybody knew what part he had to play in the scheme of things. By the time a man reached the maturity of the *Okpako* he had acquired a sound grounding in village and clan government by participation in various aspects of that government within the *itu*. In the same way and through the same channel, he learnt all there was to learn about clan law and custom which his own family or quarter had not taught him.

While age played an important part in determining who filled what office, it was by no means the sole criterion for bestowing office. All the important members of the village or clan council were expected to attain a certain age; in that sense age was a very real factor in determining in whose hands authority lay. Yet service, 'wealth' and natural talents also played their part. The *Otota* and *Olotu-rode* were key men in village and clan, with important duties to discharge, and enjoying, within limits, such freedom of action that they could, and did, overshadow their elders in the village or clan. It is clear, then, that there were offices in the filling of which services rendered and natural endowments counted as much as, if not more than, mere age. Also it was 'wealth' which made it possible for a man to join the ranks of the titled orders, and so eventually win for himself the place of 'councillor'. A very old man outside the *Ọdiọ, Ọhọnvwọnrẹn* or *Ekakuro* society certainly exposed himself to ridicule and contempt. Hence to argue that government among the Urhobo was based solely on age, leaves the picture incomplete. Similarly, the question of who was the village or clan 'head' was not always as simple as it looked. The arrangement of the offices was such that though it might be possible to single out an individual by virtue of his age or his title or a combination of these, and call him head, his authority was invariably limited by the authority conferred on other people immediately round (rather than under) him. Just as the *Ọtota* was unlikely to exceed his orders, so was the *Ọkaroro* or *Ọdiọ-ologbo* unlikely to do anything without consulting the council. In those clans where there was a clan priest, he presided over certain ceremonies and functions while the *Ọkpako-ẹwo* or head of the titled society presided over others. Unless these two men came together the 'headship' was not complete. The fact is that the question of 'headship' did not arise or call for definition till it became necessary, with the advent of foreign control, to single out such a head and appoint him to a post which carried remuneration other than was traditional. Then it was discovered that various men vied for the position.[1] Traditionally, authority was widely diffused and everything seemed to have been done to avoid the concentration of too much power in any one hand.[2]

The social and political organizations of the Urhobo as described above, bear a striking resemblance to the social and political structure of the Benin village, for the village is the basic unit of the

---

1 The reorganization of the Uvbie (Ẹvhrọ) clan was held up for a long time because of the struggle for position between the *Ovie* who was essentially a priest and the *Ehọnvwọnrẹn* who claimed that they should constitute the clan council and that their head should be recognized by the British as Clan Head. See C.S.O. 26, File No. 29211: Intelligence Report on the Uvbie clan.
2 The description here given of the Urhobo and Isoko social and political system is based largely on my own field investigations: For details of these investigations see Obaro Ikime: *Itsekiri–Urhobo Relations and the Establishment of British Rule, 1884–1936* (thesis submitted to the University of Ibadan for the degree of Ph.D., 1965), Appendix I.

Benin kingdom.[1] The Benin village was ruled by a council of elders headed by the *Odionwere* (a rough equivalent of the *Odio-ologbo* among the Isoko), who was usually the oldest man in the village. The men were divided into three age-groups: the *iroghae* (teenagers), the *Ighele*[2] (adult men, usually under forty-five years) and the *Edio* (the elders) who sat in the village council. As with the Urhobo, these age-grades had their specific duties to perform in the community, and had their respective heads. In the *Ovie*, the Urhobo possessed the equivalent of the Benin *Onogie*, a kind of hereditary village head. As already indicated, the Urhobo title of *Ohonvwonren* is of Benin origin. This similarity in the social and political institutions of the Urhobo and the Bini, tends to strengthen further the claim by the Urhobo to have come from Benin, and is also a measure of the extent of Benin influence over the Urhobo during the early part of the latter's existence in their present locations.

Among the Urhobo, justice was regarded as just another aspect of the government of the people, and was the work of the same body which handled other affairs of government. There was no 'court' distinct from the village or clan council. The law of the clan was regarded as having been declared once and for all by the ancestors. In theory, therefore, there could be no new laws. The *Ovie, Edio* and *Ehonvwonren*-in-council did not make new laws; they merely applied to varying circumstances law which was already existing and theoretically immutable, which had received the irrevocable sanction of the 'quick and the dead'. Such applications of the law to specific circumstances did, in practice, tend to become regarded as new laws in themselves, and so to constitute part of the unwritten code of clan law.

Clan law was supposed to be well known to all clan members, as indeed it was. As the ancestors had handed it down from father to son, so it was supposed to continue. And, indeed, the family constituted the lowest 'judicial' unit. Minor cases were settled within

1 R. E. Bradbury: *The Benin Kingdom and the Edo speaking Peoples of South-Western Nigeria* (Ethnographic Survey of Africa, Western Africa, Part XIII, London, 1957), pp. 31-3. See also P. A. Igbafe: 'Benin Society in the pre-colonial Era'—paper submitted to the Postgraduate African History Seminar, University of Ibadan, 6 Nov. 1963.

2 'Ighele' has become absorbed into the Urhobo language, and is used as a term of praise for physically well formed young men and women.

the family or quarter. The village council was the place where most of the cases were heard. In addition to possessing full powers of jurisdiction over certain types of offences, these village councils also acted as preliminary investigation centres for the clan council. It is difficult to lay down any rules about where the jurisdiction of the village councils ended and that of the clan council began. Murder, serious robbery, and extreme violence, usually went to the clan council, but even this was not a general rule. Where clan unity was weak, virtually all cases were disposed of at village council level. Very often it was left to the village council to decide whether a matter should be referred to the clan council. In theory, therefore, appeals lay to the clan council, though in practice little notice was taken of this, parties usually being content with the verdict of their village council. In any case, whether as a 'court' of first instance or as an appeal court, the verdict of the clan council was final. Refusal to accept the verdict of the clan council could lead to the offender being sold into slavery and thereby for ever removed from the clan.

Procedure was simple. The complainant usually took his complaint to his family head who ensured that the appropriate council was convened to hear it. If it was a matter within the quarter, the quarter council could dispose of it. But if the cause was too serious for the quarter to handle, the family got in touch with the *Qtota* who, after consulting with the village 'head,' duly informed the complainant when the case was due to be heard. It was the duty of the council's *Ikǫ* to ensure that both parties to the case attended court on the date fixed, but it was the responsibility of these main parties to ensure that their witnesses attended. If witnesses refused to attend they could not be subpoenaed—a situation which tended to force the main parties sometimes to induce witnesses to attend by giving them presents. When the council was duly assembled, the complainant was asked by the *Qtota* to state his charge. The defendant was then allowed to plead guilty or not guilty by stating his own case. If the defendant pleaded guilty without waiting for witnesses to be called, his plea was accepted and the court merely withdrew to consider what the fine and compensation (where necessary) should be. If the defendant pleaded not guilty then witnesses were called. Most of the cross-examination was done by

27

the *Ọtota*, though the other *Ekpako* could ask whatever questions they thought relevant. When all who should be heard had been allowed to speak, the 'court' withdrew to consider its verdict. On its return, the *Ọtota* pronounced the verdict which was usually given as unanimous. It was of the utmost importance that all charges should be definitely proven, especially in the case of theft which was regarded as a very serious offence,[1] as it brought lasting disgrace not only on the offender but on his entire family. The hearing of the parties and their witnesses was done in public and the reaction of the people, who usually gathered in the courtyard when cases were to be heard, was noted and taken into consideration when the verdict was being considered—a system which obviously had its advantages and disadvantages. It was regarded as vital that nothing should be done to outrage the people's sense of justice and fair play.

Evidence was usually taken unsworn. When there was doubt as to the truth of the evidence, recourse was usually had to oaths and ordeals. This meant that the parties to the suit and their witnesses would take an oath by a certain deity or sacred object credited with supernatural powers. It was believed that if after this oath a person told a lie, the god or spirit would inflict condign punishment—a punishment which could be death. An alternative to swearing an oath was the subjection of the parties to an ordeal. The forms of ordeal in general use were:—

(i) The lobe of the ear or tongue was smeared with some medicine and a needle thrust through. If the needle penetrated easily, the man was declared innocent.

(ii) The man could be asked to pick cowries out of a pot of boiling water after his hand had been daubed with medicine. If he sustained no burns he was considered innocent.

(iii) The man might be asked to pick an axe-head from a roaring fire, after his hand had been daubed with medicine, and walk about twenty-five yards with the axe-head in his hand. Absence of burns was proof of innocence.

(iv) The sasswood ordeal was generally used to detect the guilt

---

1 For a list of offences and punishment in the Urhobo and Isoko traditional system of justice, see Appendix I.

of witches. It was believed that no witch could live after drinking the sasswood mixture.

The threat of swearing an oath and trial by ordeal had the effect of persuading litigants that it was better to tell the truth than go through the ordeal. Hence perjury was less common than in the days of British 'Native Courts' when trial by ordeal and swearing an oath by a clan god were first frowned upon and then forbidden.

The enforcement of judgements was the task of the *Iletu* and *Ikọ*. Usually the *Ikọ* acted on instructions passed to them from the council through the *Ọtota*. The *Iletu* came in when it was necessary to secure the carrying out of verdicts like the hanging of murderers or other serious judgements.

In addition to the quarter, village and clan councils, all of which exercised judicial functions, there were other bodies which had a measure of judicial authority. All the age-grades, with the exception of the *Imitete* and the *Ekpako*, had the right to try petty cases among their members and impose small fines. The *Iletu* grade could try minor cases not only within their *otu* but amongst the entire villagers, as has been already stated. The titled societies also possessed similar rights and they could try and punish members of their society, even when the offence had not been a breach of their own regulations, but a breach of clan law and custom. Thus, in the judicial as in other spheres, authority was diffuse and the people were trained to prepare themselves for the day they would sit on the village or clan council, by being encouraged to participate in the activities of their various *Itu* and societies. This was the aspect of traditional government which the introduction of the 'native court' or 'warrant chief' systems was seriously to undermine.

To the west of the Urhobo country live their Itsẹkiri neighbours. The Itsẹkiri inhabit the extreme western part of the Niger Delta in the area bounded (approximately) by latitudes 5° 20' and 6 North and longitudes 5° 5' and 5° 40' East. Their neighbours, apart from the Urhobo to the east, are the Ijọ to the south, the Bini to the north and the Yoruba of Ondo Province to the north-west. Virtually all the area lies within the mangrove swamp region. Only on the eastern fringes is there some firm land. Ode-Itsẹkiri, the capital of the Itsẹkiri kingdom, stands on part of this firm land which is only twenty feet above sea level.[1] It is not surprising therefore that the dominant feature of the vegetation is the white and red mangrove.

Itsẹkiriland is watered by three large rivers and innumerable creeks. These three rivers are the Benin, the Escravos and the Forcados. They are connected by a network of creeks, most of which are navigable only by small craft. Just as the geographical location of the Urhobo has had its effect on their development and their relations with people outside their territorial limits, so has that of the Itsẹkiri affected their history—though with very different results. From the accounts of early Portuguese and other European traders and travellers to the Niger Delta, it is clear that the Forcados and Benin Rivers were highways of traffic from an early date. Since Europeans began to trade in the area from about the fifteenth century,[2] the people inhabiting this area, whether they were then an independent people or not, had an early opportunity of contact with Europeans. This early contact has naturally influenced the attitude of the Itsẹkiri and their relations with their neighbours, especially the Urhobo. It also enabled the Europeans to have direct dealings with the Itsẹkiri, and so to appreciate their laws and customs and the working of their society. This explains the kind of remarks made about them by the European writers of the eighteenth and nineteenth centuries. While these writers scarcely mentioned the Urhobo in any detail, the Itsẹkiri were accorded prominence. Thus, Major Leonard, whose remarks on the Urhobo have been quoted, describes the Itsẹkiri as 'the most intelligent and tractable' and 'the best mannered of all the tribes'[3] in the Niger Delta.

The mode of life of the Itsẹkiri people has been determined by their environment. Thus, the Itsẹkiri are primarily fishermen and have become known in the area as suppliers of 'crayfish' which

---

1 P. C. Lloyd: *The Itsekiri* (being part of the same book by R. E. Bradbury, see p. 26, note 1), p. 174.
2 See chapter 2 for more details of this early trade.
3 Leonard: op. cit., pp. 18–19. See also Gallway: op. cit., and Mary Kingsley: *West African Studies*, London 1899, Appendix I, pp. 448–9, in which M. le comte de Cardi gives a description of 'natives' of the Niger Coast Protectorate.

was a valued article of trade between the Itsękiri and their Urhobo and other neighbours, and which today is still one of the articles of trade for which the Itsękiri are known. The manufacture of salt, which has survived till today, was a much more important industry in the pre-twentieth century period than it has since become. The salt was made from the mangrove trees: the shoots, roots and leaves of the trees were burnt; a solution of the ash was made, and the filtered solution was then evaporated. In the nineteenth century salt was also made from sea water by the simple process of evaporation.[1] This salt, which is still an article of trade, was more valued as such in earlier times when imported salt had not become as popular as it is now. Pottery, another early Itsękiri occupation, has remained essentially the concern of the women. Earthenware has therefore been another product which the Itsękiri traded with their neighbours. The Itsękiri have never been farmers to any great extent, there being very little land on which they could farm. At no time in their history did they ever grow enough food to feed themselves. Consequently they have always depended for their agricultural products on the farming folks to the hinterland, especially the Urhobo.

It is as middlemen traders that the Itsękiri made their name in history. Their location by the coast, and in positions where they could control the river mouths, helped them to develop into great traders who by the nineteenth century were doing a flourishing trade with the Europeans, first in their hulks, and later in their factories on land. It should, however, be remembered that at all times only a small proportion of the Itsękiri was engaged in large-scale trade, as distinct from the local trade in fish, crayfish, salt and so on, in which the women were, for the most part, constantly engaged. The bulk of the people remained, even at the height of Itsękiri commercial prosperity, essentially fishermen.

The traditions of origin of the Itsękiri people are more straightforward than those of the Urhobo. The most widely accepted

---

1 Captain John Adams: *Remarks on the country Extending from Cape Palmas to the Congo*, London 1823, p. 122. The brass pans which the Itsękiri bought from Old Calabar people were used in this industry. For some comments on the importance of salt and fish in the Eastern Delta, see G. I. Jones: *The Trading States of the Oil Rivers*, London 1963, p. 13.

version is that of the Ginuwa migration from Benin, at a period now usually ascribed to the late fifteenth century. According to this account, Ginuwa was a prince of an Ọba of Benin called Olua (Oluwa). Ginuwa had to escape from Benin on account of the unpopularity of both his father and himself which made the Bini people determine not to have him succeed as Ọba. Olua therefore decided to safeguard his son's future and planned that Ginuwa should found a new kingdom outside Benin. By a ruse, the Ọba succeeded in getting seventy of his nobles to send their sons with the prince, allegedly to offer some sacrifice to one of the gods. In the meantime, arrangements had been made to provide the proper royal regalia for the prince. The question of whether the party actually set off with the prince in a huge Iroko box escorted by the sons of these nobles, or whether some other means was employed, need not detain us. The story goes that the party arrived at the river after they had been smuggled out of Benin, whereupon, Ginuwa, arrayed in his royal regalia, led forth his band to a new settlement with himself as king. Their first place of settlement was Amatu, then Oruselemo, both places being in present-day Western Ijọ Division. The next place the band moved to was Ijala, where Ginuwa died and was buried. To this day Ijala remains the royal burial ground.[1]

The identity of the original inhabitants of the area into which Ginuwa and his followers moved is not known. It would appear that there were earlier immigrants around Okotomu to which place Ijiẹn, son and heir of Ginuwa, moved after his father's death. Most of these immigrants apparently fled on the arrival of Ijiẹn and his retinue. It is claimed that Itsẹkiri, the name now given to the race, was the personal name of one of these earlier immigrants who remained behind, acknowledged the suzerainty of the Olu and served him loyally. It is significant, however, that early European sources did not refer to the kingdom as Itsẹkiri but as Iwere, Aweri,

---

1 In essentials there is general agreement on this version of the origin of the Itsẹkiri people. For a fuller story and differences in detail, see William Moore, op. cit. Moore's book is based on traditions collected from the elders of his day. See also C. O. Omoneukarin: *Itsekiri Law and Custom*, Lagos 1942, pp. 13–18; Lloyd, op. cit., pp. 178–9; Egharevba, op. cit., pp. 22–3 and C.S.O. 26 File 27675, Assessment Report on the Itsekiri sub-clan in the Warri Province.

or Ourre. The term Jekri, later Itsẹkiri, did not become current till the nineteenth century.

There is another account which claims that the founders of the capital were men who came from Igala, south of the Nupe country, near the confluence of the Niger and Benue. According to this account, the migration was part of the Yoruba movement westwards from Igala. While the bulk of the Yoruba travelled in the direction of Ife, a small band followed the creeks and founded what later became the capital.[1] This view of the migration is used to explain the similarities between the Itsẹkiri and Yoruba languages.

There are, however, other possible explanations for the linguistic affinity between the Yoruba and Itsẹkiri. There is a group of people to be found in Gborodo, Omadina and Ureju, who claim to have come from Ode in Ijẹbu, a kingdom situated along the southern coast of the Yoruba country, either prior to, or at about the same time as the Ginuwa migration.[2] As these people spoke Yoruba, their language might have affected that of those they met inhabiting this part of the delta. Besides, as the creek system stretches all the way from the Dahomean coast to Old Calabar, one can postulate constant contact between the coastal Ijẹbu and Ondo and the people who inhabited the area now called Itsẹkiriland. Such contact could quite easily have affected the latter's language. Indeed it is likely that the Itsẹkiri, as they exist today, are a mixture of people of Benin and Yoruba origin. Another explanation of the linguistic affinity is that Yoruba was the court language in Benin, and therefore Ginuwa and his young nobles would have used that language even after they settled in what is now Itsẹkiriland.

Although reference has been made to 'the Itsẹkiri people' it is not known exactly when they became an independent people. It is likely that during the years immediately after the Ginuwa migration there was some contact with Benin. The exact nature of this contact is not known. It was, however, customary when an Olu was to be elected, to seek the blessings of the Ọba of Benin.[3] It

1 Saburi Biobaku: 'An Historical sketch of the Peoples of Western Nigeria', *Odu*, No. 6, June 1958, pp. 24–8. 2 Ibid. See also Lloyd, op. cit. p. 178–9.
3 As late as 1936 when the Olu Ginuwa II was about to be installed, a message was sent to the Ọba of Benin to seek his blessing. See Ughelle Papers, File 10/27: Handing over Notes Jekri—Sobo Division—J. A. Mackenzie (D.O.) to B. J. A. Matthews (D.O.) 22 Feb., 1936.

has been suggested that the development of the Itsẹkiri into an independent people was probably accelerated by Portuguese missionary activity among them, as the Portuguese sought to build up the Itsẹkiri against Benin, where their missionary endeavours did not meet with much success.[1] Be that as it may, the Olu was being referred to as an independent ruler by the eighteenth century.[2]

Whoever inhabited the area that is now Itsẹkiriland before the advent of Ginuwa, it is unlikely that they established any centralized government. It would appear that such people as there were, were content to accept the government set up by the new-comers. The system of government was clearly modelled on that of Benin. It is improbable that any formal institutions of government were set up during the lifetime of Ginuwa himself; but it is said that after the arrival of the party at Ode-Itsẹkiri, the *Olu*, the title given to the ruler, turned his band of seventy nobles into a council and gave these nobles titles similar to those in use in Benin. The more important of these titles were *Ologbotsẹrẹ* (Prime minister or Chief Adviser to the Olu), *Iyatsẹrẹ* (War Lord), *Uwangue* (custodian of the Regalia, also Chief Spokesman in Council). The seventy nobles, each called *Ojoye* in Itsẹkiri, sat in council with the Olu to advise him on the running of the kingdom. They could meet to discuss matters without the Olu being present, their decisions being conveyed to him through the more senior of the *Ojoye*. The exact order of seniority of all the nobles is not now remembered, though the *Ologbotsẹrẹ's* position as chief adviser is generally admitted. The Olu was in theory not bound to accept the advice of his councillors. In practice, when there was a difference of opinion between the Olu and his councillors the issue was referred to the oracle, the pronouncement of which was regarded as final. This arrangement made it possible for the Olu to disagree with his nobles, without necessarily coming into open clash with them. Apparently, the Olu had the right to appoint as *Ojoye* anyone from

---

1 A. F. C. Ryder: 'Missionary Activity in the kingdom of Warri to the early Nineteenth century', *J.H.S.N.*, Vol. II, No. 1, Dec. 1960, p. 1.
2 Barbot who takes after Bosman stated that 'the town of Aweri' belonged 'to a nation, independent of Benin, and only an ally . . . of it'. Jean Barbot: *A Description of the Coasts of North and South Guinea*, London 1732, p. 355.

outside the band of the original seventy nobles, in recognition of services rendered. The tendency, however, was for some of the titles to become hereditary within certain families. The Olu's council was the supreme legislative, executive and judicial body for all Itsękiriland.

It does not appear that there was any great outspread of the Itsękiri people prior to the eighteenth century. Such settlements as sprang up in the immediate environs of the capital were presumably governed by 'deputies' sent from the capital, working in conjunction with the elders of the settlements. The major movement away from the capital and its immediate environs took place in the late eighteenth and the first half of the nineteenth century. Two main reasons have been advanced to explain this movement. The first is the reputed harshness of the reign of the Olu Akęngbuwa I (died 1848) which forced a number of the *Ojoye* to leave the capital and found new settlements for themselves and their immediate kith and kin. The second reason was economic. From the late eighteenth century, the Rivers Forcados and Escravos were declining in commercial importance as European trading vessels were beginning to anchor at places like Eghoro in the Benin River instead of at Ode-Itsękiri. Consequently aspiring traders began to move to the Benin River to meet the European trade. Bobi, Jakpa, Batęrę and Ebrohimi were among settlements founded as a result of this movement.[1]

The government of the new settlements was usually in the hands of the elders headed by the *Olarę-aja* (literally, the eldest male in the settlement) and the *Okpanran* (priest). Often the oldest member of the founder's patrilineage group was regarded as the *Olarę-aja* whether he was in fact the oldest man in the community or not. Matters concerning the village were disposed of by the council of elders. The quarters and extended families handled matters within their respective competence. There was a theoretical right of appeal from the village council to the Olu's council, and serious inter-settlement disputes were also sent to that body.

The social organization of the Itsękiri differed in important respects from that of their Urhobo neighbours. The Itsękiri can

---

1 P. C. Lloyd: 'The Itsekiri in the Nineteenth century; An Outline Social History', *Journal of African History*, Vol. IV, No 2, 1963, pp. 212–14.

be broadly divided into two groups—the Ọtọn-Olu (descendants of the royal family) and the Ọmajaja (free borns). The Ọmajaja can be sub-divided into the Ojoye and the ordinary citizens. In addition to the above were the *eru* (slaves) and Ọtọn-eru (descendants of slaves).[1] The part which a man played in the affairs of state was determined to a considerable extent by his social standing. Indeed the Itsẹkiri were and are extremely touchy about their own ẹbi (descent group). Most Itsẹkiri strive to trace their genealogy to an Olu or Ojoye. Failure to produce a 'satisfactory' genealogy was likely to lead to one being classified as an ọtọn-eru. Although slaves in the Itsẹkiri community were never barbarously treated, and although many of them rose to positions of affluence, it was, nevertheless, a social stigma to be a slave. It was not allowed, for example, for an Itsẹkiri to enslave another Itsẹkiri. Consequently all slaves and their descendants were largely non-Itsẹkiri. Hence all ọtọn-eru were necessarily second-rate citizens in strict law even if in practice little notice was taken of the fact. Even among the Itsẹkiri proper, birth or status group was of supreme importance. Thus an Ọtọn-olu was likely to be accorded more respect and to take a more active part in the affairs of state than a commoner who was much older than he. Generally speaking, therefore, it is true that among the Itsẹkiri birth played a much greater part in determining the role a man played in the social and political life of his community than it did among the Urhobo.

In addition to the social divisions noted above, the Itsẹkiri also had what might be described as age groups for men and women. C. O. Omonẹukarin lists five of these for the men. At the bottom were the Ọmẹtie-ọnọkẹrẹn, made up of boys under twenty years. While a boy belonged to this group he learnt most of the trades and occupations of his people, and performed simple duties for his family and community.

The Ẹdẹma age-group was made up of young men between the ages of twenty and thirty-five years. The ẹdẹma was supposed to be able to enter into life as an independent individual, and to begin to earn his own living by fishing, trading and other occupations. The Ighele were the able-bodied men of thirty-five to fifty-five

---

1 Omoneukarin, op. cit., p. 20.

36

years who were expected to play a full and active part in the affairs of the community. The next two, the *Olare* and *Eligbo*, were elders who headed the affairs of their various communities. The *eligbo* were usually men of very old age who could no longer actively participate in the affairs of their community.[1]

From the above, it is clear that the Itsẹkiri age-groups were not comparable in their organization and functions to the Urhobo age-grades as previously described. They had very few political functions to perform. In fact they represented little more than successive stages in the life of the Itsẹkiri male.

The Itsẹkiri judicial system was, in essence, very much like that of the Urhobo already described. Procedure was virtually the same, and there was the same theoretical right of appeal from village council to Olu's council, as from village to clan council among the Urhobo. Even in matters of penalties inflicted for specific crimes and offences there was remarkable similarity between the two systems. The real difference was, as has been indicated, in the personnel of the council or 'court'. In the case of the Itsẹkiri, it has been suggested, birth and 'class' played a more conspicuous part in determining the members of the council, than among the Urhobo.

The Itsẹkiri, like most Nigerian peoples, also had recourse to trial by ordeal and to oaths when there was doubt as to the truth of the evidence, or when a party declared guilty still proclaimed his innocence and insisted on vindicating himself. The forms of ordeal used were the same as described for the Urhobo. This is the place to mention one particular form of ordeal which brought the Itsẹkiri in contact with their Urhobo neighbours. It has been stated that for the trial of suspected witches, the sasswood ordeal was generally employed. There was one other form of ordeal used which was very popular all over the Warri (now Delta) Province. This was the famous Eni Ordeal of Uzere in the Isoko country. Eni was the clan god inhabiting a lake named after it. It is not now known when it was first recognized that Eni could detect and at the same time kill off witches. By the middle of the nineteenth century, however, it is said that hundreds of suspected witches

1 Ibid., p. 23.

37

were taken to Uzere every year to undergo the ordeal and prove their innocence or take the consequences of their guilt.

To Eni came not only the Isoko and Urhobo, but also Ijọ, Itsẹkiri, Kwalẹ and Aboh. The *Ovie* of Uzere was high priest of Eni and received the fees which were paid by those who sought to undergo the ordeal. The fear of witchcraft was so widespread that Eni's power which, as it was believed, could not only detect but kill off the witches in one and the same process, wielded great influence over surrounding areas. The procedure at the trials was to take the suspected witches to the banks of the Eni Lake, in a procession headed by the *Ovie*. There the *Ovie* performed certain rites and then daubed the bodies of the suspected witches with white chalk while uttering certain incantations. After this, they were taken to the middle of the lake in a canoe and were ordered to jump into the lake and swim ashore—back to the *Ovie*. Witches were supposed, by the power of Eni, to be drawn down to the bottom of the lake and drowned, while the innocent could swim happily ashore.[1] British administrative officers claimed that Eni was one gigantic fraud. The Eni Lake, they reported, was full of ravenous crocodiles brought there while still young and accustomed to feeding on nothing but human flesh. Those who died there, they argued, died not because they were witches, but because they could not swim or were eaten up by the crocodiles.[2] The Uzere people counter this by arguing that if Eni were a fraud, they would scarcely have allowed their own citizens to participate in the trials; that the Ijọ and Itsẹkiri, who were usually good swimmers, died there as well as non-swimmers, and that others, who were not particularly able swimmers actually succeeded in getting ashore.[3] They agree that there were crocodiles in the lake, but deny that these were trained on a diet of human flesh since, as fishing in the lake was prohibited, these beasts had plenty of fish to eat. Indeed the Uzere people claim that after each trial a group of people known as the

---

1 See J. W. Welch: 'Witchcraft and Christianity in the Niger Delta', *Church Overseas*, Vol. IV, 1931, p. 319.

2 Cal. Prof. 10/3, Vol. III: Report on Uzeri Ordeal. See also Welch, op. cit.

3 I was informed, for example, that the mother of the present *Otota* of Uzere, Chief William Otobo, succeeded in getting ashore, though she could scarcely swim.

Otuada collected the bodies and buried them. Fraud or no fraud, while it remained, Eni was a powerful influence over all the peoples of Warri Province and served to draw them together at each trial.

The last Olu of Itsẹkiri to reign before the establishment of British rule was Akẹngbuwa. Akẹngbuwa's reign is reputed to have been harsh and unprofitable.[1] The consequent migration of various *Ojoye* to the Benin River and the founding of new settlements has already been noted. In 1848 Olu Akẹngbuwa died. His two sons and most likely successors, Omateye and Ejo followed him to the grave with a rapidity which Egharevba attributes to a curse by the Ọba of Benin.[2] The death of the two princes ushered in an interregnum which lasted for eighty-eight years. Tradition has it that when the head slaves of the two princes realized that neither of their masters could succeed to the Itsẹkiri throne, they held a secret meeting at which they resolved not to allow any other person to be installed as Olu of Itsẹkiriland.[3] They apparently possessed the means and men to make good this resolve, for as Moore records, 'they were so formidable in wealth and men, that no power or force could with-stand them in those days'.[4]

Exactly what happened in the Itsẹkiri capital is not clear. Apparently the slaves killed all those most qualified to succeed to the throne, or at any rate caused enough fear among the royal family to force many members of the latter to flee the capital. Ultimately Iye Idọlọrusan (the European traders called her 'Queen Dola') half-sister of the deceased Olu returned to the capital and with the help of Ebrimoni, one of the head slaves who had organized the revolt, set up a council of state made up mostly of members of the royal family. An effort was made to instal an Olu but the three princes regarded as best qualified by virtue of their wealth were unacceptable because they were children of slave mothers. The best that was achieved was the appointment of an *Olotu* or Regent in the person of Prince Eri, a son of Akẹngbuwa.[5]

It is not clear with what motive (other than that popularly ascribed to them) the head slaves of Omateye and Ejo organized the revolt which plunged the Itsẹkiri 'nation' into the interregnum.

---

1 Lloyd: 'The Itsekiri in the Nineteenth century', p. 214.
2 Egharevba, op. cit., p. 47.   3 Moore, op. cit., p. 91.
4 Ibid.   5 Ibid., pp. 90–2.

39

These slaves suffered from a number of disabilities. Although many of them had become wealthy through trade, and occupied important positions within the families in which they found themselves, Itsẹkiri society was such that they could not, in strict theory as well as in practice, become the heads of the families or groups to which they belonged.[1] They remained in essence transferable property. For this reason, in this revolt there was probably that same determination, which Dr. K. O. Dike says actuated the slave revolts of the Eastern Delta in the years 1850–70,[2] to fight for changes in the political institutions of the society in which they lived—political changes which would reflect to some extent the economic worth of the slave class. If this determination was at the back of the revolt, it was apparently limited to the slaves of the two dead princes, for the other slaves did not actively aid the revolt, though they probably joined in the various acts of lawlessness which marked the beginning of the interregnum. There was no other effort on the part of these slaves to fight for political power, even though their position after the revolt remained as it had been before. If therefore the revolt of the slaves of the dead princes was aimed at effecting a change in the political *status quo*, it failed to achieve any permanent results. Indeed, when Consul John Beecroft suggested making Ebrimoni the Olu in 1851, the princes of the royal family opposed the move on the ground that Ebrimoni was a slave.[3] They on their part could not agree on who among themselves should be made the Olu. Beecroft had to be content with getting the Itsẹkiri elders to appoint a 'chief of the Benin River' better known as 'governor of the River', in the person of Idiare.[4]

The interregnum witnessed a breakdown of that central government to which the Itsẹkiri were accustomed. This breakdown of central authority did not, however, mean for the Itsẹkiri a loss of identity as a people. Until the great exodus from the capital in the eighteenth and nineteenth centuries, the Itsẹkiri were accustomed to centralized control from the Olu and his council. Even after the

---

1 Lloyd: 'The Itsekiri in the Nineteenth century', p. 217.
2 Dr. K. O. Dike discusses the slave revolts in the Eastern Delta in chapter VIII (pp. 153–65) of his *Trade and Politics in the Niger Delta*, London 1956.
3 Lloyd: 'The Itsekiri in the Nineteenth century', p. 215.
4 Ibid., p. 216.

movement to the Benin River, the power and prestige of the Olu as ruler of all Itsẹkiriland; the fact that Ode-Itsẹkiri remained the largest of the Itsẹkiri settlements; intermarriage between members of the various settlements; the existence of religious and other rituals and ceremonies which were common to all Itsẹkiriland; these factors helped to create a feeling of oneness which even the interregnum could not completely destroy. The compactness of their territory and the comparative smallness of their population were additional factors which created a sense of togetherness.

In addition to the above there was another factor which necessitated the preservation of a measure of unity among the Itsẹkiri even during the interregnum. This was the need for some authority which could deal with the European traders in their midst. The appointment by the people of 'Governors of the River' at the instance of the British consul in the years 1851–84[1] provided an officer of state around whom the Itsẹkiri people could, and did, rally for the protection of their interests. Hence despite the interregnum and despite the foundation of new settlements, the commercial interests of the leading Itsẹkiri families helped to preserve a measure of unity, however internally uneasy. In this regard the Itsẹkiri were, at the time of the advent of British rule, more united as a people and more aware of their common interests and problems than were their Urhobo neighbours.

This unity and the awareness of belonging to a single central political unit had one important result in the context of Itsẹkiri-Urhobo relations. As has already been pointed out, it was forbidden for an Itsẹkiri to enslave a fellow Itsẹkiri. The outcome was that while the Itsẹkiri bought slaves from among their neighbours, a very few Itsẹkiri slaves found themselves in the hands of these neighbours. Such Itsẹkiri slaves as were found outside their country were people either sold because of offences against the state, or otherwise enslaved by non-Itsẹkiri and these were not many. Among the Urhobo the situation was very different. The clan was the largest political unit within which blood relationship was recognized. It was therefore allowed for a man from one clan to enslave anyone from outside that clan. Consciousness of belonging

---

1 These appointments are discussed in greater detail in chapter 3.

to a greater Urhobo community was absent until the late 1930s when events began to demand a larger unit for political action. The upshot of this situation was that Urhobo people enslaved their fellow countrymen and sold these to outsiders, prominent among whom were the Itsẹkiri. At a later period, the number of Urhobo slaves in Itsẹkiri hands was to be used by the Itsẹkiri as evidence of overlordship over the Urhobo.

In another respect the absence of an Olu had an important result. Not only did the interregnum mean the temporary end of the traditional central government, but it also meant that no titles of nobility could be conferred. Those who held titles during the lifetime of the last Olu could not exercise the functions appertaining to their titles. Therefore, in matters which had to do with the Itsẹkiri people as a whole, there grew up during the interregnum a body of men, drawn from among the most influential families, who took the necessary decisions. These men were not just the *Otọn-Olu* or leading members of the families of the *Ojoye* but included those whose wealth had raised them to positions of eminence among their people. These were the men who signed the various treaties and other agreements with the British in the years 1851–84. It was thus possible in 1851 for Idiare, Idibofun, Olomu, Numa and others, to sign with Beecroft a trade agreement binding on all Itsẹkirimen and for Nana and others to sign a treaty of protection for all Itsẹkiriland in 1884. Among the Urhobo of that age, it was impossible for any group of 'chiefs' to claim to speak for all Urhoboland, because the political organization of Urhoboland was based largely on village communities, each of which was virtually independent of the other. The British treaty-makers were to find this aspect of Urhobo political organization a source of annoyance[1] and to use it as evidence of the backwardness of the Urhobo as compared with their Itsẹkiri neighbours. Further, these years accustomed the Itsẹkiri to accepting some form of control from

---

[1] One of the reasons Gallwey gave for not immediately entering into treaty relations with the Urhobo towns he visited in 1891 was that each town was independent and therefore many treaties would have to be signed. This, together with the fact that the Urhobo had not been previously brought into contact with Europeans convinced Gallwey of their 'uncivilization'. See Gallwey's 'Report on Visit to the Oil Market of the Sobo and Abraka Districts', F.O. 84/2111, Enclosure in Macdonald to F.O. No 30 of 12 Dec. 1891.

Two scenes from the Niger delta. That below is taken from the air.
Shell photographs.

An Itsẹkiri ceremonial canoe, photographed in the 1890's.

people whose main, if not sole, claim to the exercise of such control was the wealth and position they had acquired for themselves through trade rather than just their birth or 'class' as of old. Thus the phenomenon of parvenu 'paramount chiefs' and other 'chiefs' was to be less disturbing to the Itsẹkiri than to the Urhobo during the period of British administration, as something similar to it had appeared, and had been accepted, during the interregnum. Finally, despite the absence of an Olu, central control of some description was never lost among the Itsẹkiri. Consequently, the centralizing and federalizing tendencies of the British Government during the first two decades of this century were to be more easily acceptable to the Itsẹkiri than to the Urhobo. Stresses and strains began to develop between the Itsẹkiri and the Urhobo when these tendencies, more acceptable to one group, were forced on the other in a manner which, intentionally or incidentally, gave the impression of subjecting the Urhobo to institutions—British institutions—dominated by the Itsẹkiri.

Today Itsẹkiri and Urhoboland are geographically contiguous along one of their borders (see map facing p. 10). This in itself has led to a fair amount of intermingling between the Itsẹkiri and those usually referred to as the Western Urhobo. But this proximity has also helped to accentuate such differences as do exist between the Itsẹkiri and the Urhobo. One of the problems with which the British administration was to be faced was whether to treat the Itsẹkiri and the Urhobo clans on their eastern border as one administrative unit, or to respect their ethnic differences and regard them as two separate units. That the British did, in fact, tend to treat the Itsẹkiri and the Western Urhobo clans as a single political entity was, to some extent, due to the degree of intermingling of the two groups. But that the British attitude produced a certain measure of dissatisfaction, mainly among the Urhobo, demonstrated that however close the Itsẹkiri and their Urhobo neighbours had become, there were still differences between the two peoples, as well as group susceptibilities which had to be respected. This study concerns itself with these differences and susceptibilities, as well as with Itsẹkiri-Urhobo interdependence and mutual co-operation.

Chapter 2
Early European activities and Itsẹkiri-Urhobo relations, 1485–1883[1]

The Portuguese were the first Europeans to come in contact with the people now known as the Itsẹkiri. Exactly when this initial contact was made is uncertain. For although the Portuguese are said to have known of the existence of the River Forcados before 1485,[2] there is no conclusive evidence that the Forcados River area was inhabited by the Itsẹkiri at that time. Pacheco Pereira, who visited this area towards the end of the fifteenth century, mentioned the 'Subou' and 'Jos' peoples but made no mention of the Itsẹkiri nor any other people easily recognizable as such. He, however, recorded that the inhabitants along the Forcados River were called 'Huela'.[3] It is not known for certain who these 'Huela' were. It is possible that they were an amalgam of the different peoples who lived in that area, brought together by prospects of trade. Pereira also spoke of 'a place of barter', five leagues up the left branch of the Forcados, from which the Portuguese bought slaves, cotton cloth, panther skins, palm oil and 'coris'.[4] Of the purely internal organization of this trade at the time of Pereira's visit there is no information, but it is reasonable to assume a measure of commercial contact between the 'Huela' at the coast and the surrounding peoples, among them the 'Subou' to the hinterland.

1 There is very little material available for this chapter. I am heavily indebted to Professor A. F. C. Ryder's two articles in the *Journal of the Historical Society of Nigeria* which are repeatedly cited in this chapter. These articles are based on Portuguese records. I am also indebted to Dr. P. C. Lloyd's work on the Itsẹkiri. I am drawing heavily too on my own field investigations. The inadequacy of source-material has necessarily affected the style. If therefore the inconclusive nature of some of the statements made in this chapter tends to cramp the style and render it monotonous, I hope the flaw will be excused.
2 A. F. C. Ryder: 'Early Portuguese Trading Voyage', *J.H.S.N.*, Vol. 1, No. 4, Dec. 1959, p. 294.
3 Pacheco Pereira, op. cit., p. 129.   4 Ibid., p. 128.

Professor A. F. C. Ryder has published the records of a Portuguese trading voyage to the Forcados River in 1522.[1] From this account, the articles in which the Portuguese traded in this area were slaves, pepper, ivory, 'coris', cotton cloth, some leopard skins and palm oil. In return the Portuguese bartered brass, copper manillas and later, tobacco and other assorted goods, among them linen cloth.[2] The record of two voyages to the area by one James Welsh in the years 1588 and 1590 gives a similar list of articles. According to that record the boat took home in 1589, ninety-four bags of pepper, twenty-eight elephant's teeth, 'oil of palm, cloth made of cotton, and the bark of palm tree, very curiously woven.' In return they gave cloth, linen and woollen, iron work of sundry sorts, glass beads and coral. On the next trip thirty-two barrels of 'oil of palm trees' were shipped.[3] From the above lists of the articles for which the Portuguese and other European trade, the question arises, which of the peoples who inhabited the area watered by the rivers Forcados, Escravos and Benin produced the various articles involved in the trade.

For the fifteenth and early sixteenth centuries, it is not possible to be definite about the Nigerian peoples involved in the trade both at the coast and in the hinterland. It is clear, however, that from the closing decades of the sixteenth century, the Portuguese were trading with the people now known as the Itsẹkiri. Professor Ryder's work on the Portuguese missionary activities in the 'Warri' kingdom from the sixteenth to the nineteenth century,[4] indicates that there

---

1 Ryder: 'Early Portuguese Trading Voyage'.
2 Ibid., p. 296. Also 'Two Voyages to Benin beyond Guinea in 1588 and 1590' written by James Welsh, Chief Master in the Voyage—*Astleys Voyages*, Vol. I, London 1745, p. 201. Barbot describes 'coris' which he writes 'accory' as follows: 'The blue coral grows in branchy bushes, like red coral, at the bottom of the river and lakes in Benin which the natives have a peculiar art to grind or work into beads like olives, and is a very profitable merchandize at the Gold Coast'. See Jean Barbot, op. cit., p. 369.
3 James Welsh: 'Two Voyages . . .', p. 205.
4 Ryder: 'Missionary Activity in Warri', p. 1. Ryder's 'Warri Kingdom' means the Itsẹkiri Kingdom. There exists some ambiguity about the name 'Warri'. The Itsẹkiri sometimes call themselves Iwere. Early European accounts have variants of this—Oere, Awerri, Ouwerre—which they used both as the name of the Itsẹkiri capital and that of the people. The form 'Warri' did not gain currency till the nineteenth century, and by that time there were two places

had developed, by the end of the sixteenth century, a people who could definitely be identified as the Itsẹkiri. European commercial and other activities with the Itsẹkiri people can, therefore, with reasonable certainty be dated back to the late sixteenth century.

While it is possible to speak with certainty of European trade with the Itsẹkiri at that time, it remains a matter of conjecture which of the other peoples in the neighbourhood provided the Itsẹkiri with the goods which they 'sold' to the Portuguese. From what is known of Itsẹkiri industries and the geography of their land, there can be no doubt that some of the products which the Itsẹkiri sold to the Europeans were obtained as a result of a purely local trade between them and their neighbours. It is unlikely for example that the Itsẹkiri produced any palm oil themselves, nor is there any indication that they 'produced' ivory. Both these commodities were therefore very likely to have been obtained from neighbouring peoples by the Itsẹkiri and then sold by them to the Europeans. There is a striking similarity between the list of goods bought by the Portuguese in the Forcados River (as recorded by Pereira) and those bought by James Welsh from Benin. In particular, the fact that the Itsẹkiri were selling cotton cloth to the Europeans would indicate some commercial contact between them and the Bini, who were known as weavers of cotton cloth. In addition to Itsẹkiri-Bini commercial contact, it is here suggested that the Urhobo people to the hinterland of the Itsẹkiri country were also involved in the local trade. Although, as indicated in the last chapter, one cannot be sure how long the Urhobo have been settled in their present position, it is likely (from Pereira's reference already cited) that some of them were already settled in the area behind the Itsẹkiri country by the late sixteenth century.

Pereira noted that 'the country called Subou' had a fair amount of pepper. Urhobo traditions recall the exploits of great hunters who trapped elephants in huge pits. Indeed one of the Urhobo clans, Evwreni, was founded, it is said, by elephant hunters from present-day Iboland. It would thus appear that pepper and some ivory were obtainable in the Urhobo country, and some of this probably

---

which could take the name—the Itsẹkiri capital and the present township of Warri, all of which was not an Itsẹkiri settlement. The importance of this for this study is developed later. See Chapter 6.

found its way to Itsẹkiriland as a result of commercial relations between the Urhobo and the coastal people. The Urhobo probably sold to the Itsẹkiri some palm oil[1] also. One can therefore postulate commercial relations between the Itsẹkiri and the Urhobo in the late sixteenth century. The requirements of the trade with the Europeans probably had the effect of further stimulating the commercial contact brought about by the needs of Itsẹkiri people on the mangrove fringe, and their Urhobo neighbours, an agricultural people, to the hinterland.

If the Itsẹkiri traded with the Urhobo in the sixteenth century, what, apart from the export crops, were the other articles in this trade? European traders and other visitors in the eighteenth century described two Itsẹkiri industries: salt-making, and the manufacture of earthenware.[2] These industries were being carried on before the eighteenth century, the need for both salt and earthenware being more pressing before the growth of European commerce in these commodities than after. European sources give the impression that even in the nineteenth century foreign salt was not very popular in the Itsẹkiri area.[3] Apparently, the people preferred their local brand of salt. Urhobo traditions state that the Urhobo were 'buying' salt from the Itsẹkiri long before foreign salt became a popular item of trade. The trade in this commodity is one of the oldest in the area. Pottery was obviously an industry of considerable antiquity.[4] The Itsẹkiri thus had salt and pots of various types and sizes to trade with their Urhobo neighbours. In addition to these two commodities there were the products of the fishing industry, in which the bulk

---

1 So far as is known the Itsẹkiri have never been producers of palm oil. The oil palm tree does not flourish in the mangrove swamps, and the Itsẹkiri have never acquired the art of scaling the palm tree for the purpose of obtaining the fruit for the manufacture of palm oil. Although the oil palm was plentiful in the Benin kingdom proper, it would appear as if the people have never been seriously engaged in the palm oil industry. See R. E. Bradbury, op. cit., p. 24.

2 See Ryder: 'Missionary Activity in Warri', loc. cit. and Captain John Adams, op. cit., p. 122.

3 See Adams, op. cit., p. 241.

4 See Adams, op. cit., p. 122 for comments on the raw material for the industry: 'the subsoil . . . is composed of a tenacious red clay, from which the inhabitants manufacture jars for holding water, and utensils of various forms for domestic purposes.'

of the Itsẹkiri indulged. In exchange the Urhobo bartered agri-cultural products—pepper, yam, plantain, corn and later the various products of the cassava plant,[1] and some ivory and palm oil, the latter growing in quantity as demand for it grew with its exportation into Europe. With increased European commerce, the Itsẹkiri would have benefited by having extra goods to trade to the Urhobo, these being European manufactures—often cheap glass beads, cowries, manillas, tobacco, caps, various types of cloth. The picture here painted would bear out Peter Lloyd's statement:

> It will be clear that the mangrove swamps do not permit a subsistence economy and the siting of the earlier Itsekiri settlements on the edge of the swamps and on the borders of Urhobo country may be ascribed to their need to trade with an agricultural people.[2]

The pattern of trade here described is similar to what obtained in the Eastern Delta. As Dr. G. I. Jones points out for that region, neither the delta nor its hinterland was self-sufficient in its economy. In the east as in the west, the delta provided fish and salt while the hinterland offered bulk foodstuffs and labour.[3] The one difference which emerges from a comparison of the Eastern and the Western Delta is that in the west, there was not that movement of skilled labour from the hinterland to the coastal territory which seemed to be a noticeable feature of the Eastern Delta. The Urhobo, unlike the Ibo, had no skilled craftsmen and artisans—no 'medicine men', priests, blacksmiths and carvers[4] to send into Itsẹkiriland.

If the Urhobo had no skilled labour to offer to the Itsẹkiri, they had slaves. From the beginning of Portuguese commercial activity

---

1 Plantain was reported to be an article of the local trade in the Benin area by 1588. See James Welsh in *Astley's Voyages*, Vol. I, p. 202. I have not been able to trace exactly when cassava, which is said to be native to South America, was introduced into this area. Barbot refers to 'cassaba' out of which 'Farinha de Pao' a common food of the people was made. Barbot, op. cit., p. 377.

2 P. C. Lloyd: *The Itsekiri*, p. 177.

3 G. I. Jones, op. cit., p. 13.

4 Ibid., p. 13. One looks in vain for any large-scale movement of the Urhobo to the coastal areas to meet the trade. Such movement as there was would appear to have been connected with inter-marriage and the movement of slaves from the hinterland to the coast. As will be shown later, there was some movement from the coast to the hinterland—a movement dictated by the commercial requirements of the Itsẹkiri.

in Itsẹkiriland, till the early nineteenth century, slaves were a regular item of trade. The account of the voyage of 1522 which Dr. Ryder quotes in full gives the following summary:[1]

128 slaves
19 Elephant tusks
4,029 'Coris'
280 Gallons of palm oil (by rough computation)
40 Loin cloths
1 Hide
1 Manilla worth of clay.

This represents on the whole quite modest business. Unfortunately it is impossible to compare these figures with any others similarly detailed. James Welsh's account already cited represents even more modest business. The recurrent theme of bad trade and poverty which the Portuguese put abroad during their missionary activities in the Itsẹkiri kingdom probably meant that during the sixteenth and seventeenth centuries, the trade was not very much more than as represented in 1522, and was possibly less.[2]

What was the source of the slaves the Itsẹkiri sold to the Portuguese? As one Itsẹkiri was not allowed to enslave another, the Itsẹkiri had to look outside their own ethnic group for their supply of slaves. Commenting on this issue, Dr. Lloyd wrote:

> The Itsẹkiri claim that they never raided for slaves and this seems to be true. They purchased them in the Yoruba and Benin slave markets on their frontiers (these slaves being war captives exported southwards), from the Ijaw pirates who seized defenceless canoes, and from the Urhobo and Kwale who sold into slavery their tribesmen convicted of certain serious crimes.[3]

Urhobo traditions confirm the Itsẹkiri claim that they did not raid the Urhobo for slaves except, of course, such raids as were the

---

1 Ryder: 'Early Portuguese Trading voyage', pp. 307–15.
2 Ryder: 'Missionary Activity in Warri', p. 3.
3 Lloyd: p. 196. The question might be posed as to what the Itsẹkiri did with their firearms if they did not employ them in slave raids. As this chapter makes clear later, arms were needed for self defence against Ijọ 'pirates', and for occasionally brow-beating the Urhobo oil producers. Firearms were also valuable articles of trade in themselves. Besides, like slaves and canoes, firearms constituted an index of wealth and social status.

product of trade disputes, for it was an accepted way of settling a debt, especially in the nineteenth century, to seize the slaves of the debtor.

The volume of the trade in Urhobo slaves is not at all easy to determine. In 1522, 128 slaves were exported during one trip. The over-all total for the year is unknown. Such a total, however, would have included non-Urhobo as well as Urhobo slaves. In the eighteenth century, the hey-day of the slave trade, the volume of the trade in this part of the coast would appear to have remained low. Barbot wrote of the Benin River area in 1732:

> They export from thence lusty strong slaves, much better than we have them at any other parts of Guinea. But this place will not afford at most five hundred slaves in a whole year.[1]

Captain Landolphe, who traded in this same area during the closing decades of the eighteenth century, took away a cargo of 360 slaves in 1769 and 1778—and this at a time when there were no rival slavers competing with him. On each occasion Landolphe had to wait for three months to find his cargo, buying sometimes only ten slaves in a day.[2]

The method of obtaining slaves, which is described below, explains how it was that it took such a long time to find a cargo of four hundred: slaves were obtained through a rather tortuous system, only a few being available at any one time. As the numbers cited above included Bini, and Yoruba, as well as Urhobo slaves, it is clear that the number of Urhobo slaves involved in the trade could not have been large. Dr. Lloyd claims that the Itsẹkiri kingdom must have imported at least a thousand slaves annually, and that most of these were Urhobo.[3] In the light of the available evidence it is difficult to uphold Dr. Lloyd's claim.[4] It would appear that Dr. Lloyd bases his assertion on the number of Urhobo slaves in Itsẹkiri hands

---

1 Barbot, op. cit., p. 377.
2 P. C. Lloyd: 'Captain Landolphe and the Compagnie d' Owhere et de Benin', *Odu*, No. 5, 1957, pp. 14–15.
3 Lloyd: 'The Itsekiri in the Nineteenth Century', p. 218. Dr. Lloyd was writing of the turn of the nineteenth century.
4 There is a tendency to exaggerate the volume of the trade in slaves. Dr. Lloyd produces no satisfactory evidence in support of his claim that the Itsẹkiri exported at least 1000 slaves annually.

during the nineteenth century. It should be remembered, however, that in the nineteenth century slaves were no longer being exported in large numbers and so could multiply rapidly within a fairly short period. Besides, it is one of the paradoxes of nineteenth-century Niger Delta history, that the ushering in of 'legitimate' commerce in articles like palm produce led to a greater demand for domestic slaves.[1] This development partially explains the great number of Urhobo slaves in Itsẹkiri hands during the nineteenth century.

The slaves 'sold' by the Urhobo to the Itsẹkiri were obtained from various sources. First, there were criminals of various types who on conviction were sold into slavery.[2] Next, there were the products of inter-clan wars. The fifteenth to the seventeenth centuries probably constituted the period when the various Urhobo clans were settling down in their respective localities. This would also have been the period when most clans began to spread outwards from their headquarters, as groups moved away from settlements where increasing population had begun to give rise to comparative scarcity of land, to more unoccupied areas. This expansion often led to clashes between different groups. Urhobo traditions are replete with inter-clan (sometimes even inter-village) fights resulting from a clash over settling land or fishing ponds.[3] During these fights some of the enemy captives were often quickly sold off— usually before the end of the fighting, as otherwise restitution of captives might be decided on. It is impossible to estimate the number of slaves obtained as a consequence of these wars. At all times the slave trade in Urhoboland was a clandestine and small-scale affair. The 'fairs' of the Eastern Delta[4] and the slave markets in Yorubaland and Benin[5] were totally absent from Urhoboland. There was good reason for this. The Urhobo could not organize raids against any of their neighbours—the Ijọ, renowned water

---

1 Infra, pp. 59–60.
2 See Chapter 1.
3 The Intelligence Reports of nearly all the Urhobo clans abound with inter-clan wars resulting from land disputes. My own investigations have confirmed this. See Chapter 1.
4 W. Nicholas Thomas: 'On the Oil Rivers of West Africa', *Proceedings of the Royal Geographical Society*, Vol. 17, 1872–3, p. 148. The 'fairs' spoken of referred to the Bonny and Calabar districts.
5 Lloyd: *The Itsekiri*, p. 196.

pirates, dreaded even by the well-armed Itsẹkiri; the Bini, who were infinitely better organized and had the reputation of their Ọba to frighten the neighbourhood; the Aboh who were in contact with the Eastern Delta and so in possession of firearms; the Itsẹkiri, armed with firearms and in contact with the Europeans. Any slaves obtained from these people, and there were a few, were obtained purely by accident. The Urhobo were thus forced to look among themselves for slaves. There was at that time little consciousness of belonging to a common stock, the clan being the largest unit within which consanguinity played an important part in social relations. But although the lot of the slave was not unduly hard, and although consciousness of being one people is a recent development by no means yet complete, it was generally regarded as degrading to be a slave. This meant that to enslave a man from another clan or village carried with it the possibility of reprisal should it become known by whom the enslavement was effected. In such circumstances, slave markets inside Urhoboland would have led to endless wars between clans. The outcome was the practice whereby slaves were sold off as quickly as possible after they had been obtained. When a man obtained a slave, by either force or guile, he got in touch with a friend who could dispose of the slave on agreed terms or knew a third party who could. Over the years the system became efficient and the man who first obtained the slave did not always know where the slave was finally disposed of. Generally it was the practice to remove the slave as far away from his clan as possible lest he should escape and, perhaps, organize reprisal. It is probable that in time agents with a reputation for speedy dispatch of slaves sprang up, thus giving some organization to the system, though the number involved in any single transaction was always small. It was rare for a man to hoard a large number of slaves hoping to do one great sale. Children and foreigners were differently treated, as these could not escape very easily and so did not involve the same probability of reprisal. It was from this group that farm labourers and trading hands were recruited. It would thus appear that it was largely through this system and the disposal of criminals from their clans that the Itsẹkiri and other people obtained Urhobo slaves during this period. It must be remembered that the process was not always a direct one. An Urhobo slave could, in the first instance, be sold to a Bini or an Ijọ and yet finally end up in the hands of an Itsẹkiri man. The Itsẹkiri scarcely ever got any Isoko as slaves—the method of trade already described, and a look at the map of the area, make it easy to understand why Isoko slaves should have gone more to the Aboh and Ijọ than to the Itsẹkiri.

Another source of the Urhobo slaves found in Itsẹkiriland was the system whereby the Urhobo gave their children as pledges for debt owed to the Itsẹkiri. But this belonged more to the late eighteenth and nineteenth centuries than the earlier period, and was a product of the commercial methods of the time. The system became firmly entrenched in the commercial code when palm oil became the major article of the export trade. Until then trade between the Itsẹkiri and the Urhobo was a less complicated affair, based on simple barter.[1]

The fortunes of the over-all trade in this area cannot be followed in any detail due to a scarcity of records. The Portuguese, who endeavoured to maintain missionaries at the Itsẹkiri capital from the sixteenth century right up to the beginning of the nineteenth, constantly reported that the Itsẹkiri kingdom was poor. Those reports, though not detailed, gave some useful glimpses of the trade of the area during the period. In 1597 the Itsẹkiri kingdom was described by the Bishop of São Thomé as 'very poor'.[2] This poverty did not seem to mean that no slaves were obtainable, for, around the same period, the Spanish king allowed priests who visited the Itsẹkiri capital in merchant vessels to buy slaves and sell them to defray their expenses.[3] When the son of the reigning Olu, 'Don Domingos', who had gone to Portugal to be instructed in sacerdotal duties, was about to return home around 1610, he presented a

---

1 The position as it developed in the nineteenth century is described below, on pp. 59–60. Most of the material used in this discussion of the Urhobo slave trade comes from my own field work especially in Agbọn, Agbarho, Emevọ, Iyede, Ozọrọ, Udu and Ughiẹnvwe clans.

2 Ryder, 'Missionary Activity in Warri', p. 3. While one must be cautious about these Portuguese reports as they could mean that the Olu was unwilling to maintain the missionaries, it is true from the evidence that the Itsẹkiri were able to do very little trade with the Europeans in the seventeenth century.

3 Ibid., p. 4.

number of petitions to the king, one of which sought to get the king to do all in his power to help increase Portuguese commerce with the Itsẹkiri. It would therefore seem that the trade at the beginning of the seventeenth century was far from encouraging.

The seventeenth century, on the whole, could scarcely have been a prosperous time for the area. The Portuguese were already being ousted as the leading European traders by the Dutch who, Ryder remarks, because they found 'Warri' port 'relatively inaccessible and the trade unprofitable', neglected the area, leaving it 'the one port on the coast that remained open to the surviving trickle of Portuguese trade'. Between 1620 and about 1650 we have it on the same authority that the Portuguese trade with 'Warri' 'dwindled to vanishing point'. All through the seventeenth century, there thus existed a situation in which trade was on the whole poor. The Olu, writing in 1673 to the king of Portugal to plead for missionaries, took the opportunity to remark on the rarity of call of Portuguese trading vessels.[1]

During this period most of the trade must have been purely local and internal, and between the Itsẹkiri and the Urhobo, for in 1689, the Olu stated in a letter to the Capuchin Prefect of São Thomé that Ijọ pirates made it impossible for him to go to Benin to trade.[2] This Ijọ menace seems to have been perennial. That there were some Urhobo in the area immediately to the hinterland of the Itsẹkiri with whom the latter could trade at this time, is confirmed by the fact that Monteleone, Prefect of the Capuchin mission to Warri, is reported to have got in touch with the Urhobo in 1687, though most unfortunately no details of the people are given.[3]

While the seventeenth century was on the whole not very prosperous, the succeeding century also began with noticeably unimproved prospects. The Portuguese continued to represent the Olu and his court as poor. Indeed so poor were they that they were unable, as was expected of them, to maintain the missionaries sent to them. There is record of a visitation in 1705 by a new Capuchin Prefect, Father Cipriano a Napoli, to 'Warri':

> When he reached the Itsẹkiri capital he found that two of the Capuchins who had already spent a year there had been engaged in an

---

1 Ibid., pp. 6–13.   2 Ibid., p. 15.   3 Ibid., p. 14.

extraordinary activity. In order to live they had been obliged to buy earthenware cooking pots which were manufactured in Warri in large quantities; with the help of their two slaves they carried them into surrounding areas where they could be sold at a good profit.[1]

If indeed the missionaries were driven to these straits in order to survive then the situation must have been really difficult. If the court was as poor as represented by the missionaries, it is unlikely that outside the capital the situation was any better. For the Olu was also the chief trader. First, the 'comey' was paid to him, and secondly, he is said to have enjoyed certain commercial privileges. This period then was one in which Itsẹkiri trade was, in fact, mainly with their Urhobo neighbours on whom they have always depended very largely for agricultural products.

As the eighteenth century wore on, however, the situation seemed to have improved. The Dutch had not, with time, changed their attitude towards the area. Meanwhile the Portuguese having 'established a flourishing slave trading station at Whydah paid even less attention to Warri'.[2] Yet later accounts give a slightly more encouraging picture. Nyendael, who visited the area probably around the beginning of the century, did not give any exact description of the volume of trade. Barbot, apart from his comment on the slave trade of this area (already quoted), gave no further information about the trade. But the estimate he made of the number of slaves indicated that trade was slightly better than earlier on, at least in that commodity.

The year 1786 saw the establishment in Itsẹkiri country of Captain Landolphe's 'Compagnie d'Owhere et de Benin', a company which was given exclusive rights to trade in the Benin River by the French king, Louis XVI.[3] For five years Captain Landolphe who himself stayed in the 'fort' built by the company on 'the isle of Borodo' did a profitable trade in the area, enjoying a virtual monopoly. The important thing, however, is not so much the amount of trade done

1 Ibid., p. 18. Apparently no European ships were visiting the area at the time; so that the priests could not even indulge in the slave trade. It would therefore appear that the only trade that was going on during this period was the purely local one.
2 Ibid. p., 20.
3 P. C. Lloyd, 'Captain Landolphe', p. 17.

by the company (the account of this trade is, at any rate, vague), as the effect which the establishment of the company and the continued residence of Landolphe and his men must have had on the Itsękiri. In fact, in 1783, on an earlier voyage, Landolphe took back with him to France a nephew of the Olu—Prince Boudakan as Landolphe called him. This prince was presented to the French court in 1786 and granted a royal pension of 1,500 francs a month.[1] Prince Boudakan returned to his country with Captain Landolphe later in 1786.

On the same lines as the above was the Portuguese missionary endeavour in the Itsękiri country from the sixteenth until the nineteenth century. It is difficult to assess the success of the missionary effort in Itsękiriland. From Professor Ryder's account it would appear that nearly all the effort was concentrated on Ode-Itsękiri, the capital, and that Christianity was very much a palace religion, the fortunes of which varied as the reigning Olu accepted or rejected its teaching.[2] Not much proselytizing was done in the outlying Itsękiri settlements. Only once was there a reference to the Urhobo: in 1689 Monteleone, Prefect of the Capuchin mission to 'Warri' is reported to have 'got in touch with the Urhobo where he made some impression'.[3] No further details exist of this, probably the earliest European contact with the Urhobo.

From the point of view of Itsękiri-Urhobo relations, however, the important thing is not so much the failure of the Portuguese missionaries to win over the entire Itsękiri kingdom to their faith, as the effect on the Itsękiri of the continual residence, in their land, of the missionaries. It is generally accepted that Itsękiri culture has been very much affected by their early contact with the Europeans, notably the Portuguese. 'The Itsękiri', wrote Dr. Lloyd, 'are intensely proud of their contact with the Portuguese. From it stem their claims to superiority over the neighbouring Urhobo people.'[4] Such then was the effect of Portuguese activities on the Itsękiri. It is likely, though by no means easy to determine, that the Urhobo attitude to the Itsękiri in these early days was affected

1 Ibid.
2 See Ryder: 'Missionary Activity in Warri'.
3 Ibid., p. 14.
4 P. C. Lloyd: 'The Portuguese in Warri', *Odu*, No. 4, 1956, p. 28.

by their knowledge of Portuguese activities in the latter's kingdom. The sending of an Itsẹkiri prince to Portugal for instruction in sacerdotal duties could scarcely have been unnoticed in their neighbourhood. The letters written by the various Itsẹkiri rulers during this period to the Portuguese king were couched in extremely familiar terms;[1] and though these might have been the work of resident Portuguese priests, they probably had the effect of producing, in the minds of these rulers, a feeling of intimacy with such European monarchs as the kings of Portugal and Spain. In sharp contrast stood the Urhobo hinterland dwellers as yet removed from the culture contact taking place at the coast, and dependent on the Itsẹkiri not only for such knowledge of the Europeans as they had, but for European manufactures as well. In circumstances such as these the Itsẹkiri feeling of superiority is easy to understand.

With the nineteenth century we come to a period which though still poorly documented is, nevertheless, much clearer. This century was of vital importance in the developing relationship between the Itsẹkiri and the Urhobo. The overseas slave trade, never as great in this area as in the Yoruba country or the Eastern Delta, was rendered less profitable by its abolition in Britain, and gradually in most of Europe during the first three decades of the century. The trade in palm oil, which was only a little fraction of the trade at the earlier period, now replaced the trade in slaves, calling for new methods of organization in the process. The European merchants now finding their hulks inadequate, began to build 'factories' on land. Most important of all, the closing decades of the century saw the beginning of the establishment of British rule in this area. These developments had important and lasting effects on the relations between the Itsẹkiri and the Urhobo.

There are no detailed accounts of the trade of this region at the beginning of the nineteenth century. From such accounts as exist

---

1 Ryder: 'Missionary Activity in Warri', p. 12. In a letter to the Pope in 1652 asking for missionaries to be sent to his kingdom, the reigning Olu wrote, 'I am writing to my cousin king John of Portugal asking him to help me by assisting the fathers with their passage and the necessary provisions. I believe he will do this for the Portuguese have always done me favours; also because they introduced the faith into my kingdom and my forebear King Don Domingos married a Portuguese lady. I hold them in great brotherly affection.' The letter is quoted by Professor Ryder.

with regard to the eighteenth century, it might be assumed that the trade, relatively speaking, had increased during that century. This increase might have gone on into the opening years of the nineteenth century. If so, such increase was soon arrested, at least so far as the European trade was concerned. Adams, writing in 1823, noted that the English trade 'in this place' had declined.[1] Captain Owen ten years later, and after the official abolition of the slave trade, had exactly the same view: 'during the existence of the slave trade it was a place of much resort, but now possesses very little commerce.'[2]

The decline in the European trade of the area, in the years following the abolition of the trade in slaves, did not necessarily mean a decline in the purely internal trade between the Itsẹkiri and the Urhobo, and between the former and other Nigerian peoples. Adams gave a pen portrait of 'Warre' (that is, Ode-Itsẹkiri) which indicated some opulence. The Itsẹkiri capital was 'well cultivated' and had 'much the appearance of an extensive park.' To Adams too we owe our knowledge of extensive trade between the Itsẹkiri and the people of Bonny and New Calabar:

> Much trade is carried on here with the natives of Bonny and New Calabar, who come in their canoes for that purpose.[3]

One of the principal articles of this trade, according to Adams, was 'brass pans' which the Itsẹkiri used in the manufacture of salt,

> which is here the medium of exchange and a great trade is carried on in this article with the interior country.[4]

Adams further saw a great quantity of earthenware manufactured, and came to the conclusion: 'earthenware must constitute here a considerable article of trade'. Here then is a picture of intensive industry and commerce essentially designed to meet local requirements. Undoubtedly, some of the salt and earthenware found their way to the Urhobo markets and the local trade previously described, if it did not increase, at least continued during this period of de-

---

1 Captain John Adams, op. cit., pp. 115–16.
2 Captain W. F. W. Owen: *Narrative of Voyages to explore the shores of Africa, Arabia and Madagascar*, Vol. II, London 1835, p. 357.
3 Adams, op. cit., p. 122.
4 Ibid.

clining European trade. Slaves were also still being bought and sold, and Adams noted that slaves also featured in the trade between the Itsẹkiri and their fellow middlemen—traders of the Eastern Delta.[1] It can, therefore, be assumed that whatever new developments occurred during this period, the previous Itsẹkiri-Urhobo commercial and social connexions remained essentially undisturbed.

That there were important new developments in the trade of the area remains undeniable. The trade in palm produce, which replaced to a very great extent that in slaves, called for new techniques and new organization. In the days when slaves constituted the main commodity exported, the Itsẹkiri did not, as has already been indicated, equip huge expeditions into the Urhobo country for the purpose of raiding for slaves. Further, there was no great hurry to get rid of these slaves once they had passed into the hands of the Itsẹkiri. While the European slaver was awaited, the slaves could be utilized by their master both for domestic purposes and in helping to carry on their masters' trade. Rivalry there must have been between the leading Itsẹkiri traders, but it is suggested that the rivalry of the early period was nothing to be compared to that of the later period. The organization of the palm oil trade provides the clue to this rivalry.

The earlier trade between the Itsẹkiri and the Urhobo, it has been stated, was a simple bilateral affair—an exchange of one set of commodities for another on the spot. When palm produce became the main article of trade, however, the situation altered radically. The Europeans, now as earlier, traded with the Itsẹkiri on what was called the 'trust' system. What was new was the fact that it was with the coming to the fore of palm oil as the main article of trade, that the 'trust' system became the general system of trade as between the Itsẹkiri and the Urhobo.[2] To the complications arising from this system between the Europeans and the Itsẹkiri were added similar complications arising from its becoming the general pattern

1 Ibid.
2 The chapter on Nana (Chapter 3) makes it clear that by his time the 'trust' system was already the general method of trade. Investigations on the field show that Nana was only following an already established pattern which came with the development of the trade in palm produce. Indeed it was the 'trust' which the Itsẹkiri gave that induced the Urhobo to produce the larger quantities of oil required for the export trade.

between the latter and their Urhobo neighbours. This was what made the nineteenth century such a turbulent period.

The palm oil trade called for much greater organization and drive than the trade of the earlier period. For the Itsẹkiri to be a successful trader, he had to be seen to be credit worthy. This in turn had its various implications. It meant for example an ostentatious display of wealth by the successful trader, be this in the form of dress, house furniture or lavish entertainment. It was also necessary for the trader to possess a fleet of trading canoes which could go to the various Urhobo settlements to collect the palm oil. As these canoes were usually manned by slaves, the successful trader had to possess a large number of slaves. Indeed the wealth of the trader was often measured in terms of canoes and slaves. Clearly the internal trade in slaves had to continue, and continued till the close of the century. These features of the trade led to great rivalry between the leading Itsẹkiri traders—rivalry in the display of opulence to justify continued 'trust' being given, and rivalry in securing greater quantities of oil from the Urhobo. This rivalry was sometimes serious enough to lead to wars and lasting family feuds.[1] The possibility of war was only one of the reasons why the Itsẹkiri trading canoes were armed, and why some canoes were designed primarily for war. There were two other reasons: the need for self defence against Ijọ attackers,[2] and the need to strike terror, when this became necessary, into the Urhobo and force them to meet the obligations into which they had entered with the Itsẹkiri. The trade in arms was, in fact, one of the most successful throughout the greater part of the century. It is difficult to say exactly when these canoes became a regular feature of the trade. It would appear that some of these canoes were already

1 The Tsanọmi-Olomu war was one such. See Chapter 3, pp. 78–9.
2 The Ijọ were a terror to canoes in this area. Travellers always referred to them. R. Burton writing in 1863 referred to them as 'a large and influential tribe' who were 'almost always at war with the Jakrimen, because like these they traded for oil to the Sobo country.'—R. Burton, 'My Wanderings in West Africa', *Fraser's Magazine*, Vol. LXXIII, 1863, pp. 145–6. In 1856 and again in 1857 the British Consul had to take out warships against these Ijọ because they had 'ventured in great force to within sight of the English Factories and committed great depredations, capturing several canoes with cargoes of palm oil, making captives of their crews. F.O. 84/1031, Campbell to F.O. (Slave Trade) No. 3 of Feb. 1857. Also F.O. 84/1002, Campbell to F.O. (Slave Trade) No. 9 of 24 March 1856.

being used when Landolphe visited the area in the 1770s.[1] It is significant that Itsękiri legends do not speak of these great war and trading canoes either with reference to various rulers, or to individual titled nobles, till about the beginning of the nineteenth century, and it is likely that it was only at about this period that they became a general feature of Itsękiri commercial organization. They were certainly in common use in the palm oil trade of the nineteenth century.

For the Urhobo too, these new developments had important consequences. In the first place, the Urhobo were not always able to meet the obligations they undertook with regard to supplying oil. Occasionally, some of them, having received goods in trust from their Itsękiri customers, grew idle and failed to produce the agreed quantity of oil. In this situation the giving of children and slaves as pledges for outstanding debt became a common feature of the commercial code observed between the Itsękiri and Urhobo. This practice was in accord with traditional usage and even the Itsękiri practised it among themselves. The children given out were not, in strict traditional law, slaves. Unfortunately for most of them, however, their fathers did not ever redeem them and they became for all practical purposes slaves of the Itsękiri to whom they had been pledged. It is important to emphasize the fact that such a situation was regarded as perfectly ordinary, so much so that, sometimes, the Itsękiri would carry away children or slaves of Urhobo men owing them oil and *vice versa*. This practice was still being carried on even at the end of the century.[2]

Secondly, the Urhobo were as eager as the Itsękiri to establish good relations for the purpose of securing customers. Urhobo fathers, therefore, gladly gave their daughters in marriage to families of wealthy Itsękiri traders, in the hope that this would establish good relations and lead to amicable settlement of differences arising from commercial transactions. Unfortunately for those brides, their

1 I owe this piece of information to Professor Ryder of the Department of History, University of Ibadan, and to a suggestion by Lloyd in 'Captain Landolphe . . . ', p. 16, when he describes how the Olu in 1778 sent out his war captains to Landolphe when the latter was forced by inclement weather to stay for some time at Eghoro.

2 F.O. 84/2111, Gallwey's Report on his visit to the Urhobo markets: Enclosure in dispatch No. 30 of 12 Dec. 1891.

fathers did not always insist on receiving the customary bride wealth payable at marriage,[1] so eager were they to be regarded as friends by their Itsẹkiri customers. Such an attitude was understandable although, as in the case of pledged children, it sometimes resulted in such daughters being regarded as slaves when they, in fact, got to Itsẹkiriland. Fathers who gave their daughters away cheaply thus helped to swell the number of Urhobo 'slaves' in Itsẹkiri hands, and so provide one argument for a later Itsẹkiri claim to overlordship over the Urhobo people.

There was a third consequence. It was not always that disputes between Itsẹkiri and Urhobo over trade were amicably settled. Sometimes, Itsẹkiri traders, angered by the failure of their Urhobo customer to live up to their promises, sent their slaves, usually referred to as 'boys', to raid the villages of such people for slaves, the idea being that such slaves by working for the Itsẹkiri would eventually make good the loss caused by the non-fulfilment of the obligations previously agreed on. These raids tended, however, to result in indiscriminate seizure, as the 'boys' did not always confine their activities to the culprits. This practice, usually referred to as 'chopping'—a word first applied to the seizure of oil by European super-cargoes in lieu of debt owed—was to be a source of vexation to the British administrators in the years after the proclamation of a British protectorate over this part of what became Nigeria.

The years which followed the abolition of the slave trade and which saw the beginning of 'legitimate' trade were turbulent years for both the European traders and the coastal middlemen. This turbulence was the result of clashes which often arose in connexion with fixing prices acceptable to both sides. In the absence of a strong and respected central authority (the last Olu died in 1848 and there followed a long interregnum) which could regulate matters of

---

1 This impression was given to me in various Urhobo clans. In addition to the hope for amicable trade relations, fathers who gave out their daughters in the way described hoped thereby to find a lodging place, should they have cause to travel to the Itsẹkiri area for purposes of trade. This was a phenomenon which repeated itself in this century, when the Isoko used to be glad to give their daughters in marriage to Ughelle men so they could find lodgings when they travelled to Ughelle, the divisional headquarters, to attend court or other meetings.

trade, there was the tendency for European traders and coastal middlemen alike to take the law into their hands, and thereby precipitate crises which often led to some fighting and even stoppage of trade.[1]

These trade disputes, whether they arose as a result of disagreements between the Itsẹkiri traders and the white agents, or as a result of a temporary combination of white agents to lower prices, or were the consequence of personal rivalry and jealousies between leading Itsẹkiri traders, had their effects on the Urhobo to the hinterland. The Urhobo remember instances when their Itsẹkiri customers failed to turn up to collect the oil they had been storing for them. When such situations arose, the Urhobo merely sat back and waited, unable to explain the temporary cessation of trade. These instances were, however, never too frequent, as there was nearly always some trade going on all the time between the Itsẹkiri and the Urhobo. The Urhobo themselves knew about dissatisfaction arising from unacceptable or low prices, as they at times grumbled at the prices offered by the Itsẹkiri, though they did not see their way to bringing economic sanctions against the latter, because they knew the Itsẹkiri were heavily armed and could bring their war canoes to bear, and secondly, because it was imagined that the power of the white traders was behind all Itsẹkiri enterprise.

In the nineteenth century, as in the earlier period, not all the trade of Urhoboland was geared to the Itsẹkiri commercial system. Some of the trade found its way through the creeks to Ganagana where the Niger Company had a station. The Ijọ were the carriers of this trade. Later in the century, the Urhobo attempted to carry their produce themselves but Ijọ attacks forced them to appeal to the Niger Company to provide one of its barges near the creeks, to which the Urhobo could go without too much fear of attack. Most of the trade of the Isoko sector went to Patani and Ase especially from the 1860s on. Indeed, until the establishment of British rule, there was scarcely any Itsẹkiri contact with the Isoko country

---

[1] Some of the incidents caused by these quarrels are described by Dr. Lloyd in his article, 'The Itsẹkiri in the Nineteenth Century', pp. 207–31. As a background to the age of Nana reference is made to some of the incidents in the next chapter. Vide Infra pp. 76–7.

except for the one instance which was discussed in the last chapter.[1]

As already stated, the growth of the trade in palm produce led to important developments in Itsẹkiri-Urhobo relations. One such development was the establishment of trading camps by the Itsẹkiri in Urhoboland. These camps were usually established at the watersides of various Urhobo clans and were to be found in Agbọn, Abraka, Agbarho, Ewu, Udu and Uwherun clans.[2] In the days when slaves constituted the major export commodity, it was not necessary for the Itsẹkiri to have collecting centres within Urhoboland, as it was more profitable for the slaves to be employed in various tasks in Itsẹkiriland while the slavers were expected, than to keep them in or near their areas of origin where they might more easily escape. With the advance of the trade in palm produce, however, it became necessary to have the camps which served as collecting centres to which the Urhobo brought their oil for sale to the Itsẹkiri. In the nineteenth century, these Itsẹkiri trading camps were mostly peopled by the head slaves and other slaves of leading Itsẹkiri traders, though freeborn men were also found in them. From the purely commercial viewpoint, the Urhobo welcomed these camps as they were near to them and so saved them the long journey to the Ode-Itsẹkiri or Benin River areas. In the more general context of Itsẹkiri-Urhobo relations, these Itsẹkiri settlements in Urhobo country served to bring both peoples closer together. A number of leading Itsẹkiri traders married Urhobo women from these clans at the watersides where their trading settlements were established.[3] These marriages were useful in bringing Itsẹkiri and Urhobo families together and so forging ties of friendship. They were also important in promoting amicable trade relations during the turbulent years of the palm oil trade. This development, together with the general commercial contact, explains the fact that many Urhobo people in those clans in which the Itsẹkiri had trading settlements understood and spoke the Itsẹkiri language

---

1 This has to do with the Eni 'juju' of Uzere to which the Itsẹkiri, Urhobo, Aboh and Kwalẹ used to take their suspected witches for trial. Uzere is in the heart of the Isoko country. See Chapter 1, pp. 37–9.
2 See map facing, p. 10.
3 Among leading Itsẹkiri traders who married Urhobo women were Olomu, Nana, Numa, Tsegbọnẹ and Ẹda. Details of how these marriages affected commercial and other relations are discussed in Chapters 3 and 5.

(and still do), while many Itsẹkiri people can understand and speak the Urhobo language. While these Itsẹkiri settlements thus served the purpose of bringing both peoples together and paving the way for friendly relations, they were also the centres of conflicts arising from trade disagreements, and were to be, in the years after the establishment of British rule, centres of conflicts arising from certain aspects of British administrative policy.[1]

Another feature of the nineteenth century which was important for Itsẹkiri-Urhobo relations was the development of domestic slavery among the Itsẹkiri, after the abolition of the overseas slave trade. Whereas during the period of the overseas slave trade most of the Urhobo slaves 'bought' by the Itsẹkiri were exported and so removed from Itsẹkiriland, from about the third decade of the last century, these slaves were integrated into the Itsẹkiri social system. Indeed, these slaves became the Itsẹkiri labouring class. They cultivated such land as was cultivable and looked after most of their masters' trade. As the years passed, so the number of these Urhobo slaves increased, not only as a result of new additions through the usual channels of the internal slave trade, but also through repro- duction among the slaves themselves. Thus, even if the number of Urhobo slaves bought by the Itsẹkiri during the era of the overseas slave trade was small, it has to be remembered that from about the middle of the nineteenth century, the number of Urhobo slaves in Itsẹkiri hands rapidly increased. When in the 1930s the Itsẹkiri began to make the claim that the Urhobo were their slaves in the past, they no doubt had the nineteenth century in mind. If this claim was an over-generalization, and the result of certain conflicts which arose between the Itsẹkiri and the Urhobo in the 'twenties and 'thirties of this century, it nevertheless sprang from the fact that at a point in history, fairly large numbers of Urhobo slaves were to befound in Itsẹkiri land—a situation which, as commonly happens, made the Itsẹkiri regard as inferior to themselves not only the slaves they bought, but the stock from which these slaves came.

One question which has often arisen in connexion with Itsẹkiri- Urhobo commercial relations is whether the Itsẹkiri used their

---

[1] See Chapter 5.

superior arms to compel the Urhobo to trade even when prices were low. In 1931 it was claimed by a British administrative officer that the Itsẹkiri were accustomed to force the Urhobo to trade with them.[1] Dr. Lloyd once put forward a similar claim, when he argued that the Itsẹkiri maintained their commercial position in Urhobo-land by superior force.[2] As a matter of fact, force was not, in normal circumstances, an instrument for compelling the Urhobo to trade.[3] The high degree of mutual interdependence involved in Itsẹkiri-Urhobo commercial contacts has never been sufficiently stressed. The Itsẹkiri were dependent on the Urhobo for most of their food and, especially after the abolition of the overseas slave trade, for nearly all their export trade. For various reasons, the Itsẹkiri found it impracticable to do trade with their other neighbours to the same extent as they did with the Urhobo. The Ijọ did not produce oil in commercial quantities, and such as they did produce, they marketed themselves. Indeed, they competed with the Itsẹkiri for some of the oil from the Urhobo markets. Furthermore, all through the nine-teenth century, the Itsẹkiri were in constant dread of the Ijọ who were reported to be seizing and selling the Itsẹkiri men into slavery. The Ijọ country was, therefore, largely closed to the Itsẹkiri. The other producers of palm oil, the Kwalẹ and Aboh, were much farther away from the Itsẹkiri than the Urhobo. To have fitted out canoes to those areas would have involved a great deal of expense. In addition, the Aboh were among the leading middlemen traders of the Niger Delta, and the Itsẹkiri would only have run into crippling competition if they had endeavoured to develop the Warri-Patani-

---

1 C.S.O. 26/2, File 11857, Vol. IX: Annual Report, Warri Province, 1931, p. 13.

2 P. C. Lloyd: 'Tribalism in Warri', *Proceedings of WAISER*, 1956, p. 102. Lloyd has now modified this view. He now maintains that legends and contemporary records do not indicate whether the Itsẹkiri used force against the Urhobo. See P. C. Lloyd: 'The Itsẹkiri in the Nineteenth Century', p. 222.

3 This is the view held by both Itsẹkiri and Urhobo elders today. An exception should always be made with regard to raids resulting from disputes over trade. I have been unable to discover any instance of the Itsẹkiri refusing as a body to trade with the Urhobo in order to bring the latter to such a plight that they, the Itsẹkiri, could attempt any political control of the source of supply. It is not clear whether the fact that the Urhobo could exist without European manufactured goods for prolonged periods and depend entirely on their farms and rivers had anything to do with the Itsẹkiri attitude.

Ase-Aboh route as a highway of Itsẹkiri commerce. These various factors forced the Itsẹkiri to concentrate their energies on the Urhobo country in matters of trade.

The Urhobo, for their part, depended heavily on the Itsẹkiri for European manufactured goods—goods which though regarded at first as luxuries, gradually became everyday requirements. In these circumstances, there was no need for the Itsẹkiri to compel the Urhobo to trade with them. Itsẹkiri-Urhobo trade was mutually beneficial and, in the particular circumstances of the Itsẹkiri as described above, and that of the Urhobo, hemmed in as they were by more powerful neighbours, a matter of necessity.

This is not to say, however, that the Itsẹkiri contact with the Europeans and their position by the coast did not place them at an advantage over their Urhobo neighbours in matters of trade. It was their contact with the European traders that made it possible for the Itsẹkiri to supply the Urhobo with manufactured goods. More important still, this contact gave the Itsẹkiri firearms with which they equipped their war canoes. It would be unrealistic to think that the possession of firearms by the Itsẹkiri did not affect the Urhobo attitude to, and estimation of, them. The surprising thing is that despite this imbalance in armaments, Itsẹkiri-Urhobo wars were not, so far as one can find out, a common feature of the relations between the two peoples. While this was largely due to the fact that the Urhobo realized their inadequacy in terms of war canoes and armaments, and so thought discretion the better part of valour, it was also explicable in terms of the mundane and mutual requirements of both peoples as described above.

On the eve of the establishment of British rule first in Itsẹkiriland, and then in Urhoboland, therefore, there were already commercial and social contacts between the Itsẹkiri and the Urhobo. There had already begun that process of intermarriage which, despite present-day tensions, has not completely died out, and which explains the fact that many Itsẹkiri familes have Urhobo connexions and *vice versa*. Itsẹkiri-Urhobo social and economic relations had the consequence of bringing the two peoples very close together, closer together than perhaps any two other people of the then Warri Province. Itsẹkiri-Urhobo wars were few, and such wars as are remembered, occurred in the nineteenth century and were mainly caused by disputes arising from the trade in palm oil.[1]

Despite what has been said above, it should be pointed out that as coastal dwellers controlling the river mouths, the Itsẹkiri were a more wealthy and powerful people than the Urhobo to the hinterland. The palm produce trade of the Urhobo was almost entirely done with the Itsẹkiri. Few Urhobo men were able, or minded, till about the beginning of the present century, to take their produce direct to the European agents. The possession of firearms by the Itsẹkiri enabled them to dominate the rivers. Such rivalry as there was for the carrying trade was not between the Itsẹkiri and the Urhobo, but between the former and the Ijọ, who were equally at home on the rivers. This Ijọ competition, however, did not prevent the Itsẹkiri from controlling the greater part of the trade of the Urhobo hinterland.

However amicable and cordial relations were between the Itsẹkiri and the Urhobo, European activities in Itsẹkiriland clearly tilted the balance in favour of the Itsẹkiri. Wealthy by contemporary standards well-armed, accustomed to have their work done for them by slaves (many of whom in the nineteenth century were Urhobo), in fairly close contact with the European traders and the British consular authorities, it was understandable if the Itsẹkiri felt better placed and superior to their Urhobo neighbours with whom they nevertheless had to co-operate in various important fields. The establishment of British rule in Itsẹkiri and Urhoboland from 1884 was, in some respects, to emphasize this balance in favour of the Itsẹkiri, while in other respects it was to begin to undermine those factors which had made Itsẹkiri predominance possible. This, indeed, was the paradox of Itsẹkiri-Urhobo relations in the years after 1884.

1 Infra, pp. 79-81.

Chapter 3
The régime of Chief Nana 1884–94

The Nana episode—the attack on Ebrohimi by the British naval and military forces in the months of August and September, 1894—was a spectacular event, perhaps the most spectacular event in the entire history of the Western Delta. Nevertheless, to attempt to study the era of Nana merely in terms of the causes and effects of the 1894 episode will be to over-look certain essential features of the period. The era of Chief Nana cannot be fully understood unless it is realized that Nana, the leading figure in the drama, was the son and heir of a great father, and that he was the product of his age, a disturbed age during which many changes took place in the political and economic way of life of the Itsẹkiri people. The study of Nana's régime must, therefore, begin with a study both of his inheritance and of his age.

Olomu, Nana's father, was the son of Asorokun and a grandson of Ofoluwa who, according to Lloyd, 'was perhaps a governor at Bobi at the turn of the century'.[1] Today, Olomu's family trace their descent through Ofoluwa's father, Mufeme, to the Olu Abejioye whose son, Udefi, was Ofoluwa's grandfather.[2] It would thus appear that by tracing his descent through five generations, Olomu could establish some connexion with the royal family. Olomu's mother was Iwereko, a daughter of the Ologbotsẹrẹ, Eyinmisarẹn. Olomu could thus claim some connexion with Itsẹkiriland's two most important families. Yet it was not this connexion so much as his own ability that determined his political and commercial fortunes.

Olomu, it has been suggested, was born about 1810.[3] He was thus born at a time when the trade of the Benin River was suffering

---

1 Lloyd: 'The Itsekiri in the Nineteenth Century', p. 222.
2 Interview with Chief Newton Celleone Nana (aged 78), oldest surviving son of Nana Olomu, at Koko, 2nd Oct. 1963.
3 Lloyd: 'The Itsekiri in the Nineteenth Century', p. 222.

one of its periodic declines. He must have reached manhood just when there was a noticeable drop in the trade of the area.[1] As pointed out in the last chapter, this was the period when the trade in palm oil with all its new problems replaced that in slaves; a period when rivalry between the leading traders was a regular feature of the commercial life of the Itsẹkiri—rivalry which did not flinch from war. Indeed the years 1830–84 constituted a turbulent era in Itsẹkiri history. This turbulence was the product not only of trade rivalry between the leading Itsẹkiri traders, but of uncertain prices for palm oil in the European markets. Yet it was during this period that Olomu established himself as one of the wealthiest Itsẹkiri traders of his, and of all time.

From the point of view of internal Itsẹkiri history, the turbulence of these years was accentuated by the death of the Olu in 1848. From that time on effective power passed into the hands of two main groups: the royal family group and members of the Ologbotsẹrẹ family group. Prominent in the former group were Princess Iye, Oritsẹmọnẹ, Oritsẹtsaninọmi, Numa, and Omadọghọgbọnẹ, Numa's son. In the latter group were Idiare, Dudu, Olomu and Nana.[2] The political and commercial rivalry between these two groups was a regular feature of Itsẹkiri history during the period, and the career of Nana Olomu was deeply affected by this rivalry. At the same time, however, it was not enough to belong to one or other of these groups as of old. Henceforth wealth derived from trade increasingly became the surest means of acquiring power.

The death of the Olu raised the problem of some central authority among the Itsẹkiri who could regulate matters of trade. In 1850 Consul Beecroft attempted to get the Itsẹkiri to install a new Olu. He failed in this objective, but succeeded in getting the people to elect a 'Governor of the River'.[3] This was not a new office created to meet the needs of the interregnum, but one which had developed earlier as a consequence of Itsẹkiri commercial activities with the

---

1 Captain W. F. W. Owen, op cit., p. 357.
2 Lloyd: 'The Itsekiri in the Nineteenth Century', p. 217. The names Oritsẹt-saninọmi and Ọmadọghọgbọnẹ are usually shortened to Tsanọmi and Dọghọ respectively. Hereafter these shortened forms are used. The British records give the names as Chanomi and Dore.
3 Cal. Prof. 5/7, Vol. I, Beecroft to F.O., 20 March 1851.

Europeans. The duty of the Governor was to collect the 'comey' or duties due to the Olu from the trading vessels, before the Europeans were allowed to trade. The Governor, armed with a staff from the Olu, could board the trading vessels and demand the comey. Because the office of governor was thus closely connected with state revenue, it acquired great importance and was regarded by the beginning of the nineteenth century as one of the more important offices of state. As the Olu was himself the nation's chief trader, the Governor had the added responsibility of supervising all the Olu's commercial transactions. The appointment of the Governor was the sole responsibility of the Olu. He did not have to consult the Council, nor had the bearer of the office to be an *Otọn-Olu* or a descendant of one of the noble houses.[1]

As long as there was an Olu, the appointment of a Governor was a relatively unimportant matter, as he was essentially the Olu's servant. In the situation created by the interregnum, the status of the Governor became radically altered. First, there was the fact that from this time on the British consular authority or European traders resident in the area sought to influence the election of the Governor. Secondly, having been elected, he became the only duly appointed executive authority among the Itsẹkiri—a circumstance which, while enhancing the stature of the Governor, rendered his position extremely difficult.

On 1 April 1851, Idiare, son of Uwankun, was elected Governor of the River. One of the first things he had to do was to sign an agreement with Beecroft, laying down regulations for trade between his people and the European firms.[2] Thirty-three other Itsẹkiri 'chiefs' signed the agreement. Immediately after Idiare's and Idibofun's (Idibofun was Idiare's brother) came Olomu's 'mark'. This means that by 1851 Olomu had become one of the most important traders in the Benin River area. Twenty years later, he was unquestionably the leading trader, for on the death of Idiare in 1870, Consul McLeod wrote to the British Foreign Office, suggesting that Olomu be made Governor, as he was 'the only chief having intellect and a force sufficiently organized to keep peace in

---

1 C. O. Omoneukarin, op. cit., p. 28.
2 Cal. Prof. 5/7, Vol. I, Enclosure in Beecroft to F.O., 19 April 1851. See Appendix II.

the river'.[1] Olomu did not, however, become Governor until 1879; for some reason Tsanọmi was appointed to the post.

Commercial success in the nineteenth century was not easy to come by. Olomu's success must therefore be seen as evidence of considerable powers of organization and resourcefulness. With the development of the trade in palm oil, as has been pointed out, there grew the system of 'trust' as between the Itsẹkiri and the Urhobo. This trust system led to the development of the same kind of relationship between the leading Itsẹkiri traders and the Urhobo, as had earlier developed between the former and the European agents. In the interest of their trade, the European agents found it expedient to give credit, in the form of goods, to those Itsẹkiri whose wealth enabled them to wield political power.[2] Similarly, in order to be sure of a regular supply of oil from the Urhobo, it was the custom of the Itsẹkiri traders to advance to leading Urhobo men goods in trust, and to make outright presents to those who were in positions of authority, and who could influence their men to sell oil to the 'boys' of their Itsẹkiri friends.

Olomu's main sphere of influence was along the Ethiope River and also up the Warri River, through Ẹvhrọ (Effurun), to the various settlements of the Agbarho clan—Ukan, Mọgba and so on. Along the Ethiope, the main centres were Okpara, Ukhuokori (Kokori), Ẹku, Igun, Oriah and Abraka—in short the Agbọn and Abraka clans. In all these places there is a vivid remembrance of Olomu's trading methods. In the Agbarho clan, his commercial success was closely connected with his deep friendship with Ovwha who was the clan head (*Osivie*) at the time. Olomu, it is said, used to give generous presents to Ovwha as well as advance goods with which to secure oil. Ovwha on his side encouraged his people to sell their oil to Olomu's 'boys'.[3] Relations between these two families were consequently very cordial. Although this friendship with the Agbarho clan head enabled Olomu to enjoy great trading privileges,

1 F.O. 84/1326, McLeod to Vivian, 11 May 1870.
2 Lloyd: 'The Itsekiri in the Nineteenth Century', p. 218.
3 This account of the organization of Olomu's trade and his connexions with the Urhobo, as well as what follows, in the pages below, of Nana's own connections, are based on my field work over a period of six months. In the Agbarho clan Okpalefe, the present Ọtota is the son of Ovwha, Olomu's great friend.

it did not lead to the complete exclusion of other Itsẹkiri traders from the clan. Indeed, a similar alliance to that already described existed between Numa, the father of Dọghọ, and the Mowarin family of Mọgba. In the other places where Olomu traded, the pattern was the same. In Ẹvhrọ, not only did he have friends, but he married Memese, Nana's mother, from there and so established a friendship which not even the rockets of the British navy succeeded in shattering.[1] Both at Okpara waterside and at Igun, Olomu is remembered as having brought greater trade to the area by widening the creeks so that his trade canoes could more easily use them, and in both places he established depots to which the Urhobo brought their oil.[2] It is said that though it was Olomu who really opened this area to large scale-trade in palm oil, other Itsẹkiri traders like Tsanọmi, Numa and Dudu also traded there in Olomu's lifetime, though they did not succeed to the same extent.

Olomu also traded with the Abraka area. Here, however, there was not the same cordiality which characterized Olomu's activities in the Agbọn, Uvbiẹ and Agbarho clans. In this area, there were disputes over trade which led to war. One probable reason for this state of affairs was the relationship between the Abraka and their Orogun neighbours. The Abraka claim that their Orogun neighbours were constantly making incursions into their territory and causing unrest. Such unrest led to a dislocation of trade which in turn led to tensions between the Abraka and their Itsẹkiri customers. It is not known exactly which group of people in the Abraka district demanded that Olomu and other Itsẹkiri traders should pay a comey amounting to two-thirds of the oil they carried through the Ethiope River, as represented by Nana to Consul Hartley in 1876.[3] Such a demand was clearly inimical to Itsẹkiri trading interests. There was, apparently, another group of people in the Abraka area, who raided all canoes that passed up and down the river. The Orogun were probably connected with some of these raids. This was the kind of situation which forced Olomu to launch an attack against the Abraka in order, according to Nana's testimony, to ensure a

1 An account of the burning of Ẹvhrọ is given later in the chapter.
2 See Chapter 1.
3 F.O. 84/1455, Hartley to F.O., No. 54, 24 November 1876.

continuous flow of trade. Olomu was successful and carried away as prisoners eighty people, among whom were three 'chiefs'. A rumour that these prisoners had been murdered in cold blood brought Consul Hartley to the Benin River in 1876. Nana assured the Consul that the captives had not been murdered, though one of the 'chiefs' had died of starvation, and the other two had committed suicide by hanging—an act which Nana attributed to the preference of the 'chiefs' to die rather than return to their country after the ignominy of being taken prisoners.[1] It is significant that the Consul did not feel horrified about the seizure of these eighty prisoners, though he warned against a recurrence of such an incident. Events such as the above were inseperable from the commercial ventures of the time. Failure to meet one's commercial obligations was, not infrequently, met by some form of conflict during which it was customary to take prisoners who, if not redeemed, became slaves of their captors. Olomu's trade in the Abraka area was thus not as peaceful as elsewhere. Today, the Abraka people merely explain the conflict in terms of disputes over trade, and claim that Olomu was in fact their friend, but that occasionally disputes arose about prices and the conduct of Olomu's 'boys' which resulted in armed conflict. This relationship continued during Nana's time, and all through the period of Nana's ascendancy, there was always this undercurrent of hostility between his people and the Urhobo of the Abraka area.

A commercial organization like Olomu's required a large number of slaves to man the trade canoes, and arms and ammunition to defend them. Although it is not possible to express in definite terms Olomu's strength in arms, he could scarcely have become the richest trader in the river, as Consul Hopkins described him in 1878,[2] without amassing a huge armament to safeguard his canoes against Ijọ attacks, as well as against his fellow Itsẹkiri traders, whose envy of his success could, and did, lead to war. Nana must have inherited considerable armament from his father. The same thing applied to slaves: a trader of Olomu's stature required an immense number of slaves to man his trade canoes which altogether must have numbered hundreds. Each war-canoe was said to be

1 Ibid.
2 Lloyd: 'The Itsekiri in the Nineteenth Century', p. 222.

The British Vice-Consulate at Warri c. 1892.

Traditional authority in Urhoboland. On the dais (r.) the Okaroro, the oldest man of the village, regarded as 'head'; (l.) the Otota (spokesman) holding his staff of office. Between them is the shrine and above them the skulls of sacrificial victims. Photographed at Igun, 1962.

Chief Nana Olomu, from a photograph taken in Accra during his exile.

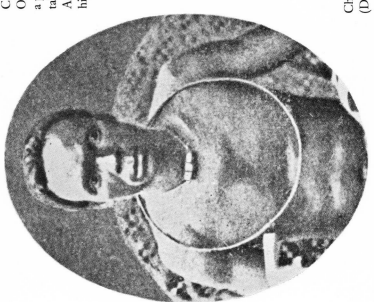

Chief Dogho (Dore Numa).

capable of taking thirty-six paddlers as well as forty armed men.[1] These war canoes were used to convey ordinary trade canoes going into the Urhobo country to load oil. Olomu lived at a time when the external slave trade had been abolished. Consequently, he did not sell the slaves he obtained, but used them for the purpose of his trade, for this was the age when domestic slavery was the backbone of the Itsẹkiri economy. Olomu's slaves have been variously numbered at 1,000, 3,000 and 4,000.[2] These slaves together with the arms and ammunition were inherited by Nana on Olomu's death.

Olomu organized his trade with the Urhobo at a time when political power in Itsẹkiriland was far from stable. The Governor remained the only recognized authority among the people. Around him clustered his immediate kin, constituting themselves into a well organized unit for purposes of trade. The office of Governor, as it developed after 1851, was full of difficulties. From the point of view of the Europeans, the Governor was a necessary officer of state who could keep some hold on the Itsẹkiri, and protect the European factories from what the white traders regarded as outrages. They looked on the Governor as head of the Itsẹkiri, whose responsibility it was to ensure peace and order in commerce; a figure who could be taken to task for any act of violence or breach of faith committed by the Itsẹkiri. The agreement of 1851 charged the Governor, referred to as 'the Chief', with the duty of seeing that 'all . . . agressions, and depredations, committed upon British subjects crossing the Bar or otherwise within the limits of the Chief of the River Benin dominions' were 'satisfactorily adjusted'.[3] As the 'dominions' were not defined, the position was such that the 'Chief' could be called upon to 'adjust' acts committed by people over whom he had no *de facto* jurisdiction. Such was the European concept of the duties of the Governor. The Itsẹkiri had their own ideas about the Governor's duties. They saw in him their leader, behind whom they could combine against the white traders in the difficult matter of fixing acceptable prices. This was clearly incompatible with the European conception of the duties of the

---

1 George W. Neville: 'Nana Oloma of Benin', *Journal of the African Society*, Vol. 14, 1914–15, pp. 162–7.
2 Lloyd: 'The Itsekiri in the Nineteenth Century', p. 218.
3 Cal. Prof. 5/7, Vol. I, Enclosure already cited.

office and was to be productive of future misunderstanding and strife.

Between 1851 and 1884 when Nana became Governor of the River, there were three Governors: Idiare (1851–Feb.May 1870), Tsanọmi (1870–9), and Olomu himself (1879–83). The tenure of office of the first two Governors revealed some of the difficulties of the office. A perennial source of trouble between the European traders and the Itsẹkiri was the debt which was the inescapable concomitant of the trust system. Most of the 'outrages' reported to have been committed by the Itsẹkiri on the factories of the white traders arose from some quarrel over the amount of debt out-standing. When such a situation arose, the Governor was expected to step in and prevent the Itsẹkiri from attacking the Europeans. In 1862, Idiare had to send an armed guard to Mr. Henry's factory to protect it against the slaves of Ikebuwa, who was preparing to storm it, because Mr. Henry had 'chopped' his oil. In this particular case, Henry ordered Idiare's guard out of his premises, boasting that he could defend himself. Yet a week later, his factory was attacked and looted. Despite Idiare's intervention, and despite Henry's rude rejection of the proffered help, Consul Freeman nevertheless fined Idiare and the other chiefs thirty-five puncheons of oil for not preventing the outrage, in addition to the fine of twenty puncheons which he inflicted on Ikebuwa himself.[1] Such actions by the British consul were little calculated to promote mutual confidence. In 1871 there arose a similar disagreement over debt involving an Itsẹkiri and Mr. Theobold of Messrs. J. H. Louch & Coy. On this occasion, Tsanọmi the Governor, sent an armed guard and so prevented an attack.[2]

If the Governors saw it as their duty to protect the white traders against the attack of their fellow Itsẹkiri, they did not fail to ap-preciate their duty to their own people. It was not only the Itsẹkiri who behaved in a manner to warrant fines being imposed on them. The European traders were equally guilty of seeking to take the law into their hands. When there arose a general situation of crisis, or when prices were unacceptable, the Itsẹkiri realized that the only effective way open to them was to stop trading with the Euro-

---

1 F.O. 84/1201, Freeman to F.O., No. 9, April 1863.
2 F.O. 84/1343, Hopkins to F.O., No. 12, 2 July 1871.

peans, in the hope that this economic sanction would force the white traders to raise their prices for palm produce. But clearly such a sanction could only be effectively enforced by the Governor acting on behalf of all the leading Itsẹkiri traders. Thus in 1866, Idiare, the then Governor, stopped all trade with the whites, by 'placing armed canoes on the river and occupying the beach with an armed force'.[1] The reason for this was that an agent of Messrs. Harrison & Co. had refused to pay a fine which Idiare had imposed. This was an example of the difficulty which existed. The white traders expected the Governor to exact fines from any Itsẹkiri who used force against them or refused to pay their debt. But they would not subject themselves to the Governor's jurisdiction. In 1879, Governor Tsanọmi stopped trade for what Consul Easton reported were 'purely personal reasons'[2]—a personal dispute with one of the agents. These stoppages of trade would appear to have been fairly effective. They were certainly much more effective than attempts by the Europeans themselves to combine in an endeavour to lower prices of palm produce. In 1879 for instance, despite the alleged personal nature of Tsanọmi's stoppage of trade, Olomu, who was by that time the wealthiest of the Itsẹkiri traders, observed it. The more various consuls looked into the circumstances which surrounded such stoppages of trade, the more they discovered, as Acting Consul Ehnes did in 1866, 'that there was a considerable cause for complaint on both sides'.[3] Stoppages of trade were not just a mere pastime indulged in by capricious trader-tyrants. Rather they arose out of the commercial organization of the time.

It was natural that there should have been rivalry among the Itsẹkiri traders both at the Urhobo markets and at the factory beaches. Such rivalry probably led to skirmishes between 'boys' of rival masters. As for the leading Itsẹkiri traders themselves, there were remarkably few instances of wars between them, remembered or recorded. It is all the more significant, therefore, that Olomu was involved in the few wars that there were among the Itsẹkiri during his lifetime. The probable explanation for this was his phenomenal success in trade which won for him the envy of the

1 F.O. 84/1265, Ehnes to F.O., No. 4, 9 June 1866.
2 F.O. 84/1541, Easton to F.O., No. 4, 18 Dec. 1879.
3 F.O. 84/1265, Ehnes to F.O., No. 5, 8 July 1866.

other leading Itsẹkiri traders of his day. Olomu fought three wars against his fellow Itsẹkiri. Two of these were connected with his trade to the Urhobo country: the war against the royal princes led by Oritsẹmọnẹ, and that against Idiare in 1867. The former was occasioned by the success which attended Olomu's efforts to open up trade at Ukan in Agbarho clan. Oritsẹmọnẹ resented Olomu's penetration into an area he probably desired to retain as an exclusive sphere of influence. In the war which resulted from Oritsẹmọnẹ's attempts to push Olomu out of the area, Olomu emerged victorious.[1] The latter war resulted from Olomu's instistence on reopening trade with an Urhobo market to which Idiare had closed all trade, because his canoes had been robbed there. Olomu was again victorious. The third war was against Tsanọmi, and resulted from a debt which the Olu Akẹngbuwa owed to Olomu. This debt remained unpaid at the time of the Olu's death. After the Olu's death, Olomu requested Iye, the Olu's princess, to pay her father's debt. Iye regarded Olomu's request as an insult, and Tsanọmi, Iye's son, mustered his war canoes against Olomu only to be beaten.

It was said earlier that after the death of the Olu Akengbuwa I, effective power passed into the hands of two groups. Some effort would appear to have been made to maintain a balance between these groups. It will be recalled that Idiare who was elected Governor in 1851 belonged to the *Ologbotsẹrẹ* group. Tsanọmi, his successor, belonged to the royal family group. Olomu, who as will be seen succeeded Tsanọmi, again belonged to the *Ologbotsẹrẹ* group. Undoubtedly this attempt at maintaining a balance was aimed at preserving a measure of peace among Itsẹkiriland's two most important family groups. In this regard Olomu's victory in war over both Oritsẹmọnẹ and Tsanọmi disturbed this delicate balance as it underlined the predominance, at least for the time being, of the *Ologbotsẹrẹ* group. Indeed the Olomu-Tsamọmi war in particular was the beginning of a lasting family feud between the two families concerned. Numa, Tsanọmi's cousin, inherited this feud and Dọghọ, Numa's son, was to carry on a bitter vendetta against Nana, Olomu's son. In fact it is only against this background that the role Dọghọ

---

1 These wars are mentioned by Neville, op. cit.; by Lloyd, 'The Itsekiri in the Nineteenth Century', loc. cit. See also William Moore, op. cit., pp. 95–9 for an account of these and the wars discussed below.

played in the events which led to Nana's fall in 1894 can be adequately appreciated. The other importance of the wars described
above is that they demonstrate that commercial success in those
days had its peculiar hazards, and that on the whole Olomu had
the means of defending his 'commercial empire'.

Against the Urhobo, Olomu fought two wars—the Igun war and
the Ogiegba war. The Igun war resulted from a quarrel over runaway slaves. The Igun people had given some slaves to Olomu in
lieu of oil. A number of these slaves later ran back to Igun, and
Olomu demanded their return. The Igun people refused and Olomu
fought and defeated them, and probably took more slaves than had
run away in the first instance.[1] Ogiegba was an Urhobo trader from
Amukpẹ in Okpẹ clan. The Okpẹ people, because of their nearness
to Itsẹkiriland, were semi-middlemen who did a profitable trade in
slaves. Ogiegba, a leading trader, noticed that the Itsẹkiri were
increasingly going via the Ethiope into the interior, thereby reducing
the trade of the Okpẹ people. He decided to oppose this tendency
by raiding Itsẹkiri trade canoes. Olomu, whose canoes were involved
in Ogiegba's raids, took the 'field' against him and defeated him.
These wars indicate the general pattern of trade relations in the
age, and reveal the fact that the Urhobo were not mere passive
spectators in a turbulent age, unresisting victims of Itsẹkiri depredations.

It was perhaps a fitting end to an illustrious life, that Olomu
should have filled the highest office of state available at the time,
in his last few years. For following the deposition of Tsanọmi in
1879 for stopping trade, Olomu was appointed Governor of the
River.[2] His tenure of office is devoid of any official records from
which he can be judged. References to him in earlier years confirm
his wealth and portray him as a friend of the Europeans.[3] There
was always an element of apparent contradiction in the life of Olomu,
and of his son after him. While it would appear that they were on
the whole disposed to be peaceful, they did not hesitate to use force
when there was the need for it, in an age in which force (or at least

1 This war is very well remembered by the Igun people—Interviews with the
Ọkaroro and elders of Igun, September 14–16 1963.
2 F.O. 84/1851, Easton to F.O., No. 41, 18 Dec. 1879.
3 Lloyd: 'The Itsekiri in the Nineteenth Century', p. 223.

a show of it) was necessary to back up one's claims and rights. Olomu died in 1883.

Nana who succeeded his father as head of the family was in fact one of Olomu's younger sons born, according to Neville, in 1852 at Jakpa, that is, before Olomu founded the settlement Ebrohimi,[1] which Nana was to make famous. Nana was thus still a boy when his father's wars depicted above were fought. These wars must have left a deep impression on his young mind. Neville, a great admirer of Nana, whom he knew personally, claims that Nana served his apprenticeship in his father's war canoe, first as a paddler, then as one of his father's bodyguards.[2] Nana's impressionable mind must have conceived of his father as fighting for his rights to trade where he pleased. He probably realized early in his life, that in the age in which he lived, the successful trader had also to be a good and courageous fighter himself.

It is not clear how it was that Nana succeeded to his father's entire heritage. The more usual practice was to divide the inheritance among all the children. Nana's son today says that this was because Nana was very attentive to the needs of his father during the latter's old age; a legend attributes it to some supernatural 'opening' of Olomu's eyes, which enabled him to see that of all his sons, Nana would made the most worthy successor; Neville suggests that it was Nana's brilliance and courage as a warrior that determined his father to single him out as his successor.[3] Whatever the reason for Nana's choice as successor, by 1876, he was already playing the leading role in his father's affairs. It was he who defended his father against the charge of murder of Abraka prisoners before Consul Hartley in 1876, and was probably among those who had fought the war that let to the captives being taken. In that year Hartley described Nana as 'a very intelligent young man and well acquainted with the English language'.[4]

---

1 Olomu first lived at Jakpa with the rest of the *Ologbotsẹrẹ* group. Later he decided to branch out on his own in order to be better able to organize his trade. Ebrohimi was founded by him as a result of these movements. See Lloyd: 'The Itsekiri in the Nineteenth Century', pp. 212–13, and William Moore, op. cit., p. 93.

2 Neville, op. cit., p. 162.

3 Neville, op. cit.

4 F.O 84/1455, Hartley to F.O., No. 54, 24 Nov. 1876.

Nana himself probably began his early career with a war. This was the war against Ẹku, which arose out of the fact that one of Nana's half-brothers, called Igbẹn, committed adultery with one of Olomu's wives and then fled to Ẹku, his mother's town. Nana pursued him there, and demanded that Igbẹn be given up, but the Ẹku people refused, and a war followed. Ẹku appealed to Abraka to come to their aid, which the latter did. Despite the Abraka aid, Ẹku suffered a very severe defeat, after which Nana carried the war to Abraka and forced the people to flee into settlements farther into the hinterland in order to escape Nana's severe punishment.[1] It will be shown later that most of Nana's troubles with the Urhobo came from this part of the country. The tradition of hostility begun during Olomu's régime was never lost, even if it was driven underground from time to time. When British administrative officers assumed, as they tended to do in the 1890s, that all the disturbances in the Abraka and Agbọn clans were the work of Nana and his slaves, they failed to realize in their ignorance that there was this undercurrent of hostility and that the Urhobo of these areas were themselves a turbulent people. The British were to discover for themselves this fact of the people's turbulence, when they attempted to penetrate this same area after Nana's fall.[2]

Nana was appointed Governor of the River in his father's place in 1884, the year after the latter's death. Nana did not succeed to his father's title only; he inherited his father's entire business connexions and with these his slaves, his armaments, his trade and war-canoes and (this is a point which ought always to be remembered) his enemies both among the Itsẹkiri and the Urhobo. In this connexion it should be pointed out that the appointment of Nana as Governor in succession to his father went contrary to the convention observed since 1851 whereby the office was held alternately by members of the royal family group and the *Ologbotsẹrẹ* group. By that convention the former group should have provided the candidate for the governorship after Olomu. Apparently Nana's obvious pre-eminence in wealth and power decided the issue in his favour. But this was unlikely to have mitigated the growing tension

1 This war is today well remembered both at Ẹki and Abraka – Interviews with elders of Ẹku and Abraka during the month of September 1963.
2 See Chapter 4.

between the two groups already touched off by Olomu's victory in war over both Oritsẹmọnẹ and Tsanọmi. The Tsanọmi—Olomu feud was thus further intensified.

If the position of the Governor was a difficult one in the years before 1884, it was to become even more so in the post-1884 era. For Nana succeeded to the office (12 July 1884) at a time when, as a result of international diplomacy, the British were seeking to establish a claim through treaties to the Niger Delta as a British sphere of influence. This was to complicate the situation even more. In accepting the people's election of Nana, Hewett, the British Consul, said that he 'looked to him [Nana] to keep peace and good order in the country and settle disputes at the markets'.[1] Hewett was no doubt referring to the markets from which the oil came, i.e. the Urhobo markets. In other words, by virtue of his office, Nana was expected to get involved to some extent in Urhobo affairs. In 1876 Olomu had interfered in force in the Abraka area when trade was allegedly being interrupted. Was Nana being asked to be prepared for a similar act? The events of 1894 were to show that part of Nana's troubles was his endeavour to settle disputes at the markets in accord with the practice of the time.

The staff of office was formally handed over to Nana by Vice-Consul Blair on 6 May 1885. On that occasion the Vice-Consul assured Nana that he had the support of the British Government in exercising the authority which had been entrusted to him, so long as that authority was used in the interest of good government, amicable relations with his neighbours and the furtherance of trade and civilization.[2] Nana was to regard himself as the executive power through which the decrees of the British Government and consular courts were to be enforced. Blair assured the assembled chiefs that there was to be no interference with their 'native laws and customs', so long as these did not conduce to 'barbarism' and degradation. Each of these charges and assurances was pregnant with difficulties.

The tone of Blair's address was obviously dictated by the fact that Itsẹkiriland was already, in 1885, part of the British protectorate that was being gradually established over the Oil Rivers. For one of Nana's first acts as Governor was to sign, together with other

---

1 F.O. 84/1660, Hewett to F.O., 28 July 1884.
2 F.O. 2/64, David Boyle Blair to Nana, 6 May 1885: Exhibit E at Nana's trial.

leading Itsẹkiri men, a treaty which made Itsẹkiriland a British protectorate. The treaty which was signed on the 16 July 1884, was in the usual form, except that at the end there was this addition, namely, that the treaty was to come into force as soon as practicable, 'except as regards Articles VI and VII' which were 'to be left for negotiations on a future occasion'. According to Hewett, Nana, Tsanọmi and the other elders had refused to accept these two articles. Article VI laid it down that:

> The subjects and citizens of all countries may freely carry on trade in every part of the territories of the kings and chiefs parties hereto and may have houses and factories therein.[1]

Article VII provided for freedom of religious worship and freedom for all ministers of the Christian religion to practise in the area. It is of the greatest significance that the Itsẹkiri leaders refused to accept these two articles, especially Article VI. As middlemen, the Itsẹkiri realized that to accept the article which provided for 'free trade' would be prejudicial to their commercial prosperity. Nana was clearly not alone in holding this view, nor was it only the Itsẹkiri middlemen who refused to accept Article VI of the treaty. The preliminary treaty signed by Consul Hewett with 'the king and chiefs of Opobo' on the 1 July 1884, did not include this clause.[2] When a fuller treaty was finally signed on 19 December 1884, Article VI as printed in the treaty form was expunged on the insistence of King Jaja and his chiefs.[3] During the conflict which later developed between the British Consul and Jaja, the latter argued that his refusal to accept Article VI of the 'protection' treaty justified his seeking to protect his hinterland markets from direct exploitation by British merchants.[4] It would appear that in Jaja's, as in Nana's case later, the British administrative officers

---

1 F.O. 93/6/10, Treaty with Chiefs of Jakri (Benin River). See Appendix III. Professor J. C. Anene did not apparently take note of the stand of the Itsẹkiri elders, for in his *Southern Nigeria in Transition*, Cambridge 1966, p. 58, by implication he contrasts the intelligence of Jaja with the simplicity of the rulers of Benin River, New Calabar, Bonny and Old Calabar which places, he argues, 'proved easy acquisitions' to the British.
2 Jaja 3, Preliminary Treaty with the King and Chiefs of Opobo (1 July 1884).
3 Jaja 3, Treaty with King and Chiefs of Opobo: 19 Dec. 1884.
4 See Jaja 1/3, Cockey Gam and others to Salisbury 27 Aug. 1887; Jaja to Queen Victoria, 30 Aug. 1888.

found it convenient to pay little attention to the fact that these middlemen traders had deliberately, and after full discussion, rejected 'free trade' as part of the obligations which they undertook to fulfil when they accepted British 'protection'. 'Free trade' might have been necessary in the interest of British commerce and the development of the hinterland. Nevertheless, coastal middlemen like Jaja and Nana were, strictly speaking, within their treaty rights when they refused to allow 'free trade', or sought to protect their own interests in the face of growing 'free trade' tendencies.

There has been some confusion as to the area over which Nana was appointed Governor, and the area which thus became a British protectorate by virtue of the 1884 treaty signed by Nana and others. First, Neville in his eulogy on Nana states that Nana was appointed 'Governor of the whole Province'.[1] If by this he meant Warri Province, then he was widely off the mark. In the 1930s British administrative officers who wrote reports on various Urhobo clans stated loosely that when Itsẹkiriland was declared a protectorate, certain Urhobo clans were included, implying that these clans were under the suzerainty of the Itsẹkiri.[2] Professor J. C. Anene states that in 1884 'Nana . . . signed the treaty of protection on behalf of himself and the Itsẹkiri and Urhobo communities west of the Forcados river'.[3] Neither the terms of the treaty, nor the events which followed its being signed, can justify any of the above conclusions. It will be recalled that when later some Ijọ towns were brought under the 1884 treaty, this was a deliberate act accomplished as a result of a visit to the towns concerned by Hewett and Nana. No such visitation was undertaken with regard to the Urhobo country. Further, whereas Nana protested against the Royal Niger Company making treatries with the Ijọ towns that had acceded to the 1884 treaty, he made no such protests when the same company and later the Niger Coast Protectorate signed treaties in Urhoboland. Urhoboland was clearly not included in the 1884 treaty.

Since the interregnum, appointment to the office of Governor was, to some extent at least, a recognition of the power, commercial and therefore political, of the man appointed to that office. At the

---

1 Neville, op. cit., p. 163.
2 C.S.O. 26, File No. 20655, Intelligence Report on Ewu clan, 1930, p. 23.
3 J. C. Anene, op. cit., p. 152.

same time, having been appointed, the Governor was in a position to attract trade to himself and his immediate kin, since the European agents did all in their power to win the Governor over to trade with their respective firms. The Governor was thus in a position to enhance his economic standing.

If Nana had a 'goodly heritage', he was not content to sit back and squander it. On the contrary, he applied himself to the task of improving on his inheritance. Like his father before him, Nana concentrated on the Urhobo markets along the Ethiope and Warri Rivers. In the Agbarho clan, he continued the friendship with the Ovwha family, cementing the relationship by marrying Ejemutohwo, a daughter of that family, and another woman, probably the product of an Urhobo-Itsẹkiri alliance, with the Itsẹkiri name of Ẹmẹbirẹn, also from the Agbarho clan. These marriage alliances became a matter of general policy. In the Udu clan, Nana took to wife Ikogho of Ovwhia, mother of Chief Newton Celleone Nana, who now heads the Nana family. In the Abraka area, Nana sought to improve the relations by marriage alliances, and took two wives from Abraka: Agbemeta, daughter of an influential trader called Madubi, and Oghọrọ, daughter of another trader.[1] Where his father did not leave behind friends who could ensure that trade was attracted to him, Nana proceeded to make new friends. Thus in Okpara he sought and obtained the friendship of some of the leading local traders like Nwajeri, Ukavwe and Owere. These men could then influence others to trade with Nana and his 'boys'.

These links of friendship and marriage fitted well into the organization of the trade which remained very much along the lines established by his father. He sent his head slaves to establish depots along the watersides of Urhobo towns which lay more to the hinterland. There were many such depots dotted along the rivers, the most important being those at the watersides of Okpara, Ukhuokori, Ẹku, Abraka and Otumara. No annual rents were paid to the elders of the Urhobo towns where these depots were established. It was customary, however, for the Itsẹkiri to give presents to the elders of the towns concerned before actually settling down to trade.

---

1 Even Nana's son, the late Johnson Nana, married from Abraka, and a product of the marriage, Okwovbera by name, today lives at Abraka, his mother's place.

These presents served to win the goodwill of those who were in a position to influence the movement of trade. The head slaves and their aides did not tour the Urhobo areas buying palm oil and then arranging to transport the oil down to their waterside stations. They depended on the Urhobo to bring the oil to them. This was one reason which made Nana seek to have friends at the most important centres, so that those friends could attract trade to him. For the Urhobo, the system had the result of producing people who bought small quantities of oil locally and finally took their stock to the Itsẹkiri traders at the watersides. A generous advance of trade goods to friends and leading customers further helped to ensure a supply of oil. At Abraka for instance, it is said that despite the hostility which flared up from time to time, Nana remained by far the best man with whom to trade. He was seldom behind in payment for oil supplied. If anything it was more usual for the supply of oil to be in arrears. This picture of Nana as a great and trusted trader is general in the Urhobo areas with which he traded, including even Ẹku which holds his memory in great hostility because of the Ẹku War previously described. He seemed never to have allowed past quarrels to influence his general trade relations.

The head slaves and their followers stayed almost permanently at the markets to which they were posted, going back to Ebrohimi occasionally to report their progress to their master. Ologun, one of Nana's head slaves, is remembered as having stayed at Okpara, and apparently controlled the trade at Ẹku and Abraka as well. Another head slave was stationed at Amukpẹ to tap the trade of what is now the hinterland of Sapẹlẹ. As Nana is often compared with Jaja, it is here relevant to mention that the trade organization described above was very similar to Jaja's. Like Nana, Jaja had his slaves residing in the hinterland markets where they collected the palm produce and then conveyed it to Opobo for sale to European merchants.[1] If Acting Consul Johnston's[2] accounts are to be given

---

1 Jaja's trading methods are vividly portrayed in Johnson's dispatches to the Foreign Office. See Cal. Prof. 2/2 Vol. 5, Various correspondence from Johnson to F.O.

2 Johnston, Sir Harry Hamilton: artist, zoologist, explorer and administrator, born 1858. Royal Academy of Arts 1876–80. Explored Portuguese West Africa and Congo River 1882–3. Commanded Scientific Expedition of Royal Society to Mount Kilimanjaro, 1884. Her Majesty's Vice-Consul in

any credence, there was at least one occasion on which Jaja was influential and powerful enough to have secured the deposition of the headchief of a hinterland town, and to have replaced him with his own head slave. This was at Ohambele where Johnston reported that Jaja removed Baba, who was the chief of that town, because the latter favoured direct trade with Europeans, and replaced him with one 'Ekike Notshe', his own head slave, who proceeded to reverse Baba's policy.[1] No such active intervention in the political life of the Urhobo has ever been attributed to Nana. There is no truth in the report by one of the English merchants that Nana described a three-mile limit around his markets with broken glass, obliging all those within the three-mile radius to take their oil to his markets.[2] The setting up of such a frontier would have been a most foolish undertaking, for the distance between his markets and most of the inland towns which fed these markets was often much more than three miles. Indeed, such a limit would have secured for him comparatively few customers at each of his markets.

Nana was not content to leave his commercial affairs entirely in the hands of his senior slaves, but toured the more important markets from time to time in order, personally, to strengthen his connexions with the Urhobo traders. If Nana was thus eager to maintain friendly relations with the Urhobo with whom he traded, he did not, it would appear, allow such relations to derogate from a proper appreciation of his own importance. He seemed to have been conscious of his wealth and power, and to have wished others to see and recognize these, and treat him with due deference. The story is told of a visit which Nana paid to Okpara. One of his closest friends in that town, by name Ukavwe, went out to meet him. Nana insisted that this man, who was much older than he, should kneel down publicly before him as a token of respect. When Ukavwe refused to do this, Nana ordered his 'boys' to seize him as a slave, the close friendship notwithstanding. Ukavwe's son had to redeem him with nine

the Cameroons 1885. Acting Consul in the Oil Rivers 1887. Consul for province of Mozambique 1888. Commissioner and Consul-General, British Central African Protectorate, 1891. Consul-General for Uganda Protectorate, 1899–1901. Author of various books on Africa. Died July 1927.
1 Cal. Prof. 2/2 Vol. 5, Johnston to F.O., No. 12, 1 August 1887.
2 F.O. 2/63, Coxon to Pinnock, 1 July 1894.

slaves.[1] This awareness of his power and of his position was one of the traits which were to annoy British administrative officers like Gallwey and Moor. The reaction of the Urhobo man in this episode is interesting. Ukavwe as a friend of Nana's was fully aware of the power of his friend, yet he refused to kneel down before him, no doubt because he felt that this was against his own custom. He preferred to stand on his rights and face seizure rather than suffer humiliation. While the knowledge of Nana's power must have affected the Urhobo in their dealing with him, incidents such as this show that the Urhobo were not always overwhelmed by fear of such power being used against them. Other episodes already described confirm this.

If Nana himself was guilty of such excesses and show of power, his head slaves were even more so. Everywhere in the Urhobo country where Nana's 'boys' traded, one hears of their exploits. It is said that it was their practice, sometimes, to invite children and women to their canoes to 'buy' fish and other local and imported goods. These women and children would carry their own wares into the canoes, and when the bargaining had started, the head slaves would give the order to 'shove off' and all these people would be carried off as slaves; some of the women would be married to other slaves and their issue helped to swell the number of Nana's slaves. These exploits are said to have been more frequent when trade was bad, as the head slaves sought to have something to show for their ventures, rather than merely report that trade was bad. But these incidents were never too frequent, as it was necessary that time be allowed for the restoration of confidence after each trick. It is not known whether Nana himself was always aware of these events, for the number of slaves who traded for him was so large that it is unlikely that he knew all of them, or that they all reported back directly to him. It is said, however, that on some occasions when he did know of the actions of his 'boys', he made amends. Thus, the mother of the present head of the Nana family, Chief Celleone Nana, was first carried away as a slave in the way described above. Tradition has it that the head slave who seized her presented her as a wife to Nana. Nana, however, made enquiries about how she was

1 The story was told by Oraka (son of the Ukavwe who was seized) at Okpara at an interview on 16 September 1963.

obtained. On being told that she had been deceived into the canoe and carried away, not only did Nana order the head slave to be punished, but he sent the woman back to her people, with an offer to marry her if her people would let him. The woman's people, overjoyed at Nana's action, readily agreed and Nana married her. On another occasion, one of Nana's 'boys' killed an Urhobo girl from Udu clan because the girl refused to enter into his canoe. When Nana got to hear of the matter, he ordered that two canoes be filled with goods and a seemly slave girl found, to be sent to the family of the murdered girl as compensation.[1] This was accordingly done. Acts such as these restored the confidence of the Urhobo in Nana himself, as a man of peace and a lover of justice—the view which even today still persists.

Nana also obtained Urhobo slaves through pawning, as indicated in the last chapter. At his trial in 1894, Nana denied that he raided the Urhobo for slaves to the number of 200 a year, as claimed by Ralph Moor. 'It is the custom', Nana declared, 'with the Sobos when they take trust to give one of their children as security'.[2] Any such pledges not redeemed automatically became, for practical purposes, if not in strict law, slaves. If Nana did not normally order raids against the Urhobo, that is not to say that there were no raids at all. As there were other Itsẹkiri trading to the areas in which Nana was interested, it is likely that 'boys' of rival masters fell out among themselves, and that the resulting chaos, the neighbourhood was raided. Besides, when the Urhobo took the offensive by seizing Itsẹkiri trade canoes, such an action was followed by a raid of reprisal during which slaves were usually taken. From Nana's own account, there was such a raid against the Abraka people in 1885. This raid was occasioned by the seizure of Nana's canoes, by Abraka people, and the killing of one of his men in the process. Nana claimed that when he sent a force against Abraka, he captured only one old man who was subsequently ransomed.[3] He could not take more captives because most of the people ran away from their

1 Interview with Chief Aya Yovbake of Aladja, 22 July 1962, and elders of Udu clan, 21 September 1963.
2 F.O. 2/64, Evidence of Nana at his trial—Enclosure in Macdonald to F.O., No. 49, 13 December 1894.
3 Ibid.

homes. The Abraka recall this war, and say that Nana's force was so overwhelming that they had to run away to a place called Umebu near Orogun territory, till Nana recalled his force. There were probably similar raids elsewhere about which no records exist.

It should be remembered that the Urhobo people themselves continued to deal in slaves throughout this period. Therefore, Urhobo slaves found in Ebrohimi were not the products of the escapades of Nana's boys and of raids only, but also the products of the normal trade in slaves which was described in the last chapter. As the children of slaves were slaves, and as slaves were not so barbarously treated as to postulate a higher rate of mortality among them than among the free-born, the slave population, irrespective of annual replenishments, was bound to increase from year to year.

Nana became Governor at an extremely difficult time. The British were seeking to establish a more permanent foothold on the Delta than they had done during the tenure of office of other Governors. Thus in 1885 the Oil Rivers Protectorate over the territories which had entered into treaties with the British was promulgated. Itsẹkiriland was part of this protectorate by virtue of the 1884 treaty. In fact, after the signing of the 1884 treaty, Hewett took Nana and Tsanọmi on a tour of the Rivers Escravos, Ramos and Dodo. According to Hewett, the Ijọ towns along these rivers acknowledged Nana's suzerainty, and they were therefore told of the treaty of July 1884, and informed that since they were Nana's subjects, the treaty was binding on them. The Ijọ people, including those of Burutu, accepted the treaty signed by Nana as binding on themselves. On this trip, one can imagine how much was made of Nana by the British Consul. He was, for instance, allowed to give instructions to the Ijọ and to warn them that if they failed to abide by his orders, he would return and punish them.[1] Two years later, Acting Consul Johnston confirmed that Nana had jurisdiction over these people.[2] At the beginning of British rule in Itsẹkiriland, therefore, not only was Nana used for the purpose of forwarding British ambitions, but his power and authority were confirmed by this very fact. Only three years after Johnston's confirmation of Nana's

1 F.O. 84/1660, Hewett to F.O., No. 18, 25 August 1884.
2 F.O. 84/1882, The Extent of Chief Nana's Rule in the Bight of Benin— Memo by Johnston.

jurisdiction over the Ijọ people, that jurisdiction was called in question by a British special commissioner. The questioning of Nana's power and authority was basic to the quarrel of 1894.

From the commercial point of view, the 1880s were bad years for trade. The price of oil in Liverpool fell by half.[1] For the Itsẹkiri this meant lower prices for palm produce. Nana as the head of his people was directly involved in this situation. In 1886, he stopped trade with the whites in an endeavour to force up the price of oil.[2] It is fair to assume that Nana did not stop trade in order to secure benefits to himself alone, though as the greatest of the Itsẹkiri traders, he stood to gain from an increase in prices. It was not mere coincidence that it was in 1886 that there was this stoppage, for 1886 was in fact 'a singularly bad year for business'.[3] In 1887 Nana was forced to write to the British Consul to the effect that his people were unable to accept the prices offered by the white traders, and could not therefore trade with them. Hewett's reply to Nana is interesting. The Consul attributed the stoppage of trade to two causes only: either Nana was incapable of dealing with the matter of the lowering of prices with the people at the producing markets, or he was unwilling to do so for selfish ends. The Consul saw three possible solutions to the problem: Nana's removal from office as Governor; the establishment of factories at the markets by the agents of the European firms; the annexation of Itsẹkiriland instead of its being a mere protectorate.[4] Nana was ordered to resume trade immediately on receipt of Hewett's letter. In Nana's letter and the reply to it can be seen, first, the dilemma of the Governor whose actions in his official capacity and on behalf of the Itsẹkiri traders as a whole could so easily be interpreted as being for selfish

1 Lloyd: 'The Itsekiri in the Nineteenth Century', p. 225.
2 F.O. 84/1749, Paton to Hewett, 2 December 1886—Enclosure in Hewett to F.O., 23 December 1886.
3 *The Liverpool Review*: 1 January 1887. The fact that 1886 was a bad year for trade is important, too, as part of the background of the quarrel between the British merchants and Jaja, which ended with the deposition of the latter in 1887. In the face of low prices for produce, both sides were undoubtedly eager to get the best possible out of their investments. For Jaja, this meant control of the hinterland. For the British merchants and their consul, it meant freedom to penetrate the interior and trade direct with the producers. The resultant clash was, in the circumstances, understandable.
4 F.O. 2/64, Hewett to Nana, 24 Feb. 1887—Exhibit F at Nana's trial.

reasons; secondly, the change in the tone of the British Consul in the new circumstance of Itsẹkiriland being a British protectorate. There was clearly a new authoritativeness in the tone of the Consul's letter. This was to become more noticeable in the years ahead, and to cause a certain amount of tension between Nana and the British.

Earlier writers on Nana have been so obsessed with trying to find reasons for the British offensive against him in 1894 that they have failed to draw attention to certain events which helped to shape Nana's attitude to the British.[1] One such event was Macdonald's[2] mission of 1889. In 1884 as described above, the people along the Rivers Escravos, Ramos and Dodo, had acknowledged themselves to be under Nana, and had agreed that they were bound by the 1884 treaty signed by him. Yet in 1888 these very people signed treaties with the Royal Niger Company. When Nana heard of these treaties, he immediately asked the Governing Council of the Benin River to protest on his behalf, at a meeting held on 18 September 1888.[3] This protest was probably responsible for Hewett's tour of the area that year. He went to Burutu and 'Goolah', the two towns reported to have signed these treaties, and discovered that they had actually done so. Hewett reported that the two towns handed over the treaties to Nana, and that he permitted Nana to inflict severe punishment on these people for signing another treaty after they had undertaken not to do so four years earlier. He argued

---

1 None of those who have done any work on Nana seem to have thought it necessary to study the events of the years 1891–93 as a background to the crisis of 1894. A few like Bindloss and Michael Crowder say that Nana co-operated for a time and then fell foul of the British, but they make no real attempts to explain this. See: Harold Bindloss: *In the Niger Country*, Edinburgh 1898, p. 206; Michael Crowder: *The Story of Nigeria*, London 1962, p. 181; A. F. Mockler-Ferryman: *British Nigeria*, London 1902, pp. 98–9; William N. M. Geary: *Nigeria Under British Rule*, London 1927, p. 109.

2 Sir Claude Maxwell Macdonald. Born 1852. Trained Royal Military College, Sandhurst. 74th Highlanders 1872. Served throughout the Egyptian campaign 1882, and through the Suakin Expedition of 1884 as a volunteer with the 42nd Highlanders. Decorated with Khedive's star and 4th class Osmanieh. Military Attaché to British Agency in Cairo 1882–7. Acting Agent and Consul General at Zanzibar 1887–8. Special Commissioner to Niger Territories 1889. Commissioner and Consul-General in the Oil Rivers Protectorate 1891. Envoy Extraordinary and Minister Plenipotentiary at Peking 1896–1900. Ambassador at Tokio 1900–12. Died 1915.

3 F.O. 84/1881, Hewett to F.O., No. 34, 10 November 1888.

that to let the Royal Niger Company occupy the Forcados area and impose their high duties would cripple the trade of the Warri River area, since the Forcados afforded the best entrance to steamers in the whole of that region. He recalled the dissatisfaction which even then existed in the Akassa area over the Company's duties, and forecast that in a similar way, the traders established along the Benin and Warri Rivers would be subjected to 'vexatious obstructions and troubles innumerable' if the Royal Niger Company's treaties were ratified by the British Government. The commercial repercussions aside, Hewett advanced the argument that these treaties could not be valid because 'the native signatories thereto had no power to enter into them they being subjects of Nana and . . . included in the Jekri Protection Treaty of 1884'.[1] Hewett was clearly inclined to uphold the authority of Nana. The British Government did not, however, consider that this was a matter of importance. As Salisbury noted in a minute, whichever British authority signed the treaties, the areas were secured to the Crown.[2] Nevertheless, it was probably as a result of the strong protest of Hewett, that Johnston was asked to write a memorandum on the extent of Nana's jurisdiction. As already pointed out, Johnston confirmed Hewett's views in his memorandum, pointing out that the people concerned had on various occasions admitted to him that they were under the suzerainty of Nana.

When Major Claude Macdonald was appointed Special Commissioner in 1889 to examine and report on various complaints made against the Royal Niger Company, he was asked to take the opportunity to make a special study of the Forcados question. Macdonald's report was a blow to Nana:

> After careful consideration, I cannot see that Nana and his advocates had made out a case with regard to Burutu and Goolah.[3]

Macdonald based his conclusion on what the people of these places told him. At Goolah he was told that Nana was a friend, not their overlord; that they had handed over the treaty to him because

1 F.O. 84/1881, Hewett to F.O., No. 34, 10 November 1888.
2 F.O. 84/1881, Salisbury's Minute on Telegram From Hewett, 5 November 1888.
3 F.O. 84/2109, Macdonald's Report: Chapter III—The Forcados Question.

Nana had taken them out into a British man-of-war and threatened them there.[1] The Burutu people told a similar story. It is probable that it was the yearly subsidy paid by the Company that influenced the Ijọ in their choice of the company. Perhaps, from the point of view of this work, the important thing is not whether, in fact, Nana did exercise a *de facto* suzerainty over these Ijọ people; what is important is to realize what Macdonald's report meant to Nana. In 1884, Hewett had used Nana's power to bring these Ijọ under British protection. In 1888 Hewett had again confirmed and emphasized Nana's authority over the Ijọ of Goolah and Burutu. Then in 1889 Macdonald's report questioned, and indeed denied, the very power which had been utilized by the British five years earlier. The crisis of 1894 was, partially at least, the outcome of the dissatisfaction which arose from situations such as this. The longer Nana associated himself with the British, the less he had cause to like them, the less he trusted them, and consequently the less popular he grew with them.

At the time of the Macdonald mission, there was general uncertainty at the British Foreign Office as to how best to administer the Oil Rivers. Up till the time of the mission, little had been done by way of effective administration. British authority still consisted largely in the periodic visits of the British Consul. The advocacy of Hewett and Johnston[2] for a more formal and effective form of administration had not, up to that time, produced any results. Macdonald was therefore further asked, as part of his task during the mission, to seek the opinion of the Nigerian coastal peoples as to what form of British administration they would prefer. The choice was between government by chartered company (the Royal Niger Company, or the African Association or both) and direct imperial control in the form of a colony or protectorate.[1]

---

1 Ibid. The Goolah people claimed that the reason for their friendship with Nana was that his mother was a Goolah woman. As a matter of fact Nana's mother was an Urhobo woman from Ẹvhrọ (Effurun). It is hoped that this was not typical of the accuracy of the Goolah chiefs.

2 F.O. 84/1881, Johnston to F.O., 16 March 1888.

3 Dr. J. E. Flint discusses the Macdonald mission in detail in his *Sir George Goldie and the Making of Nigeria*, London 1960, Chapter 7. At Old Calabar some of the chiefs did not see cause for any change whatsoever; they would have preferred to remain as they were.

When Macdonald visited the Benin River for the purpose of finding out the wishes of the Itsẹkiri on this matter, Nana was the chief spokesman. He was categorical in his rejection of Company rule. He was, however, prepared to have a 'Queen's Government' provided two conditions were met: that he and his people should be allowed to keep slaves, and that their polygamous way of life should not be tampered with.[1] For the Itsẹkiri, the question of being allowed to keep slaves was of vital importance. The whole of their economy hinged on slavery. It was the slaves who manned their trade and war canoes, carried on most of the actual trading, and cultivated their food on such land as was cultivable. The issue of slavery was a difficult one. Even the British consuls realized how vital slaves were to the economic system of the coastal peoples. It was not surprising that most of the coastal states insisted on the institution of slavery being guaranteed to them.[2] It was probably in recognition of the complications involved over slavery, that the Foreign Office decided to reject the crown colony system for the Oil Rivers till such a time as 'the way had been prepared by an administration resembling that of a colony in that all officials would be directly servants of the Crown, but without the cumbersome machinery'.[3] The upshot was the establishment of a protectorate over the Oil Rivers. Major (by now Sir) Claude Macdonald himself was appointed Commissioner and Consul-General, and sent out with a team of vice-consuls and other staff to inaugurate the new era in 1891. In many ways the troubles of Nana began with the inauguration of this more regular, more formal machinery of government. For although no final decision had been reached on the thorny issue of slave-holding, Macdonald and his successors sought to prepare the way for its final abolition. As Dr. Flint points out, it was part of Macdonald's policy to achieve the necessary social reforms that would prepare the way for establishment of a

---

1 F.O. 84/1940, Enclosure 8 in Macdonald to F.O., No. 11, 12 January 1889.
2 At Bonny, Opobo, New Calabar and Brass Macdonald discovered that the people wished to retain the institution of slavery. See Flint, op. cit., pp. 133–4.
3 Quoted by Flint, op. cit., p. 153. Macdonald had originally recommended the establishment of a crown colony. The decision to establish a protectorate was a modification suggested by Macdonald himself, partly because of the difficulty over the slavery question.

British colony.[1] This policy was diametrically opposed to the wishes of Nana and all the other coastal middlemen, who frowned on any type of social reform that not only struck a blow at their prestige and status in their communities, but undermined their economic position in one and the same process.

Macdonald began his assignment with a tour of the entire area committed to his charge, establishing vice-consulates at suitable points along the rivers. In the area covered by this work, two such vice-consulates were set up: at Warri on the River Forcados, and in the Benin River. Macdonald's first visit in his new official capacity indicates what the lines of future policy were to be, and with respect to Nana's position, foreshadowed what lay ahead.

The Consul-General first visited Warri (19 August 1891). He admitted that 'the chiefs of Warri' were under Nana. But according to him, these 'chiefs' were very anxious to become independent of Nana (he did not say how this issue arose) and,

> as the trade here promises to be one of the most flourishing in the Protectorate, and as Nana is already sufficiently powerful, and threatens to be another Ja Ja, I thought it politic to establish a separate vice-consulate at this place and to conclude with the chiefs of Warri a separate Protection Treaty.[2]

Thus, at the very beginning of his administration and before he had had more time to study Nana for himself, and even before the meeting he held with the white traders at the Benin River two days later, Macdonald had come to the conclusion that Nana was a danger. The establishment of a vice-consulate at Warri would therefore appear to have been a premeditated act, directed towards reducing the power of Nana. Because the trade of the district promised to be profitable, Nana was to be excluded from it if possible.

From Warri, Macdonald proceeded to the Benin River where he held a meeting on the 21 August. One of Macdonald's main aims during these tours was to explain to the people the implications of the import duties which he was imposing, in order to raise a revenue for the proper administration of the territory placed under him.

---

1 Ibid.
2 F.O. 84/2111, Macdonald to F.O., No. 2, 1 September 1891.

Both at Warri and Benin River, he reported that the 'chiefs' consented to this imposition and thoroughly understood the implications. He did not, unfortunately, indicate whether he spoke to the people about the full implications of the establishment of British rule in their territory. By his instructions, he was directed to let the chiefs rule their people as previously, but he was to watch them 'so as to prevent injustice and check abuses'. The chiefs were to be made to understand that misgovernment would result in forfeiture of powers. Macdonald was empowered, 'in special cases', to insist on the delegation to himself of the powers of the chiefs if this would be 'for the benefit of the natives'. Finally, Macdonald was 'to take under immediate control of the inter-tribal and foreign relations of the native chiefs'.[1] It is not known whether in 1891 Macdonald fully explained these instructions to the people, or whether he preferred first to establish his régime, and let the chiefs learn, with time, what the new conditions of their lives were to be. It is strange that Macdonald did not report to the Foreign Office what he had told the 'chiefs' about the question of slavery. The Itsẹkiri 'chiefs' had categorically asked for the preservation of this institution. Apparently, in 1891, no definite ruling was laid down. Yet this was one of the issues which ostensibly led to the crisis of 1894.

The Benin River meeting gave Macdonald another opportunity (the first was during his mission in 1889) of sizing up Nana. Some measure of Nana's wealth at the time can be seen from Macdonald's account of his entourage. Nana arrived for the meeting in a war canoe, 'paddled by upwards of a hundred slaves, with four or five similar canoes in attendance'. He had a personal escort of 'twenty men armed with Winchester repeating rifles'.[2] His business sense was shown by the fact that he had a copy of the proclamation containing Macdonald's import duties' schedule which, Nana assured Macdonald, he had carefully studied in order to be ready for any white traders who might seize the opportunity to increase prices beyond the level justified by the duties. Macdonald could not but come to the conclusion that Nana was 'a man possessed of great power and wealth, astute, energetic and intelligent'.[3]

---

1 F.O. 84/2110, F.O. to Macdonald, Draft No. 2, 18 April 1891.
2 F.O. 84/2111, Macdonald to F.O., No. 2, 1 September 1891.
3 Ibid.

After the meeting with the Itsẹkiri, Macdonald decided to hold a separate meeting with the European traders. As a result of this meeting, he once again noted that he would have 'to combat another Ja Ja difficulty'. The Europeans gave conflicting views of Nana, no doubt according to their trade relations with him. Some of them complained that they could not trade at the hinterland markets because they could not get fair play 'owing to Nana's great power and influence'. Macdonald told these traders that it was for them to decide whether they went to the markets to get the oil themselves, or trusted the middlemen to do so for them. His concern was that those who did decide to go to the markets should obtain protection against all forms of molestation.[1]

The question of Nana preventing the Europeans from going into the interior which was raised during this visit was again to come to the fore during 1894. Yet there is no record of attempts by Europeans to penetrate into the Urhobo country prior to 1891 which were stopped by Nana or some other Itsẹkiri trader. In 1891 Gallwey reported that some Europeans had in the previous year attempted to go into the interior, but had not done so because they were afraid of the hinterland peoples.[2] The account given by Lloyd of the attempts to find a route to the Niger proper, via Patani, can hardly be regarded as penetration into the interior.[3] Admittedly, in 1873 Tsanọmi and other Itsẹkiri traders, as well as the European members of the Court of Equity had signed an agreement to the effect that all trade at Warri should cease.[4] This was designed to protect their own position as middlemen not against European penetration into the Urhobo country, but against another set of Itsẹkiri middlemen whose base was Warri. Had the Patani route become well developed and regularly used, all that would have happened was that the trade of the Benin River would have suffered, while Patani and other places would have grown up as new centres for middlemen trade, for the bulk of the oil was not produced along the main Forcados

---

1 F.O. 84/2111, Macdonald to F.O., No. 2, 1 September 1891.
2 F.O. 84/2111, Gallwey's report on his visit to the Oil Markets of the Sobo and Abraka Districts—Enclosure in Macdonald to F.O., No. 30, 12 December 1891.
3 Lloyd, 'The Itsẹkiri in the Nineteenth Century', p. 226.
4 Ibid.

River but in the hinterland; there is no evidence of any attempt by the Europeans to move into this hinterland in the period before 1891. That was no doubt why Nana and the other Itsẹkiri traders were so welcome in the Urhobo area.

It might be argued that the Europeans did not make any attempt to penetrate the interior because they knew that the Itsẹkiri would oppose such a move. The point is whether in the 1880s and 1890s the European firms would necessarily have made larger profits if they had decided to go to the hinterland themselves, buy the oil, and transport it in barges (where these could be used) to the main river mouths, at a time when they were not at all sure of the kind of reception they would have got from the hinterland peoples. During his mission in 1889, Macdonald himself was surprised that although 'Ogbe Sobo' (Aladja) which was only '20 minutes launching above Warri' was a rich oil market, the European agents did not make any effort to go there themselves.[1] On that occasion even though Nana was already the most powerful trader, no complaints were brought against him. One wonders whether the Europeans merely put forward these complaints because they knew that they were in line with the new policy which the Macdonald administration was bound to pursue. At any rate, the fact that as late as 1905 the firms were still content to remain at the centres where government stations were established, and were not setting up depots in the hinterland even when it was clear that the Itsẹkiri could not stop them, is evidence that these traders did not consider it necessary to take on the added responsibility of sending their agents direct to the producer areas.[2] The reluctance of the European firms to move into the interior was also noticeable in the Eastern Delta. There was no immediate move into the hinterland after the fall of Jaja. In fact, as late as after the Aro expedition, Moor[3] complained that the European merchants were still unwilling to invest money in the

1 F.O. 84/2109, Macdonald's Report—Chapter III: The Forcados Question.
2 C.O. 592/3, Annual Report, Central Province, 1906.
3 Sir Ralph Denham Rayment Moor. Born 1860. Educated at home. Served as District Inspector, Royal Irish Constabulary 1881–1891. Deputy Commissioner and Vice-Consul in the Oil Rivers (later Niger Coast Protectorate) 1892. Acting Commissioner and Consul-General 1892–5. Commissioner and Consul-General 1896–1900. High Commissioner, Southern Nigeria, 1900–3. Retired 1903. Died 1909.

development of road transport, which would enable them to trade direct with the hinterland producers. They were apparently satisfied with their trade at the coastal 'factories'. Moor complained that in this instance trade was waiting for the flag to take the initiative, a reversal of the more usual process.[1] The explanation for the attitude of the firms lay in the fact that the road system of the protectorate was as yet undeveloped.[2] In the circumstances, it was cheaper for the agents to rely on the middlemen using their canoes and slaves, than for them to hire canoes and labour and penetrate the hinterland.

The real problem which was posed in 1891 was whether Nana was still to be regarded as Governor, following the establishment of the Macdonald administration. Dr. Lloyd states that with the appointment of Gallwey as Vice-Consul in charge of the Benin River in 1891, Nana's office as Governor ceased to exist and he had no further control over trade.[3] It is almost certain that Nana did not see things in this light. Clearly, he attended the August meeting in his official capacity, and actually made a very impassioned speech about Consul Annesley who had apparently broken his staff of office and declared him deposed. Nana had protested to Lord Salisbury in a petition dated 14 December 1890,[4] but up to the time of Macdonald's meeting no reply had been received by Nana. Macdonald himself still regarded Nana as head of the Itsẹkiri. It was not till 1894 that he wrote to Nana to the effect that he was no longer to regard himself as head of the Itsẹkiri, but of his own family only.[5] No doubt the other Itsẹkiri continued to regard Nana as their head. Yet his position was bound to get increasingly untenable. He stood for a system based on power, wealth and slavery; the new order stood for a system which, while directed towards increasing the wealth available, sought to make itself the only, or at least the ultimate, power in the whole of the protectorate. It was in Nana's interest that the social, political and economic *status quo* should be

1 Tamuno, op. cit., p. 131.
2 See Tamuno, op. cit., p. 364 for a comment on the road-development policies of Moor and Egerton.
3 Lloyd: 'Nana Olomu—Governor of the River', *West Africa*, June 1957, p. 609.
4 F.O. 2/64, Nana to Salisbury, 14 December 1890—Exhibit G at Nana's trial.
5 F.O. 2/64, Macdonald to Nana, April 1894—Exhibit M at Nana's trial.

maintained; the new order was for a reorganization of this *status quo*. A clash of interests was therefore likely, and events moved rapidly towards such a clash.

It probably will never be fully known how Nana reacted to the new situation created by the inauguration of the 1891 administration. Matters were not made any easier by the fact that the years 1891–3, which preceded the year of crisis, were years of commercial uncertainty. One reason for the uncertainty was the establishment of the Niger Company in the Forcados River area, which made it impossible for the Itsẹkiri traders to go to some of their old markets in the Urhobo country unless they were prepared to pay export duties which, even by Macdonald's own account were high, and the enforcement of which he considered injurious to trade.[1] In 1891 Macdonald fixed a provisional boundary with the Company. By 1892 he was seeking to have this boundary modified because he had discovered that it did not conform to any 'fiscal boundary'.[2] In May 1892, the Liverpool Chamber of Commerce sent a strongly worded protest to Lord Salisbury, in which it argued that not only would the Company's duties 'harass the merchants of the Oil Rivers', but they would also 'probably lead to conflicts with the natives on the grounds of objection'.[3] The Niger Company's duties were at first seen as affecting only the Warri district rather than the Benin River, but as one of the protest letters pointed out, those in the Benin River were bound to suffer equally, because 'a certain portion of the Warree produce' was taken over to the Benin River.[4] Unfortunately, the Foreign Office, preoccupied during these years with boundary negotiations with France in various spheres in Africa, could not immediately give any definite ruling.[5] As the Niger Company's claims to territory around the Niger and Benue

1 F.O. 84/2194, Macdonald to F.O., No. 12, 8 March 1892.
2 F.O. 403/171, Macdonald to F.O., No. 23, 12 November 1892.
3 F.O. 403/178, Liverpool Chamber of Commerce to Salisbury, 25 May 1892.
4 F.O. 403/171, Messrs. Ellis, Fislingbury & Co. to Salisbury, 12 January 1892. That there was general apprehension about the effect of the R.N.C. duties on trade was shown by the number of protest letters from firms interested: F.O. 403/171, African Association to Salisbury 5 December 1891; Mr. Pinnock to F.O., 14 January 1892; Elder Dempster to Salisbury, 13 January 1892; Highgate Brothers to Salisbury, 15 January 1892.
5 For a discussion of these negotiations see Flint, op. cit., Chapter 8.

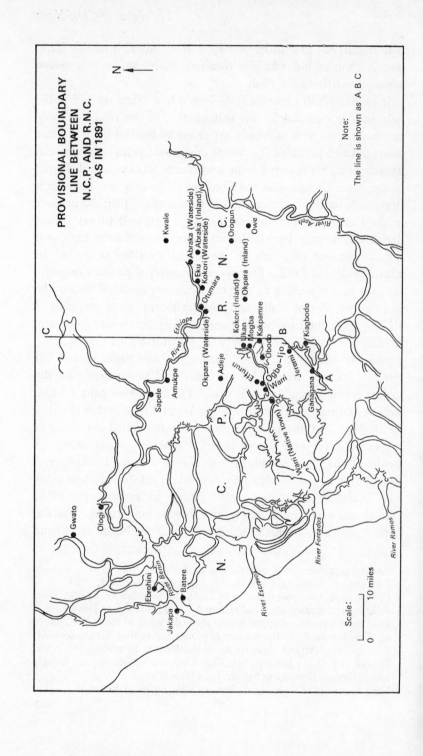

PROVISIONAL BOUNDARY
LINE BETWEEN
N.C.P. AND R.N.C.
AS IN 1891

Note:

The line is shown as A B C

N

Kwale

Abraka (Waterside)
Abraka (Inland)
Eku
Kokori (Waterside)
Otumara

Orogun
Owe

R.   N.   C.

Okpara (Waterside)
Okpara (Inland)

Kokori (Inland)

River Ethiope

Adeje

C

Sapele

Amukpe

Efurun

Ukan
Mogba   Obodo
Kakpamre
Ogbe—Ijo
Warri

Jeremi
Ganagana

Kiagbodo

B

A

River Aseh

P.

C.

Warri (Native town)

Gwato

Ologi

N.

River Escravos

River Forcados

River Ramos

Ebrohini
Batere
Jakapa
River Benin

Scale:

0   10 miles

were a useful diplomatic weapon in the international bargaining that was even then going on, the Foreign Office was tempted to uphold the Company's claims. In a letter to the various firms interested in the Forcados River trade, the Foreign Office maintained that the company was perfectly within the rights of its charter, if it decided to establish in the Forcados River area.[1] Towards the end of 1892, the prevailing confusion led to bloodshed in the Warri district, when two canoes loaded with oil attempted to pass the revenue hulk of the Niger Company. The Company's launch gave chase. One of the canoes escaped, but the crew of the other was forced to run into the bush and when pressed, fired at the launch, killing one person. The launch returned fire, killed one man and wounded two. This caused general excitement in the area. Harper, Acting Vice-Consul for the district, reported that the Itsẹkiri people were all so very excited that there could be a crisis any moment.[2] Macdonald, who was on leave at the time, realised the urgency of the situation and urged the Foreign Office to do something to ease the tension. In his report for 1892, Macdonald stated categorically that trade had suffered as a result of these duties.[3] Nana, like any other trader, must have suffered from the general uncertainty which seemed to have prevailed, especially during the second half of 1892. Such were the events and developments which preceded the crisis of 1894.

By 1892 Nana was clearly the greatest of the Itsẹkiri traders. In a report covering the years 1891–4, Macdonald noted that the trade of the Benin River was 'almost entirely in the hand of a powerful Jekri chief of the name of Nana', acknowledging thereby Nana's commercial success. But Macdonald went on to add that Nana was 'accustomed . . . to rule the river by terrorism'.[4] While it is true that Nana did, in fact, win a near monopoly of the trade, it is questionable whether he did this through terrorist tactics. His trade organization in the Urhobo country, to a large extent, belies this

1 F.O. 403/171, T. V. Lister to various firms interested in the Forcados River trade, 18 January 1892.
2 F.O. 84/2194, Harper to Macdonald, 8 November 1892—Enclosure in Macdonald to F.O., 8 December 1892.
3 F.O. 2/51, Macdonald to F.O., 12 January 1893.
4 F.O. 2/63, Report on the Administration of the N.C.P. 1891—July 1894.

accusation. As for the other Itsẹkiri, the Urhobo claim that men like Awala, Dudu and Numa were not prevented from trading in the areas to which Nana traded.[1] Nana got the better of them by sheer superior wealth and ability. This is not to say that Nana's power, in terms of armaments, did not play some part in building up his commercial position. The Urhobo realized fully the danger of crossing his path, and his rival Itsẹkiri traders probably considered it wiser to keep out of his preserves—thereby facilitating the building up of Nana's monopoly, for as it has been said, nothing succeeds like success.

The report on the Benin District for the year 1891–2, gave the fullest account of the position in that area. In it Gallwey,[2] the vice-consul in charge of the district, gave reasons for the slackness of trade during the year. He topped his list of causes with 'the predominating influence of Chief Nana and the monopoly of trade held by him in the early part of the year'. The report indicated that Nana was already beginning to lose the monopoly. For while recalling past occasions on which Nana had stopped trade on account of unacceptable prices, and pointing out that the 'Sobo markets' were almost entirely ruled by Nana, he indicated that Nana, 'a fairly sensible man', was beginning to accept the fact that he must allow others to trade where they would.[3] In other words, Nana was beginning to adjust to the new policy advocated by the Government —that of free trade.

---

1 Nana is very well remembered among the Urhobo, and they use 1894, the year of his fall, to date births and other events. Gallwey in his explanation for trade being bad in 1891 wrote, 'I am of the opinion that the slackness of trade has been, and is due, to the monopoly held by Nana and one or two big traders' thus confirming the Urhobo people's claim that there were other Itsẹkiri traders operating—F.O. 84/2111, Gallwey's report on Visit to Urhobo Markets—Macdonald to F.O., No. 30, 12 December 1891.
2 Lt. Colonel Henry Lionel Gallwey. Born 1859, educated Cheltenham College and Sandhurst. Entered army 1878. Major 1899. Lt. Colonel 1901. Deputy Commissioner and vice-consul, Oil Rivers Protectorate 1891. Deputy Commissioner and consul, Niger Coast Protectorate 1897. Acting Consul-General Niger Coast Protectorate, Aug.–Nov., 1896, Jan., 1897, Feb., 1898–Jan., 1899. Acting High Commissioner, Southern Nigeria March–December, 1900, Governor St. Helena, 1902. Governor Gambia, 1911. Governor South Australia, 1914.
3 F.O. 2/51, Report on the Benin District Oil Rivers Protectorate for the year ending 31 July 1892—Enclosure in Macdonald to F.O., 12 January 1893.

The second reason given by Gallwey was the continual quarrels which occurred between the middlemen and the oil producers. These quarrels, he reported, were of frequent occurrence and followed the failure of the Urhobo producers to pay oil for the goods with which they had been entrusted. They took the form of fights between the 'boys' of the Itsẹkiri traders and those who owed the oil, and ended up as slave raids. According to Gallwey, there was such a raid just before he took up his duties in 1891, as a result of which Nana had taken 200 slaves from one man in the Urhobo country. These slaves, however, Nana had returned on the intervention of the Vice-Consul.[1] These fights usually led to temporary stoppages of trade, stoppages which were almost invariably blamed on Nana. This second explanation given for the prevailing unsatisfactory state of trade is important for Itsẹkiri-Urhobo relations. It calls in doubt the general impression created by other works on Nana, that the Urhobo were a helpless, harmless people, the passive victims of a powerful, dominating Itsẹkiri trader-tyrant. It has come to be accepted that the Urhobo were far too ill-organized and too powerless to oppose Nana, or the other Itsẹkiri during this period.[2] Admittedly, the Urhobo could not equip their own canoes and face the Itsẹkiri on the rivers, for they were not as a people 'water men', and those who were had not the same access to firearms as had the Itsẹkiri. But they found another way of retaliating: refusal to supply oil. It is not unlikely that some such refusals were the consequences of dissatisfaction with the methods adopted by Nana's 'boys', whose actions were not always pleasant, or in line with their master's known wishes. Gallwey, at this stage, realized that the raids and fights were likely to continue till it was possible to establish government stations in the hinterland.[3] As Gallwey himself had undertaken a tour of the Ethiope River area in the closing months of 1891, he had first-hand knowledge of the true situation at that time. Thus, at Ẹku he noted that the people were continually

---

1 Ibid. It is important to note that the raids were as a result of disputes over trade, not out of pure bravado; and that Nana surrendered his captives—an indication that he was already modifying his way of life in line with the new administration.

2 Lloyd: *The Itsekiri*, p. 181.

3 F.O. 2/51, Report on the Benin District, Oil Rivers Protectorate for the year ending 31 July 1892.

in a state of war with the Itsẹkiri traders or the neighbouring clans. At Oria the people pleaded that they wanted more traders to buy their oil, for only Nana's people were coming, and so could dictate their own price which was usually too low. At Okpara, Gallwey discovered that as a result of raids which were part of the commercial relations between the Itsẹkiri and Urhobo, the Okpara people had seized '15 Jekri men' and the Itsẹkiri '13 Sobo men'. Gallwey ordered mutual restoration.[1]

According to Gallwey, there were three other explanations for the slackness of trade. One was the policy of the Ọba of Benin, who insisted on Itsẹkiri traders who operated in his dominions paying a kind of trade tax, and who stopped trade if this was not paid. Another was the difficulty of the middlemen in understanding fluctuating prices in the European markets. The third explanation was the establishment, by European agents, of factories 'up country'.[2] It is likely that the factories referred to were those opened at Sapẹlẹ, where a vice-consulate was established during the year. This had caused less trade to flow to the Benin River, the traders preferring to stop at Sapẹlẹ and thereby save themselves miles of canoe journey. It is significant that even though the opening of Sapẹlẹ meant establishing a trading centre at a point much nearer the Urhobo oil producers, Nana is not recorded as having done anything to oppose the government. In fact, he claimed during his trial that he assisted the government in getting land at Sapẹlẹ.[3]

The situation in 1892, therefore, was one in which Nana and the other Itsẹkiri traders, as well as the Urhobo were, to a very great extent, pursuing their accustomed ways of life despite the new fact of the establishment of British rule, and using the old sanctions with regard to securing trade, and tackling the perennial question of debt. At the same time, the presence of British political officers was beginning to affect this situation, and to demand a modification of the old ways of doing things. Both sides by 1892 were beginning,

---

1 F.O. 84/2111, Gallwey's report on visit to the Oil Markets of the Sobo and Abraka districts.
2 F.O. 2/51, Report on the Benin District, Oil Rivers Protectorate for the year ending 31 July 1892: Enclosure in Macdonald to F.O., 12 January 1893.
3 F.O. 2/64, Evidence of Nana at his trial: Enclosure in Macdonald to F.O. No. 49, 13 December 1894.

however slowly, to react to the new situation. Nana, by Gallwey's own testimony, was definitely attempting to modify his position. Gallwey, for his part, realized and reported that time must be given to the Nigerian peoples to adjust their way of life. It looked as if there would follow a period during which the Nigerian peoples and the British would seek to find an acceptable *modus vivendi* through co-operation. Yet in 1894 there came a crisis which ended in war. What is the explanation for this?

A few of Nana's papers captured after the expedition of 1894 provide some clue to the gradual worsening of relations between him and the British administration. In June 1892, Gallwey in a peremptory note ordered Nana to recall Ologun, his head slave, from the markets and to restrict him to Ebrohimi. He gave no reason necessitating this action.[1] In another equally brusque and mysterious note a week later, Gallwey wrote: 'You are playing a very dangerous game and I warn you that if I do bring gun-boats into the River, I shall use them'.[2] Short of a request that Nana was to see him, this was all the letter contained. It probably will never be known what called for these letters, or why Gallwey chose to couch them in such terms. Possibly, Gallwey had heard one of the many complaints put abroad by envious Itsekiri traders in their effort to discredit a rival. The unfortunate thing was that Nana was not, as a close study of his letters to the Acting Consul-General in 1894 reveals, easily frightened, and it is unlikely that Gallwey's threats impressed him.

In August of the same year, Hally Hutton, the Benin River Acting Vice-Consul, wrote to Nana, informing him that the Vice-Consul at Warri had written to say that the Itsekiri traders there were still frightened to trade at Warri and Sapele, because Nana had not sent them word to the effect that they should. According to Hutton, Nana had promised to send such a message and he now held him to his promise.[3] This letter confirms the fact that Nana was a great power in the area, and further serves to emphasize the difficulty in which this power placed him. It would appear, from a letter by Gallwey in December, 1893, that Nana did keep his promise in this regard, asked the traders to resume trade, and himself sent up a great

1 F.O. 2/64, Gallwey to Nana, 15 June 1892—Exhibit A at Nana's trial.
2 F.O. 2/64, Gallwey to Nana, 21 June 1892—Exhibit H at Nana's trial.
3 F.O. 2/64, Hally Hutton to Nana, 9 August 1892—Exhibit I at Nana's trial.

quantity of goods to buy oil—for which act Gallwey charged him with enlightened self-interest.[1] In this letter, Gallwey informed Nana that it was the policy of the British administration that everybody should be free to trade where he pleased. Everything seemed to revolve round Nana, and it is only too likely that other people, both Itsẹkiri and Urhobo, aware of the fact that any disturbances were likely to be attributed to Nana and his 'boys', took the opportunity of causing such disturbances.[2] Tension was being steadily built up between Nana and the British officers.

In December 1893, the position deteriorated. In that month, Gallwey went to Okpara to see what the state of trade was like. He returned 'very dissatisfied with the state of affairs up there'. There were various reasons for this dissatisfaction. He charged Nana and his boys with 'spreading lies about the Government' to the Urhobo people and thereby setting the latter against the government. If he caught anyone so doing, he warned, he would make a lasting example of him for the benefit of Nana, his boys and his 'Sobo friends'.[3] Secondly, Eddu, whom Gallwey described as Nana's headman, had refused to see him when he (Gallwey) had summoned him, on the grounds that Nana had not indicated that he should do so. Here was a perfectly understandable relationship between a headman and his master; but it annoyed Gallwey beyond measure. Another of Nana's men, Ubari, refused to let his people sell chicken to the Vice-Consul saying, according to Gallwey, that Nana had not given him any such instructions. These incidents so offended Gallwey that he wrote in his letter to Nana, 'Had my soldiers been with me I would have made prisoners of Ubari and Eddu—and probably burnt Ubari's house'.[4] These incidents are illustrative of the control Nana had over his men. Although Okpara was so far from Ebrohimi, they would not do anything which they thought would enrage their master. Gallwey's reaction to the situation

---

1 F.O. 2/64, Gallway to Nana, 7 December 1893—Exhibit K at Nana's trial.
2 Ibid. In the same letter Gallwey remarked that 2 buoys which he had put in the river had been removed. He was convinced nobody but Nana's 'boys' could do such a thing. He requested that Nana should find the culprits.
3 F.O. 2/64, Gallwey to Nana, 1 December 1893—Exhibit J at Nana's trial. Apparently, Gallwey had not caught any person spreading lies about the Government. The question is who told him and with what motives?
4 Ibid.

suggests that he regarded Eddu's and Ubari's attitudes as a personal insult, for there was scarcely any matter of government policy involved in these two incidents, except in so far as they helped to demonstrate that the ordinary people did not yet regard the British government as the final authority in the land. Gallwey ordered Nana to remove Eddu and Ubari from Okpara and punish them. When this letter was tendered as evidence to prove Nana's misdeeds during his trial, he began his defence with, 'I could not understand why Captain Gallwey had spoken so strongly'.[1] According to Nana Eddu was not a slave but a freeborn man and head of the Itsẹkiri community at Okpara. He had not sent Eddu to Okpara. Yet on receipt of Gallwey's letter he had recalled Eddu from Okpara 'and put him in chains'. He had inquired of Gallwey whether he should send Eddu down to the consulate. But Gallwey had sent to say that since Eddu had been removed from Okpara he was satisfied.[2] In the same letter Gallwey charged Nana with injuring trade (without saying how) adding in a postscript that Harrison, a rival trader, and a relation of Dọghọ who was also a government interpreter, was of the same opinion. 'Should I find you out', he concluded, 'you must expect full punishment'.[3] The year 1893 thus ended with an atmosphere of tension and suspicion between Nana and the British. Apart from the charge of setting the Urhobo against the government which was not definitely brought home to Nana, most of the incidents were of a relatively minor nature, and yet it would appear that they were used to set the stage for the drama that was to be enacted during the following year. One can hardly avoid the suggestion that in all this, there was some element of a clash of personalities.

In March, 1894, Hugh Lecky, Acting Vice-Consul at the Benin River, wrote to Nana to the effect that he had heard that Nana was intending to 'chop' some Urhobo at Uria near Abraka. Lecky warned that as such action was likely to lead to a stoppage of trade, Nana would be held responsible for any such stoppage.[4] It was probably this alleged intention of Nana to raid some Urhobo that

---

1 F.O. 2/64, Nana's evidence at his trial.
2 Ibid.
3 F.O. 2/64, Gallwey to Nana, 1 December 1893—Exhibit J at Nana's trial.
4 F.O. 2/64, Hugh Lecky to Nana, 27 March 1894—Exhibit L at Nana's trial.

led Macdonald to write to Nana in April, informing him that, as the British administration, was already fully established, he was no longer to regard himself as 'Governor' but as head of his house only.[1]

In May, A. F. Locke (Consular Agent) reported that he heard that the trade up the Benin River was stopped. He went on to investigate and was told by 'several of the Abraka and Uriah chiefs' that they had done no trade for a number of months. They blamed this on Chief Nana who, they said, had not allowed them to trade at the waterside. At the same time 'in their interior villages their people were always being seized and taken away by Nana or by people acting under his orders'.[2] Locke obtained a list of those who had been seized and wrote to Nana asking that these people be returned.[3]

It was this 'unsettled state of affairs' which brought Acting Consul-General Ralph Moor to the Benin River in June 1894. He discovered that trade was 'almost entirely stopped owing principally to the acts of the people of Chief Nana in seizing Sobo people and generally terrorizing the locality of the Ethiope River'.[4] Accordingly, he wrote to Nana on 23 June, inviting him to the vice-consulate to discuss the situation.[5] Nana replied that as a result of deaths in his family and the illness of his brother, he would not be able to attend the meeting, but offered to send Tonwe, a relation and trusted messenger, to represent him.[6] Moor, while regretting the misfortunes which had befallen Nana, thought the issues involved so vital, that he urged Nana to attend at the Vice-Consulate the next day.[7] But Nana pleaded that the custom of his people forbade him to leave home so soon after the deaths he had mentioned in his previous letter.[8] On receipt of this, Moor wrote a detailed letter in which he gave Nana certain directives. First, Moor indicated that the Urhobo 'chiefs' up the Ethiope were being prevented by Nana's people from trading down the waterside markets—and that this was

---

1 Ibid., Macdonald to Nana, April 1894—Exhibit M at Nana's trial.
2 Ibid., Evidence of Locke at Nana's trial.
3 Ibid., Locke to Nana, 10 July 1894—Exhibit B at Nana's trial.
4 F.O., 2/63, Moor to F.O., No. 22, 6 August 1894.
5 F.O. 2/64, Moor to Nana, 23 June 1894—Exhibit N at Nana's trial.
6 Nana to Moor, 24 June 1894—Exhibit O at Nana's trial.
7 Ibid., Moor to Nana, 24 June 1894—Exhibit P at Nana's trial.
8 Ibid., Nana to Moor, 25 June 1894—Exhibit Q at Nana's trial.

in direct contradiction of government policy and orders. Nana was to order his men to desist from so doing, and to send a message to the Urhobo, informing them that he had so ordered his men. Secondly, Moor ordered that Nana should recall his head slave Ologun from Ẹku because this man was generally terrorizing the people; and lastly, that Nana should release the Urhobo people seized by Ologun. Nana was given two weeks within which to comply with these instructions. In the meantime,

> No canoe belonging to you or your people will be allowed to pass up the Ethiope River for any purpose whatsoever.[1]

In his reply of the same date, Nana stated his case. He denied that he had given orders to his 'boys' to stop the Urhobo from going to the waterside markets, and promised to send to warn the 'boys' concerned, and to inform the Urhobo accordingly. As for the Urhobo seized by Ologun, these were men given in payment to Ologun for outstanding debts. The Ẹku people, argued Nana, owed him 200 puncheons of oil out of which they had paid only twenty-one. Ologun, he pointed out, had been resident at Ẹku for a long time and was familiar with the way things were done there. However, since it was the government's desire that Ologun should be recalled, he would recall him, though he added a plea that the Consul-General would allow Ologun to return at a later date to collect the debt still outstanding.[2] As it transpired at the trial, Nana did recall Ologun from his station.

After the above exchange of letters, the two weeks allowed Nana to carry out his instructions were allowed to pass. Moor returned thereafter to the Benin River and, according to him, discovered that his instructions had not been carried out (even though Ologun had definitely been recalled). Therefore,

> I stopped the trading of Nana and his people in the Ethiope River, establishing a blockade against them at its mouth and seizing any of their canoes that attempted to pass.[3]

Nana was kept informed about the above decision. At the same time, a proclamation was issued generally banning war canoes from

---

1 F.O. 2/64, Moor to Nana, 25 June 1894—Exhibit R at Nana's trial.
2 F.O. 2/64, Nana to Moor, 25 June 1894—Exhibit S at Nana's trial.
3 F.O. 2/63, Moor to F.O., No. 22, 6 August 1894.

the rivers—war canoes being described as 'any armed canoe, or canoe carrying armed men'.[1] In the letter in which Moor informed Nana of the steps he was taking, he argued that by seizing people because of debt, Nana was taking the law into his own hands; Nana was to remember that he was only head of his house, and should not endeavour to settle disputes which arose outside that house. If he desired to claim the debt owed to him by the Ẹku people, he had first to hand over the people seized, then make his case at the consular court.[2] In other words, while other people were still using the old sanctions for making good their debt, Nana was expected not to use these sanctions.

From this point on, Moor was determined that only force, or at least a show of force, would satisfactorily meet the developing situation. When he returned to the district in July, he brought with him one officer and twenty men of the Niger Coast Protectorate Force to strengthen the one officer and fifty men in the district. His main reason for this action was that he had heard, while at Bonny, that Nana intended to attack 'two friendly chiefs, Dore and Dudu'. By now he had a total force of three officers and eighty-seven men. Not satisfied with this force, he wrote for H.M.S. *Alecto* to be in attendance. The *Alecto* duly arrived on 30 July 1894. Moor then summoned a meeting of all the Itsẹkiri chiefs to discuss the situation.[3]

In the meantime, Nana had written to Moor, telling him that he had heard rumours that if he attended at the vice-consulate, he would be seized and deported like Jaja, and that therefore, he was afraid to attend the meeting summoned.[4] Moor wrote back to reassure him on this point, informing him that he could come in his war canoes for the meeting.[5] By this time Nana himself had apparently lost faith in Moor, and was genuinely afraid. Up to 2 August, he still pleaded to be represented by some other chief at the meeting. In a letter dated 2 August, he asked that Chief Ogbe be allowed to represent him. In the same letter he complained that

---

1 Ibid.
2 F.O. 2/64, Moor to Nana, 10 July 1894—Exhibit T at Nana's trial.
3 F.O. 2/63, Moor to F.O., No. 22, 6 August 1894.
4 F.O. 2/64, Nana to Moor, 23 July 1894—Exhibit U at Nana's trial.
5 Ibid., Moor to Nana, 31 July 1894—Exhibit V at Nana's trial.

canoes carrying food for him and his people were being seized on the orders of Mr. Locke, and that this act increased his fear. He argued that his rivals were spreading many 'tales' against him, ending with a promise to accept the decisions that the other chiefs would arrive at.[1]

Nana did not attend the meeting of 2 August. At that meeting the chiefs present (virtually all the important traders) signed a treaty of the 1884 type, with an additional clause which regarded the 1894 treaty as a ratification of that of 1884. Offences committed in the past would be forgiven on the signing of this treaty, and the faithful observance of its terms. The new treaty did not exclude clauses VI and VII as in 1884. Moor sent a copy of the treaty to Nana and told him he was at liberty to sign it, but only at the vice-consulate. Through the same letter he observed that Nana had placed an obstruction—'a gate'—across the creek leading to Ebro-himi. Nana was ordered to remove this 'gate' at once, or face 'serious consequences'. The blockade of his town was to be intensified and any of his canoes found 'on any of the waters of the Benin or Warri districts', would be seized and forfeited. If occupants of such canoes refused to stop when hailed, they would be fired upon.[2] Nana's reply was to the effect that the 'gate' had been placed there by his father, as a means of defence against attacks by rival Itsẹkiri traders, and not for purposes of war against the government. Rather foolishly perhaps, he added that if he saw government launches going up the creek, he would regard such an act as a declaration of war.[3]

On 3 August, as Nana had not ordered the removal of the barrier, Moor ordered Lieutenant-Commander Heugh of the *Alecto* to remove it with mines. This took some time to accomplish as the barrier was well built, and required ten mines each with fifteen charges to destroy it. During this operation 'four or more shots' were fired by Nana's men, the British party replying with about half a dozen shots and two 'rockets'. The first shots had been exchanged and Moor considered that a state of war now existed, though

---

1 F.O. 2/64, Nana to Moor, 2 August 1894—Exhibit X at Nana's trial.
2 F.O. 2/64, Moor to Nana, 2 August 1894—Exhibit Y at Nana's trial. A copy of the new treaty was attached to this letter.
3 F.O. 2/64, Nana to Moor, 4 August 1894—Exhibit Z at Nana's trial.

he still hoped that Nana would surrender. In his dispatch to the Foreign Office, he informed his employers that should Nana decide to surrender, he would only accept such surrender if Nana agreed to pay a fine of £500, and gave up all arms and ammunition which he would not be entitled to have under an Arms and Ammunition Ordinance which had been approved by the Secretary of State and which was shortly to come into force.[1]

From this time on, Moor concentrated on building up evidence against Nana. He reported that 'a party of Idzos from a village under the control of Chief Nana' had attacked and burnt down the village of Bobi. The Ijọ chief was summoned to the vice-consulate to account for the action of his men but refused to turn up. Moor attributed this refusal to the advice given by Nana. A force under Major Copland-Crawford and Captain Scarfe of the Niger Coast Protectorate Force, together with a party of marines under Heugh, were sent to sack the Ijọ village.[2] Another incident at Ẹvhrọ, home town of Nana's mother, was also attributed to Nana. A dispute had arisen among the local traders at the Ẹvhrọ market on 26 July 1894. Erigbe, the 'chief', apparently ordered his fighting men to attack the disputants. As a result, goods were destroyed and a number of people injured. As in the former case, Erigbe was ordered to report to the vice-consulate but failed to show up. On 8 August, Moor himself led a force of the military and a detachment of the marines under Heugh to Ẹvhrọ and sought to get Erigbe 'to palaver'. When this proved unsuccessful, Ẹvhrọ was attacked and 'the greater part of the town was fired and burnt down'. Moor hoped that the 'severe lesson' would have an excellent effect in settling the disturbed state of the district.[3]

The explanation for the rather heavy punishments inflicted on the Ijọ village and Ẹvhrọ was that the Ijọ chief and Erigbe were, as seen by Moor, 'staunch adherents' of Nana, and therefore their actions constituted a demonstration in favour of Nana. By July and August, the general state of the Benin and Warri districts was disturbed; yet Moor seemed to have thought that in the circumstances, men like Erigbe would willingly travel to the vice-consulate.

1 F.O. 2/63, Moor to F.O., No. 22, 6 August 1894.
2 F.O. 2/63, Moor to F.O., No. 23, 8 August 1894.
3 Ibid.

There was little evidence to show that either the Ịjọ chief or Erigbe acted on the instructions of Nana. Moor himself reported that Erigbe had 'caused much trouble for a long time past by his piratical acts in seizing boys, canoes and produce passing down his town'.[1] If this was based on fact, and not on a desire to paint Erigbe in such colours as would excuse his action in burning down the town, it would further strengthen the argument that the whole process of seizing 'boys', canoes and produce was not confined to Nana or the Itsẹkiri. All those whose geographical locations and power enabled them to do so, seemed to have indulged in it. It was part of the risks of commercial enterprise during that age. Again, if the actions of the two chiefs was a demonstration in favour of Nana, then Nana must have been well worth such demonstration. It should be remembered that by this time, Nana's town was under blockade and he himself was unable to leave Ebrohimi. The trial of force between him and the British had, in fact, already begun, and the two chiefs in question were doubtless aware of this fact. If despite the evidence of British hostility towards Nana, these men chose to stand by him and risk their towns being burnt, it is unlikely that Nana was the 'sable tyrant' and perpetrator of 'sickening atrocities' portrayed by Bindloss.[2] Such a tyrant would scarcely have kept the loyalty of the victims of his tyranny—for so are the Urhobo generally portrayed—when once a new and presumably superior force arrived on the scene.

In the meantime, Nana continued to write to Moor to plead for a settlement though refusing to accept Moor's essential condition that he must report to the vice-consulate in order to settle the dispute. By 22 August, Moor had come to the conclusion that a greater show of force was necessary, and sent for another gun boat and seven powder field piece from Lagos. The *Phoebe* was sent by the naval authorities in answer to Moor's demands and he himself took two officers and 100 men to reinforce troops already concentrated in the Benin river region. If this show of force failed to persuade Nana to come to terms, Moor thought that more active measures would have to be taken, and Chief Nana and his advisers removed from the District.[3]

---

1 Ibid. 2 Bindloss, op. cit., pp. 206, 209.
3 F.O. 2/63. Moor to F.O. No. 25, 22 August 1894.

There was considerable levity on the part of the marines about the impending encounter with Nana. It was not fully realized that Ebrohimi was particularly difficult of access, and that it was strongly fortified and well supplied with arms and ammunition, and Nana's men on the whole well organized. These arms and ammunition had not been amassed for the definite purpose of 'trying conclusions' with the British, as Moor was later to argue. All leading traders were fully armed for their own self-defence, and arms and ammunition constituted a most valuable article of trade. The foretaste of what Nana was capable of doing came when Lieutenant-Commander Heugh decided to reconnoitre, with a view to fixing the exact position of Ebrohimi. The reconnoitring party ran into heavy fire from a masked battery, which resulted in at least three deaths and five injured. As Lugard, who was then passing through to Jebba, noted in his diary, 'the result of this business' was 'a great scare'.

> These young chaps see what *War* means—they were horrified and I fancy it has cooled off their martial ardour a good deal and they no longer 'hope to goodness Nana won't give in without a fight after all our preparations' as they said to me before.[1]

Moor reported that Heugh's venture was against his orders but, as Heugh argued, the venture had indicated what the British were to expect from Nana. From now on preparations for a full-scale war were made.[2]

On 29 August, what Moor described as a 'reconnoitring in force' was attempted. This could be regarded as the beginning of the real war. The entire force available was landed, and an effort was made to get through to Nana's town by cutting a road through the mangrove swamp. This was found impossible under the circumstances, as heavy though inaccurate fire was kept up by Nana's men all through the period of reconnoitring. Nevertheless, the exercise helped to show that the town was well fortified and armed, and gave the attacking British an even clearer idea of the task ahead. It was decided that if the town was to be taken, at least two more

---

1 Margery Perham and Mary Bull: *The Diaries of Lord Lugard*, London 1963, Vol. IV, p. 78. Lugard's comments show that there was, until this incident, a real desire to fight against Nana.
2 F.O. 2/63, Moor to F.O., No. 25A, 31 August 1894.

gunboats were needed, and these were immediately sent for. Pending the arrival of these gunboats Ebrohimi was subjected to incessant shelling in an endeavour to force Nana and his men to surrender.[1]

It will be seen that nothing new, save the reported actions of the Ijọ chief and Erigbe of Ẹvhrọ, had happened since May when Nana was alleged to have seized Urhobo people. Ologun, the offending head slave, had been recalled; and according to Nana, three of the men seized from Abraka had been returned to the vice-consulate.[2] The war was being fought now because the administration had come to the conclusion that Nana's power had to be broken. The dispatch of 15 September did not give any new reasons for the war. The old story of Nana's terrorism over an area alleged to be 120 miles inland and fifty to sixty miles broad was repeated, and the impossibility of allowing such a situation to continue stressed. According to this dispatch, Nana had written to plead for peace, but his letter showed that 'he was under the impression that a settlement could be effected by which he could retain his position and power to a great extent'.[3] Moor replied to the effect that the only solution was absolute, unconditional surrender; and, to his superiors at the Foreign Office, Moor suggested Nana's deportation as the only rightful and effective punishment.[4]

The ships requisitioned arrived on 18 September, together with the supreme commander on the West Coast, Rear-Admiral F. G. Bedford himself. The entire naval strength on the West Coast was thus concentrated on Ebrohimi, with virtually all the military forces of the protectorate, undoubtedly the most impressive battle array ever assembled in the protectorate, and in a sense, a tribute to Nana's power and organizational ability. Shelling and the blockade were intensified until 23 and 24 September, when it was again decided to cut a path through under heavy but erratic fire. On the 25th, the final attack was made at 5.30 a.m., and it speaks well for the vigilance of the beleaguered that this attack was anticipated, for, fifteen minutes after it had begun, heavy fire was

1 Ibid.
2 F.O. 2/64, Nana's evidence at his trial.
3 F.O. 2/63, Moor to F.O., No. 27, 15 September 1894.
4 Ibid.

opened on the attackers from the town. By 9 a.m. Ebrohimi was taken.[1]

Nana and some of his henchmen, were, however, no longer in the town. During the shelling and blockade, Nana had conceived the idea of digging a canal to the river through which to escape. This work was not finished before the attack of the 25th, so he escaped in a canoe through the creeks. On the 28th this canoe together with his belongings and papers were found, Nana himself having again escaped capture.[2] He eventually got to Lagos where he surrendered himself to the Governor. The power of the last, and the greatest, of the coastal chiefs had been broken.

It would appear that the war just concluded was fought in order to put right the 'unsettled state of affairs' brought about by 'acts of the people of Chief Nana in seizing Sobo people',[3] or in order to reopen the trade which Nana was alleged to have stopped in the Abraka area. Indeed, this has been the official view and that of all the British writers on the subject.[4] This view requires careful examination. Enough has been said about Nana's relations with the Urhobo for it to be clear that the events in the Urhobo country which immediately preceded the war were no more than normal occurrences typical of the age. The closure of markets was an economic sanction designed to help in settling disputes arising over trade. It was a phenomenon common to many West African peoples at this time, a phenomenon which, as will be shown, the British often used as the excuse for furthering their imperial ambitions.

The real clue to Nana's fall lay partly in the internal rivalries among the Itsẹkiri traders, but chiefly in the aims and ambitions of the British administration. There can be little doubt that most of what reached the ears of the consular authorities were the tales of Itsẹkiri traders outrivalled by Nana. Chief Dọghọ and his cousin, Harrison, were two such rivals, and as Nana stated in his defence, it was the ancient feud between his father and the Numa faction that lay at the bottom of some of his trouble. Indeed, he charged Dọghọ with having openly declared that he (Dọghọ) would see that

---

1 F.O. 2/64, Moor to F.O., No. 28, 5 October 1894.
2 Ibid.
3 F.O. 2/63, Moor to F.O., No. 22, 6 August 1894.
4 See footnote 1, p. 92.

he got into trouble.[1] In the circumstances, it was no surprise that Dogho and those generally described as 'friendly chiefs', but who, in fact, constituted a rival group who chafed under Nana's commercial success, performed such useful services during the active operations and during the mopping up organized by Macdonald, that Dogho, now regarded by the British as the leading Itsekiri, was awarded a commemorative medal, the first of a number he was to win in a career of faithful, if extremely profitable, service to the British administration in the then Warri Province.[2] The rancour of the Tsanomi-Olomu war in which Olomu defeated Tsanomi was accentuated by the unprecedented success of Olomu's son in trade, a success which drove most of the other traders from the area in which Nana operated, thereby giving him a monopoly. In this internal, purely Itsekiri situation, is to be seen part of the reason for Nana's fall.

By 1894 Nana's position had become incompatible with the aims of the British administration. Indeed, the establishment in 1891 of a more formal system of government in the Niger Delta was a pointer to the fact that the British Government had abandoned their policy of indifference in the affairs of the various Nigerian peoples, and adopted a new one of active intervention. The 1890s and the early years of this century were, therefore, occupied by various expeditions to 'pacify' the hinterland of the coastal districts. In the process of this 'pacification', not only were the hinterland peoples to be brought more directly under British rule, but all recalcitrant coastal chiefs and people were to be reduced. The Nana episode must be seen therefore, as no more than one in a series designed to achieve Britain's imperial ambition, in the face of French and German rivalry in other spheres. Parallels to the Nana drama could be found elsewhere along the West Coast of Africa.

The Ijebu expedition of 1892, as Dr. A. B. Aderibigbe has so clearly pointed out, was organized not because it was necessary to break up 'the intransigent Yorubas of the "coast" and force them to surrender their control of the trade routes' in order that 'Christianity, commerce and civilization' might flourish in the hinterland, but because the forward party at the British Colonial Office, ably

1 F.O. 2/64, Evidence of Nana at his trial.
2 Dogho's career is more fully discussed in Chapter 5.

represented by Gilbert Carter in Lagos, wanted British rule extended to Ijẹbu and beyond. But it would have been naïve to put forward this as the reason for the expedition. Instead, the Ijẹbu were accused of trade monopoly, refusing to allow free passage through their territory and dishonouring the terms of a spurious treaty signed on behalf of the Ijẹbu by Carter's own nominees.[1] In Sierra Leone, the Government was also busy extending its rule into the interior. Governor Fleming was reported to have said at a banquet in England in June 1893:

> Let us do all in our power to preserve the possessions we now have. . . .
> Let us do all in our power to extend their boundaries into the interior
> of the continent.[2]

The preservation and extension of these possessions entailed loss of independence on the part of the West African peoples concerned. When after 1890 the British Government in the then Gold Coast decided to alter its policy of non-intervention in Ashanti, it sent the Badger mission to the Asantehene to complain that the unsettled state of Ashanti resulted in bad trade, and that this would have to be rectified. But it was not bad trade that was exercising the mind of that administration, so much as the fact that by 1890, as Ward argues, 'circumstances had changed. The British were no longer . . . the only colonizing power in this part of West Africa'. There were the French in the Ivory Coast; the Germans in Togoland; and both powers had their eyes on the Gold Coast. British imperial interests demanded that Ashanti should be reduced. Occasion had to be found to translate this desire into practical reality. When in 1890 the Asantehene refused the British offer of 'protection', it was clear that he would have to be removed. By 1895, the year after Nana's fall, the assault on the Asantehene began. The ultimatum which was sent to him charged him with failure to keep open the roads; with hindering trade; and with encouraging human sacrifices.[3] There is a striking similarity between these charges and those

---

1 A. B. Aderibigbe: 'The Ijebu Expedition, 1892: An Episode in the British Penetration of Nigeria Reconsidered', *Historians in Tropical Africa*, September 1960, p. 267.
2 Quoted by J. J. Crooks: *A History of the Colony of Sierra Leone, West Africa*, Dublin 1903, p. 313.
3 W. E. F. Ward: *A History of Ghana*, London 1958, pp. 300–3.

levied against Nana only the year before, and those which were to be levied against the Ọba of Benin, a year after the Ashanti expedition of 1896.

The fall of Nana was, therefore, not accomplished in order to save the Urhobo from the ravages of his 'boys', or in order to increase the trade of the area. These were no more than plausible excuses. If the fall of Nana saved some of the Urhobo from the occasional raids of his 'boys', this was only incidental. As in the case of Ijẹbu and Ashanti, so in this, the real reasons for the expedition 'could not be openly avowed, and so other reasons had to be found'.[1] The Ebrohimi expedition of 1894 became necessary because the British administration in the Niger Coast Protectorate was determined to demonstrate to the Nigerian people concerned that it was the supreme, the ultimate, power in the land. In fact Moor gave the case away when he wrote:

> It has too long been the custom of the people of Benin and Warri districts to say that they know no government but Chief Nana and it has now become necessary to convince them to the contrary.[2]

This declaration, rather than the case which Moor built up in his dispatches to justify his action, explains the Ebrohimi expedition of 1894. If the above reason explains the expedition, it cannot justify it. Both Gallwey and Macdonald had, by their own reports, shown that Nana was aware of the need to modify his mode of life to suit the changing circumstances. It is strange, therefore, that it was found necessary after only three years to wage a war against him. Surely, it was difficult to expect Nana to resign so much power, so much wealth, and so much influence, within so short a period.

In the circumstances, Nana's trial, which followed the end of the war, could be no more than a mere formality designed to satisfy anyone who might raise the cry of 'British justice'. Moor had made it clear that only one solution—the deportation of Nana—could meet the case. The trial was designed to secure that end. Macdonald himself hurried back from leave to handle this phase of the episode. Nana was charged with making war on 'Her Majesty the Queen in the Niger Coast Protectorate' in an endeavour to avoid

1 Ward, op. cit., p. 307.
2 F.O. 2/63, Moor to F.O., No. 23, 8 August 1894.

carrying out the terms of the 1884 treaty (a treaty which had definitely excluded free trade); with committing a breach of the peace and inciting others to commit a similar breach; with failing to carry out the terms of the 1884 treaty in so far as he acted in opposition to the British consular officers in the execution of the duties allotted to them, and refusing their advice in matters related to the administration of justice, the interests of commerce and the resources of the country.[1]

The evidence was carefully called to show that Nana, both at home and in the Urhobo markets, had been guilty of terrorism and frightful barbarities, rather than to prove the charges officially levelled against him. The chief prosecution witness was Ralph Moore himself, who displayed remarkable ability in misrepresenting the facts contained in the various letters which he tendered in evidence.[2] Tonwe, Nana's trusted messenger, virtually turned Queen's evidence, and detailed acts of barbarism committed by his fallen master in Ebrohimi, perjuring himself in the process as Nana's cross-examination of him showed.[3] Nana's own statement of defence has been constantly referred to elsewhere in this chapter. Here only a few more points need be raised. He argued that he planned no attack on Dudu and Dogho as alleged by the prosecution; that as he was confined to Ebrohimi, he could not be held responsible for events along the Ethiope during the period; that when he heard about the Ẹvhrọ incident, he had sent to investigate, and had left a warning that 'the white man' was not to be fired at. As for the acts of injustice which Nana was alleged to have committed in Ebrohimi, he explained that he had merely acted according to the laws of his people, and had kept Gallwey informed.[4] Nana was found guilty on all counts and sentenced to deportation for life.

Nana was first deported to the Cross River, from where in 1896,

---

1 F.O. 2/64, An account of Nana's trial.

2 F.O. 2/64. See evidence of Moor at Nana's trial. His summaries of the various letters handed in at the trial were nearly always wrong in detail, and designed, it would appear, to paint Nana in the worst possible colours.

3 F.O. 2/64. See evidence of 'Towery' at Nana's trial: he said for instance, that Nana had locked him up after he (Tonwe) returned from a trip to Lagos, for failure to procure a lawyer for Nana. Under cross examination he confessed that he had voluntarily shut himself up out of fear.

4 F.O. 2/64, Nana's evidence at his trial.

he was removed to Christianbourg Castle in Accra, and granted an allowance of ten shillings a day (later increased to 12/6d) for himself and four members of his family.[1] He remained in Accra till 1906 when, after a series of petitions in which he pleaded to be allowed to return to his country, he was allowed to return to the town of 'America' (now known as Nana town) near Koko, where his brother was then staying.[2] By this time Moor and Gallwey, his implacable enemies, who had reported adversely on all his petitions up to 1902, had left the scene, and the British were sufficiently well established in the area to be more accommodating than during the earlier period. The government seemed as eager to treat him well on his return, as they had been to find fault with him in 1894. He was granted an allowance of £10 a month for two years, during which time it was hoped he would have settled down sufficiently well to look after himself.[3] The fears expressed earlier by Moor, and in 1906 by Mr. Fosbery, that Nana would find it extremely difficult, if not impossible, to settle down to life as a private individual[4] did not materialize, as the ex-governor with characteristic vigour and application, built a new town on the model of Ebrohimi, and was soon contributing his share to the general development of the Province and of Koko in particular.

Nana's home-coming was greeted with jubilation by some of the Itsẹkiri, and even more so by the Urhobo people with whom he had had connexions. Canoe-loads of people from Ọvwia, Aladja and other places in the Udu clan, Mọgba and Ukan in Agbarho clan, and Okpara in Agbọn clan went to meet him with presents to rejoice at his return. Gifts of 'bullocks' came from Mọgba, Ukan and Okpara. Constant visits by private individuals continued for a long time after his return, and some of those who had been 'freed'

---

1 C.O. 444/2, Moor to C.O., No. 159, 23 September 1899.

2 C.S.O. 12/25, File 1971/06, C.O. to Officer Administering the Government of Nigeria, No. 259, 6 July 1906.

3 C.S.O. 12/25, Provincial Commissioner, Warri, to District Commissioner, Sapele, 10 September 1906. The Provincial Commissioner wrote: 'His Excellency, is anxious that Chief Nana should be well treated by the Government and he hopes that Interpreters and Police do not unnecessarily "rub it in" that he is not the powerful chief he once was'.

4 C.O. 520/35, Minute from Mr. Fosbery, 19 April 1906—Enclosure in Egerton to C.O., No. 124, 12 May 1906.

by the British expedition of 1894 willingly went back to work for him. These manifestations of love and loyalty were so genuine and obvious, that they excited the envy of Chief Dǫghǫ, by now the leading figure in Itsẹkiriland. Dǫghǫ therefore grabbed at the first opportunity he got, to ask the government to reassure him that Nana would not be allowed to become the powerful personage he had been before.[1] Ten years after his return, Nana died on 3 July 1916.[2]

The régime of Chief Nana continued, and in certain ways, inten-sified the process of intermingling between the Itsẹkiri and the Urhobo to which reference was made in the last chapter. Nana's trade organization was such that many of his 'boys' were resident for long periods in Urhoboland. He himself went on occasional tours of the areas in which he had trading interests. His commercial connexions led him to marry from a number of Urhobo clans—Abraka, Agbarho and Udu—and to make friends in others. Al-though attention has been focused on Nana, it should be remem-bered that other Itsẹkiri traders like Dudu, Awala and Numa also traded with the Urhobo during this period. They too, like Nana, had their own friends, relations by marriage, and trading settlements in Urhoboland. There was thus increased social and commercial intercourse between the Itsẹkiri and the Urhobo during the closing decades of the nineteenth century.

It is perhaps a pity for Itsẹkiri-Urhobo relations that it was Nana's relations with the Urhobo that provided the occasion for Nana's fall. The events of 1894 which preceded the British offensive were so magnified by the British administration as to create the im-pression that the Urhobo were a weak, downtrodden people, ill-used by Nana. This, as has been constantly pointed out in this chapter, was not really so. As a matter of fact, the régime of Chief Nana provides, perhaps, the clearest illustration of the relations which existed between the Urhobo and their Itsẹkiri neighbours, before the establishment of British rule began to introduce new factors into the lives of both peoples. Itsẹkiri-Urhobo relations in

---

1 C.O. 520/37, Enclosure 4 in Egerton to C.O., Confidential, 31 October 1906.
2 C.S.O. 14/8, Telegram from Resident, Warri, to Secretary, Southern Pro-vinces, 4 July 1916. For a more detailed study of Nana Olomu, see Obaro Ikime: *Merchant Prince of the Niger Delta*, London 1968.

these years were mostly social and economic. Nana was a powerful and successful trader who controlled virtually all the trade of the Abraka, Agbarho, Agbọn, Ẹvhrọ and Udu clans. Nana's power in terms of men, canoes, and armaments enabled him to keep control of the trade which he and his father before him had secured through friendship and inter-marriage with leading Urhobo families having both political and social influence in their respective clans. He became so powerful and wealthy that the Urhobo held him in awe and great respect, the more so since all those Urhobo who took the field against him were defeated. In these circumstances, it was easy for the outside observer (especially if he were a foreigner like the British administrative officers) to see Nana as the overlord and ruler of the Urhobo. And because Nana's success was, to some extent, based on the physical force he could muster, it was also easy to see in him a tyrant, who maintained his position in Urhoboland by superior force.

Yet Nana was not really the tyrant Moor would have us believe. Nor did he regard himself as the ruler of the Urhobo people, despite his undoubted power and the great control he exercised over the economic life of those clans with which he traded. His preoccupation with seeking the co-operation of those who today would be described as the political leaders of the Urhobo clans with which he was associated, shows that he did not conceive of himself as the ruler of those with whom he traded. The fact is that in those days nothing called for a definition of the political relations between the Itsẹkiri and the Urhobo. The fact that Nana was the son of an Urhobo woman, and that he himself was married to a number of Urhobo women was enough for him to be regarded as a brother, in an age when marriage connexions meant much more than they have come to mean in our own time. This same fact affected Nana's treatment of the Urhobo people and explains his tendency to put right the wrongs committed by his 'boys'. But it was not always possible for Nana to maintain perfect amity with the Urhobo in a turbulent age. Quarrels and fights there were—quarrels and fights which only served to show Nana's superior might.

If Nana and the men of his age did not see Itsẹkiri-Urhobo relations in terms of ruler and ruled, Nana's régime did, nevertheless, provide a proud reference point for later generations of Itsẹkiri men. It was easy for them to see in Nana's great power and his success in his wars against the Urhobo, a symbol of Itsẹkiri pre-eminence and overlordship. When in the twenties and thirties of this century, tensions and conflicts began to arise between the Itsẹkiri and the Urhobo, it was natural for the Itsẹkiri, in their bid to enhance their 'national' pride, to refer back to the glorious days of Nana, as a period of Itsẹkiri overlordship over the Urhobo. Yet the conflicts of the thirties, as will be demonstrated, had very little to do with Nana and his relations with the Urhobo. They were, in fact, largely the product of a new age—the age of effective British rule in Itsẹkiri and Urhoboland.

Chapter 4
The British penetration of
Urhoboland, 1891–1914

In an earlier chapter the point was made that by comparison with
the coastal areas of what is now southern Nigeria, European penetration into the Urhobo country took place rather late.[1] It has also
been noted that contrary to the views expressed by British administrative officers in the 1930s and by a recent historian of southern
Nigeria, there is no evidence to suggest that the Itsẹkiri 'protection'
treaty of 1884 was meant to apply to part or the whole of Urhoboland.[2] British penetration of the Urhobo country did not, in fact,
begin until some ten years after the signing of the 1884 treaty.

The Nana episode, as shown in the last chapter, was symptomatic
of a new British attitude to the peoples of West Africa. It was a
token of the fact that the British had abandoned that indifference
relieved only by haphazard interference in the affairs of the West
African peoples which had characterized their colonial policy of an
earlier period, for a new forward and active policy. This new policy
entailed not just the removal of recalcitrant coastal middlemen
chiefs like Nana but also a determined push into the hinterland in
an effort to exploit more effectively the resources of the country.

For Nana as for the Urhobo the year 1891 marked a real turning
point. In that year Sir Claude Macdonald began the inauguration
of what was to be the first really effective government over the Oil
Rivers. Vice-consulates were established in the Benin River and
Warri, and for the first time ever British consular and other officials
began to reside permanently at these places. In the same year
Macdonald introduced, again for the first time, the payment of
duties on all imports into the protectorate in an endeavour to raise
revenue for the proper government of the territories committed
to his charge.[3] If import duties were seen as a source of revenue,

---

1 See Chapter 1.   2 Supra, p. 84.
3 F.O. 84/2111, Macdonald to F.O., No. 2, 1 September 1891.

it was realized that far greater revenue could be derived from developing the export trade of the protectorate. To this end it was necessary to penetrate the hinterland and help develop its agricultural and other resources. Such penetration would also have the ultimate effect of undermining the position of the middlemen traders who, it was argued, by preventing European traders going to the hinterland, and the oil producers coming to the coast, were making 'tremendous profit'.

The pioneer of British penetration into the Urhobo country was Henry Lionel Gallwey, the first Vice-Consul of the Benin River. Acting on instructions from the Consul-General, Gallwey paid a visit to 'the Oil Markets of the Sobo and Abrakar districts' in October 1891. According to Gallwey,

> The objects of the visit were manifold, the most important being the establishment of law and order; the selecting of suitable sites for a vice-consulate, barracks and constabulary posts; to impress upon the natives the great advantages to be gained by the cultivation of such crops as coffee, cocoa, etc., and enquire into the reasons for the slackness of trade in the Sobo district generally.[1]

The British preoccupation with the development of trade is thus clearly stated. The Urhobo people were not only to be persuaded to pursue their old lines of trade more assiduously; they were also to branch out into new fields. It was held out to them that coffee, cocoa and the like would find a ready market in Europe. But as Michael Crowder points out, the British fully realized that 'if trade was to be carried on to [their] advantage then the highest authority in the land would have to be that of the British Government and not that of the African chief'.[2] Consequently more vice-consulates backed by 'barracks and constabulary posts' were set up—a clear indication that the British anticipated the resistance which the hinterland peoples would put up. Between the enunciation of the policy summed up in the aims of Gallwey's visit and its complete and effective implementation in Urhoboland, over twenty years were to elapse. The time lag is in itself a measure of the opposition

---

1 F.O. 84/2111, Gallwey's Report on his visit—Enclosure in Macdonald to F.O., No. 30, 12 December 1891.
2 Crowder, op. cit., p. 134.

encountered in the establishment of the *pax Britannica* in Urhobo-land.

Despite the fact that Gallwey covered a fairly extensive tract of country during this visit, he entered into no treaties bringing the Urhobo areas through which he passed under British 'protection'. His reason for this was that the Urhobo were so 'uncivilized' that they could 'not well understand the nature of a Treaty', and so were unlikely to adhere to treaty terms. The implications of the absence of such treaties did not seem to have worried Gallwey in the slightest, for he found what he thought was a substitute for well defined, even if one sided, treaty terms. 'The influence of the white man', he wrote, 'and the wonderful belief the uncivilized African has of the white man's power, would, I consider, be quite sufficient guarantee to ensure the establishment of law and order on a sound footing'.[1] In so far as this visit was regarded as a prelude to the effective establishment of a British Protectorate, Gallwey's assessment of the attitude of the Urhobo people was seriously at fault. Later events were not only to demand that treaties should be signed, but to demonstrate that the Urhobo in their 'uncivilization' and naïvety, were not as awestruck of 'the white man' as Gallwey antici-pated. The penetration of Urhoboland was to be met with a most stubborn passive resistance which called for armed patrols. The enthusiasm with which Gallwey reported he was received[2] was not to last for very long. In 1891 the Urhobo had no idea what this, the first visit of 'the white man' to their country, was going to mean to their way of life. His advent was seen by the Urhobo as a possible means of improving their lot *vis-à-vis* the Itsẹkiri coastal dwellers who had, for a long time, been in contact with Europeans—a situation which had, without question, been of definite economic advantage to the Itsẹkiri. The price they were expected to pay for this resetting of the balance was not yet apparent.

Gallwey did not, with the exception of the Sapẹlẹ case discussed hereafter, attempt immediately to set up any agencies of government similar to what was already in existence at the vice-consulates, or to the 'warrant chief system' that was later to be established. No

1 F.O. 84/2111, Gallwey's Report referred to above.
2 Ibid. 'I was on all occasions received most enthusiastically by the natives who evidently hailed the advent of the whiteman with great satisfaction'.

doubt this was one reason for his enthusiastic reception. He proclaimed 'free trade' to the Urhobo and urged them to endeavour to increase their output. The Urhobo received this very well, doubtless because they thought that Gallwey would immediately be followed by European traders who would establish depots in their territory and so save them the journeys to Sapęlę or Benin River or Warri.[1] Any such hopes were not immediately met. The European traders did not, for all their outcry against the Itsękiri traders, move into the hinterland at this stage. They were content to go to where the Government established vice-consulates like Warri, Sapęlę and Benin River. The failure of the European traders to come to them, together with their realization that their mode of life was to be radically affected, combined to turn the enthusiasm of the Urhobo to hostility or at best insolent indifference.[2]

The first move into Urhoboland was thus almost purely exploratory. There was, however, one important outcome, namely, the establishment of a constabulary post and vice-consulate at Sapęlę. One of Gallwey's objects in undertaking the tour was to find sites suitable for the establishment of such posts. In his report to Macdonald he wrote, 'I consider Sapele to be a very good place to establish a vice-consulate.'[3] In November 1891 Macdonald himself visited Sapęlę to inspect the site and agreed with his vice-consul's estimation. He realized that a great deal of clearing would be required; but any worries he might have entertained as to the difficulty of meeting this problem were removed by the people of Sapęlę themselves: 'The people of Sapele informed me that if I would come and build there, they would clear as much ground as I wished.'[4] But the need for the post was so urgent that Macdonald did not even wait till the clearing had been made, and permanent buildings erected. Rather, a hulk was purchased at a cost of £1,800 and fitted out at Sapęlę to serve as consulate, prison and barracks.[5]

From the point of view of Itsękiri-Urhobo relations, the establish-

---

1 Interviews with 'chiefs' and elders of Okpara 7 July 1962 and with elders of Ęku 10 July 1962 and elders of Ukhuokori 14 July 1962.
2 C.O. 520/25, Political Report on the Kwale Expedition: Enclosure in Dispatch No. 260, 3 June 1904.
3 F.O. 84/2111, Gallwey's Report.
4 F.O. 84/2111, Macdonald to F.O. No. 3 of 12 December 1891.
5 F.O. 84/2194, Macdonald to F.O., December 1892.

ment of a vice-consulate at Sapẹlẹ was a significant development. It would appear as if Macdonald's original idea was to open new posts in addition to the vice-consulates already established. In the event, however, the setting up of the Sapẹlẹ vice-consulate led to the closure of the Benin River vice-consulate. By 1895 for instance, the latter only served as a customs port, and the officers were agitating that even this aspect of the establishment should be transferred to Sapẹlẹ in order to avoid the delay involved in the shipping having to go to the Benin River 'to clear'.[1] Hence the establishment of a vice-consulate at Sapẹlẹ meant that there was a deterioration in the relative importance, economically and politically, of the lower Benin River. For hundreds of years, that part of the river had been the focus of European activity. Any Urhobo who could take their own produce to the factories, had to take it right into the heart of Itsẹkiri country. Now the situation began to change. Sapẹlẹ was much nearer to the oil producers of the Ethiope hinterland. As early as 1894, the Urhobo were reported to be already taking advantage of the new development:

> now that Sapele is well opened, and every native being allowed to trade at every market . . . very little produce from the rich Ethiope country will find its way to the lower river factories—as the natives are beginning to appreciate the fact that by selling their produce at Sapele they save 90 miles of canoe journey.[2]

The establishment, for the first time ever, of a British post in Urhobo country proper[3] was thus already beginning to produce noticeable results.

The establishment of a vice-consulate at Sapẹlẹ had another effect on Itsẹkiri-Urhobo relations. It has been argued that the closure of the Benin River vice-consulate in favour of Sapẹlẹ, 'broke the barrier almost completely of the Itsẹkiri middlemen in the matter

---

1 Cal. Prof. 8/2 Vol. 1, Report on the Benin District for the quarter ending 30 June 1895.

2 Cal. Prof. 8/2 Vol. 1, Benin District Report for quarter ending 31 December 1894.

3 It has been established as a result of a legal suit that Sapẹlẹ is Urhobo-owned (see next page). The establishment of a vice-consulate there meant that future attempts to open up the Urhobo country were made from Sapẹlẹ and not Benin River, a fact which in itself is of considerable psychological, if not political, significance in the development of Itsẹkiri-Urhobo relations.

of trade'.[1] In fact the situation was far less simple. If anything, the establishment of Sapẹlẹ as a vice-consulate helped to create a problem which was not solved till the Sapẹlẹ land case was disposed of in the law courts as late as 1941.[2] As the trade of the area moved from the lower Benin River to Sapẹlẹ, and as Sapẹlẹ grew to become an important government centre, so more and more Itsẹkiri traders, as is the wont of all traders, moved with the trade and settled in Sapẹlẹ. In those early days such movement and settlement would not have involved the payment of regular rents by the Itsẹkiri to the Urhobo landowners, the payment of annual rents for land being, in fact, quite a recent development which probably followed on the 'Public Lands Acquisition Proclamation' of 1903,[3] which put a new value on the land. Over the years, the Itsẹkiri population grew, and as there was no documentary evidence to prove the ownership of the land the Itsẹkiri elements occupied, it was possible for them, many years later, to put forward a claim to such land. The issue of Sapẹlẹ land was rendered more complicated by the fact that when the government wanted to acquire some of the land, it was Dọghọ who, as political agent, signed the lease.[4] The chance event of Dọghọ being an Itsẹkiri gave the Itsẹkiri additional grounds for claiming ownership of the land. It was this claim which led to the court action referred to above. Thus, although the establishment of a government post at Sapẹlẹ was in a way a blessing to the Urhobo, who were relieved of many miles of canoe journey to the Benin River factories, it also posed new problems for them, as they now found themselves living closer to the Itsẹkiri than they had done before, and so called upon to work out a formula for peaceful co-existence.

---

1 A. Salubi: 'The Establishment of British Administration in the Urhobo Country', *J.H.S.N.*, Vol. 1, No. 3, December 1958, p. 191. Salubi appears preoccupied, in this article, to demonstrate that the British penetration of Urhoboland was an event accomplished with ease and happily welcomed by the Urhobo. The present writer cannot, in the light of the evidence, accept this view.

2 Salubi deals with this land case in his article 'The Origins of Sapele Township', *J.H.S.N.*, Vol. 2, No. 1, December 1960, pp. 115–29

3 C.O. 588/1, Proclamation No. 5 of 1903.

4 I have not been able to find the record of the exact date on which Dọghọ was appointed Political Agent. In 1897, however, Moor referred to him as such. F.O. 403/218, Enclosure No. 1 in Moor to F.O., 29 January 1897.

Gallwey's visit to certain parts of the Urhobo country[1] in 1891 was, as already stated, the result of instructions given by Macdonald for efforts to be made to penetrate the interior, and not only establish law and order and encourage the expansion of trade, but also to endeavour to bring the people in the hinterland more directly under British 'protection' and control.[2] Gallwey could not see his way to making treaties with the Urhobo people on his first trip on account of the latter's 'uncivilization'. But his colleague in Warri did not, it would appear, consider the stage of civilization attained by the Urhobo a bar to entering into treaty relations with them. Between December 1892 and August 1893, consular officers based in Warri entered into treaties of protection with Urhobo towns, all of them near to the Warri vice-consulate.[3] Gallwey himself signed a similar treaty with the Abraka people in May 1892.[4] The years 1891–3 therefore constituted the period when the British Government made the first moves to bring Urhoboland under their 'protection'. But the mere signing of treaties did not accomplish the aims which Macdonald had set forth. For although treaties had been made, and the foreign power had laid down its terms of 'free trade' and the abolition of all abhorrent 'native' customs, nothing more had been done either to ensure the carrying through of these aims, or to lay down firm lines for future development. And nothing really of lasting effect was to be done till the opening years of this century.

The time lag between the signing of the first treaties and the beginning of really ordered administration in Urhoboland demands explanation. After the treaties of 1893 the attention of the Government was fully occupied over the Nana issue. As has already been pointed out, the Nana episode can, in fact, be seen as having been the outcome of the determination of the British Government of the Niger Coast Protectorate to penetrate into the Urhobo country, and to establish itself as the sole and unrivalled authority in the area. In thus seeking to establish itself, the Government of the Niger Coast Protectorate counted without the Royal Niger Company,

1 The places visited were Sapẹlẹ, Okpara, Ẹku, Uria, in the Abraka clan.
2 F.O. 84/2111, Macdonald to F.O., 21 May 1891.
3 F.O. 2/168: These towns were Asagba, Tori, Ajeba, Agbassa, Ogulu, Obodo, Ogọ, and Ogbe-Sobo (Aladja).
4 F.O. 2/64, Enclosure 3 in Macdonald to F.O., No. 40, 26 November 1894.

which was equally eager to extend the area within its jurisdiction, with the hope of attracting more trade to itself.

One of the disputes which Macdonald was instructed to look into in 1889 when sent out as Special Commissioner was that between the Niger Coast Protectorate and the Royal Niger Company over the right to administer the Forcados River area. Following his appointment as Commissioner and Consul-General charged with the responsibility for administering the Oil Rivers Protectorate, one of Macdonald's first actions was to come to an agreement with the Royal Niger Company over the boundaries between the two authorities. This, always referred to as the Provisional Boundary Line, was:

> . . . On the West of the Nun mouth of the Niger River; A line starting at a point at the mouth of the Forcados River midway between the right and left bank, following that River to the mouth of the so-called 'Warri creek' following this creek up to a point two miles before reaching the mouth of the creek leading to Oagbie and Akiabodo.[1]

Territory on the right bank was to be under the Niger Coast Protectorate and on the left bank under the Royal Niger Company. It was noted that this line was drawn subject to modification by the requirements of local circumstances.[2]

Until 1894 nothing of great significance occurred to raise the issue of the boundary. In that year, however, began a dispute over the boundary, which was not finally solved till the charter of the Royal Niger Company was abrogated in 1899. In September 1894 while Acting Consul-General Moor was still involved in the Nana expedition, information reached him to the effect that the Royal Niger Company was busy making treaties 'at the back of the Benin and Warri districts', where the boundary was only a provisional one. In his fury not only at the attempt by the Royal Niger Company to force the boundary issue, but also at what Moor considered the company's meanness in taking advantage of his being preoccupied with the expedition against Nana, he dispatched a telegram to the Foreign Office in which he urged it to declare invalid any treaties entered into by the Company in the Benin and Warri districts, 'Warri and Benin being the natural outlets to Sobou

---

1 F.O. 84/2111, Macdonald to F.O., 13 June 1891.   2 Ibid.

country'.[1] In a dispatch explaining the telegram, Moor argued that the area into which the company was seeking to penetrate was under his jurisdiction as it had previously been under the sway of Nana. He pointed out that to hand over the area to the Royal Niger Company would cripple the trade of the two districts concerned, and compel the Urhobo to pay the prohibitive export duties of the company. His officials, he argued, had been prevented from entering into more treaties with the Urhobo, because of the provisional nature of the boundary line. In the light of the Company's action, Moor suggested a modification of the boundary to suit local needs. Giving his own views on the boundary, Moor wrote,

> The waterway of the Kiabodo creek, as far as it can be made use of, would being natural boundary, be the best point on which to commence and the course of a permanent boundary should then be determined by the difference of race, the Sobos being under the Protectorate and the Mahins under the Royal Niger Company's jurisdiction.[2]

Macdonald, home on leave, suggested that until a final readjustment could be made, both sides to the dispute should take up the positions they held prior to the Royal Niger Company's treaty-making expedition of which Moor complained.[3]

The Foreign Office, unable to understand this struggle for territory between the two British authorities, happily handed over the dispute to the arbitration of Sir John Kirk, who was appointed to inquire into the circumstances which led to the Akassa Raid. After investigations, Sir John was only able to report that some agreement had been reached by both sides on what was to be regarded as the provisional boundary. The old boundary, Kirk declared in his report, was unworkable but, at the same time, it was his opinion that the time had not yet arrived for a final settlement. Such a settlement, Kirk recommended, had to await the time 'when the geography of the Sobo and Assay markets is better known, and the relations of the tribes and their trade markets better understood'.[4] The situation thus created was scarcely better than it had been before Sir John's mission.

1 F.O. 2/64, Moor to F.O., Telegram, October 1894.
2 F.O. 2/64, Moor to F.O., No. 29, 10 October 1894.
3 F.O. 2/64, Macdonald to F.O., No. 52, 12 October 1894.
4 F.O. 403/316, Kirk to Kimberly, 30 June 1895.

It was too much to expect that having successfully got rid of Nana, Moor would remain inactive while the Foreign Office waited for time to solve the question as to which of the Niger Coast Protectorate and the Niger Company was to hold sway over Urhoboland. Besides, the Royal Niger Company had already made treaties with Egoo (Igun), Okpara, Okpare, Odokpo, Ughelle and Ovwo between 14 and 24 September 1894.[1] Despite Moor's plea that these treaties be nullified, the Foreign Office had not done so. As a fight back, for Moor loved a fight, he ordered his officials to go ahead with treaty-making. Between 28 September 1894 and June 1895, thirteen treaties were signed with Urhobo towns, among which were Okpara, Kokori, Ẹku, Allagigun and Uria.[2] Immediately, the Royal Niger Company protested to the Foreign Office, declaring that the Niger Coast Protectorate treaties were with towns which had already entered into treaty agreements with it, and that the apparent difference in names was no more than a difference in spelling.[3] Caught between the ambitions of these two authorities, the Foreign Office asked the Niger Coast Protectorate to desist from further action in Urhoboland, though the treaties already entered into were not disallowed. Macdonald, whose views were sought by the Foreign Office, merely suggested that if the treaties made by the Royal Niger Company were to be ratified, the Company might as well be saddled with responsibility for the coastal districts of Warri and Benin.[4]

Meanwhile, Moor was quite prepared to go on with his declared policy of penetration. The year 1896 was a busy one for the officers of the Sapẹlẹ vice-consulate, who made journeys into the hinterland, settling differences between Urhobo towns and making three more treaties in the process.[5] In 1897 the Foreign Office, determined not

1 F.O. 2/167, pp. 167–74.
2 F.O. 2/168, pp. 34–5 and 107–23.
3 F.O. 2/168, Moor to F.O., 18 April 1895.
4 F.O. 2/83, Macdonald to F.O., No. 25, 3 May 1895. The implication of Macdonald's comment was that it was impossible for one of the contesting authorities to administer the coastal districts, while the other held sway in the hinterland.
5 These treaties were with Obiaruku, Owe and Orogun, Moje and others. F.O. 2/168, pp. 178–80. The visits were paid to Ukhuokori, Orogun and Owe—F.O. 2/102, Lecky to Commissioner-General No. 10, 14 September 1896.

to allow the struggle for territory between the Company and the Protectorate to deteriorate any further, sent an official dispatch to Moor, urging him to do nothing that would lead to friction between the two contesting authorities.[1] Moor only grudgingly obeyed this injunction. He pointed out in his reply that the 1891 agreement had been meant to be temporary, subject to modifications to suit local requirements. He stressed that the Foreign Office had approved the treaties made by his officials, and that in practice, the area which the Royal Niger Company claimed as its territory had been administered by the officials of the Niger Coast Protectorate. Nevertheless, in view of the injunction from the Foreign Office, he had instructed his men

> to take as little action as possible in the direction of the left bank of the Ethiope and the Sobo country . . . but I consider this a retrograde movement and one that will result in the work already done in that direction having to be done over again in the future.[2]

Thus from 1897–9 there was a pause in the penetration of Urhoboland.[3] It was not till the Royal Niger Company lost its charter, and its territories were handed over the Niger Coast Protectorate in April 1899, that full attention could once more be paid to bringing the Urhobo systematically under control.

It is necessary to examine in more detail the treaty-making activities of both the Royal Niger Company and the Niger Coast Protectorate during this first phase of the penetration. The Niger Coast Protectorate treaties were negotiated by protectorate officials from Warri and Sapęlę. No detailed reports exist of the negotiations which preceded the actual signing of the treaties. The British administration was determined to establish its authority in the hinterland and to tap the economic resources of the country. In the circumstances, it is scarcely necessary to argue the case as to whether these treaties were signed with the Urhobo (or any of the other Nigerian peoples) because these people requested to be brought under the protection of Her Majesty the Queen of Great Britain.

---

1 F.O. 403/267, F.O. to Moor, No. 192, 2 September 1897.
2 F.O. 403/267, Moor to F.O., No. 11, 12 January 1898.
3 Other reasons which explain the pause, apart from the boundary dispute, were the greater attention given to Benin affairs following the murder of British officials in 1896, and to disturbances up the Cross River.

The important thing is that once the treaties were signed, the British administration of the Niger Coast Protectorate had a legal right to take over control of the affairs of the people concerned. The Urhobo were to learn that the signing of these treaties meant the beginning of a tremendous change in their mode of life, a change which they neither always appreciated nor welcomed. At the beginning, however, the British were enthusiastically received after the initial fear always inherent in a first contact. Gallwey recorded in 1892 for instance, that the Urhobo were very anxious to be placed under Her Majesty's protection, and in fact, considered that they were so placed already.[1] Gallwey probably misunderstood the reason for this enthusiasm. Yet one can understand the Urhobo attitude. For years, all knowledge most of them had about the European had come through the Itsẹkiri. They knew of the power of men like Nana, and realized that this power had been made possible by the contact between the Itsẹkiri and the Europeans. They were witnesses of Itsẹkiri commercial prosperity. Now it began to appear as if these blessings would be theirs too. From a commercial point of view, they hoped for better prices for their produce and for cheaper imported goods. It was to take some time before these hopes were realized.

The entourage of the treaty-making officials usually consisted of an interpreter, who was sometimes also the messenger and guide and one or two other Europeans, attached to the vice-consulate or constabulary, who signed the treaties as witnesses. R. A. Alder and Harrison were the two interpreters who accompanied the consular officials on their treaty-making trips at this stage. Harrison was an Itsẹkiri who had featured prominently in the Nana episode. He had no great influence with the Urhobo and is not remembered as having been important on his own account. It is a commentary on how well the Urhobo understood the treaties they signed, that Alder, who attended as interpreter for eighteen different treaties with the Urhobo during these years, was reported in 1897 as 'being unable to talk Sobo'.[2] The Urhobo, as already indicated, had their

1 F.O. 2/51, Report on the Benin District Oil Rivers Protectorate for the year ending 31 July 1892—Enclosure in Macdonald to F.O., 12 January 1893.
2 Cal. Prof. 8/2 Vol. II, Warri District Quarterly Report for Quarter ending 31 March 1897.

own reasons for accepting British 'protection'—reasons which probably outweighed any irregularities which marked the signing of the treaties.

It is interesting to compare the treaty-making activities in Urhoboland and those in the Burutu area. In the 1880's when Hewett sought to prepare the way for the establishment of a British Protectorate, it was noticed that he did not sign separate treaties with the Ijọ of Burutu and 'Goolah'.[1] He was content to accept the declaration by these Ijọ that they were subject to Nana's rule. No such incident is recorded or remembered in connexion with the events described above. Indeed, what struck the consular officials was the complete independence of every little Urhobo settlement.[2]

Treaties, however legally desirable, were not in fact an end in themselves. They were simply a means to the desired end of placing Urhoboland under British control. Consequently, both in this first phase and in the later phase of British penetration, great emphasis was placed on visits by administrative officers. The year 1896 was an active year for such visits. Lecky, Assistant District Commissioner at Sapẹlẹ, paid two visits to what was generally described as Kwalẹ country, though this area included both the Urhobo clan of Agbọn and the Isoko clan of Owe.[3] During the second visit, Lecky entered into treaties with Orogun and Owe, Owe thus becoming the first, and as it turned out the only, Isoko clan to enter formally into a protection treaty with the British.[4] More important than these treaties, however, were the pains Lecky took to get the people to bring their standing disputes to him; to convince them to give up reprisals against each other such as seizing people whenever there was a dispute; and most important of all to warn them that the roads must be kept open for trade and that the practice of levying tolls on passing produce had to be given up.[5] The people were beginning to realise that it was one thing

---

1 Supra, p. 90.
2 This was one of the reasons that made Gallwey wonder whether treaties could be made with the Urhobo. F.O. 84/2111, Gallwey's Report.
3 F.O. 2/101, Enclosure in Moor to F.O., No. 58, 18 July 1896.
4 F.O. 2/102, Lecky to Acting Commissioner No. 10, 14 September 1896.
5 Ibid.

to enter into treaties, but quite another to satisfy the British terms embodied in, or implied by, these treaties.

During Lecky's first journey in April 1896, he was accompanied by Captain Ruger of the Niger Coast Constabulary at the head of a small escort. Tonwe, Nana's former messenger now in the service of the government, went as messenger and was always sent ahead to announce the coming of the main party. Then to quote Lecky himself,

> I took the Jekris representing the Native Council at Abraka with me, so that they could make friends with the Kwalis and open up trade.[1]

During the second visit. Lecky took with him chiefs Jim Etchie and a certain 'Chichilu'[2]—Itsẹkiri members of the Benin River Native Council. The role which these two played is not detailed in the report of the tour. This practice of taking on chiefs from one station to another was a common one adopted not only with the aim of 'opening up trade', but also of bringing the different peoples to know more of one another, in the hope that inter-clan and other disputes could thereby be more amicably settled. During the same journey, Lecky insisted on the Urhobo chiefs of Asagba and Abraka accompanying him to Abbi to meet the chiefs there.[3]

While Lecky was busy as already described, Mr. P. W. G. Copland-Crawford was undertaking a land march from Warri to Sapẹlẹ (the first European to do so), with the aim of opening up communication between the two stations. The journey, quite apart from its importance so far as the future Warri-Sapẹlẹ road was concerned, also served to enable Copland-Crawford get in touch with the Urhobo settlements along the route, among them Adeje and Amukpẹ and to explain to these settlements the new order that was being established.[4]

If the Urhobo were, at the beginning, eager to welcome the advance of the British into their country, they soon had cause to resist this advance. The aims of the British Government were not always compatible with their old customs, and the people therefore

1 F.O. 2/101, Lecky to Acting Commissioner No. 10, 14 September 1896.
2 The real name was Tetsọla. In some other records the name is also given as 'Tetchalla'—See C.S.O. 26/2 File No. 11329/S.33.
3 F.O. 2/101, Enclosure in Phillips to F.O., No. 101, 6 November 1896.
4 F.O. 2/100, Copland-Crawford to R. Moor, No. 5, 22 January 1896.

began to prove much more recalcitrant than Gallwey's early enthusiastic report would lead one to expect. Even during these first
years of really active penetration, the reactions of certain Urhobo
towns were already strong enough to cause the District Commissioners considerable worry. In the closing quarter of 1896,
the District Commissioner, Warri, had to deal with the intransigence of 'Jeremy' (Ughięnvwe) and Obodo. As he put it,

> During the commencement of last quarter the chiefs of the Sobo
> towns Jeremy and Obodo which adjoin each other became too inde-
> pendent. One chief in particular by the name of Capue it was found
> necessary to remove as he totally ignored the orders of the government.[1]

In the same year, Effurun which had suffered during the Nana
episode was again visited with a patrol under Captain Cockburn
and forty men of the Niger Coast Protectorate Force, with Mr.
Locke as political officer.[2] The year 1897 was no easier, since the
Benin expedition gave rise to widespread unrest. Not only did the
Urhobo refuse to have anything to do with supplying carriers for the
expedition, but they also refused to submit to any authority outside
that of their own people. In his report for the year, the Acting vice-
consul wrote in very strong terms:

> The Sobos, however, are most truculent and nothing but the strong-
> est measures will reduce them to a proper state of submission. . . . It
> has now become an imperative necessity that a few soldiers should be
> stationed at Warri or Sapele who could enforce the orders of the
> Government which are now utterly ignored even in the immediate
> vicinity of the consulate.[3]

Thus at the end of the first phase, although many Urhobo towns
near Warri and Sapęlę had either signed treaties or been visited
by the British political officers, these towns as well as the rest of
the Urhoboland were far from being fully under control.

As for the treaties made by the Royal Niger Company, there
are no details of the negotiations which preceded their signature.
Annual subsidies were paid by the Company to the various treaty

1 Cal. Prof. 8/2 Vol. I, Warri District Quarterly Report for Quarter ending
31 December 1896.
2 Ibid.
3 Cal. Prof. 8/2 Vol. II, Annual Report, Western Division for the Year ending
31 March 1897.

towns. These subsidies varied from place to place in accordance
with what was considered the commercial prospects of the area.
Thus, Ughelle received fifty-five pounds worth of goods, while
Okpare received twelve pounds.[1] At Ughelle there is a very vivid
remembrance of the coming of the company's officials. Their
coming created a great stir as no Europeans had previously visited
that town. McTaggart who led the treaty-making expedition was
thus the first white man to visit Ughelle. After the signing of the
treaty he charged the Ughelle people not to have similar agreements
signed with any other Europeans, but rather to show them a copy
of the company's treaty. The Ughelle elders say that after signing
the treaty, they were encouraged to direct their trade towards
Ganagana where the Company had a depot.[2] It was against this
sort of influence on trade routes that the Niger Coast Protectorate
protested. Apart from the attempt to influence the direction of
trade, the company did little more. They certainly did not set up
any institutions of government over which they exercised control
or supervision. Much earlier than the 1894 treaties were those made
with Ivǫrǫgbǫ and Ase in the Isoko area.[3] Ase was already an
important centre to which the Isoko took their produce. Ivǫrǫgbǫ
was to become a depot of the Niger Company after it had lost
its charter—the only truly Isoko town with a European trading
station, and one to which people from as far away as Ughelle
went after it began to function.

After the various attempts described above, no further steps
were taken to visit and further open up the Urhobo hinterland
during the years 1897–9. Moor, who had only reluctantly accepted
the Foreign Office injunction to put an end to further penetration,
was by 1899 thoroughly disgusted with the inaction imposed on his
staff. Reports of unrest in the country around Abraka and Orogun
were used by Moor as evidence of the chaos reigning in the interior
following the inability of the Niger Coast Protectorate officials to
visit the area.[4] Earlier in the year, he wrote to the Agent General

---

1 The treaties can be found in F.O. 2/67.
2 Private and public interviews with various elders and Ovie-in-council of
Ughelle during the period 8–11 January 1962.
3 F.O. 84/2109, Chapter 1 of Macdonald's Report.
4 C.O. 444/1, Moor to C.O., No. 77, 23 May 1899.

of the Royal Niger Company at Burutu, informing him that as a result of the reported unrest, he had instructed the Acting Vice-Consul, Western Division, to visit the subsidized towns 'with a view to putting matters right'.[1] In a lengthy dispatch to the Colonial Secretary in April 1899, Moor insisted on the Urhobo areas being definitely placed under the Niger Coast Protectorate and urged the necessity for setting the administration of these areas on a much firmer footing.[2] With the abrogation of the charter of the Royal Niger Company at the end of 1899, the Protectorate Government took over all the territories of the former in the south, and the way was thus left open for the next and final phase of the penetration of Urhoboland.

As early as 1896 Moor had outlined, in response to a Foreign Office demand, the steps which he intended to take for the opening up of, and further development of trade with, the interior, and for gaining the confidence of the various Nigerian peoples in the Protectorate.[3] The more important of these steps were:

I. Small expeditions of a peaceable nature in all directions that can be penetrated by such means with a view to explaining the aims and objects of the Government and to open up friendly relations.

II. At all towns and villages visited where a friendly reception is met with a native council of chiefs is organized for the adjustment more particularly of external 'palavers' with the neighbouring tribes and at the same time for the settlement of internal troubles . . .

---

1 F.O. 2/186, Moor to the Acting Agent General, R.N.C., No. 2, 25 January 1899.
2 C.O. 444/1, Moor to C.O. No. 66 of 14 April 1899. Moor did not attempt to argue that the areas in dispute were legally under the jurisdiction of the N.C.P. His argument was rather that the N.C.P. had, in practice, controlled those areas and had been responsible for removing Nana who, argued Moor, virtually ruled over the area before his defeat in 1894. Moor argued that since the R.N.C. did not raise the matter at the earlier period when Nana was in control, it had not moral right to raise it now that the N.C.P. had fought against, and removed, Nana. He was not questioning the R.N.C.'s legal rights. He was merely urging the modification of the boundary line to bring it more into accord with the practical situation in the interests of the trade of the Itsẹkiri and those Urhobo traders who were under the jurisdiction of the N.C.P.   3 F.O. 2/101, Moor to F.O. No. 50, 14 June 1896.

III. Treaties of peace and friendship in the usual form are made with all tribes and peoples willing and anxious to enter into them and every effort is made to ensure friendly reception in future at all towns once visited though the original reception may have been most unfriendly.

IV. Instructions are given that all complaints no matter how trivial their nature are to receive prompt and active attention and in serious cases or those of general importance the scene if within possible range is to be visited as speedily as possible on first opportunity . . .

V. Continuous attention is given to the patrolling of the waterways, the main routes of trade, and prompt measures are taken for the suppression of piracy the commonest offences at the time this Administration started . . .

VI. Attention is give to the opening of land trade routes to the waterways and the stoppage of the system of land piracy carried on and tolls levied by the tribes through whose country such routes pass.

VII. I propose with sanction, establishing permanent posts further in the interior from time to time to act as bases for further development and to render secure the interior ends of roads which may in future be made from existing stations.

Some efforts were made to implement this policy in the years 1892–7. The task was now taken in hand with new vigour following the establishment of the Protectorate of Southern Nigeria which incorporated the former Niger Territories in the south.[1]

The new phase of penetration began on an encouraging note. The areas near to the centres of government gave the administrative officers cause for satisfaction. Native courts, which were already functioning in other parts of the Protectorate, were now opened for the first time in the hinterland areas. By September 1900, there were three such courts, at Okpare, Ajareyube (in Agbarho clan)

---

1 The new Protectorate was broken up into three Divisions: Western, Central, and Eastern. Warri and Sapęlę Districts which concern us in this work were in the Western Division. The bulk of the Isoko were in the Agbəri District of the Central Division. The opening up of the hinterland was from now on to be directed from Warri, Sapęlę and Agbęri.

and Gbogidi.[1] As will be explained in the next chapter, these courts were seen not only as judicial institutions, but as instruments for bringing under effective administrative control the areas in which they were established. Hence the opening of a Native Court was always viewed with satisfaction by the District Commissioners, as this meant not only that they had a body of people charged with performing definite duties for, and on behalf of, the Government, but also that the administrative officers were left with a freer hand to tackle new areas and new problems.

Further away from the Government stations, however, the situation was not so satisfactory. In 1900 Copland-Crawford noted that the Uzere Eni 'juju' was still functioning and would have to be tackled, as it constituted trial by ordeal, a process which the Government had been trying to wipe out.[2] In 1901 there was need to send a patrol to the Orokpo area in Agbon clan in order to bring the people ther under firmer control. Although the details of this patrol are not available in the records, it is well remembered because of the fact that George Eyube, one of the three political agents during this period, died during that patrol, from an accidental shot fired from his own pistol.[3]

Records showing the dates of appointment of the political agents do not seem to have survived. Tom Fallodun, a Yoruba, was already working in the Abraka area in 1897.[4] Chief Dogho featured prominently in the Benin expedition of 1896, the records of which refer to him as a political agent.[5] George Eyube died in 1901. The inscription on the marble grave erected by the government reads

---

1 Cal. Prof. 10/3 Vol. 1, Warri District Quarterly Report for quarter ending 31 March 1900.
2 Cal. Prof. 10/3 Vol. 1, Warri District Quarterly Report for quarter ending 31 March 1900.
3 In appreciation of the work done by Eyube, the government erected a marble grave in his memory. The grave can still be seen today in his home town of Gbogidi.
4 Cal. Prof. 8/2 Vol. II, Annual Report, Western Division for year ending 31st March, 1897—Burrows wrote, 'This [i.e. the truculence of the Urhobo] applies to the whole of the Division with the exception of the neighbourhood of Abraka and great credit is due to Tom Folladoh for the way he administers that part.'
5 The records of this Expedition are quite clear on this point. F.O. 403/218, Enclosure 1 in Moor to F.O., 29 January 1897.

that he was 'for five years political agent in the Warri District'. It would therefore appear that the appointments were made in 1896, that is, soon after the fall of Nana.

George Eyubẹ was born about 1855. He was the son of Atsemudiara, an Urhobo man of Gbogidi, and Inumameje, an Itsẹkiri woman. The mother, like most Itsẹkiri women, was a keen trader and it is said that it was from her that George learnt the techniques of the commercial world of his time. He developed into a great trader himself and is said to have done very well as a trader even during the Nana era. He carried his produce from the Urhobo markets to the European beaches in his own canoes. In his commercial career his mixed parentage served him well at both ends of the market. During this process of commercial intercourse, he acquired the English language and was able to converse intelligently with the Europeans. This, together with the undoubted knowledge he had of the ways of his countrymen, secured for him appointment as a political agent. His sphere included his own clan of Udu, Ughiẹnvwe, Agbarho, Olomu and surrounding areas. In all these places he is remembered as one who laboured with varying degrees of success, to explain the aims of the British Government to the Urhobo. When the Native Courts of Gbogidi, Ajareyubẹ (named after him), and Okpare were opened, it was he who helped to explain to the court members exactly how the courts were to be run.

There are only a few references to Eyubẹ in the administrative records, a fact which makes it difficult to assess his contribution to the British penetration of Urhoboland. The one tribute paid to him was in 1900, a year before his sudden death. Writing of the political situation of the Warri District in 1900, the District Commissioner, Mr. W. E. B. Copland-Crawford, commented,

> The new Minor Court at Ajarejubi has been completed and courts are now being held there—and a large number of cases are forthcoming. The chiefs attend regularly and appear to be gradually improving in the manner of the conduct of the court. Chief Ayubah, at this court as at the others had rendered great assistance.[1]

---

1 Cal. Prof. 10/3 Vol. I, Warri District Quarterly Report 30/9/1900. The other facts recorded here in connection with Eyubẹ I have obtained from his sixty-three year old son who is now a Roman Catholic Catechist in Warri—interview on 20 December 1961.

The first decade of this century was an extremely busy period for the officers of the Warri and Sapęlę districts. During those ten years, the whole of the Urhobo country was brought as much under control as could be expected, before the Native Courts and other paraphernalia of British administration had had time to produce the desired effects. Up to 1901 the penetration of the Urhobo country by Protectorate Officers had been centred on the area now known as West and Central Urhobo. The Isoko country, with the singular exception of Owe which had signed a Protection treaty in 1896, was left very much to itself because it was well within the former territories of the Royal Niger Company, which did little to penetrate into the hinterland. Attention was now focused on the Isoko country as well. Forwarding to the Colonial Office his plans for penetration in the dry season of 1902–3, Moor reported that the area around Ase Creek had 'always been an area giving serious trouble both in the days of the former Royal Niger Company and laterly to the Government'. This area was therefore to be visited by a patrol in 1902–3. Further, whereas trial by ordeal had, in many parts of the Protectorate, been abolished, it still flourished at Uzere in the Isoko country, in the form of the famous Eni 'juju' used for the trial of accussed witches. Moor argued that the time had come for this particular form of trial to be suppressed and the whole of the surrounding area brought under regular governmental control.[1]

It did not, however, require a military patrol to solve the problems of Eni. Mr. Copland-Crawford, who in 1903 was Acting Divisional Commissioner of the Central Division, had earlier on, when he served as District Commissioner in Warri, made efforts to get the *Ovie* of Uzere to abolish the Eni ordeal. But the *Ovie* made it clear at that time that he could not stop people coming to Eni, the abolition of which would entail a great financial loss to himself, as he usually received fees and presents from all those who came to Eni, of which he was high priest.[2] Copland-Crawford in 1903 now undertook to persuade the *Ovie* to agree to abolish the ordeal, holding out on the one hand, the veiled threat of a punitive

---

1 C.O. 520/15, Moor to C.O., No. 388, 22 August 1902.
2 Cal. Prof. 10/3 Vol. I. Quarterly Report, Warri District, 30/9/1900. Also Cal. Prof. 10/3 Vol. III, 'Report on Useri Ordeal'.

expedition should he fail to do so, and on the other, the post of Vice-President of the Native Council (with an annual salary of fifty pounds) which the Government intended to open at Uzere, should he see his way to agreeing to the abolition of the ordeal, convincing the other elders, and faithfully supporting the new régime which would take the place of Eni. The *Ovie* eventually gave in and Eni was declared duly abolished on the 9 December 1903. The Government made its abolition a really grand occasion. Representatives of the Itsẹkiri, Ijọ, Aboh, Kwalẹ, as well as a great number of people from the other Isoko and Urhobo clans were brought to Uzere for the occasion. Those who appended their 'marks' to the resolution abolishing Eni included 106 elders from virtually all the Urhobo and Isoko clans; 15 from various Ijọ towns; 13 Itsẹkiri; 11 from the Agberi and Ndoni Districts and 20 from Ase.[1] So important an achievement was the successful abolition of Eni regarded by the Government, that Copland-Crawford, who was on a probationary term as Divisional Commissioner, was confirmed at the post, following the recommendation of Fosbery, the then Acting High Commissioner.[2]

The work thus begun in 1903 at Uzere was quickly followed up the next year. Part of the Kwalẹ Patrol of 1904 under Captain Wallis, accompanied by Mr. C. A. Wordsworth, District Commissioner, Agberi, visited Ozọrọ, Ọfagbe and Oleh. Apart from Ozọrọ, where there was some trouble over the failure of 'the head chief Amawe', to give up men who had committed murder, no resistance was offered to the column.[3] Earlier in the same year Mr. Wordsworth while still in charge of Warri, had made a tour of inspection through part of the Isoko area and got the towns of Olomoro, Ẹmede and Igbide to agree to attend the Native Council that was to open shortly at Uzere in the Agberi Districts.[4] By June Mr. Wordsworth

---

1 C.O. 320/24, Copland-Crawford to Acting High Commissioner, 14 Dec. 1903—Enclosure in Fosbery to C.O., No. 15, 15 January 1904.

2 C.O. 520/24, Fosbery to C.O. No. 15, 15 January 1904. Also C.O. Draft to the High Commissioner, Protectorate of S. Nigeria No. 427, 18 November 1904.

3 C.O. 520/25, Wordsworth's report on the tour—Enclosure in Fosbery to C.O. No. 260, 3 June 1904.

4 C.O. 591/2, Govt. Gazette (S. Nigeria) No. 10, 30th June, 1904, Quarterly Report Warri District, Jan.–March 1904, p. 187.

reported that the Uzere Native Council was already functioning.[1] The Uzere court was later incorporated in a joint Uzere-Patani court which sat in both places in turn. This followed a minor re-organization when, in 1906, the Protectorate of Southern Nigeria and the Colony of Lagos were amalgamated into a single administrative unit. The Isoko, following this reorganization, were now included in the new Aboh District.[2]

The Isoko sector was not, however, fully brought under control till about 1911. In 1909 it was reported that the Isoko towns were giving so much trouble that they had to be fined.[3] The next year, Owe, Ozọrọ and Oleh had again to be visited and persuaded to give up their age-old custom of blinding those convicted of theft by the cruel method of pouring boiling oil into their eyes. Oleh only grudgingly consented. Copland-Crawford was not deceived by the promises to reform made by these towns and made it clear, in his annual report on the Central Division, that stronger measures would be necessary before these and other Isoko towns could be brought under full and effective control.[4] His fears were justified in 1911, when it was discovered early in the year, that the towns were persisting in their old habits and boasting that if any white men again visited them such white men would be cruelly man-handled. As a result of this recalcitrant attitude, three sections of the Southern Nigerian Regiment were sent into the area to deal with the three towns mentioned above, and to bring all the surrounding towns and

---

1 C.O. 591/2. Report on the Agberi District for Quarter ending 30 June 1904—Government Gazette No. 16, 23 September 1904, p. 311.
2 As part of the preparation for the amalgamation of the administrations of the Protectorate of Southern Nigeria and the Colony of Lagos, the districts were rearranged. The Western Division was now divided into the districts of Warri, Forcados, Sapẹlẹ, Kwalẹ, Benin City, Agbor, Ishan and Ifon. Of these districts, Warri, Sapẹlẹ and Kwalẹ fall within the area covered by this work—the Kwalẹ District included the Urhobo clan of Agbọn. The Isoko were included in a new district, Aboh, which was formerly part of the Central Division. In 1906 all these districts including Onitsha, constituted the Central Province with headquarters at Warri. C.O. 591/3. Annual Report Western Division 1905—Government Gazette No. 2, 9 May 1906, p. 50.
3 C.O. 592/7, Annual Report Central Provinces 1909, p. 737.
4 C.O. 592/9, Annual Report Central Provinces 1910, p. 661. Wrote Coplan-Crawford, 'It will probably be found that before such pernicious customs are destroyed more active measures will be necessary to ensure protection of life and property in these parts.'

villages under control. Various sections of the respective towns were burnt down to impress upon the people the type of punishment they should expect every time they showed themselves disinclined to do what Government desired. Awed by this visitation, the area submissively quietened down after that. By the end of the year, Mr. R. A. Roberts, then in charge of the Central Provinces, could write of the Isoko area: 'the country is now under complete control and trade is flourishing, a condition which now maintains throughout the district.'[1]

At the same time as the Isoko area was being brought under control, the rest of Urhoboland was also being visited and 'pacified'. In 1902 Mr. Raikes, the Acting District Commissioner, Sapẹlẹ, visited Okpara, Ukhuokori, Orogun, and Owe. These towns seemed to have received the constant attention of the officers, for although they were among the areas first visited by British political officers, it was by no means easy to get them to obey instructions. At Okpara, Raikes found that the Itsẹkiri doing trade at the waterside had complaints against the Agbọn people of Okpara inland. The Itsẹkiri complained that the Agbọn people sometimes stopped trade going to the waterside, and threatened them (the Itsẹkiri) with violence. The Agbọn people argued that they merely stopped sending produce down to the waterside when they found it impossible to accept the prices which the Itsẹkiri were prepared to offer. The old trouble over acceptable prices had not been solved. Raikes, however, got Ogun, the Itsẹkiri elder, and the Agbọn elders to agree to put an end to this process of holding up produce and threatening violence against each other. At Ukhuokori Raikes reported that the people did not really wish to surrender to the control of the British administration but were merely playing up to the administrative officers. Mr. Raikes put the blame on the 'headman', Evigare, whose removal from his position he urged. On the whole this visit did not, it would appear, inspire Mr. Raikes with much confidence, for he wrote:

> I am of opinion that no permanent good will result from visiting the country around Ukpara, Kokoree and Arogun, unless the officer visiting is prepared and able to stay there some considerable time, say

---

1 C.O. 592/13, Annual Report Central Provinces 1911, p. 136.

six weeks . . . and is in a position to enforce his wishes if not carried out otherwise.[1]

Mr. Raikes' views were fully upheld when it was found necessary for the Kwalẹ Patrol of 1904 to visit this same area. James Davidson, the Acting District Commissioner, who accompanied the Kwalẹ expedition, recalled why it was necessary to re-visit the area:

> Ever since the Government has been established in the Sapele District this particular portion of the country has always resolutely pursued its own course, retaining all its native habits and customs in spite of the many warnings received at frequent intervals from every Divisional or District Officer. . . . This disinclination they have carried to the length of turning the Officers from their towns and even when their presence has been tolerated, the towns have always displayed the greatest indifference to all they have been told.[2]

The other main reason for the patrol was the need to get the people to put an end to the policy of 'seizing', pledging or selling individuals either as a settlement for outstanding debt or as a result of land and other disputes. There was also the pressing need to get the roads under proper repair and to ensure that they could be safely used by all who so desired. Finally, the policy of 'free trade' was to be further emphasized and insisted on.

The patrol visited Orogun, Okpara, Ukhuokori and Owe. Ukhuokori was the town which gave the greatest trouble. In addition to its many misdemeanours (which included refusal to treat with the Divisional Commissioner some months previously, assault on a Native Court Messenger, and a standing feud with Orogun) this town, it was reported, harboured a criminal society which called itself the 'Arukpete Club' whose main occupation seemed to be raiding the waterside markets, and generally terrorizing the neighbourhood. The town was brought to book and fined twelve puncheons of oil. A number of 'chiefs' were arrested pending the payment of this fine. These chiefs were given out to be Naturo, Obiri,

---

1 Cal. Prof. 10/3 Vol. III, 'Report on visit to Okpara, Kokori and Owe', April 1902.
2 C.O. 520/25, Political Report on the Kwale Expedition—Enclosure in dispatch No. 260, 3 June 1904. It will be recalled that this was the same area with which Nana had most of his trouble. The British were now discovering for themselves that the people were not easy to handle. See Chapter 3, p. 81.

Napoma, Bweni, Otogbogbo and Ologbode. Davidson suggested that Naturo, the 'headchief', should be deposed and one Itowe, described as 'the third chief of the town' and a member of the Native court, put in his place. Itowe, it was argued, 'would be a useful man for the place as he has always shown himself as well disposed towards the Government and at all times had done his best to display a more friendly attitude towards us'.[1] It is not clear, however, whether Davidson's suggestion was carried out.

One other place where stern measures were taken was Agbassa, which drove back the messengers sent there to inform the town of the patrol's intention to visit it. When the patrol arrived, it was discovered that the town was largely deserted. But the people eventually came in, and put the blame on two of the elders, Okwe and Emouria. The farms and houses of these men were accordingly destroyed.[2]

Finally, Mr. Davidson succeeded in getting Orogun, Owe and Ukhuokori to come to some agreement and so end their long-standing feud. The patrol stayed in the area for two weeks. During this period, various meetings were held at the different centres at which the policy of the government was fully explained to the people. As in the earlier period, the political officer reported:

> I made it a point that the towns we had visited should attend as many future meetings as possible with the double object of further impressing our policy on their minds and of bringing the towns into contact with each other in a friendly manner.[3]

This confirms the point made earlier that the practice of taking people from one centre to another was calculated to promote more harmonious relations between the different peoples being brought under British administrative control. At the end of the patrol, the political officer was of the opinion that the expedition had had the desired effect, and that the people themselves were beginning to see the need to adapt themselves to the new ideas which the British Government was trying to impress upon them. He observed, however, that in order to achieve permanent results, not only would

1 Ibid.
2 C.O. 520/25, An account of proceedings in Kwalę country: Officer commanding Kwalę Expedition to Officer commanding Southern Nigeria Regiment— Enclosure in Despatch No. 26, 3 June 1904.
3 C.O. 520/25, Political Report on the Kwalę Expedition.

frequent visits be necessary, but more courts would have to be established so that people would not have to go long distances to get their disputes resolved.[1] In pursuance of this suggestion new courts were established at Ughiẹnvwe and Ughelle by the end of the year 1904.[2]

The next three years saw generally satisfactory progress. The Urhobo people were beginning to settle down to the new system. In 1907, however, unrest was reported in Agbassa and Iyede. Captain Beamish led a small patrol to these areas and endeavoured to settle things.[3] Despite this visitation Agbassa remained so obstinate that yet another patrol was sent there, this time under Captain Wayling, with Major Swanston as political officer. As a result of this patrol the two head chiefs of Agbassa were deported.[4] By 1909 Agbassa was at last reported settled, and included in the Okpare-Ughelle Native Court area.[5] Here, as in the Isoko section, therefore, the area was generally under full control by 1911.

One, if not the main, reason for the British penetration of the coastal hinterland was the desire to increase the trade of the Protectorate by creating an atmosphere in which trade could flourish. The constant aim of the administrative officers on their many tours was to stop the 'seizing' of debtors and the blocking of trade routes, as well as to venture out into new branches of trade. Great emphasis was laid on free movement of persons as of trade. For both these purposes, there had to be roads, and these roads had to be safe from robbers and terrorists. The same applied to the waterways: they had to be cleared both of physical obstacles and of 'pirates'.

First then let us examine the steps taken by the Government to quicken the development of trade. The Government very much hoped that by getting the people in the hinterland to accept their

1 Ibid.
2 C.O. 591/2, Govt. Gazette No. 21 of 18 November 1904—Order No. 10 of 1904.
3 C.S.O. 1/19 Vol. 16, Annual Report Central Province for the year 1907— Enclosure in Dispatch No. 38, 19 January 1907. The cause of the unrest in Iyede was the refusal of the people to have an Itsẹkiri chief imposed on them. Infra, p. 182.
4 C.O. 592/5, Annual Report, Central Province, 1908, p. 407.
5 C.O. 592/7, Annual Report, Central Province, 1909, p. 735.

rule, the way would be open for the various trading firms established in Warri, Sapẹlẹ and Ganagana to open depots in the interior for tapping the trade of the area. As it turned out, however, not many firms were eager to move into the Urhobo hinterland even at this stage. Thus, until 1905, no European firm had established a permanent depot in the Urhobo area, though the annual report for that year held out some hopes of the Niger Company and John Holt and Company moving into the interior. In 1906 it was reported that the firms were actually going to meet the trade in the hinterland.[1]

The firm of John Holt and Company took energetic steps, in the years after 1905, to get the Urhobo people to trade more directly with it. In the years 1906–7 Mr. Wood, John Holt's agent at Frukama, made strenuous efforts to convince the Urhobo to trade with his firm. According to him, the firm had secured a plot of land on which to build a beach and depot at Otọrughiẹnvwe ('Otu-Jeremi') by November 1906. All that remained to be done before the firm could establish a station there, was 'to get papers signed in front of the District Commissioner'.[2] Throughout 1906 and most of 1907, Wood toured the entire Urhobo country, including part of the Isoko country, convincing the people to take their produce to the John Holt depots. Wood hoped that most of the people around Okpare, Ewu, Ughelle and Iyede would send their produce to the new station that was to be established at Otọrughiẹnvwe.[3] Later, John Holt established a 'factory' at Okpare in the Olomu clan in the period after 1914. On the whole Wood's tramping around the Urhobo country gave the trade of the area a new impetus and encouraged the Urhobo to take their produce to the nearest John Holt station themselves. As for the Isoko, they were encouraged to take their produce, via the Owodokpokpọ creek, to Patani where John Holt had a well established factory.

While Wood was busy attempting to establish a trading station at Otọrughiẹnvwe the agent of the Niger Company based in Ase was doing a similar thing in the Isoko country. As pointed out in

---

1 C.O. 592/3, Annual Report, Central Province, 1906, p. 317.
2 John Holt Papers Box 1/6, Wood to John Holt, 9 August 1906.
3 Ibid. I have not been able to find a report to the effect that the Ughiẹnvwe station was actually opened. The Ughiẹnvwe elders say, however, that the firm regularly sent a 'barge' to their town. This barge was towed to Frukana when fully loaded with produce.

the last chapter, most of the trade of the Isoko area was directed towards Ase and Patani in the days of the Royal Niger Company. When the company lost its charter and became merely a trading concern, this flow of trade was not interrupted. At Patani the Niger Company was soon in competition with John Holt and Company. Even at Asaba-Ase which had been a Niger Company stronghold, John Holt was to appear too. In order therefore to secure more effectively the trade of the Isoko area, Mr. J. P. Dunn of the Niger Company established the first trading station in Isokoland proper at Ivọrọgbọ in 1908. Dunn undertook a tour of the Isoko area (very much like what Wood had done in the other part of Urhoboland) and from Ivọrọgbọ visited Ozọrọ, Oleh and adjacent towns.[1] Ivọrọgbọ only some twelve miles from Ase, was to become a busy trading station to which a fair amount of the produce of Isoko went. Even people from as far away as Ughelli and Okpare were known to attend Ivọrọgbọ market.

This development of trade and trade routes had its effect on the trade of Itsẹkiri middlemen. First, as for the Isoko section of the country there was little or no Itsẹkiri interest at this time, though a few Itsẹkiri traders later settled at Ivọrọgbọ where they bought produce from the Isoko at the local market and then sold to the Niger Company at their station there. Most of the people, however, took their produce direct to the Niger Company at Ivọrọgbọ or Patani. Hence now, as earlier, there was little or no Itsẹkiri influence over this area.

With regard to the rest of Urhoboland, the Itsẹkiri continued in their role as carriers, though doing diminishing business as more and more Urhobo were by 1906 carrying their own produce to the various stations where the European firms were established. As the road transport system became more developed, so the Urhobo became more and more their own carriers, using bicycles which became very popular and constituted an index of affluence very much like the Itsẹkiri trade canoes of an earlier period; and so the Itsẹkiri had less of the produce passing through their hands; but this took over a decade to develop. As Warri and Sapẹlẹ remained the chief trading stations, so the Itsẹkiri remained the leading

---

1 J. W. Welch: 'An African Tribe in Transition', *International Review of Missions*, Vol. XX, 1931, p. 563.

middlemen. The old disputes between them and the Urhobo and Kwalẹ continued very much as before, except that new solutions were found for them. In 1905 for instance, the perennial question of prices came up again. The Urhobo and Kwalẹ felt that the Itsẹkiri to whom they sold their oil and kernels were not paying them a fair price. The reaction to such a situation in the earlier days would have been to stop production till the prices were put up. Under the new circumstances, the Native Council at Sapẹlẹ met and fixed a minimum price for both oil and kernels. This price was to be subject to revision every month to meet local and foreign price fluctuations.[1] One source of constant friction between the Urhobo producers in the interior and the Itsẹkiri at the coast in past years was thus avoided and regularized.

The British penetration of Urhoboland had another consequence for Itsẹkiri-Urhobo relations. After the fall of Nana, it was the policy of the British Government to encourage Itsẹkiri traders to continue their custom of settling at the waterside of Urhobo towns and carrying on their trade from there. Thus at Okpara waterside, Ukhuokori waterside and other riverain areas the Itsẹkiri settled as traders, buying the produce from the Urhobo and taking this down to the European stations. When the Itsẹkiri moved into Urhobo areas it does not appear that any formal agreement was reached regarding the land on which they settled. The casual manner in which the settlements grew up was typical of the prevailing attitude towards land as already explained.[2] It has been suggested by some British administrative officers that the Urhobo dared not question the right of the Itsẹkiri to settle as they did, because they looked up to the Itsẹkiri to defend them against slave raids.[3] This was scarcely true. During the Nana régime, his agents settled in Urhobo areas and yet slave raiding went on. The real explanation, now as earlier, was that the settlement of the Itsẹkiri in Urhoboland served a practical commercial purpose: it saved many of the Urhobo from travelling to the European firms in Warri, Sapẹlẹ or Ganagana before they could sell their produce.

However convenient such an arrangement might have been from

---

1 C.O. 520/31, Egerton to C.O., No. 258, 22 June 1905.
2 Supra, p. 132.
3 C.S.O. 26/2 File 11857 Vol. VIII, Annual Report, Warri Province, 1929.

the purely commercial viewpoint, it did, nevertheless, raise certain problems. Disputes arose now and again like that in 1902 at Okpara, which required the personal intervention of the District Commissioner, Sapęlę.[1] When Native Courts began to be established, these Itsękiri settlers were allowed to send representatives to sit on the courts of the areas in which they lived. This was to be resented by the Urhobo and to lead to bickerings and dissatisfaction which will be discussed in their proper place.[2]

A number of enactments was necessary to meet the requirements of the penetration era. Directly connected with the question of penetration was the Slave Dealing Proclamation of 1901 which made it illegal to indulge in buying or selling human beings or aiding in the process.[3] As slavery and the traffic in slaves constituted one of those customs on which the British frowned, this enactment was, from their point of view, of great significance as people could now be more definitely charged with breaking the law. Even more important was the long term effect of this enactment on the relations between the Itsękiri and the Urhobo. It has been pointed out, in an earlier chapter, that the possession of Urhobo slaves by the Itsękiri has been used as one argument to support a claim of Itsękiri domination of, and overlordship over, the Urhobo people. Although the enactment of the above law did not immediately put an end, once and for all, to slave dealing, yet it was to do so within the period covered by this work. Thus, one avenue through which Itsękiri claims of superiority and overlordship could be driven was eventually closed.

Another important enactment was the Roads and Creeks Proclamation of 1903.[4] This ordinance put the responsibility for maintaining the roads and creeks on the elders of the towns and villages through which these ran. As the opening of roads was one of the main concerns of the British administration, this ordinance was important in providing a means for the accomplishment of this aim. While there was some basis for such an enactment in traditional usage,[5] it did tend to produce occasional dissatisfaction. Sometimes

1 See p. 150.   2 See Chapter 5.
3 C.O. 591/1, Proclamation No. 5 of 1901.
4 C.O. 588/1, Proclamation No. 15 of 1903.
5 See the duties of the *Evrawa* age-grade in Chapter 1, pp. 15–16.

people were called upon to work on roads and creeks for rather long periods, and at times inconvenient to them. The provision for a fine for failure to keep roads under repair also produced occasional grumbling. Yet with the funds available and the pressing need for roads to connect village to village and clan to clan, some measure like the above ordinance was called for. If in some places, and on certain occasions, the ordinance led to 'forced labour' and ugly incidents like the Crewe-Read affair,[1] these only demonstrated that like most enactments, the proclamation was open to abuse.

It was under the provisions of this proclamation that the development of roads in this area was first taken in hand. Great emphasis was placed on the maintenance of roads as this was necessary not only for trade purposes, but to enable the people to know more of their fellow countrymen. In 1896 work began on a road between Warri and Sapẹlẹ.[2] It took many years before the road was completed, but by 1911 it was reported that a light car could use it. In 1904, while the road was still only a track, seven chiefs of towns along it were arrested and fined for failure to keep their respective sections under repair. Apart from this major road, other minor roads received constant attention. In 1904 there was a road linking Gbogidi to Okpare.[3] In 1906 the people began cutting a road from Sapẹlẹ to link up with Kwalẹ.[4] In addition to the Kwalẹ road referred to above, another road was being built to connect Sapẹlẹ to Agbor, and another from Ugharefe ('Warifi') to Sakpoba. In the Kwalẹ District a road was being built from Okpara to the boundary of the Warri district, while within Agbọn clan, another road ten miles long was under construction to link Ukhuokori Waterside to Ukhuokori Inland.[5] In the Isoko area similar work was being done, although here the annual floods were a constant

---

1 The Crewe-Read affair is discussed by S. M. (now T. N.) Tamuno: *The Development of British Administrative control of Southern Nigeria, 1900-1912* (thesis submitted to University of London, October 1962), pp. 236-9.

2 F.O. 2/100, Copland-Crawford to Moor, No. 5, 22 January 1896.

3 Govt. Gazette No. 10, June 30, 1904, p. 187: Quarterly Report, Warri District, January-March 1904.

4 C.S.O. 1/19 Vol. IV, Annual Report, Central Province, 1906.

5 Supplement to Southern Nigeria Government Gazette 30 September 1908, pp. iv-ix: Annual Report on Roads Construction in the Central Provinces, 1907.

menace which rendered the building of roads a much less effective and satisfying affair. By present standards these roads were no more than tracks but they served the immediate purpose for which they were designed. By 1911 it was reported: 'It is now possible to motor in a light car from Warri to Sapẹlẹ, Benin-City, Kwalẹ, Agbor and Asaba on the west side of the Niger.'[1]

The linking up of various places by road was of definite commercial and social significance. As far as the relations between the Urhobo and their Itsẹkiri neighbours were concerned, the construction of roads had the effect of enabling the Urhobo to get in touch with centres of administration and commerce. So, as the years wore on and communications by water and land improved, the Urhobo depended less and less on the Itsẹkiri to bring manufactured goods to their markets. The Urhobo realized this early. Commenting on the significance of the Sapẹlẹ-Kwalẹ road, Mr. F. S. James, who was Provincial Commissioner for the Central Province, remarked that the people already appreciated

> being able to get down to the trading centres, where they may either trade or obtain employment rather than have to depend on a middleman's canoe.[2]

The opening up of communications therefore had the effect of ending the comparative isolation of the bulk of the Urhobo from what were regarded as centres of civilization and progress. With the end of this comparative isolation began an era in which the Urhobo was to shed that feeling of dependence on the Itsẹkiri coast dweller for the supply of European manufactured goods, and that respect towards the Itsẹkiri for being very close to the white man. This changed attitude was to lead to the growth of a new type of relationship between the two neighbouring peoples.

One more aspect of the penetration of Urhoboland remains to be discussed, that is the coming of missionaries to the area. In the areas immediately to the hinterland of the government stations of Warri and Sapẹlẹ, missionary endeavour began in earnest during the second phase of the administrative penetration, that is, in the opening years of this century. In the Isoko sector and the more

---

1 Cd. 6007–35, Colonial Reports—Annual: S. Nigeria, 1911, p. 28.
2 Cd. 372–18, Colonial Reports—Annual: Colony and Protectorate of Southern Nigeria, 1906, p. 77.

remote Urhobo areas, real missionary work did not begin till about 1913, when the British had all but established their administrative control over the country. The missionary effort was directed from three different bases: Warri, Sapẹlẹ and Patani. The Warri and Sapẹlẹ aspect was under the superintendence of the Niger Delta Pastorate Church, a more or less independent section of the work of the Niger Mission. Patani was immediately under the Niger Mission, and so the missionary work which at the beginning was directed from there was regarded as being directly under the purview of the Niger Mission.

The first recorded attempt by the Niger Mission at evangelization in the Itsẹkiri-Urhobo area was in 1875, when Bishop Crowther accompanied by his son, the archdeacon, visited Olomu, Nana's father, in the Benin River, and asked for permission to open a mission station. Olomu, suspicious of the effect Christianity might have on the customs and traditions of his people, refused to be persuaded,[1] and the idea of a mission station was dropped for over fifteen years. With the establishment of the Niger Coast Protectorate there were renewed efforts at establishing mission stations in this area. In 1893 the C.M.S. Committee in England was informed that 'Captain Harper, the Consul at Warri', earnestly begged for a missionary to be sent into the district.[2] In 1898 Bishop Tugwell put the plea of the British and other traders in the Warri district for a missionary before the Parent Committee of the C.M.S.[3] Apparently, this Committee was not prepared to extend the sphere of its ministration and apart from a grudging consent to Bishop Tugwell's proposal that the Reverend Henry Proctor, superintendent of the Ijọ district of the Niger Mission, be allowed to pay occasional visits to the Warri area,[4] nothing more effective was immediately done.

Bishop Tugwell would not, however, be so easily shaken off. In 1899 he again addressed himself to the Parent Committee. He pointed out that the power of the Oba of Benin had been

1 C.M.S. Papers, CA/013; D. C. Crowther: 'A Missionary Trip to the Benin River', October–November 1875.
2 G3. A3/06, Hill to Wigram, No. 21, 2 January 1893.
3 G3. A3/07, Tugwell to Baylis No. 79, 14 April 1898.
4 A3/P1–6, Resolution passed by C.M.S. Committee in London, 6 June 1898.

broken two years earlier, and argued that it was necessary to introduce Christianity into the surrounding area if the people were not to return to a worse form of idolatory. He suggested that Benin be made a mission centre.[1] The Niger Mission did not, however, take over the Benin work. It was given to the Niger Delta Pastorate Church under the supervision of Bishop James Johnson. Sapẹlẹ and Warri were created sub-districts of Benin and missionary penetration of the area began in earnest in 1902.[2]

From Warri and Sapẹlẹ the work was carried into the Urhobo areas immediately to the hinterland. The organization of this endeavour was at the beginning necessarily rudimentary. The work was done by volunteers and a few Yoruba agents—'Bishop Johnson's men'—who were sent into the Urhobo country. Very little effective evangelization could be carried out in the circumstances, the Yoruba agents being unable to speak Urhobo, and such translation as was done, being done in the Itsẹkiri language by local lads who happened to have picked up a smattering of that language. Ukhuokori in Agbọn clan was the most important centre from which a 'Johnson man' operated.[3] The agent from Ukhuokori was supposed to supervise the 'church' in that town and the 'Christian' communities that were springing up in surrounding areas like Evbreni, Okpare and Ughelli. On the whole, little attention was paid to the Urhobo areas in the years before 1914. More effective work was done in Warri and Sapẹlẹ and the areas within a five-mile radius of these towns, like Ẹvhrọ (Effurun) and Amukpẹ. This was because in these centres educated men in the employ of government or commercial houses offered their services to the young and struggling churches.[4] It was not, in fact, till Warri and Sapẹlẹ became full-fledged missionary centres with resident priests that the work which had been started earlier began to be really consolidated, and this was

---

1 G3. A3/08, Tugwell to Baylis, No. 168, 12 December 1899.
2 G3. A3/09, Bishop Johnson's Presidential Address—Third Conference Niger Delta Church, 23 January 1904.
3 Niger Mission Papers: Attachment to No. 80 of 1913: 'Report of an Itineration in the Agabo Country, February 8th to June 23rd 1913', by Rev. J. D. Aitken.
4 Niger Mission Papers: No. 110 of 1904: 'A Report of a Missionary Journey Within and Beyond the Southern Nigeria British Protectorate', by Bishop Johnson.

not till 1920 when Warri and Sapẹlẹ were placed under the Yoruba Mission.[1]

The missionary penetration of the Isoko country was directed from Patani. Patani was, for the Isoko of Ẹrohwa, Umẹ, Igbide and Ẹnwẹ clans, one of the biggest markets where both the Niger Company and John Holt had stations. It was through commercial contract with Patani that the Isoko got to hear of Christianity.[2] In 1911 Proctor reported that the Isoko were visiting Patani in large numbers and attending Church there. Proctor suggested that a missionary be definitely assigned to these people as they spoke a language different from Ijọ.[3] In 1913 the Executive Committee of the Niger Mission specifically commissioned the Reverend J. D. Aitken, who was attached to the Patani station, to undertake an itineration of the Isoko country.[4] In the years 1913 and 1914 Aitken, the pioneer missionary in the Isoko country, undertook extensive tours of the area, visiting Igbide (which was in these years the centre from which Aitken operated), Ẹmede, Oleh, Uzere, Olomoro, Owe, Uwherun, Evbreni and some of the towns in which 'Johnson's men' laboured. He reported that he was enthusiastically received wherever he went, though it was too early to say how well Christianity would flourish among the Isoko.[5] Here, as in the Urhobo areas, not much could be done in these first years until more staff could be found. But in 1914 the C.M.S. definitely agreed to create an Isoko district and to carry on, under the Niger Mission, the work begun by the Rev. Aitken.[6] From that time till now the C.M.S. has been of very great service to the Isoko people.

The real importance of the missionary penetration of Urhoboland

---

1 *Proceedings of the C.M.S.*, 1918–19, p. 27.
2 Rev. J. W. Welch gives an account of how an Itsẹkiri native court clerk, Mr. Eda Oruẹdon who had heard Bishop Johnson and his men preach Christianity in Warri and Benin, introduced the new faith to the people of Uzere where he was working in 1909—J. W. Welch: 'An African Tribe in Transition', pp. 568–9.
3 Niger Mission Papers: Enclosure in No. 44 of 1911: H. Proctor to Editor, *C.M.S. Gazette*, 29 April 1911.
4 Niger Mission Papers: No. 24 of 1913: Minutes of the Niger Mission Executive Committee, January 1913.
5 Attachment to No. 80 of 1913: J. D. Aitken's Report already cited.
6 G3. A3/013 No. 45 of 1914, Minutes of the Niger Mission Executive Committee, July 1914.

lay not so much in the number of people who claimed to have 'thrown away their jujus', as in the education which the missions took to the people. 'Education in Isoko', wrote the Rev. J. W. Welch 'has been the hand maid of the church'.[1] This, very true for Isoko, has been true of all Urhoboland. This aspect of missionary work was even the more important because in this area no 'government' schools were opened throughout the period covered by this work, and Native Administration schools were not established till the 1930s. The C.M.S. has therefore been to the fore in the matter of education. The thirst for education was felt from the very beginning. J. D. Aitken in his report already cited claimed that everywhere he went, the people asked for schools to be built for their children. The C.M.S. began its educational work early. A school was opened at Sapẹlẹ in 1902 and at Warri in 1903.[2] In the hinterland, however, it was not till the 1920s that regular schools were to be established. In the meantime all that could be done was itinerant teaching by the few available and poorly qualified teachers.[3] The missionary effort was welcome, not so much because of the salvation it brought to men's souls, as for the practical use to which its educational achievements could be put. The position was neatly summarized in 1915:

> Heathen people are ready to subscribe the money necessary to support a school teacher. The conscious need for the Gospel though it is shown occasionally, it most frequently obscured by the demand for education. Our religious instruction is tolerated and accepted because it is compulsory and is a means of the acquiring of English, the language of trade, the law courts, and government administration.[4]

The Government itself established schools only at the government and commercial centres: Warri and Sapẹlẹ, Aboh and Ase.[5] In the schools at Warri and Sapẹlẹ, the majority of the pupils were Itsẹkiri

1 Welch: 'An African Tribe in Transition', p. 570.
2 G3. A3/09 No. 99 of 1904, Bishop Johnson's Presidential Address—Third Conference of the Nigeria Delta Church, 23 January 1904.
3 See Chapter 6 for some discussion of later missionary work in the field of education.
4 *Proceedings of the C.M.S.*, 1914–15, p. 43.
5 Cd. 2238–10, Colonial Reports, Annual, No. 433, S. Nigeria, 1903 p. 26, and Cd. 2684–4, Colonial Reports, Annual, No. 459, S. Nigeria, 1904, p. 27.

and children of other Nigerian peoples working in the commercial houses and government departments. With the opening of schools in the Urhobo country by the C.M.S., and the development of road communications, the Urhobo gradually began to pay more attention to education. The result was that by the 1920s the Urhobo were producing young men educated enough to compete with the Itsẹkiri and other Nigerian peoples for jobs in the various provincial establishments.

A few conclusions, significant for Itsẹkiri-Urhobo relations, can be drawn from the above account of the British penetration of Urhoboland. As has been shown, the penetration was in two definite phases. The first phase began shortly before the fall of Nana and ended shortly before the fall of the Ọba of Benin. These two events had their effects on the attitude of the Urhobo to the coming of the British. Nana was known to have been a very powerful chief. The power that defeated Nana had to be a great power. The Ọba of Benin was regarded with awe and veneration because of his former suzerain power and the superhuman attributes associated with him. Yet the British had the better of him. These two British victories must have filled the Urhobo with wonder and fear. But it is easy to exaggerate the influences of these victories on the Urhobo. Thus, it has been argued that with the capture by the British of Nana and the Ọba of Benin, the Urhobo people had no choice but to submit to them when they (the British) began penetrating into Urhoboland.[1] The events so far described show clearly that the Urhobo submission was more apparent than real in the years before 1910. Not only did some of the people positively refuse to accept the new régime until they were forced to bow to superior force (a mere show of force being sufficient for this purpose) but, all through the years of penetration, the people put up a stout even if passive resistance to the new order. This sort of opposition was, in the event, more difficult to combat than active hostility which could have been more easily met by armed force. The British penetration of Urhoboland was far from easy.

While the British were busy bringing Urhoboland under their administrative control, nothing spectacular was happening in

---

1 A. Salubi: 'The Establishment of British Rule in Urhoboland', p. 199.

Itsẹkiriland. There was therefore, a striking difference in the respective reaction of the Itsẹkiri and the Urhobo to the British administration during the years of penetration. While the Urhobo naturally
found it hard to accept the new control which the British sought to
impose, the Itsẹkiri, with a longer tradition of association with the
British, were far less restive. There were good reasons for this.
First of all, the Itsẹkiri had learnt from bitter experience that they
were geographically placed in such a way that the British navy could
be effectively used against them should they prove difficult. Besides,
the Itsẹkiri were only settling down to normal life after the disturbances connected with the Ebrohimi expedition of 1894 and the
Benin expedition of 1897. The removal of Nana was not only a
potent display of British might, but a happy event for those Itsẹkiri
traders who had feared his power and envied his commercial
success. Similarly the Itsẹkiri stood to gain from the fall of the
Ọba of Benin. As early as 1892 Gallwey complained of the 'heavy
tax' which the Itsẹkiri had to pay in the areas controlled by the
Ọba before they were allowed to trade, and came to the conclusion
that it would 'be necessary to break down the Benin king's rule'.[1]
Commercial self-interest therefore disposed the Itsẹkiri to welcome
the break-up of the power of the Ọba of Benin. It was understandable
in these circumstances for the Itsẹkiri to accept the power that had
rid them of the 'over-mighty' Governor of the River, and the
dreaded Ọba of Benin. This Itsẹkiri acceptance of the British, in
contrast to the Urhobo intransigence of which the administrative
officers complained, won for the Itsẹkiri, at least for the time being,
the favour of the British administration. It was not till the 1920s
that under changed conditions the Itsẹkiri were to begin to resent
certain policies of the British administration.[2] In the meantime
they enjoyed the goodwill of the British administration.

Not only did the Itsẹkiri find themselves in a position in which
prudence demanded that they accept British control, but they also
found themselves playing a useful role in the British penetration
of the Urhobo hinterland. As the Itsẹkiri were already familiar with
Urhoboland, it was possible for the British to employ them as

---

1 F.O. 2/51, Report on the Benin District Oil Rivers Protectorate for the Year
  ending 31 July 1892—Enclosure in Macdonald to F.O., 12 January 1893.
2 See Chapter 6.

guides, messengers and interpreters. Furthermore, the main aim behind the opening up of the interior was the development of the trade of the protectorate. As the Itsękiri were the leading traders in this part of the protectorate during these years, it was natural that the British should have used them in their bid to develop and increase the trade of the Benin River and Warri Districts. Thus leading Itsękiri traders were made to accompany various British patrols and visiting teams in the hope that they would make contacts with the hinterland producers which would be in the overall interests of trade.[1] As the European firms only began to establish branch 'factories' in the Urhobo hinterland about 1908, it was a matter of some importance for the British to encourage the Itsękiri to tap the produce of Urhoboland more effectively. There can be little doubt that in this regard, the Itsękiri contributed a great deal to the development of the commerce of this part of the protectorate.

Itsękiri activity in Urhoboland during this era has given rise to the claim by British political officers who served in the area at a later date, that 'it was by means of Itsękiri influence that the neighbouring Sobo clans were brought under control'.[2] One other factor which contributed to this claim being made was the general belief that all the British political agents who operated in Urhoboland were Itsękiri. In fact, of the three such agents who served in the area only Dǫghǫ was Itsękiri, and until about 1912 he was responsible only for the Benin River District, a purely Itsękiri area. Of the other two, Tom Fallodun was a Yoruba whose area of service was the Abraka and Agbǫn clans. The third, George Eyubę, described by a British political officer as 'an influential Jekri',[3] was in fact of mixed parentage, his father being Urhobo and his mother Itsękiri. While the services rendered by these political agents must have facilitated British penetration of the Urhobo hinterland, it will be stretching the point to argue that it was through their influence that Urhoboland was brought under British control. The decisive factors in this regard were clearly British military patrols and the frequent visits of British political officers.

---

1 Supra, pp. 140 and 152.
2 C.S.O. 26/2 File 11857 Vol. IX, Annual Report, Warri Province, 1931, p. 21.
3 C.S.O. 26 File 26770, Intelligence Report on Olomu Clan, p. 18.

Yet the above claim is important for Itsẹkiri-Urhobo relations. In a sense, the claim was a mark of British gratitude for the role played by the Itsẹkiri during the years of penetration. Not only was this gratitude not forfeited for a long time, it also disposed the British to favour the Itsẹkiri in times of Itsẹkiri-Urhobo conflict.[1] More important, however, is the fact that over the years, the Itsẹkiri themselves did tend to believe and amplify the claim made for them, and to see themselves as the agency through which Urhoboland was 'opened up'. The questioning of both the claim and the belief by the Urhobo in the thirties of this century was to generate considerable tension between them and the Itsẹkiri.[2]

Finally, by 1914, when British penetration of Urhoboland can be said to have been completed, Itsẹkiri-Urhobo relations were undergoing a silent revolution brought about by the resulting developments: improved land and water communications, the establishment by the European firms of branch 'factories' in Urhoboland, and the spread of education which followed missionary activity among the Urhobo people. Until now the Itsẹkiri (because of their position at the coast, and their contact with the European traders and British administrative officers) had been the suppliers of slaves to the European dealers, had controlled the greater part of the Urhobo palm produce trade, were the main channel through which the Urhobo obtained European manufactured goods, and supplied the guides, interpreters and messengers needed by the British in their Urhoboland campaign. As a result, they had acquired an importance and reputation for loyalty and service to the British government, out of proportion to their comparatively small numbers. Now this importance gradually began to diminish, as the Urhobo to the hinterland grew less isolated from European commerce and influence as a result of British penetration, and became, in many ways, rivals to their Itsẹkiri neighbours. This changed situation was to lead to new developments in Itsẹkiri-Urhobo relations in the years ahead.

---

1 See Chapter 5.
2 This question is discussed in Chapter 6.

Chapter 5
The native court system and the career of Chief Dogho, 1900–25

British political penetration of the hinterland of Southern Nigeria was accompanied by the establishment of 'Native Courts'. These courts, as will be shown, were not only expected to serve as tribunals of justice, but were also regarded as the local executive arms of the central government. It was therefore not surprising that in 1900, at the beginning of the last phase of the effective subjugation of the hinterland by the British, Sir Ralph Moor, the High Commissioner, should have promulgated the Native Courts Proclamation, 1900, replaced by a similar proclamation the next year.[1] These proclamations formally inaugurated the native court system in Itsẹkiri and Urhoboland, as elsewhere.

It should be pointed out, however, that these proclamations merely legalized institutions which were already in existence. From the time Europeans first began to build 'factories' on land along the Niger Delta, the need was felt for some authority that could settle disputes not only among the Nigerian peoples but also between them and the white traders. The European traders, in particular, desired some authority among the Nigerians sufficiently powerful to settle disputes before these led to strife, trade stoppage and general unrest. The establishment of 'Courts of Equity' and later of 'Governing Councils' at various points along the Delta was designed to satisfy the above desire, at a time when consular administration consisted solely of chance visits in a gun boat, and when the consular establishment was such that one solitary figure was expected to keep control over hundreds of miles of the Niger Delta.[2]

Courts of Equity and Governing Councils situated at chosen centres along the coast might have fulfilled the purposes for which

---

1 Cal. Prof. 10/2 Vol. I, 'Native Courts Proclamation, 1900' (No. 9 of 1900). C.O. 588/1, 'The Native Courts Proclamation, 1901' (No. 25 of 1901).
2 F.O. 84/1881, Johnston to F.O., No. 12 (Africa), 16 March 1888.

168

they were established. Yet at best they were only suited to a period when the British Government had not made up its mind to extend its sway into the coastal hinterland. The establishment of the Oil Rivers Protectorate (later Niger Coast Protectorate), ushered in a new era which called for new and more efficient instruments of administration. Sir Claude Macdonald, the first Consul-General, did not immediately inaugurate a system of native courts. Rather, he set up what were known as 'Consular Courts' at those centres where vice-consulates were established in 1891. In the area covered by this work, there were thus two consular courts: at Warri and at the Benin River. No administrative records about the working of these courts have come to light. But Harold Bindloss, writing about them, states that the Nigerian peoples willingly sent their offenders and criminals to be tried by the consular courts, which consisted of the vice-consul or his assistant as sole judge. An interpreter translated the evidence into what Bindloss in characteristic style describes as 'fantastic English'. The commonest charges were wife-snatching, child stealing, slave dealing, firing at trade canoes and attempted murder.[1]

According to Dr. Tamuno, there was doubt as to the legality of these courts. Macdonald's and Moor's desire for 'elucidation' on this point did not call forth any response from the Foreign Office.[2] Nevertheless, the courts continued to function. By 1896 new courts, which consisted of Nigerian people sitting as judges, had already been started. Thus there were 'Native Councils' at Warri and Benin River and was what described as a 'Native Court' at Abraka.[3] It should be stated at this point that, so far as evidence at present available indicates, no effort was made to pattern these native councils and courts along traditional lines in the respective areas. The court members were invariably the leading middlemen traders, whose antecedents were not scrutinized by the British authorities. Where there was an obvious ruling group some of the members of

---

1 Bindloss, op. cit., p. 145. The consular court at the Benin River was transferred to Sapẹlẹ in 1893 when a vice consulate was opened in the latter place.
2 S. M. Tamuno, op. cit., p. 60.
3 *Southern Nigeria Government Gazette*, No. 8, 30 March 1905, pp. 192–5. A full list of all the early native courts is given. The list shows the dates of establishment, names of members and the 'places' these members represented.

these courts were no doubt drawn from it. Where there was no such obvious group, no special effort was made to discover how the people concerned ordered their political and social life with a view to forming the courts on a similar pattern. The preoccupation was with finding *some* rather than *the* authority that could settle disputes.

The Benin River Council was exclusively an Itsẹkiri tribunal with jurisdiction only over Itsẹkiri settlements. The Warri Native Council however, had jurisdiction over Itsẹkiri as well as over a number of Urhobo settlements—Effurun, Tori, Efuruntor, Mọgba, Asagba, Agbassa, Adeji, Ogbe-Sobo (Aladja).[1] Apart from the Abraka court no other court was sited in the Urhobo hinterland in this pre-1900 period, despite the fact that treaties had been concluded with a number of Urhobo towns by 1896. It is not known for certain what were the factors which guided the British administrative officers in their choice of court members for the Warri Native Court at this stage. Although the court was expected to serve a number of Urhobo settlements, there was not a single Urhobo on the 'bench' of the court: of the sixteen members in 1896, fifteen were Itsẹkiri and one Ijọ.[2] From the predominance of Itsẹkiri members one can only conclude that the British appointed to the court those with whom they were already familiar, namely, the Itsẹkiri at the coast. It was impossible for the British to have selected members from some of the Urhobo settlements like Mọgba, Adeje and Efuruntor, for it must be remembered that in 1896 the British penetration of Urhoboland had hardly begun. Effurun was burnt down in 1894 during the Nana episode, and it was probably felt that the people were still too anti-British to react favourably to British sponsored native courts. It will therefore be unfair to suggest that the British deliberately subjected the Urhobo to an Itsẹkiri dominated court. Nevertheless, the issue of Urhobo attendance at the Warri Native Court was to lead to considerable Urhobo agitation in the years ahead.

The proclamations legalized the two sets of courts (Native Councils and Minor Courts) already in existence. Native Councils were to be presided over by the District Commissioners who could appoint deputies to act for them in their absence. These deputies

1 Ibid.   2 Ibid.

had to be European officials.[1] The presidents of the Minor Courts were to be selected by the members on a three-month rotational basis. Members of the Court were to be appointed by the High Commissioner or his representative. Once so appointed they could not be removed from office without 'the special sanction of the High Commissioner'.

The courts were to administer 'native laws and customs not opposed to natural morality and humanity', and any new laws or modifications of old laws sanctioned by the government.[2] They were to have jurisdiction over such criminal and civil cases to which 'native law' applied, and in which all the parties concerned were natives. Non-natives could, by their own consent, be tried by these native courts.[3]

Clause XII of the 1901 Proclamation set it down:

> Where a Native Court is established in any district the civil and criminal jurisdiction of such court shall as respects natives be exclusive of all other native jurisdictions in such districts, and no jurisdiction shall be exercised in such district by any other native authority whatsoever.[4]

This clause rendered illegal the judicial powers which the village councils as well as various age grades had been accustomed to exercise until that time. As the courts were also to be regarded as executive organs, this same clause rendered illegal, in practice if not in law, the executive powers of the traditional institutions as well. This provision made the new system highly unpopular with the majority of the people.

The Native Councils had wider powers than the Minor Courts. In civil cases the former could try personal suits involving damage, debt, demand; or suits over land held under 'native tenure'; or suits involving succession to the goods of a deceased person; provided that these different types of suits did not involve money or goods valued at more than £200 sterling. Minor Courts could try similar cases where the money or value of goods involved did not

---

1 Cal. Prof. 10/2, Vol. I, 'Native Courts Proclamation 1900' Clause X.
2 Ibid. The clauses to which references has so far been made are IV–VII.
3 C.O. 588/1, 'The Native Courts Proclamation, 1901' Clause XI (This provision was made subject to such other provisions as were contained in the proclamation.)
4 Ibid., Clause XII.

exceed £25 (except in the case of goods of a deceased person, which goods could be worth as much as £50). The defendant had always to be resident in the district over which the court trying him had jurisdiction. In criminal cases the native councils had authority to try offences committed, wholly or in part, within their respective districts, for which the punishment could be:

(i) imprisonment for a term not exceeding two years with or without flogging not exceeding fifteen strokes;
(ii) imprisonment for a term not exceeding one year with or without hard labour, and a fine not exceeding £100;
(iii) a fine not exceeding £100.

The minor courts could try similar cases where the punishment could be:

(i) imprisonment not exceeding six months with or without hard labour, with or without flogging not exceeding fifteen strokes;
(ii) imprisonment for a term not exceeding three months, with or without hard labour, and a fine not exceeding £25;
(iii) a fine not exceeding £50.[1]

Appeals lay from the minor court to the Native Council, and from there to the Supreme Court. Where the debt, damage or claim ordered to be paid, or the fine imposed did not exceed £50, or where the term of imprisonment was not longer than three months, there could be no appeal. The Supreme Court decision was final. The District Commissioner was granted general powers to transfer cases from the native courts to the Supreme Court, acting in his discretion. A case could also be transferred to the Supreme Court if a defendant applied to, and secured the approval of, the District Commissioner for such a transfer.[2]

The proclamation provided for a fine of £50 on any unauthorized persons who sat as court members. Anyone who sought to influence the decision of the court in favour of himself or any party to a suit was liable to a fine not exceeding £100, or imprisonment for two years. The High Commissioner reserved to himself the right to

1 Ibid. See Clauses XIII–XVI.
2 Ibid., Clauses XXX–XXXII and XXXIV.

dismiss any court members for misdemeanour, provided such members were given an opportunity to defend themselves before being dismissed.[1]

In 1903 an amendment proclamation was issued. The District Commissioner was by this proclamation made a member of all native courts in his district.[2] This was important because it meant that whenever the District Commissioner sat on any of the minor courts, he conferred on such courts by that very act, the jurisdiction of a native council, and could hear appeals against decisions of the minor courts. The Assistant District Commissioner was, by another amendment, enabled to sit on, and act as president of, any minor court in his district in the absence of the District Commissioner. The District Commissioner was further empowered to appoint as vice-president any member of any native court nominated by such tribunal, and subject to the High Commissioner's approval. Such a vice-president acted for the District Commissioner and his assistant in their absence. Another provision conferred on the minor courts equal jurisdiction with the native councils in civil cases.[3]

The Native Courts Proclamation of 1906, which was issued on the amalgamation of the Protectorate of Southern Nigeria and the Colony of Lagos, did not materially alter his provisions of the earlier ones. There was, however, one important innovation: the High Commissioner was empowered to appoint any member of any native court to be the president of such a court.[4] This was the first time that such a provision was made. These were the provisions which guided the working of the native court system until 1914.

Between 1900 and May 1906, nine minor courts were opened in Urhoboland. These courts were those of Gbogidi, Ajareyubẹ (Agbarho) and Okpare which were opened in 1900; that at Sapẹlẹ which was probably constituted between 1901 and 1902; and those of Okpara, Abraka Jeremi (Ughiẹnvwe), Ughelle and Uzere which were opened in 1904. In addition to these courts, three others not in Urhobo or Isoko territory proper served various sections of the

---

1 Ibid. See Clauses XLI–XLIII.
2 C.O. 588/1, 'The Native Courts Amendment Proclamation' (No. 17 of 1903) Clause 3.
3 Ibid. See Clause 4(1)—4(3) and 5.
4 C.O. 588/2, 'The Native Courts Proclamation, 1906' (No. 7 of 1906).

Urhobo and Isoko people. These were the Ase court which Isoko people from the Aviara and Ivọrọgbọ areas attended; the Patani court which served Ẹrohwa and Umẹ clans, and the Frukama court which served part of Ughiẹnvwe clan.[1] The native councils of Benin River and Warri continued to function and to exercise their jurisdiction as previously described. In 1903, as a result of a tour of inspection and reorganization, Mr. Justice Menendez decided to convert the minor court at Sapẹlẹ to a native council with effect from 10 October that year. In November, a native council was similarly established at Ase.[2]

It would appear that in these years the administration was unwilling to open many courts in this area. In pre-British days, the Urhobo clan was self-sufficient in matters of justice and mode of government. With the new régime, and in view of the clause in the Native Courts Proclamation which rendered traditional tribunals illegal, a number of clans found that they had to travel outside their own clans in order to be able to attend court. Many of the thirty-two 'places' under the jurisdiction of the Ajareyubẹ native court were outside the confines of that clan. Ewu, Iyede and Ughelle had to attend the Okpare court till they got their own courts. Part of the Ughiẹnvwe clan attended court at Gbogidi before a court was opened in their clan, while part continued to go to Frukama even after a court was established at Otọrughiẹnvwe. The Uzere court served most of the Isoko towns. If the arrangements depicted above had the long term advantage of bringing the various Urhobo clans closer together, this advantage was not immediately apparent. Rather, considerable dissatisfaction was felt. Those clans which had to travel outside their territory viewed with distaste a system which appeared to subject them to those clans in which the courts were situated, clans with which until then, they had dealt on nothing but terms of perfect equality. This dissatisfaction was more keenly felt by those Urhobo areas like the Uvbiẹ (Effurun) clan which had to attend an Itsẹkiri court. In later years the issue of Urhobo people attending courts over which Itsẹkiri influence was supreme was to cause considerable tension between the two ethnic groups.

The problem of siting native courts was not an easy one. From

1 *Southern Nigeria Government Gazette*, No. 8, 30 March 1905, pp. 192–5.
2 C.O. 520/18, Enclosure in Moor to C.O., No. 16, 7 January 1803.

the point of view of the administration, the decisive factor was that of efficient supervision. As an administrative officer observed, the government faced a dilemma: on the one hand, enough courts had to be established to leave no excuse for the Nigerian people's refusing to take their disputes to the courts for settlement on grounds of prohibitive distances; on the other hand, to establish courts which could not be under 'frequent European supervision' was, from the government point of view, utterly unsatisfactory.[1] It was a dilemma which was extremely difficult to resolve, especially during a period when the British administrative officers had no confidence in the ability of the 'warrant chiefs' to perform their duties efficiently, and when these chiefs, exposed to new influences, and called upon to carry out the functions of government in new ways, were finding it difficult to adjust. Indeed, it was a problem which constantly exercised the minds of the administration throughout the period covered by this study.

The establishment of native courts was regarded as a very important aspect of government policy. The courts were seen as being of immense value because they rendered 'material assistance in the control of the territories' which were only just being brought under British rule. They were also seen as a means of teaching the chiefs 'the proper methods of government and . . . the administration of justice'. The native councils were, in addition to ordinary judicial work, to be encouraged to make 'necessary native laws' for the government of the people over whom they had jurisdiction. The proceeds from court fees and fines were to be applied by the court members to the building of roads and 'other works of public utility'.[2] The courts were charged with responsibility for 'all administrative and executive work among the natives themselves, and for the furtherance of trade, education, agriculture etc., throughout the territories'.[3] From this formidable list of duties, it is clear that these tribunals were, in effect, local arms of the central government. Here in fact was the system which was later to be called indirect rule being put into practice without any of the fanfare that was to be

---

1 Supplement to Government Gazette, No. 30, June 1904, p. 180: Annual Report Western Division 1904 (Year ending 31 March).
2 Colonial Reports No. 289 (Cd. 3–12): Niger Coast Protectorate 1898–9, p. 9.
3 C.O. 520/18, Moor to C.O., No. 16, 7 January 1903.

noticeable during the Lugardian era. Now as later the impelling reason for adopting the native court or warrant chief system was the obvious inadequacy of the British staff available for the effective administration of the vast areas being rapidly brought under British rule. Admittedly some British administrative officers were inclined to argue that by adopting the above policy they were preserving the traditional systems of government of the peoples concerned.[1] As many of these officers knew little of the traditional systems in the period before 1930, they were hardly in a position to know what to preserve. Whatever good the warrant chief system did, it also undermined some of the more salient features of the traditional systems of government in this as in other parts of Nigeria. Be that as it may, because the native courts were seen as the local arms of the central government, dissatisfaction with them became tantamount not to dissatisfaction with a judicial system, but with the entire governmental set up.

The selection of those to sit on the courts was quite a problem. Among the Itsẹkiri, however, it was not very difficult to find a solution to the problem, for with them there had grown up over the years, as was pointed out earlier,[2] a group of men who were regarded by the bulk of the Itsẹkiri people as their leaders. Most of those in this group were men who had become important because of their success as traders. It is interesting to note that the early court members numbered among them most of those who signed the earlier agreements and treaties with the British, or descendants of such people.[3] Whether these men who were appointed to sit on the courts would have been so appointed had there been an Olu in the years 1900–4, it is difficult to say, for by this time many titles of nobility were unfilled and there can be no saying who would have been honoured by the Olu. The point here stressed is that the majority of the Itsẹkiri who did obtain 'warrants' to sit on Itsẹkiri courts were, in the circumstances, men who for a number of decades

1 See Anene, op. cit., p. 250.
2 See Chapter 1, pp. 42–3.
3 Awala, Fregene, Etchie, Brigby, Numa, Nesame, Ogbe, Okorofiagbe— these were among the men who signed the agreement of 1851 and the treaty of 1884. See Cal. Prof. 5/7 Vol. I and F.O. 93/6/10, Treaty with Chiefs of 'Jekri'. They or their descendants (like Dogho in place of Numa) were the most prominent court members. See Gazette No. 8, 30 March 1905, p. 195.

had been accustomed to exercising authority and influence among their people, irrespective of whether such authority was traditional in content, or acquired as a result of success in trade.

With the Urhobo the state of affairs was very different. The Urhobo had not lost their traditional system of government, nor had that system been modified as was the case in Itsẹkiriland, following on the interregnum of 1848. Thus even as the British were introducing their system, the Urhobo knew who among them performed specific duties according to their own system. The traditional system of office holding was rather complicated. It was not possible to speak of the 'rulers' of the people in the exclusive terms of the British. There was, therefore, greater suspicion of the new order in Urhoboland than in Itsẹkiriland. The *Ekpako*, *Ehǫnvwǫnrẹn*, *Ediǫ* and other title holders tended to sit back and watch the developments before committing themselves. That was why there were, among the first group of court members, people who would not have been on such tribunals under normal conditions. This is not so say, however, that even among these early court members there were no people who held positions of traditional responsibility in their respective communities. The District Commissioners did not always merely handpick anyone who had the courage not to run away on their approach.[1] In Urhoboland the earliest courts were established in places which already had some prior contact with the white man.[2] His coming to establish courts was not therefore a frightening phenomenon. Tradition has it that there was always some consultation between the District Commissioner and some at least of those, who were until that time, charged with responsibility for ruling their people. In Agbarho clan for example, the sixteen court members appointed in 1900 were said to have been chosen at a meeting in the *Osivie's* house.[3] As a result, the earliest court members included some of the most prominent men in their

1 See Anene, op. cit., p. 259. Anene rightly warns that any generalization about how the chiefs were selected is open to objection.
2 Abraka, Ajayube, Gbogidi, Okpara, Ughelle, Uzere—these places all had contact with Europeans a number of years before native courts were established in them. See Chapters 3 and 4.
3 C.S.O. 26 File 27999, Agbadu clan Intelligence Report. (The *Osivie* is the Agbarho clan head.) A similar thing happened in some of the other Urhobo clans.

respective communities: Ogharisi of Ughelle, Buluku of Oteri, Asagba of Amukpẹ, Okpalefe of Mọgba, Fekanrurhobo of Oginibo— —these were men who occupied positions of authority in their towns and villages.[1] It was only after the people had indicated their choice of court members that the District Commissioner put their names on an already prepared warrant which, on approval by the High Commissioner, constituted the legal instrument establishing the court. It was from this warrant that the members got their name of 'warrant chief' which, by 1927, had become the symbol of the opprobium in which the native courts were then held.

It should always be remembered that the opening of courts in this as in other areas was seen as a means of further consolidating British rule, and that the process was going on at the same time as the British were effecting the political subjugation of the area by means of patrols and punitive expeditions. Indeed, the native courts were the visible symbols of British rule in the rural districts. It was in connexion with these courts that the political agents appointed by the British administration performed their most useful services. As pointed out in the last chapter, the two such agents who laboured in Urhoboland proper in the pre-1914 period were Fallodun and Eyubẹ.[2] One other name which crops up in connexion with this period is that of Cheke, an Itsẹkiri, who served for a short while at Iyede.

As the use made of the Itsẹkiri by the British during the penetration of Urhoboland led to the claim that it was through Itsẹkiri influence that Urhoboland was opened up, so a number of claims have been made by, and for, the Itsẹkiri in connexion with the establishment of native courts in Urhoboland. In 1915 a certain Itsẹkiri, by name Ekeke, petitioned the Lieutenant Governor, Southern Provinces, requesting that the government pay him a subsidy for services which he had rendered to it.[3] He numbered

---

1 These names can be found on the list of 1905 to which reference has already been made. The present *Ovie* of Ughelle is the son of Ogharisi; an Okpalefe is the present *Ọtota* of Agbarho clan; Fekanrurhobo, son of the 'warrant chief' is one of the most respected local leaders in Ughiẹnvwe. His father was the *Odede–Ade*—see Chapter 1, p. 17.

2 See Chapter 4, pp. 145–6.

3 C.S.O. 26/2 File 11329/S.I., Petition from Ekeke to Lieut. Gov. dated 13 October 1915.

among these services the fact that in the early days of the native court system, he acted as president of nine minor courts (there were only nine such courts in Urhoboland until 1907) in Urhoboland. According to him, those courts included those of Okpare, Ughelle, and Ughiẹnvwe.[1] After Ekeke's death, his brother in pleading that the subsidy paid to the deceased be transferred to him, put the claim more clearly:

> Chief Ekeke was a Political Agent for Ganagana Western Ijǫ Division. I was send with Chief Ekeke to assisted him [*sic*]. Then after this Copland Crawford and Chief Ekeke proceeded into the bush and opened the Native Courts. The courts opened by them are Frukama, Okpare, Ughelle and Jeremi.[2]

British administrative officers in later years made an even stronger claim for the Itsẹkiri. The report on Warri Division for 1925, for instance, stated:

> When the Native courts were being established in the outlying districts of the Division leading Jekris with trading interests in these parts were given warrants in order to show the Sobos and other less enlightened tribes how the working of the courts should be carried on.[3]

Writing of the Ughiẹnvwe native court in 1932, Mr. S. E. Johnson (District Officer, Warri Division) claimed that in the early years of this court's existence it was presided over by the District Commissioner or 'by a Jekri Agent who took his place as vice-president'.[4]

On the one hand, the above claims demonstrate that constant intermingling between the Itsẹkiri and the Urhobo, which was a regular feature of Itsẹkiri-Urhobo relations. On the other hand, they represent the type of claims which gave rise to tension and hostility between both peoples. Commenting on Ekeke's petition, the Resident, Warri Province, stated that Ekeke was an Itsẹkiri trader who toured various parts of Urhoboland in the interest of his trade. The subsidy which he claimed was formerly paid to his

---

1 Ibid. Ekeke is not at all remembered in Ughelle. The Okpare court as was stated in the last chapter was supervised by George Eyubẹ. It was not till 1916 that Ekeke sat on the Okpare court and by that time he was a mere trader resident in Okpare. Vide infra p. 207.

2 C.S.O. 26/2 File 11329/S.I., Teren Kenusi to Governor, 5 August 1925.

3 Ughelli Papers File 96/1925A, Annual Report, Warri Division, 1925.

4 C.S.O. 26 File 27630, Intelligence Report on Jeremi (Ughienvwe) Clan, p. 18.

father, Kenusi, and arose out of the government's policy of paying some compensation to those coastal chiefs who, prior to the establishment of British rule, used to receive a share of the comey collected from European traders. According to the Resident, Ekeke was 'utterly useless from a government point of view'.[1] Ekeke was, however, a member of the Warri Native Court. It is possible that people like Ekeke posed as government servants in the Urhobo areas (although in this case Ekeke is not at all remembered in the areas where he claimed he was vice-president) as such a pose would have been of definite advantage to their commercial ventures. The Urhobo, aware of the fact that the British used Itsẹkiri men in such capacities, would scarcely have had cause for suspicion.

The reference to the Ughiẹnvwe court is evidence of the general belief held by a later generation of British administrative officers, that it was the Itsẹkiri who played the leading role in the establishment of British rule in Urhoboland. The 'Jekri Agent' alluded to was probably George Eyubẹ who, as already stated, was of mixed Urhobo-Itsẹkiri parentage, and who was, at any rate, dead by the time the Ughiẹnvwe court was established. In fact, the record of the opening of this particular native court completely invalidates the claim made by Mr. Johnson. After the death of Eyubẹ no one was appointed to take his place. In the sphere previously supervised by Eyubẹ, the District Commissioners seemed to have determined to establish the new courts on sound and proper lines by going to sit there themselves. Thus, the District Commissioner wrote of the Ughiẹnvwe court in March 1904:

> During the quarter I have opened a minor court at Jeremi. . . . I have made arrangements to sit or send the Assistant District Commissioner to sit each sixteen days at Jeremi.[2]

The Uzere Native Council which was established at about the same time was similarly handled:

> The Uzere Native Council is now fairly started. It sits only when I or Mr. Crewe-Read can be present, and I am trying to arrange for it

---

1 C.S.O. 26/2 File 11329/S.I, Resident, Warri Province, to Secretary, Southern Provinces, Lagos, No. C3064/1909, 26 April 1919.
2 Supplement to Government Gazette, No. 10, 30 June 1904, p. 188: Quarterly Report Warri District, January–March 1904.

to be visited on the 7th and 21st of each month so as to have sittings about once a fortnight.[1]

In the light of clear evidence such as quoted above, the claims made for the Itsẹkiri are seriously called in doubt. Yet the claims are important as revealing a noticeable tendency on the part of the Itsẹkiri, and some British officers in the twenties and thirties, to exaggerate the role which the Itsẹkiri played in the process of the consolidation of British rule in Urhoboland. The British officers presumably did this partially out of gratitude to the Itsẹkiri, and partially out of genuine ignorance of the exact position of affairs at a time when they had not joined the service. As for the Itsẹkiri, they were probably forced to exaggerate their past services in an endeavour to enhance their reputation in the face of increasing Urhobo competition in commerce and other spheres.

The assertion that Itsẹkiri men were given warrants to sit on Urhobo courts in order that they might show the Urhobo how to run the courts may now be examined. The first thing to note is that it was Itsẹkiri men with trading interests in the areas concerned who were so appointed. This is fully borne out by the table below:[2]

Court (and when established)	Total no. of members	No. of Urhobo	No. of Itsekiri
Abraka-Okpara	17	11	6
Ajareyube (Jan. 1900)	19	16	3
Gbogidi (Jan. 1900)	18	17	1
'Jeremi' (June 1904)	16	16	–
Okpare (Jan. 1900)	16	15	– (one Ijǫ)
Sapele (as in 1902)	11	16	5
Ughelle (Oct. 1904	32	32	–
Uzere (May 1904)	25	25	–

Itsẹkiri warrant chiefs were to be found in Abraka, Okpara (Agbǫn clan), Ajareyubẹ (Agbarho clan), Gbogidi (Udu clan) and Sapẹlẹ in the years before 1914. These were the areas in which, as already pointed out, the Itsẹkiri traders were particularly active. As a matter of fact, virtually all the Itsẹkiri who were given warrants to sit on

1 Government Gazette, No. 16, 23 September 1904, p. 311: Report on Agberi District for quarter ending 30 June 1904.
2 The summary is culled from lists given in Gazette No. 8, March 1905, pp. 192–5.

these courts were men resident in the Itsẹkiri settlements in those clans. If the Urhobo accepted their appointments without demur, it was not only because they were afraid of government action in the event or their agitating against the appointments, but also because they were already familiar with the Itsẹkiri men concerned and scarcely regarded them as foreigners.

It is difficult to assess how successfully these Itsẹkiri warrant chiefs fulfilled the purpose for which they were allegedly appointed. An examination of the names concerned reveals that not one of the men who served in these Urhobo courts had had any previous experience in the older courts at Warri and Benin River.[1] It is therefore not easy to see how they were expected to teach the Urhobo the working of a system which was as new to them as to the Urhobo. There is no evidence in the records from which it can be judged whether the courts with Itsẹkiri chiefs were more efficiently run than those on which no Itsẹkiri chiefs sat.

What was the Urhobo reaction to the presence of Itsẹkiri chiefs on their courts during this pre-1914 period? Generally, the Urhobo were apparently unaware that the appointment of Itsẹkiri chiefs to their courts was regarded as a commentary on their inability to run these courts. The Itsẹkiri concerned were so well known to the Urhobo, that they worked happily together at the beginning. In the post-1914 period this amity was to give way to hatred and suspicion which will be discussed later.[2] There was, however, one incident in this earlier period which foreshadowed things to come. Cheke, it has been said, was placed in charge of Iyede court as a political agent. But he was so unpopular with the Iyede people that they drove him from their clan. Partly as a result of this action, Iyede was visited by a patrol in 1908 and certain sections of the town burnt down as punishment for their attack against 'Cheke, the Jekri Agent'.[3] It was not clear whether Cheke's expulsion was due to the mere fact of his being Itsẹkiri, or was the result of certain objectionable traits of character.[4] At any rate the burning of Iyede

1 See various lists of court members given in Gazette No. 8, March 1905, pp. 192–5.   2 Infra., pp. 207–9.
3 C.S.O. 26 File 27994: Intelligence Report on Iyede clan, p. 10.
4 The Iyede people today say that they expelled Cheke because he was Itsẹkiri—Interview with Kaghọ Omomadia (aged over 80 years) and other elders at

by the British, while understandable as a demonstration of the need to respect constituted authority, was hardly calculated to increase Itsẹkiri-Urhobo harmony.

There is little to go on in attempting an assessment of the working of the native courts in the pre-1914 era. The constant theme that they were popular and working satisfactorily was based on the large number of cases which went before them. In 1906 it was reported for the central provinces:

> The number of cases heard and determined is ample proof . . . of the confidence the people as a whole have in the administration of justice by the system of native councils and minor courts so happily inaugurated by . . . Ralph Moor.[1]

The number of cases determined is unacceptable as an adequate criterion for assessing the success or popularity of the courts. With the provision which rendered traditional tribunals illegal being enforced, many of the people had to take their cases to these courts. For some people, the courts became instruments with which they could fight their opponents in local feuds.[2] On the whole, it took a long time before the people reconciled themselves to the new system. In 1902 it was reported that 'considerable difficulty' was being 'experienced in getting the natives to attend the courts'. As a way out, Moor suggested that the court messengers be made to take the summonses to the 'Head Chief' of the village concerned, and that it be impressed on all such chiefs 'that their neglect to ensure the attendance of persons summoned would result in

---

Iyede on 21st December 1961 and 7 September 1963. In view of Itsẹkiri-Urhobo tension at the time of the inquiry there is room for scepticism about the opinion of the Iyede elders. It should be noted, however, that as there was little Itsẹkiri contact with this westernmost part of the Isoko section before this time, there might be some truth in the assertion by the Iyede people that Cheke was expelled because he was Itsẹkiri—a stranger to them. The situation was different with Urhobo clans like Abraka, Agbǫn or Agbarho.

1 C.S.O. 1/19 Vol. IV, Annual Report Central Provinces 1906. See also: Supplement to Government Gazette No. 10, 30 June 1904: Quarterly Report Warri District January–March 1904 and C.S.O. 1/19 Vol. 16: Enclosure in No. 33, 19.1.09: Annual Report Central Provinces 1907.

2 This accounts for the reputation of the Urhobo as a litigious people. In the new system a man was likely to win his case if he called sufficient evidence to back his claim. In the traditional system, the fear of trial by ordeal made men wary of raking up false evidence.

punishments to themselves.'¹ In 1911 troops had to visit Ọzọrọ and the surrounding area because the people were still persisting in their habit of blinding thieves, clear proof that the traditional system had not been given up. In 1914 Owe had to be burnt down because the people attacked their court messenger and killed him, his wife and children.² The Urhobo people were still not completely reconciled to the new system in 1914.

Between the chiefs and the people, and between these and the District Commissioner, stood the figure of the court clerk. In many ways he was the central figure in this novel set-up. While the District Commissioner could only be occasionally present at each court, the court clerk was present every time his court met. Various 'rules' made by the High Commissioner laid out the duties of the court scribe. It was his duty to summon three members (the official quorum) to attend each day's sitting; anybody who desired to inspect the records of a case with a view to obtaining a copy had, after securing the approval of the District Commissioner, to do so 'under the personal supervision of the clerk'. On the first day of every month the clerk had to travel to the divisional headquarters in order to submit his monthly returns to the District Commissioner.³ In addition, there was his primary duty of keeping the record of cases heard, summonses taken out, fees received and the like. If the District Commissioner had any information or instructions he wanted to pass on to the court members, he did so through the court clerk. The court clerk was, therefore, in the eyes of the warrant chiefs and the generality of the people, an extremely powerful and influential personage. It was this power and the corrupt way in which the court clerks used it that made them unpopular with the people. Very often they sought to arrogate to themselves more powers than they were legally allowed to wield. As early as 1904 the District Commissioner, Warri reported:

---

1 Cal. Prof. 9/2 Vol. II, Moor to Divisional Commissioner, Western Division, Draft No. 9, 22 May 1902.

2 C.S.O. 26 File 27898, Intelligence Report Owe Clan, pp. 19–20. The Owe clan elders confirmed this report at an interview on 8 September 1963.

3 Various Government Gazettes: Vol. II, No. 18, 30 September 1901, p. 361; Vol. III, No. 6, 30 April 1903, p. 122; Vol. III, No. 15, 15 November 1902 (Supplement), p. xxii.

I have had to remove the clerk of minor courts of Bogidi and Aj'Eyubi for various misdemeanours chiefly arising from his idea that he was a kind of Native Consul in these parts.[1]

The task of regulating the position of the clerk *vis-à-vis* the court members and the people remained one of the ever present problems of the native court system.

The amalgamation of Northern and Southern Nigeria became effective on 1 January 1914. At the start of the régime of Sir Frederick Lugard as Governor-General of the new administration, the native court system was further developed. The Native Courts Ordinance, 1914, and the Native Authority Ordinance, 1916, provided the legal framework of the system as it developed after 1914. But before examining the ordinances and their effect on the native court system, it is necessary to introduce the man whose career had a profound effect on the working of the system in Itsẹkiri and Urhoboland, namely Dǫghǫ Numa.

Dǫghǫ was the son of Numa, whose mother Uwala was a princess of the Olu Erejuwa I. Dǫghǫ's mother was Ejuǫnẹnowo, daughter of one Ogie, a son of an Ologbotsẹrẹ. On both sides, therefore, he was well connected, though it must be pointed out at once that his connexions both with the royal family and with the noble house of Ologbotsẹrẹ were on the female side—a fact which in strict Itsẹkiri law debarred him from holding any important office of state based on the hereditary principle. Not a great deal is known about Dǫghǫ's early days. In the dissensions which featured among the Itsẹkiri in the years after 1848, the Numa family stood in opposing camps to the Olomu family. The role played by Dǫghǫ during the Ebrohimi expedition of 1894 has already been noted. Dǫghǫ entered into the good books of the administrative officers as early as 1891. In that year, Gallwey made a journey through the creeks to Lagos. Nana supplied him with 'a large gig canoe' but refused to supply the crew, arguing that once his slaves got to Lagos they would run away. Dǫghǫ promptly made good the deficiency by giving thirty 'boys'

---

1 Supplement to Government Gazette, No. 10, June 1904, p. 187: Annual Report, Warri District, March Quarter 1904. The Urhobo elders recall how the court clerks used to threaten them with what Idisi (the Urhobo rendering of 'D.C.') would do to them if they failed to carry out the clerk's bidding.

to man the canoe,[1] thereby earning the gratitude of Gallwey. He was never to forfeit this gratitude. In 1892 Gallwey, in a report on his district, spoke of the two factions which existed in Itsẹkiriland. He explained the differences between these factions in terms of the people on the left bank of the Benin River objecting to being dictated to by Nana. Numa was the head of this left bank group. Numa died in February 1891 and Dǫghǫ became head of the Numa house, and leader of that faction. Commenting on this change, Gallwey wrote:

> Numa was a particularly weak minded and incapable chief, but his son, who succeeded him, is a very superior man altogether, and in time is likely to improve very materially on his father's rule and further, he is not afraid of Nana. In addition to all this, he is a very loyal supporter of Her Majesty's Government—His name is Dore.[2]

William Moore suggests that Dǫghǫ's faction carefully built him up in wealth and social status, in order that he could oppose Nana during the latter's term as Governor of the River. Dǫghǫ's position as interpreter to the council which Nana summoned to discuss various trade matters enabled him to become attached to the vice-consular officers, and Moore suggests that he used this position against Nana, by enlarging on the reports of disaffection brought up by various people against Nana.[3] Harrison Dudu, who featured prominently during the Nana war, was also Dǫghǫ's henchman. Dǫghǫ himself rendered useful service to the British during the Ebrohimi expedition. It will be recalled that one of the charges brought against Nana by Moor was that Nana planned an attack on Dǫghǫ and Dudu, 'two friendly chiefs'. The war canoes of Dǫghǫ and Harrison were used against Nana's supporters in the Sapẹlẹ area. It was Dǫghǫ's 'headman', Omota, who led a force of fifteen war canoes and 400 men to attack Okotobo, to which place Nana had fled after he escaped from Ebrohimi.[4] Antagonism to

---

1 H. L. Gallwey: 'Journeys in the Benin Country', *Journal of the Royal Geographical Society*, Vol. I, 1893, p. 124.
2 F.O. 2/51, Report on Benin River District, Oil Rivers Protectorate for year ending 31 July, 1892—Enclosure in Macdonald to F.O., 12 January 1893.
3 Moore, op. cit., p. 108.
4 F.O. 2/64, Enclosure in Macdonald to F.O., No. 49, 13 December 1894. See evidence of Moor and Omota at Nana's trial.

Nana, loyalty to the British, a certain shrewd opportunism, these were the factors which made Dogho one of the greatest agents of the British administration in Southern Nigeria between the years 1894 and 1932.

Dogho was appointed the political agent for the Benin River District about the year 1896, the same year that he was put in charge of the Benin River Native Council. In his capacity as Vice-President of this council, he won the encomiums of Gallwey in 1900. Gallwey, after reading a report on Sapẹlẹ District for the September quarter of that year, noted that Captain O'Riordon, the acting District Commissioner, had not commented on the state of affairs of the Benin River Native Council. 'I am afraid', he minuted, 'that supervision by the Acting District Commissioner could not have been very close; but it is fortunate that they have a man like Chief Dore who thoroughly knows his work'.[1] In short, the presence of Dogho was a guarantee that things were being properly run. This gives some idea of the respect and esteem in which the man was held by the British.

Dogho again won the deep gratitude of the British Government during the Benin expeditions of 1896 and 1897. Although he warned the foolhardy Phillips not to proceed with his plans of visiting Benin, he, nevertheless, furnished him with 180 of the 240 carriers required for the trip as well as canoes to convey them.[2] It was he who reported that the Phillips expedition had been fired upon and the white men killed. He furnished the canoes that patrolled the creeks to pick up information and any survivors after the disaster. During the punitive expedition of 1897, Dogho (this time aided by Dudu and Etchie) was again to the fore in procuring carriers at a time when both the Itsẹkiri and the Urhobo were unwilling to accompany the British on another Benin venture. Already the proud winner of a British commemorative medal for his services during the Ebrohimi expedition, he was awarded yet another medal for his services during the Benin expeditions.[3] Forwarding the diary

1 Cal. Prof. 10/3 Vol. I, Gallwey's comments on Sapẹlẹ District Quarterly Report, September 1900.
2 Alan Boisragon: *The Benin Massacre*, London 1897, p. 56.
3 C.O. 444/3, Moor to C.O., No. 236, 30 December, 1899. Also Macgregor (War Office) to Under-Secretary of State for the Colonies, 29 May 1899.

of the Sapẹlẹ District Commissioner which gave the details of the preparations of the Phillips expedition, Moor remarked of Dọghọ, 'Chief Dore is the most able and trustworthy native Political Agent in the division.'[1] The testimony of Bindloss, a British traveller in the 1890s, gives an even clearer picture of the esteem in which Dọghọ was held by the British administration. The Vice-Consul (Warri) was entertaining Bindloss and his fellow travellers to a dinner to which Dọghọ was invited. Bindloss wrote:

> There sat down with us a Niger man attired in plain white linen whose name is a power in the delta and whose counsel has been taken by Government in times of anxiety. His fine white gig lay alongside the bank, flying the jack above her stern; and the writer was informed that when a newly arrived and zealous official ordered its owner to abandon the use of a flag sacred to the imperial service, he received a hint to let Chief Dore alone.[2]

In 1906 Governor Egerton sought to allow Nana to return from exile. He naturally asked the opinion of those officers who had actually worked in the Benin River area. Mr. F. S. James, then the Provincial Commissioner, Central Provinces, consulted Dọghọ before forwarding his own opinion, which was in favour of the return of Nana. According to James, Dọghọ was of the opinion 'that Nana's return, or non-return, would have no political effect on this portion of the Protectorate'.[3] But Dọghọ had no intention of allowing his former rival to become, on his return, the important and influential personage he had been earlier. He therefore sought and obtained an assurance to this effect from Governor Egerton himself, when the latter granted him an interview in October 1906.[4]

In 1908 and 1911 various parcels of land in the present Warri township were leased to the government for ninety-nine years. Dọghọ and Ogbe signed these leases 'on behalf of themselves and the Itsẹkiri people'.[5] In 1908, 510 acres of Sapẹlẹ land were leased

1 F.O. 403/218, Moor to F.O., No. 1, 29 January 1897.
2 Bindloss, op. cit., pp. 194–5.
3 C.O. 520/35, Minute by Mr. F. S. James, dated 3 May 1906—Enclosure in Egerton to C.O., No. 124, 12 May 1906.
4 C.O. 520/37, Interview between Governor Egerton and 'Chief Dore' on the S.V. *Ivy* on 15 October 1906.—Enclosure 4 in Egerton to C.O., Confidential, 1906.
5 Moore, op. cit., p. 111.

to the government for ninety-nine years. The lease was signed by Dogho 'acting for and on behalf of the chiefs and people of Sapele'.[1] Both these transactions led in after years to court cases in which first, the validity of Dogho's signature was challenged and then the ownership of the lands involved called in question. The leases were executed under the Public Lands Acquisition Ordinance, 1903, Clause 6 of which provided that:

> Where lands required for public purposes were the property of a native community, the Head Chief of such community may sell and convey the same for an estate in fee simple, notwithstanding any native law and custom to the contrary.[2]

Thus by 1908, Dogho was already regarded as the *de facto* 'native authority' of the Warri district, though it was not till 1917 that he was to be so appointed. As a political agent, the only one still in active service, he was building for himself a considerable reservoir of power. The British administration aided and abetted him in this process by the use they made of him.

By 1914 the British administration was firmly established in Southern Nigeria. New developments were taking place in various spheres of the people's lives. These new developments, like the acquisition of public land for government purposes, called for new men and new measures. Dogho was one of those men called upon to implement policies in the formulation of which they had no say. The implementation of these essentially 'foreign' policies in the then Warri Province led to complications between the different ethnic groups, especially between the Itsekiri, now presided over by Dogho, and the Urhobo.

In Southern Nigeria the 'classical' period of the native court system is usually regarded as having begun in 1914, with the amalgamation of Northern and Southern Nigeria, and the introduction of Lugard's concept of administration. Lugard was extremely critical of the native court system as it operated in the South before his time. It was his view that the courts had not been able to develop along the right lines, because they had been presided

---

1 Evidence and Exhibits: Sapele Land Case Suit No. 2/37/1941.
2 C.O. 588/1, The Public Lands Acquisition Proclamation, 1903 (No. 5 of 1903).

over by European officials, who could not be expected to understand fully the mentality of the people over whom they sat in judgement.[1] It was necessary to make the native courts more 'native', and to effect a general improvement of the system. Accordingly, a new Native Courts Ordinance came into effect on 1 October 1914. The new ordinance empowered the Resident,[2] subject to the Governor's approval, to establish native courts at such places within his province as he saw fit. There were to be various categories of native courts. Apart from the Alkali courts in Northern Nigeria, there were two other categories provided for. The first type was to consist

> of a paramount or head chief with or without minor chiefs or other persons acting either in conjunction with the paramount chief or head chief as judges or sitting as assessors.

The second category of court was to have as members

> chiefs or other persons representing the communities inhabiting the area within which the court exercises jurisdiction as may from time to time be appointed by the Resident.

The Resident was empowered to appoint the presidents and vice-presidents of these two categories of courts from among the court members.

In addition to the two types of courts, the Governor was granted powers to declare the court of 'a paramount chief or head chief' a 'judicial council'. It was then provided:

> A judicial council may exercise such executive functions as may be approved by the Governor in addition to the judicial powers conferred upon it by warrant under which it was established as a native court.

Where there was a 'paramount chief', the Resident was to appoint the members of the native courts or judicial council, 'in consultation with or on the nomination of such paramount chief'. The Resident was further empowered, with the approval of the Governor, to appoint the judicial council or native court

> at the capital city of his province, to be a court of appeal from all

---

1 C.O. 657/1, Blue Book Report (Nigeria) 1914, p. 32. See also F. D. Lugard: *Notes for Political Officers*, Lagos 1914, para. 2.

2 As from 1914 the provinces were put in the charge of Residents. Warri Province included not only the Urhobo and Itsẹkiri but the Kwalẹ, Aboh and Western Ijọ peoples.

other native courts or judicial councils in the province, or any part thereof or for such of them as he may name in the order.

As in the older proclamations, the ordinance imposed penalties on all who exercised any other form of judicial authority within the area of a native court's jurisdiction. Penalties were also prescribed for clerks of native courts who rendered false returns of the cases tried or the penalties inflicted.[1]

The new ordinance contained a number of important innovations. First, European administrative officers were no longer to be presidents of the native courts. Lugard set great store by this. It was his view that the native courts could not attain that independence and sense of responsibility which he considered that they should, 'if dominated by the presence of a European'.[2] Secondly, the idea of a 'paramount chief' or 'head chief' was now written into the ordinance and as can be seen from the provisions quoted above, the 'paramount chief', where he did exist or was created, was likely to develop into a more important personage than he ever was before. This was more likely to be the case if the 'paramount chief' was given authority over people who did not traditionally come under his jurisdiction. Chief Dọghọ was to acquire an influence out of all proportion to any traditional authority that he might have possessed. The provision which laid it down that the Resident should appoint members of the native courts of his province in consultation with, or on the nomination of, the 'paramount chief', was pregnant with difficulties if it operated in an area where two or more different ethnic groups were arbitrarily subjected to the sway of a British-made 'paramount chief'. The third innovation was the constitution of a native court of appeal. A native court of appeal was different from an ordinary British type court of appeal under the Supreme Court Ordinance for example. In the latter case, all the courts, irrespective of their location, administered the same code of laws, and the procedure was virtually the same. In the case of the former, especially where different ethnic groups were involved, the 'code' of 'native law and custom' as well as procedure varied from place

1 C.O. 656/1, Native Courts Ordinance, 1914 (No. VIII of 1914). The clauses to which reference has been made are 3, 5(b & c), 6, 7, 23, 26–8.
2 F. D. Lugard, op. cit., para. 2.

to place. Was it, therefore, legally advisable to ask people with varying customs and traditions of justice to attend the same appeal court? It took nearly fifteen years before this was seen as an unworkable proposition.

The establishment of native courts, along lines which he considered an improvement on the old system, was only one aspect of Lugard's policy. He came down to the south determined to set up there the system which he had operated in the north, and which has been called 'indirect rule'. It was held that it was necessary for the working of this system, that there should be traditional rulers or paramount chiefs, to use the name that became popular, who were to continue to rule their own people, though along lines directed by the British, and implementing policies dictated by that same power. If there were no paramount chiefs, then they had to be created. This done, they could be declared legal 'Native Authorities' and given certain powers. In 1916, therefore, Lugard promulgated, as a logical corollary to his Native Courts Ordinance, the Native Authority Ordinance, 1916.[1] This ordinance empowered the Governor to appoint as a 'native authority' any 'chief or other Native or any Tribunal'. The Governor could 'make the Native Authority of any area subordinate to the Native Authority of any other area'.[2] Other provisions listed the duties of the native authorities. Thus, as from 16 May 1916, the two essential legal instruments of the new policy had been provided and all was ready to usher in Lugard's 'indirect rule' throughout the Southern Provinces.

This work is not a treatise on indirect rule. But as the system deeply affected Itsẹkiri-Urhobo relations, as will be presently demonstrated, one may be permitted a few comments. There has been the tendency to see in the period before the amalgamation of Northern and Southern Nigeria one of *direct* rule while the period which followed the amalgamation had been seen as one of *indirect* rule. According to the protagonists of this view indirect rule was not introduced into parts of the south until well after the amalgamation. There is no evidence to justify this view.[3] The pre-1914

---

1 C.O. 656/2, The Native Authority Ordinance, 1916 (No. XIV of 1916).
2 Ibid., Clause 4.
3 The warrant chief system as it worked in the Urhobo area was very similar to that in the former Eastern Nigeria. Dr. A. E. Afigbo [*The Warrant Chief*

period was no more direct that the post-1914 period. As has already been indicated, the origins of the native court or warrant chief system date back to the era of Courts of Equity and Governing Councils, formalized and institutionalized by Ralph Moor in his enactments of 1900 and 1901. From the duties which the courts were expected to carry out and by Moor's own testimony there was no doubt that the system he was trying to carry out was one of rule through the 'chiefs' of the respective peoples of the protectorate.[1] He was fully aware that this was the only wise policy, seeing that the available staff was hopelessly inadequate to cope with the details of local government. If it is charged against Moor and Egerton, his successor, that the 'chiefs' employed were not the traditional rulers of his people (an accusation which is not valid for all cases) then a similar charge must be brought against Lugard and his successors, for the personnel of the courts changed little after the enactments of 1914 and 1916. If anything, in the area covered by this study, the advent of the Lugardian concept of indirect rule merely worsened the situation in this regard. Lugard did no more than transplant to the south ideas and concepts which had worked in the north with its differing traditions and culture. This transplantation was not always successful.

The first appointments under the Native Authorities Ordinance were made in 1917. The Governor-General, by a gazette notice, conferred on certain people the status of 'Recognized Chiefs' and then proceeded to appoint such 'recognized chiefs' native authorities. In the whole of the Warri Province, only one person was so appointed—Chief Dọghọ who was appointed a second class chief and native authority for Warri Division.[2] The Governor-General also appointed certain native courts to be the native authorities for

System in Eastern Nigeria 1900–1929 (Ph.D. Thesis, University of Ibadan, 1964)] and I are agreed on many grounds about this. The subject here briefly mentioned is taken up in detail by Afigbo in his 'The Warrant Chief System in Eastern Nigeria: Direct or Indirect Rule', *J.H.S.N.*, Vol. III, No. 4 June 1967, pp. 683–717.

1 C.S.O. 1/13, Moor to E.O., No. 139, 18 August 1898.
2 *The Nigerian Gazette*, Vol. IV, No. 45, 13 September 1917 (Notice No. 104) p. 351. As from 1914, the Warri Division included all Itsẹkiriland and all the Isoko and Urhobo clans except the Agbọn clan which was in the Kwalẹ Division.

their respective areas of jurisdiction. All the native courts of the Warri Division were so appointed.[1] But a further provision laid it down that in the Warri Province,

> The Native Authorities of the Warri Division other than Dore Numa are made subordinate to Chief Dore Numa.[1]

Two things are important. First, Ḍoghọ was now legally recognized as paramount chief. His new position entitled him to nominate who should sit on the native courts of the Warri Division, or at least to be consulted by the Resident when appointing such members, for the native courts were also the native authorities. Secondly, all the native courts in the Urhobo and Isoko clans, having been created native authorities, were arbitrarily subjected to Ḍoghọ. For a system designed to enhance the position of traditional rulers throughout the country, nothing could be more self-contradictory.

The appointment of Ḍoghọ as native authority for Warri Division, was a further, and perhaps the greatest, proof of British gratitude for the services which he had rendered since 1894. By 1917 the British penetration of Urhoboland was already complete. It could no longer be pleaded that the British were unfamiliar with the Urhobo people. The subordination of the Urhobo to Ḍoghọ is, in the circumstances, difficult to explain. It can only be assumed that now, as earlier, the British were still perplexed by the difficulty of finding some authority acceptable to all the Urhobo clans, and therefore decided to appoint a foreigner over them. It would appear, however, that little or no consideration was given to the implications of the appointment. Accustomed to the idea of emir-type native authorities to whom authority could be delegated, the Lugardian administration paid little regard, in this instance, to ethnic differences between the Itsẹkiri and the Urhobo. The presence of a man like Ḍoghọ already ranking high as a loyal supporter of the British administration merely made the slip easier.

In 1924 a new gazette notice altered the *status quo* created in 1917. Ḍoghọ retained his position as native authority. The Native Court of Sapẹlẹ and the Native Court of Appeal for Kwalẹ Division were made native authorities independent of all other native authorities

---

1 Ibid., p. 355.
2 Ibid., p. 351.

in the province.[1] Nothing was said about the other native courts in Urhoboland, but Dǫghǫ as native authority of the Warri Division was empowered to appoint, with the concurrence of the Resident, subordinate native authorities.[2] The new notice worsened the situation for the Urhobo. Dǫghǫ was now the only person who could initiate the move for the appointment of native authorities among the Urhobo. Nothing could have been better calculated to enhance the prestige of Dǫghǫ and to humiliate the Urhobo. However, Dǫghǫ did not make use of the powers conferred on him before the issue became a matter of practical administrative difficulty.

It was part of the aim of Lugard's policy, as initiated in the years 1914–16, to make a legal distinction between the native courts as judicial bodies on the one hand, and native authorities on the other. That was why a Native Authority Ordinance was necessary in the first instance. If the Itsẹkiri and Urhobo did not make these legal distinctions, the administrative officers certainly did. There were thus no legally constituted native authorities in the Urhobo clans after the notice of 1924. In a memorandum to the Resident in September 1925, Mr. Murphy, the District Officer in charge of the Warri Division, pointed out this fact. He reported that as a result of the non-existence of legal native authorities, the native courts could not be taken to task for failure to keep roads, rest houses and court houses in good repair. He urged that all the native courts in the division be created native authorities, but warned:

> These authorities should not with the exception, perhaps of Warri court, be declared subordinate to Chief Dore as such a system would be bound to end in failure.[3]

As nothing had been done by November, the District Officer again addressed a memorandum to the Resident re-stating his case:

> The proposal that Chief Dore should appoint Sobo chiefs as subordinate authorities among the Sobos is, I think quite impracticable. The Sobos own no allegiance to Chief Dore who is of the Jekri tribe

1 *The Nigerian Gazette*, Vol. II, No. 32, 26 June 1924 (Notice No. 59), pp. 256 and 260.
2 Ibid., p. 260. Section 6 of the Notice cancelled 'all previous notifications published in the Gazette relating to the appointment of Native Authorities'.
3 Ughelle Papers, File 41/1929, Murphy to Resident, Memo of 25 September 1925.

and any attempt to give him an artificial dominion over the Sobos would be opposed by them.[1]

The Urhobo case could not have been more clearly put. Murphy reminded the Resident that the Urhobo in the Kwalę Division had protested vigorously against being forced to attend the Appeal Court at Warri, because this court was presided over by a permanent president who was an Itsękiri. As a result of the protest, a separate appeal court had to be established for the Kwalę Division. That, thought Murphy, ought to be a guide to the administration in deciding what should be done in the existing circumstances. Finally, he pointed out what should have been obvious from the beginning:

> The proposal that Chief Dore should issue orders to Sobo chiefs appears to be the negation of the principles of Government through tribes and clans which administrative officers have recently been exhorted to carry out.[2]

On the strength of the District Officer's strong representations, the Resident, after initial hesitation, wrote to the Lieutenant-Governor proposing that the Urhobo native courts be gazetted native authorities independent of all other such authorities in the province.[3] Consequently, in June 1926, the necessary notice was inserted in the gazette, by which, though Dogho remained a native authority over the Itsękiri area, all the Urhobo courts (these were listed in the gazette) were declared independent native authorities, with jurisdiction over their respective native court areas.[4]

It is interesting to notice the difference in attitudes between the District Officer and his superior officers. The former, more in touch with Urhobo feelings, realized that the proposed measure would infuriate the people. The Resident and, presumably, the Lieutenant-Governor, were apparently more concerned with the need to build up some 'paramount chief'. These more senior officers failed to realize that in the Warri Province (more than perhaps any other) there were various ethnic groups, each of which

---

1 Ughelle Papers, File 41/1921, Murphy to Resident, Memo of 3 November 1925.
2 Ibid.
3 Ughelle Papers, File 41/1921, Resident, Warri Province, to Secretary Southern Provinces, Memo of 21 June 1926.
4 *The Nigerian Gazette*, Vol. XIII, No. 35, 17 June 1926 (Notice No. 79) p. 311.

had a tradition of complete independence. Therefore, however much a 'paramount chief' facilitated the working of the new system, to foist the 'paramount chief' of one group upon the people of another, was to undermine the guiding principles of the very system they were operating. Urhobo resentment of the new order and the understanding of the District Officer averted, in this instance, the evils and conflict of arbitrary 'paramountcy'. In other respects, however, Dǫghǫ's position and power continued to lead to conflict between the Itsẹkiri and the Urhobo.

As for the native courts themselves, the first result of the new order was the increase in their number. In the early years, the administration was inclined to limit the number of these courts. But Lugard regarded it as essential that there should be a sufficiency of courts to stop complainants travelling prohibitive distances to take out summonses.[1] By 1922 there were twenty-four courts as compared with eight before 1914.[2] With this increased number of courts, the problems of the native court system became more noticeable than they had been earlier.

It has been stated that during the earlier period, it was the practice in many cases for the administrative officers to consult with the leaders of the people before deciding who were to sit on the native courts. There was good reason for this. Faced with the problems of introducing a new order and without ready-moulded instruments to hand, they were virtually forced to go to the people to obtain these instruments. By 1914, however, there was already a core of people, 'the warrant chiefs', with some experience in running these courts. It was easy for the British political officers to ask these chiefs to help select prospective members of the courts, without their going through the laborious process of seeking the opinion of the village elders as a whole. The warrant chiefs thus became, largely through no fault of theirs, a class of 'king makers', who filled the vacancies that occurred within their ranks. This was one way by which people became warrant chiefs in the new era.[3] The moment the people realized that the warrant chiefs could secure appointment

1 Lugard, op. cit., para. 9(b).
2 Ughelle Papers, File 49/1922, H. G. Aveling (D.O., Warri) to Resident, Warri Province, Memo No. 894/1922, 6 December 1932.
3 Ughelle Papers, File 25/1919, Memo No. 233/1919, 16 April 1919.

for prospective candidates, abuses began to creep into the system. The title of 'chifi' (as the Urhobo call it) became a marketable commodity bought from existing warrant chiefs.

If the nomination of warrant chiefs by those already in office was a deviation from strict traditional usage, the practice whereby a retiring chief recommended his brother or son to succeed him was even more so. This practice sought to render hereditary an office which had been conferred on the retiring holder as an individual, on account of his age, title and personal abilities and attributes. Despite this irregularity, the District Officers seemed to have accepted such recommendations without demur.[1]

A third channel through which people became warrant chiefs was by direct application to their District Officers. Occasionally, such applications were sent by the village on behalf of an individual of their choice.[2] More often, the individual himself applied for the post, and either took a clientele to the District Office to prove his popularity, or invoked the services rendered by him or his forebears to the government. When in 1920 one Sam Itsẹkiri of Ẹvhrọ applied for appointment as warrant chief, he was said to have taken 'a considerable number of supporters' with him to the District Officer. In the same year a retired police constable sought similar appointment. He concluded his plea with 'simply look upon my long services and good work I have done when I was in the service.' Two years later, Chief Skin urged the appointment as warrant chief of a son of Ogbe, arguing that the late Ogbe had rendered services to the government which were valuable enough to justify recognition along the lines suggested.[3]

Perhaps the surest way to secure appointment as warrant chief

---

1 Ughelle Papers, File 25/1919, Shelton to Resident, Memo No. 233/1919, 16 April 1919. Mr. L. H. Shelton (D.O.) recommended the appointment of a certain Okoro of Iyede to take the place of his father, 'Okukor' who was retiring on account of old age. There were other instances in the same year. (See same File.)

2 Ughelle Papers, File 35/1928, *Ekpako* of Ikwuewu Town to D.O., Warri, 22 November 1928. The *ekpako* wanted a certain Esemuo to be appointed as their chief.

3 Ughelle Papers, File 25/1919, Wood to Resident, Memo 46/1920, 23 January 1920; Ughelle Papers, File25/1919, Petition from Tom Ofia to Resident, 14 August 1920; C.S.O. 26/2 File 11329/S.21, Chief Skin to Resident, Warri, 19 December 1922.

was to win the favour of Chief Ḍọghọ who, by virtue of the powers conferred on him, had to be consulted by the Resident before the latter finally approved the appointment of any warrant chief. In this regard, Ḍọghọ's influence was keenly felt in Urhoboland. Prospective candidates (Itsẹkiri and Urhobo) used to send canoe loads of presents to him to secure his support for their applications. Some Urhobo elders even sent their children and relations to Ḍọghọ to do private work either in order him to get to support their candidature or else to influence him in a case pending in court over which Ḍọghọ was to preside.[1] It was not till the 1920s that this practice was discouraged.

Each of the methods described above by which people became warrant chiefs was, strictly speaking, a deviation from traditional usage, and open to abuse. Some efforts should have been made to ascertain who, according to the customs of the people, were really qualified to be court members. Yet one must concede the fact that the issue of court membership was a complicated one. It was not altogether unreasonable for the administrative officers to see in the existing chiefs the rulers of their people, and to trust them to select the right man to join their ranks when a vacancy occurred. Besides, authority in traditional society was widely diffused. Most of the age grades possessed not only executive authority but a measure of judicial power. Viewed in that light, virtually any adolescent could have been delegated to sit on the native courts, if the elders thought fit to do so. Such an appointment would, however, have been basically delegatory in nature, and terminable at the pleasure of the elders-in-council; while in office, the appointee would have had constantly to report back to his village council. What really went wrong with the new system, was not so much that the wrong people were appointed (though this must be granted in a number of cases), but that the delegatory nature of clan and village representation

---

1 Chief William Otobo who is the present *Otota* of Uzere, was one of the clerks who worked with Ḍọghọ in the 1920's. He described to me how both Itsẹkiri and Urhobo used to take presents to Ḍọghọ thereby confirming what various Urhobo elders admitted to me. According to Chief Otobo most of the time Ḍọghọ did not even bother to see these people. He merely asked one of the clerks to receive the presents and take the names of the applicants. Almost invariably, such applicants were appointed on the strength of Ḍọghọ's recommendation.

was utterly lost after the system had operated for some years. At the same time, it was difficult for the warrant chiefs to see themselves as mere delegates, when they probably bribed their way into office, and were answerable to the administration which held them responsible for failure to perform their duties as set down in the various ordinances. These duties were many, and included not only sitting as judges in the courts, but performing all the executive duties usually associated with local government authorities. In the place of the village council and age-grades, a few men in each village found themselves the only recognized judicial and executive authorities. A concentration of power of this magnitude was unknown to the Urhobo in their traditional system of government. It was easy in a situation like this, for the warrant chiefs to look on themselves as lords over their people. The problem of court membership was never satisfactorily settled throughout the period covered by this work. For the real question posed was whether government, in framing its administrative policy, was to look backwards or to the future. In 1920, for instance, should government have sought to enthrone the *ekpako* and titled men who ruled in the 1890s, or should they, taking into consideration the new economic and social factors which even then were making themselves felt, have sought a new ruling class? That is not a question which admits of easy pronouncements.

The warrant chiefs did not find their work any easier as a result of the powers they enjoyed. The people, no more associated with the ruling group in the work of government, refused to give that traditional (almost instinctive) loyalty that was expected from them. At the same time the spread of Christianity added to the difficulties of the chiefs, as the 'Christians' found excuses for dodging duties that they should normally have performed in and for their community. In Agbarho clan in 1919, for example, a group of 'Christians' refused to help clear one of the clan roads, on the grounds that it led 'to one fetish known as Oloku'. It required the personal intervention of the District Officer to force the young men to carry out the orders of their chiefs.[1] The law that was administered in the courts presented yet another difficulty. Their traditional laws the

---

1 Ughelle Papers, File 16/1919, Petition from Charlie Esewu and others to D.O., Warri, 15 February 1919.

chiefs probably knew well; but the government ordinances were very strange to them and the task of administering a mixed 'code' of laws was not easy.[1] Many of the chiefs appeared to the administrative officers to possess little sense of duty. In 1921 a District Officer complained:

> The chiefs have little idea of keeping order in their courts and generally take little interest in their duties; their main idea is to sit as often as possible and so draw sitting fees.[2]

In September of 1921 Iyede court was closed as a result of the disorderly manner in which it was conducted.[3] Ozǫrǫ court was similarly closed in 1925.[4] To the difficulty arising from the position of the chiefs among their own people, was added the unpleasantness of the visitations of the administrative officers when things went wrong.

Power breeds temptations, and these warrant chiefs who suddenly found themselves with powers which they could never otherwise have had, did not always succeed in withstanding the temptations of office. The complaints most frequently brought against the chiefs, included aiding and abetting criminals, holding court at home, unlawful arrest and accepting bribes. In 1919 eight warrant chiefs were suspended (three were later dismissed) for 'demanding and receiving' with a view to perverting justice; one was dismissed for being implicated in stealing; three were convicted for unlawful arrest.[5] In 1921 some chiefs in Ewu had their warrants cancelled because they were suspected of murder.[6] In 1926 the warrant chiefs of Agbǫn were charged with generally aiding criminals and thereby creating an unsettled state in the Kwalę Division.[7] The victims of the malpractices of the warrant chiefs were, of course, the ordinary people.

---

1 C.S.O. 26 20653, Intelligence Report, Ewu Clan, p. 51.
2 Ughelle Papers, File 68/1921, Annual Report, Warri Division, 1921.
3 Ibid.
4 Ughelle Papers, File 96/1925A, Annual Report, Warri Division, 1925.
5 Ughelle Papers, File 26/1919, List of Warrant Chiefs sentenced.
6 Ughelle Papers, File 68/1921, Annual Report, Warri Division 1921.
7 Kwalę Papers, File K/10/1923, Letter from a group of night guards to D.O., Kwalę. See also C.S.O. 26/2 File 11857, Vol. IV, Warri Province, Annual Report, 1926. Mackay, the D.O., Kwalę, confirmed in this report that the warrant chiefs were helping the criminals.

That was not all. The chiefs tended to grow arrogant with the years. They harassed any elders who attempted to settle disputes outside the courts. It used to be customary for various age grades to make rules governing their members. Now such rules had to be registered in court if they were to be of any effect. The *Eweyae* (women folk) of a town in Ughięnvwe clan, for example, made a rule which imposed a fine of twelve shillings on any woman found guilty of adultery. In 1924 a woman of that town committed adultery but refused to pay the prescribed fine. The case was taken to court. The 'Otu-Jeremi' Native Court found the woman guilty of adultery but held that she could not be made to pay the twelve shillings because the rule had not been registered in court. According to the court:

> All native laws and customs are made before the court and registered and not by *common people* at home.[1]

The chiefs might only have been carrying out instructions, but they need not have created the impression that they were a class apart from the 'common people'. It was not for nothing that in 1927 the people took their revenge on these chiefs when an opportunity offered itself.

The position of the court clerk remained as strong as before. He still remained the medium of correspondence between the District Officer and the chiefs. He was allowed to give orders to the chiefs on the instructions of the District Officer.[2] He alone could read the written law, and so could easily mislead the chiefs if it suited his purpose to do so. His custody of the court records gave him added prestige, and his frequent trips to headquarters increased the respect in which he was held by the chiefs and people. His position and his powers made him equally, if not more, amenable to bribery and the people recall how they used to give 'presents' to their court clerk to influence him in their favour. The court clerks were in many ways a law unto themselves. In 1922 Mr. Aveling, the

---

1 Ughelle Papers, File 43/11/1921, Case of Ebi V. Akoh and two others, heard at 'Otu-Jeremi' Native Court, 11 December 1924. (The italics are mine.)

2 See War Prof. Papers, File 30/10, D.O., Warri, to Clerks, Native Courts—Memo No. 512/5/1921. See also Ughelle Papers, File 43/U/1921, D.O., Warri, to clerk, Native Court, Jeremi, 12 November 1921 and File 43/V/1921, D.O., Warri, to Clerk, Ivǫrǫgbo Native Court.

Assistant District Officer, Sapęlę, complained that the native court clerks were in some cases the actual judges. He pointed out that as the depositions the clerks took down in court could not be read by the presiding chiefs, it was easy for them to distort the evidence and the verdict. He recommended the inclusion in the courts of educated young men who could check the records of the court clerks.[1] It was not, however, till the beginning of reorganization in the 1930s that the position of the court clerks was reviewed. In the meantime they enjoyed tremendous power. Even Chief Dǫghǫ could not escape the authority and arrogance of these clerks. In 1925 he reported to the District Officer that the clerk of the Benin River Native Court was always interferring with the court's decision and would not let the chiefs pass judgement as they saw fit. (We do not know whether the interference was in the interest of justice or not.) More galling to Dǫghǫ perhaps was the clerk's impertinence in smoking in court, a privilege reserved for 'his paramountcy' Chief Dǫghǫ.[2]

In the years before 1914 there were only a few court clerks to serve the limited number of courts then functioning. Of these clerks, Esiri and Okitikpe were Urhobo; Bar Rolle was a Sierra Leonian; and Otuędon was Itsękiri.[3] It is understandable that there should not have been more Itsękiri or Urhobo clerks, for it was only in 1902–3 that schools were opened at Warri and Sapęlę,[4] while in the Urhobo hinterland regular schools were not to be founded till the late 1920s. There were, therefore, few men who could write well enough to perform the duties of court clerk. By the twenties the position had improved considerably. The Sapęlę and Warri schools had had time to turn out a number of young men who could serve as court clerks. In 1922, of the seventeen court clerks who served in Itsękiri and Urhoboland, seven were Itsękiri and only one was

---

1 Ughelle Papers, File 49/1922, A.D.O., Sapęlę, to Resident, Warri, 26 September 1922.
2 Ughelle Papers, File 93/1925, D.O. Warri to Resident, Memo of 9 December 1925. According to the D.O., no other member of the court apart from Dǫghǫ was allowed to smoke.
3 These are the only names to be found in the various Government Gazettes: No. 2, 28 February 1903; No. 110, 31 August 1903; No. 12, 30 September 1903.
4 See Chapter 4, p. 163.

Urhobo.[1] To some extent the numbers indicate the relative index of literacy as between the Itsẹkiri and the Urhobo. Until the thirties, most of the literate men who could take service in government departments and commercial houses were Itsẹkiri. The Warri and Sapẹlẹ schools, in their earlier years, served Itsẹkiriland more effectively than they served Urhoboland. This is a fact which is of significance in Itsẹkiri-Urhobo relations. The British found the Itsẹkiri useful in the penetration era. In the running of the native courts and some of the other government offices, it was again the Itsẹkiri who produced the men. It was only natural that the British should regard the Itsẹkiri as the enlightened people in this part of the protectorate. Some of the claims which the British made for the Itsẹkiri must, therefore, be seen against this background of services rendered to the administration by the Itsẹkiri.

It is not known for certain how the Itsẹkiri court clerks behaved in the Urhobo courts. It is striking that all the Itsẹkiri clerks served in Urhobo courts, while the one Urhobo clerk served in the predominantly Itsẹkiri Warri Native Court. It might well be that this was a deliberate government policy, pursued in the hope that the clerks would thereby be less susceptible to local political and other influences. The Urhobo elders do not remember the Itsẹkiri court clerks as having been more corrupt or overbearing; they claim that the court clerks were all much of a type. Whatever the relations might have been between these Itsẹkiri clerks and the Urhobo court members, the time was to come when, as the Urhobo began to produce their own literate young men, it became necessary to review the position of the Itsẹkiri court clerks still serving in courts in Urhoboland.

There was an increase in the number of native courts in Urhoboland after 1914. But this increase was not such that all clans had courts opened for them. The Uvbiẹ (Effurun) clan was among those which had no courts of their own. The Uvbiẹ people therefore still had to attend the Warri Native Court, which not only had a preponderance of Itsẹkiri members (the figures in 1928 were seventeen

---

1 Ughelle Papers, File 33/1922, Handing Over Notes, Warri Division: H. G. Aveling (D.O.) to H. B. Butler (D.O.), 18 December 1922. A full list of all the courts and clerks is given. Of the others, two were Benin. One was a Sierra Leonian; the others were from the former Eastern Nigeria.

Itsẹkiri chiefs to eight Urhobo), but a permanent Itsẹkiri president, in the person of Chief Skin.[1] It should be pointed out that with the exception of the Native Court of Appeal, and after 1924, the Benin River Native Court, both of which had Chief Ḍọghọ as permanent president, no other courts in the Warri Division had such presidents. The office was made rotational among the court members in all the other courts. No explanation was given for making the Itsẹkiri-controlled courts an exception to this general practice. In November 1923, the Effurun chiefs addressed a petition to the Resident on the issue of their attending the Warri Native Court. They protested against the practice whereby one Urhobo chief sat with three Itsẹkiri chiefs to hear cases in the court. They contended that there was perversion of justice as it was impossible

> for one Sobo chief to debate or argue three Itsẹkiri chiefs for justice, especially in a case Itsẹkiri v. Sobo as their judgment may be more aristocratic than democratic.[2]

The petitioners requested that the arrangement be revised so that two Urhobo chiefs could sit with two Itsẹkiri. The petitioners suggested that if the Resident was unable to grant this request, different days of the week be set apart for the hearing of Itsẹkiri and Urhobo cases, so that the Itsẹkiri chiefs could adjudicate over purely Itsẹkiri cases while the Urhobo chiefs handled their own cases.[3] Apparently, the Resident turned down the request of the Urhobo chiefs, for two more petitions were addressed to the Resident on the same issue in 1924 and 1926 respectively, before he agreed to alter the arrangement so that the quorum for hearing cases could consist of two Itsẹkiri and two Urhobo chiefs. The Effurun chiefs accepted this arrangement but, as the District Officer himself pointed out, it was unlikely that they were entirely satisfied.[4]

---

1 Ughelle Papers, File 112/26, Annual Report, Warri Division, 1926. The 1928 figures are given in Ughelle Papers, File 86/1928, Handing Over Notes Warri Division: S. E. Johnson (Acting D.O.) to J. W. C. Rutherfoord (D.O.) 24 August 1928. This was two years after the Resident had agreed to modify the arrangement.
2 Ughelle Papers, File 53/1924, Petition from Effurun chiefs to Resident, Warri Province, 18 November 1923.
3 Ibid.
4 Ughelle Papers, File 112/26, Annual Report, Warri Division, 1926.

This chapter cannot be concluded without a further discussion of the effect, on Itsẹkiri-Urhobo relations, of Dọghọ's role in his various capacities as permanent president of the Warri Appeal Court, and as 'paramount chief'. Chief Dọghọ, like many men who find themselves in positions of great power and influence, was not only fully aware of his theoretical and legal powers, but tended to amplify them in practice. If he had authority to nominate chiefs, he had no power to remove or suspend the chiefs once they had been appointed. Suspension or removal was the sole prerogative of the Resident, using powers delegated to him by the Governor. Yet in 1920 Dọghọ instructed the clerk of the Patani Native Court to suspend a warrant chief for not carrying out his instructions. The District Officer protested strongly against Dọghọ's action. He wrote to the Resident:

> Will you please . . . inform me if Chief Dore has authority to temporarily suspend chiefs without reference to yourself or the D.O. . . . . Even if Chief Dore has authority to suspend chiefs in this way I strongly object to his writing to the court clerks except through me and I beg to point out that if any trouble occurred through such orders I should have to enquire into and settle the disputes and not Chief Dore.[1]

A similar incident occurred at Evbreni.

Dọghọ abused his office in other ways as well. In 1919 it was reported by the District Officer, Warri, that Dọghọ was in the habit of using his position to obtain oil from Urhobo villages at £5 a puncheon, and then retailing the oil to the factories at £20 a puncheon. The District Officer did not consider Dọghọ's methods a fair way of making money, and asked the Resident to advice him on what steps to take.[2] It would appear that the Resident made no comments on the issue. In the same year Dọghọ used his position to force the chiefs of the Frukama Native Court to supply him with 200 'sticks' (presumably hewn from what in that area is called 'iron wood') for the building of his house, using the veiled threat

---

1 Ughelle Papers, File 58/19, D.O. to Resident, 14 May 1920, and D.O. to Resident, Memo No. 349/1920, 31 May 1920. The Resident in his reply stated that Dọghọ had no right to suspend chiefs and promised to warn him and make it clear that if he persisted in such actions he would lose his presidency of the Appeal Court—Resident to D.O., Memo No. 330/1920, 31 May 1920.

2 Ughelle Papers, File 58/19, D.O. to Resident, Memo No. 601/1919.

of issuing a summons against the chiefs if they failed to do his bidding.[1] The District Officer again reported the incident, but apparently nothing came of it. Dọghọ quite clearly exercised a great deal of authority and influence over the Urhobo. It is obvious, however, that he was able to do this because of his official position with the British, rather than as a result of any rights or powers which he, as representing the Itsẹkiri, had over the Urhobo. It was only after his appointment as 'paramount chief' in 1917 that incidents like those depicted above occurred. His power lay at headquarters and he seemed to have been on extremely good terms with the Residents.[2]

Dọghọ's position benefited other Itsẹkiri too. As shown earlier there were, on the whole, only a few Itsskiri chiefs actually sitting in Urhobo courts in the pre-1914 period. After 1914 the number increased. At Ewu, Uwherun, Ivọrọgbọ, Okpare, where there were no Itsẹkiri warrant chiefs in the earlier period, these could now be found. Ekeke, who until 1916 was a member of the Warri Native Court, had his warrant transferred to Okpare Native Court, because he decided to settle at Okpare as a trader.[3] The District Officer commented:

> I cannot quite understand why he [Ekeke] should hold an official position as warranted chief in a town which being composed entirely of Sobo he by no means represents.[4]

Yet Ekeke was allowed to sit on the court for some four years before

1 Ibid., D.O. to Resident, Memo No. 15/58/19.
2 Interview with Mr. E. R. Chadwick in London, 20 December 1962. Chadwick served first as A.D.O., Warri and Ase, and later D.O., Warri, from 1929–33 and is one of the best-remembered D.O.'s in Urhoboland. He remained in Nigeria till 1954. He was Development Secretary, Eastern Nigeria, at the time of his retirement. At the time of the interview, he was Director of the Voluntary Service Association, London. Chadwick remarked that it was generally known among the junior administrative officers that Dọghọ was abusing his office but that he was clever enough to choose the right time and place. With the Residents he had officially an extremely good reputation.
3 C.S.O. 26/2 File 11329/S.I., Resident, Warri, to Secretary, S. Provinces, No. C3064/1909, 26 April 1919. Cheke similarly settled at Eruregbedi (a waterside settlement) in Ewu clan, and had his warrant transferred to the Ewu court from Warri: Interviews with Ọtota and elders of Ewu clan, 24–6 September 1963.
4 Ughelle Papers, File 25/1919, Shelton (D.O. Warri) to Resident, Memo No. 230/1919, 16 April 1919.

his warrant was cancelled. In the case of Apo, the Itsẹkiri who sat in the court at Uwherun, the Resident while agreeing that it was a mistake to have 'Jekri chiefs as warrant chiefs in Sobo Native Courts', could not see his way to removing Apo despite the protests of the Uwherun people, conveyed to him in a memorandum from the District Officer.[1] Not only were these Itsẹkiri appointments irregular, but the Itsẹkiri representation was out of proportion to their numbers. By 1930 in the Agbọn clan, there were seven Itsẹkiri warrant chiefs representing an estimated population of 180 (one chief for every twenty-six people) while nine Urhobo chiefs represented an estimated population of 4,652[2] (one chief for every 517). Admittedly, the courts were not houses of representatives, but it was a peculiar system in which the stranger elements were more adequately represented in the courts than the indigenes. One cannot but conclude that Dọghọ's position at headquarters, and the powers which he enjoyed, were partially (if not wholly) responsible for this anomaly. At first these appointments did not cause any strife between the Urhobo and the Itsẹkiri so appointed. The Urhobo were accustomed to having Itsẹkiri men live in their water-side settlements and regarded them as friends.[3] By the 1920s, however, the Urhobo were already beginning to agitate for the removal of the Itsẹkiri chiefs as the latter's attitude became increasingly overbearing, because they knew that their views would be sympathetically considered at headquarters, where they were regarded as performing essential services for the administration.

In fairness to the British administration, it must be put on record that it was realized, especially in the 1920s, that it was time to remove Itsẹkiri chiefs from Urhobo courts. The same officer who claimed that Itsẹkiri chiefs were given warrants to sit in Urhobo courts to show

1 Ughelle Papers, File 26/1919, D.O., Warri, to Resident, Warri, Memo No. 15/1920, 8 January 1920.
2 C.S.O. 26 File 28903, Intelligence Report, Agbon Clan, p. 30.
3 A number of Itsẹkiri warrant chiefs married from clans in which they settled. In Abraka clan these 'diplomatic marriages' led to very cordial relations. Tsẹgbọnẹ (Itsẹkiri) married Onokpese Ifeta; Eda (Itsẹkiri) married Yabe Ifeta. Ifeta was the *Qtota* of Abraka clan. It was difficult for the clan spokesman to spearhead any movement that would lead to the expulsion of his daughters and sons-in-law. There were similar marriages elsewhere. Interview with Uwumiakpo, the oldest member of the founder family and other elders of Abraka, 27–9 September 1963.

the Urhobo how to run the courts, also agreed that these chiefs had served their purpose by 1925 and that their continued presence in Urhobo courts was in many cases a source of trouble.[1] At the end of 1925 the warrant of Apo was transfered from the Uwherun court to Warri, and that of Memiafo, who sat on the Ivọrọgbọ Native Court, was cancelled.[2] The real problem which the administration had to face was to find the proper excuse for removing the Itsẹkiri warrant chiefs whose appointments it had sanctioned in the first place. The reorganization of the 1930s provided the opportunity. Their attempt, at that time, to put right the anomaly, had the effect of straining Itsẹkiri-Urhobo relations.[3]

Clause 23 of the Native Courts Ordinance, 1914, conferred on the Resident of a Province the right to appoint a Native Court of Appeal at the capital city of his province. In accordance with this provision, a Native Court of Appeal was opened at Warri, and Dọghọ was appointed its permanent president. Appeals to this court came from all over the Warri Province as it was then known. In this as in the case of the Warri Native Court, there was a preponderance of Itsẹkiri chiefs over Urhobo, Isoko, Kwalẹ, Aboh and Ijọ chiefs. A Native Court of Appeal by its very nature demanded proportionate representation from among the ethnic groups which attended it. Instead of such an arrangement, people travelled long distances only to face a court with a majority of Itsẹkiri chiefs presided over by Dọghọ.[4]

The Urhobo people did not leave any doubts about their dislike of the Warri Native Court of Appeal. The unpopularity of the court is mentioned in virtually all the intelligence reports on the Urhobo clans.[5] There were three main grounds for complaint. First, there

---

1 Ughelle Papers, File 96/1925, Annual Report, Warri Division, 1925.
2 Ibid.   3 See Chapter 6.
4 No figures showing the comparative numbers of Itsẹkiri and Urhobo members are available. But there is general agreement the court was 'predominantly Jekri' in composition. See C.S.O. 26 File 27630, Intelligence Report on Ughienvwe (Jeremi) Clan; also File 21943, Intelligence Report 'Ukpe' Clan, in which the court is described as 'virtually an Itsẹkiri court'.
5 See for example:
    C.S.O. 26 File 39797, Intelligence Report, Udu Clan
              File 28903,   „   „   Agbọn „
              File 26770,   „   „   Olomu „
              File 20653,   „   „   Ewu „

was the predominance of Itsẹkiri chiefs over the Urhobo. This meant that the Urhobo members of the court were so few (and they were usually the nominees of Dọghọ), that the majority of Urhobo clans had no representation at all.[1] Such unrepresented clans hardly considered it necessary to take their appeals to the court.[2] Secondly, the more hinterland Urhobo clans had considerable distances to travel in order to attend the Appeal Court. It was scarcely worthwhile to travel what, in those days, must have appeared great distances to attend a court which, as a result of its composition, could not guarantee (at least so the Urhobo felt) equitable judgements by the standards of the time. Rightly or wrongly, the Urhobo people felt that with the court composed as it was of an Itsẹkiri majority, their own laws and customs were not being adequately represented. In 'mixed' cases (that is in cases involving Itsẹkiri and Urhobo) the Urhobo had no confidence in the ability of the court to give an equitable verdict. Even such Urhobo chiefs as were members of the court could not always be present to act as a check on the Itsẹkiri, because of the distances they had to travel. Finally, there was the person and position of Dọghọ, the permanent president of the Appeal Court. With the Urhobo already prejudiced against the court, Dọghọ did not have to be a bad judge to arouse their suspicion. One of the reasons why the Urhobo so often bribed Dọghọ—by sending 'presents'—was that they knew that though he was only a president, and had to take into account the views of the other chiefs, his own view was very often accepted. Such a position could very easily be abused. The impression which persists today among the Urhobo, is that Dọghọ could be an extremely competent judge when he was not biased in favour of any party to a suit. When he was biased, he displayed an impatience towards detailed evidence which seriously undermined his integrity. The Urhobo elders remember his favourite peremptory orders on such occasions, '*Ja gbọnrọn*' and '*Kuwẹrẹ*',[3] both of which convey im-

---

1 C.S.O. 26 File 27630, Intelligence Report, Jeremi Clan.
2 C.S.O. 26 File 27998, Intelligence Report, Evbreni Clan.
3 '*Ja gbọrọn*' is an impertinent way of saying 'shut up' and is normally used by an elder to a junior, or a superior to his inferior. '*Kuwẹrẹ*' literally means 'get out of there' and, depending on the inflection of the voice, could be an extremely contemptuous remark.

patience and a certain autocratic disposition. As late as 1930, Dọghọ
was still being charged with this tendency. In that year the Resident
reported that the District Officer, Warri, complained to him that he
(the District Officer) had to use the powers conferred on him to
review cases heard in the Appeal Court on a number of occasions,
because Dọghọ sometimes displayed 'an amazing disregard for
evidence'.[1]

The administration had to face Urhobo protests against their
attending the Appeal Court soon after the inception of that court.
Apparently, the matter was so serious that the Governor's ruling
had to be sought. The Governor ruled that the Urhobo should not
be compelled to take their cases to the Appeal Court, but could
take them to the District Officer if they preferred to do so.[2] In the
last six months of 1921 for instance, the District Officer heard 396
appeals with 100 summonses still outstanding.[3] This policy, which
was clearly designed to meet the Urhobo protest, was altered in 1921
when, after a visit to Warri, the Lieutenant-Governor ruled that he
saw no evidence of the Appeal Court's unpopularity (despite the
many appeals heard by the District Officer) and that therefore all
appeals from the native courts were to go to that court without
reference to the District Officer. The District Officer, Mr. Wood,
was rather disappointed by this ruling. In handing over the Warri
Division, soon after, to Mr. Maddocks, he wrote:

> The best way for the natives to convince His Honour that they
> do not get justice is for them to appeal against it [the Appeal Court]
> freely.[4]

---

1 C.S.O. 26/2 File 11857, Vol. VIII, Annual Report, Warri Province, 1930.
2 Ughelle Papers, File 28/1921, Handing Over Notes, Warri Division: B. G.
  Wood (D.O.) to H. Maddocks (A.D.O.) June 1921. To quote Wood in full,
  'You will remember the dislike of the Sobos to the Appeal Court and the
  ruling of His Excellency that they were not to be compelled to have their
  cases tried there. The Lieutenant-Governor practically washed that out on
  his recent visit here, saying he saw no evidence of its unpopularity, and that
  cases were to go there without reference to the D.O.'
3 Ughelle Papers, File 68/1921, Annual Report, Warri Division, 1921.
4 Ughelle Papers, File 28/1921, Handing Over Notes, Warri Division:
  B. G. Wood (D.O.) to H. Maddocks (A.D.O.) June 1921. Even if the Urhobo
  did not appeal against the court's decisions, one should have thought that the
  D.O. of the Division was, in this matter, in a better position to judge the
  popularity of the court.

In order to offset, to some extent, the adverse effect of the Lieutenant-Governor's ruling, the Resident promised to increase the number of Urhobo chiefs in the court.[1] There is no evidence as to whether this promise was fulfilled or not. Here once more was that clash between the administrative officer on the spot who could better feel the pulse of the people among whom he laboured, and his superior officers at headquarters who were concerned with upholding the strict theory of the established system.

The Lieutenant-Governor's ruling did not stop the Urhobo agitation against the Appeal Court. As a result of their 'many protests against being compelled to attend a court the permanent president of which was a foreigner to them,'[2] a beginning towards meeting their protests was made in 1923, when another appeal court was established in the province. In that year the Kwalę Division, which included the Urhobo clan of Agbǫn, (this clan was most vociferous in its protests) had a separate appeal court established for it.[3] Sapęlę was also removed from the jurisdiction of the Warri Appeal Court, though it is not clear whether appeals from Sapęlę had to go to the Kwalę court or to the District Officer. The Resident commented on the Sapęlę decision:

> No appeals from Sapele Native Court are now allowed to be taken in Warri Appeal Court over which Dore dominates.[4]

The establishment of the Kwalę appeal court and the exclusion of Sapęlę from the jurisdiction of the Warri Appeal Court were thus, in effect, a demonstration against Dǫghǫ's power and influence, and a recognition of the Urhobo dislike of the Warri Appeal Court.

In 1926 yet another section of the province was removed from the jurisdiction of the Warri Appeal Court. In that year, the Isoko clans were constituted into a sub-district under the charge of an Assistant District Officer, with headquarters at Ase on the Niger.[5] The Isoko clans had, until then, been neglected on account of their distance from the headquarters at Warri, and the difficulty of finding transport for regular visits. With the establishment of the

---

1 Ughelle Papers, File 68/1921, Annual Report, Warri Division, 1921.
2 Ughelle Papers, File 41/1921, Murphy to Resident, 3 November 1925.
3 C.S.O. 26/2 File 11857, Vol. I, Annual Report, Warri Province, 1923.
4 Ibid.
5 Ughelle Papers, File 98/1929, Annual Report, Warri Division, 1926.

Ase sub-district, the complaints of the Isoko clans against being forced to attend the Warri Appeal Court were given attention. These clans had 'for a considerable time been petitioning for a separate Appeal Court' on the grounds of differences in custom and distance from Warri. On 3 December 1926 their demand was met: an Isoko Appeal Court was formally opened at Ase.[1] In the years which followed, people from Uwherun and Evbreni preferred to send their appeals to Ase rather than Warri though the latter place was more readily accessible.

It was in keeping with the administration's predilection for Dǫghǫ, that although they thus reduced his powers by establishing other appeal courts, it would appear that they did not appoint presidents by vice-presidents for these courts.[2] Dǫghǫ apparently still possessed certain powers over these courts and their decisions. In 1927, only some months after the establishment of the Isoko Appeal Court, the administration became alarmed by the growth and spread of the *Igbe* cult[3] in the Isoko area and in Kwalę Division. In August, the Assistant District Officer reported to the Resident that the Isoko chiefs were of the opinion that the cult be suppressed, lest it undermined their authority and led to civil disturbances:

> The majority of the Isoko Appeal Court chiefs are in favour of closing down the juju. I suggest that Chief Dore's confirmation be obtained and the order promulgated in every Native Court.[4]

It would appear from the above that 'Chief Dore' was still regarded as having some powers over the decisions of the Isoko Appeal Court.

It was not only the Urhobo who, by asking for separate institutions of their own, sought to reduce Dǫghǫ's power over them. His fellow Itsękiri too began to question his position. At the end of 1922 a dispute arose among the Itsękiri themselves. According to the Resident, a faction of the Itsękiri led by William Moore, and having

---

1 Ughelle Papers, File 98/1929, Annual Report, Warri Division, 1926.
2 This is the view expressed by Chief William Otobo who was a clerk in the provincial office during these years.
3 The *Igbe* cult is said to have been started by one Ubiosa of Ukhuokori (Kokori). It started off as a little group headed by Ubiosa who was credited with curative powers. It soon grew into a religion of its own which specialized in the detection of witches. See J. W. Welch: 'Witchcraft and Christianity in the Niger Delta', *Church Overseas*, Vol. IV, 1931, pp. 328–30.
4 Ughelle Papers, File S.D. 74/1927, Memo No. S.D. 74/1922, 8 March 1927.

as a figure-head Chief Denedo, were seeking 'to deprive Chief Dore of the position he . . . occupied since the arrival of British rule in Warri, i.e. that of Paramount Chief of the Jokri'.[1] As a matter of fact, at the time of the report, Chief Denedo and William Moore, on behalf of themselves and the members of the Olu Akẹngbuwa family, had taken out court action against Dọghọ (June 1922), challenging the latter's right to give out land in Warri (Ogbe-Ijoh and Alder's Town) to the British Government, and to receive rents therefrom. They contended that as descendants of the Olu Akẹng-buwa I, they owned the land and ought to receive the rents. The case did not come up for hearing till April 1923. In his judgement which was for Dọghọ, Mr. Justice Webber is reported to have declared:

> In appointing him Paramount Chief and spokesman for all the Jekris he was officially recognized as the head of the Jekri nation and the man with whom the Government would negotiate in all matters connected with the Jekri nation and their land.[2]

Dọghọ had won legal recognition as head of the Itsẹkiri and the rightful man to execute leases on their behalf.

Although Dọghọ had won this case, the suit had its administrative repercussions. One of the reasons which led to the court action was that Dọghọ did not share the rents he received with all those who felt entitled to a share, not did he spend the money on public utilities though he argued, during the trial, that he was merely a trustee for the people. In order to find some solution that would be more satisfactory and less productive of future dissensions, the Lieutenant-Governor held a meeting with all the Itsẹkiri chiefs in November 1924. At this meeting it was decided that the rents derived from Itsẹkiri lands (which totalled about £306) should be divided into six parts; Chief Dọghọ was to receive one sixth of this, and the remainder put into an Olu Trust Fund and banked in the name of the Resident. The money was to be used for public works and other legitimate purposes in Itsẹkiriland. Three trustees were appointed: Dọghọ, Ogbobinẹ and Ọmagbemi. No expenditure

1 C.S.O. 26 File 09209, Annual Report, Warri Province, 1922.
2 Attempts made to trace the original judgement in the records of the High Court, Lagos, failed. The above quotation is as recorded by William Moore, op. cit., p. 161.

from the money banked was to be incurred without the approval of the Resident.[1] Although Dǫghǫ was by this arrangement still recognized as the chief representative of the Itsękiri nation, his overall influence and power were somewhat curtailed.

In 1925 the Urhobo people of Agbassah took court action to question Dǫghǫ's right to collect rent from land in the Agbassah area, claiming that the land was theirs and not Itsękiri land.[2] In dismissing the claim of the plaintiffs Mr. Justice Maxwell is quoted by William Moore as having said that the legal position of the defendant (Dǫghǫ) had been firmly laid down by the Full Court on 1 February 1924 in connexion with the appeal which Chief Denedo and others had filed against Justice Webber's judgement of 1923.[3] The Agbassah people were to take up the matter again in the future, and even now, they have not finally accepted their several defeats in the law courts. From the very beginning of their struggle to claim ownership of the land on which they are settled, the legal position of Chief Dǫghǫ has been one of the greatest obstacles to their success. In the judgement of the Full Court to which Justice Maxwell referred, it was argued that Dǫghǫ was a successor to the old 'Governors of the River', and that as those 'Governors' were the trustees of Itsękiriland, so Dǫghǫ, by his appointment as 'paramount chief', was the legal trustee.[4] In an intra-Itsękiri suit such an argument probably held good, despite the different historical circumstances of Tsanǫmi's time and Dǫghǫ's in the 1920s. But in an Itsękiri-Urhobo suit, it needed first to be established that the land on which the Agbassah people settled was Itsękiri land before or at the time the Agbassah moved in. It would appear that this was assumed by the trial judge, otherwise it is difficult to see the validity of the reference to Dǫghǫ's legal position as established in a previous suit. The 'Agbassah land case', as it is popularly called,

1 C.S O. 26/2 File 11857, Vol. II, Annual Report, Warri Province, 1924.
2 Ughelle Papers, File 96/1925[A], Annual Report, Warri Division, 1925. The Agbassah people in question live in a section of what is now Warri Township. It is this section that they sought to claim as their land.
3 Moore, op. cit., p. 184.
4 Records of the Supreme Court, Lagos: Full Court Record Book, Vol. 5, pp. 2–4. Judgement in the case of Chief Omagbemi (sub for Chief Denedo) and others—Plaintiffs—Appellants V. Chief Dore Numa—Defendant—Respondent, 1 February 1924. (Records of the High Court, Lagos).

has remained up till now one of the factors making for bitterness in the relations between the Itsẹkiri and the Urhobo.

For the purpose of this study, it was not only the outcome of the two suits that was important. Equally important was the very fact that these court actions were taken out at all. For over twenty years Dọghọ's position had remained unchallenged. Now both his fellow Itsẹkiri men and the Urhobo were questioning his authority and thereby undermining his position. His legal rights were well founded. The people's protests amounted, in fact, to a challenge of Government's wisdom in granting him all the powers he enjoyed. In 1925 there remained but seven years of life for Chief Dọghọ. These seven years witnessed an increasing demand for a modification of his official position, and a whittling down of his powers. Developments in the 1930s contributed towards making his position untenable, but he retained his official position till he died in 1932.

The native court system and the career of Chief Dọghọ thus had important consequences for Itsẹkiri-Urhobo relations. Until the coming of the British, the relations between the Itsẹkiri and the Urhobo had been largely social and economic. With the establishment of native courts and the appointment of Dọghọ as paramount chief, a new element was brought into Itsẹkiri-Urhobo relations. This new element was political in nature. Hitherto, the Itsẹkiri and the Urhobo had not had to share the same judicial or political institutions. Now as a result of the introduction of native courts (and native court of Appeal) the Urhobo (some more than others) found themselves sharing common judicial institutions with the Itsẹkiri. The fact that in these common institutions there was always a preponderance of Itsẹkiri chiefs over Urhobo chiefs, was a source of grievance to the Urhobo, who saw themselves being subjected to the Itsẹkiri. There was considerable Urhobo agitation against this arrangement in the 1920s. The fact that the British administration did not, from the Urhobo point of view, react quickly enough to their clamour for a revision of the arrangements about which they complained, worsened the position, as the Urhobo tended to believe that the British were deliberately bringing them under the control of the Itsẹkiri. No doubt the British attitude was determined by their concern not to establish a multiplicity of native courts, and perhaps by a feeling that as the Itsẹkiri and the

Urhobo were already closely connected in certain respects, the bringing together of these two peoples in the judicial sphere would only further encourage an already existing tendency for the Itsẹkiri and the Urhobo to co-operate in various fields. This was all very well, except that where before the Itsẹkiri and the Urhobo had decided the nature and extent of their field of co-operation, now the decision lay in the hands of a third party, a party which (whether intentionally or not) tended to favour the Itsẹkiri in its appointments and disposition. This was one of the factors which led to Itsẹkiri-Urhobo tension over the native court system.

A feature of Itsẹkiri-Urhobo relations in pre-British and early British days was the friendship which existed between the Itsẹkiri men resident in Urhobo areas and the Urhobo themselves. This friendship, which had grown up over the years and was buttressed in many cases by marriage alliances, had at its base mutual respect between the Itsẹkiri concerned and the Urhobo in whose territory they lived. This respect had in turn developed out of a recognition of the mutual interdependence that was involved in the relations between the two groups. The years after 1914 witnessed an increased movement into the Urhobo areas of Itsẹkiri traders. This movement was partially prompted by the fact that with the opening up of the Urhobo hinterland by the British, more Urhobo were enabled to handle their own trade direct with the European firms, and therefore those Itsẹkiri who desired to improve their own trade had to move farther into Urhoboland in order to secure this trade. The result was that Itsẹkiri men were to be found in places like Ewu, Uwherun, Okpare, Ivọrọgbọ, into which areas they had not penetrated in the earlier period. It was these Itsẹkiri who, together with those who had settled earlier in places like Okpara and Abraka, were appointed to sit on the Urhobo courts. As the years passed, tension developed between some of these Itsẹkiri court members and their Urhobo counterparts. The tension, it would appear, resulted from the tendency of some of the Itsẹkiri to adopt an overbearing attitude in their dealings with the Urhobo. The attitude of these Itsẹkiri men was probably born out of the realization that the British regarded them as watchdogs over the Urhobo court members, as well as their awareness of the powers enjoyed by Dogho whose position had probably made their appointments possible in the first instance. While there was Urhobo agitation for the removal of specific court members, like Apo of the Uwherun native court, and Ekeke of Okpare native court, there was as yet no general demand for the removal of all Itsękiri men sitting in Urhobo courts. Nevertheless the apparant reluctance of the British administration[1] to remove these Itsękiri court members against whom the Urhobo complained, again tended to create the impression that the British were deliberately subjecting the Urhobo to the Itsękiri. This aspect of the working of the native court system thus had the result of undermining that old friendship which had existed between the Urhobo and the Itsękiri resident within their land.[2]

It was, however, the career and powers of Chief Dǫghǫ that led to the greatest discontent of all for the Urhobo. As paramount chief and permanent president of the Warri Native Court of Appeal to which, even after 1926 (when separate appeal courts had been opened for Kwalę Division and the Isoko), many Urhobo clans still had to take their cases, Dǫghǫ exercised great authority and influence over the Urhobo—authority and influence which were both new and political in content. At no time in the past had any Itsękiri man exercised such authority over the Urhobo. Not even Nana in all his might had been able to choose for the Urhobo who were to be their judges and local authorities. Dǫghǫ's powers, conferred on him by the British, were therefore a source of great irritation to the Urhobo. Their agitation against the Appeal Court was proof of this irritation. At the same time, their awareness of the fact that Dǫghǫ was backed up by the British Government, tended to make the Urhobo seek Dǫghǫ's co-operation rather than provoke his indignation. The position of the Urhobo, in the face of the tremendous authority conferred on Dǫghǫ by the British administration, was indeed a difficult one.

Perhaps the most important outcome of Dǫghǫ's career was that it furnished the best evidence for those who, in the 1930s, argued

---

1 This reluctance was only apparent because as pointed out on page 208 the British actually recognized the need to remove the Itsękiri concerned. But it was one thing to appoint the chiefs and quite another to remove them. The right opportunity had to be found and this took time. In the meantime the Urhobo saw the delay as evidence of British partiality for the Itsękiri.

2 This was not a sudden or complete development. It took time and varied in intensity from place to place.

that the Urhobo were ruled by the Itsẹkiri in years past. It was convenient when such claims were made, to forget that Dǫghǫ was the instrument of British rather than the Itsẹkiri power, and that the Urhobo constantly protested against the authority exercised over them by Dǫghǫ. Where Urhobo protests failed to be of any effect, this was the doing of the British administration rather than of Dǫghǫ or the Itsẹkiri as a people. Indeed, the career of Dǫghǫ is the best illustration of how the policies of the British administration led to the growth of conflict between the Itsẹkiri and the Urhobo.

Thus on the eve of the introduction of taxation and native administration, that cordiality and mutual respect, which had been noticeable in Itsẹkiri-Urhobo relations, were already being undermined as a result of various aspects of British rule. British rule had brought the Itsẹkiri and the Urhobo together in new ways, and emphasized, in the process, Itsẹkiri pre-eminence. As yet there was no general crisis in Itsẹkiri-Urhobo relations, but the Urhobo questioning of Itsẹkiri pre-eminence had begun, and there was already a noticeable deterioration in Itsẹkiri-Urhobo relations.

Chapter 6
The reorganization of the 1930's

'I think,' said Sir Graeme Thomson in May 1927, 'that the most important thing that has happened during my brief term of office is . . . the extension of this system of Native Administration to the hitherto untaxed provinces of Southern Nigeria.' The system of Native Administration under discussion was that then in operation in Northern Nigeria and, by 1927, in those provinces of the South which had traditional 'paramount chiefs'. One of the great virtues of that system, as seen by the British administrative officers, was that the Emirs 'were accustomed to exact and the people to pay taxes'. Consequently, it had been possible to introduce what were called 'Native Treasuries' into which was paid half the proceeds of taxation for use in local development and public services.[1] The system was judged to have been so successful in the North that it was extended to the Yoruba country and the Benin kingdom between 1914 and 1920. It was argued in support of this extension that in these areas 'the conditions bore a certain resemblance to those prevailing in the Fulani states' of Nigeria, both in the sense that they possessed 'paramount chiefs' and in the fact that they were accustomed to the payment of tolls and tribute to some form of central authority before the coming of the British. The rest of Southern Nigeria—Warri Province and those provinces east of the Niger—was lumped together as being 'for the most part in the clan or family stage of development' and so without 'paramount chiefs' and unaccustomed to the idea of tribute. These latter areas consequently stood out of the system for the time being.

By 1927, however, the time was considered ripe for the extension of the system of Native Administration to the Warri and other untaxed provinces despite the continued absence of what was

---

1 Sir Graeme Thomson (then Governor of Nigeria): 'Some Problems of Administration and Development in Nigeria' (an address delivered at a dinner of the African Society), *Journal of the African Society*, Vol. XXVI, 1926–7, p. 306.

considered the *sine qua non* of the system, namely, the institution of paramount chiefs. Two main reasons were advanced to justify this extension. First, it was held that 'no progress could be made in the Government's policy of educating these tribes in the art of self-government unless funds to establish Native Administrations were forthcoming, in the shape of direct taxation.' Secondly it was argued that justice demanded that direct taxation be extended to the areas concerned in order to bring them in line with the rest of Nigeria.[1] It was apparently thought that the 'native authorities' which had been appointed since 1917 could become the basis of the new Native Administration system. Accordingly in April 1927 the Native Revenue Ordinance was amended to make it applicable to Warri Province and the untaxed provinces of the then Eastern Nigeria. The corollary to the imposition of taxation was the setting up of 'native treasuries'. Tax was to be collected for the first time in these provinces in 1928. If from the point of view of the British administration this innovation was seen as an important event, for the Itsẹkiri and Urhobo it was even more momentous. The introduction of taxation and 'Native Administration' had extremely important consequences for Itsẹkiri-Urhobo relations.

The year 1928 was chosen for the implementation of the policy of taxation in order to give the administrative officers time to carry out propaganda work among the people, and to compile nominal rolls of all those who would be liable to pay tax. It was realized that taxation, however necessary, was an unpleasant innovation and that the greatest care would be required in the initial campaign and in formulating a scheme for its implementation.[2] As soon as the law was passed in April 1927, the administrative officers began their propaganda tours. The attitude of the people was described at that stage as 'sullen and suspicious'.[3] When the actual counting of the people began, it became clear that the Urhobo as well as the Itsẹkiri were very averse to the idea of taxation.

According to the Resident of the province, the anti-taxation

---

1 See Obaro Ikime: 'The Anti-Tax Riots in Warri Province, 1927–28', *J.H.S.N.*, Vol. III, No. 3, June 1967, p. 559.
2 Ughelle Papers, File 174/1947, Handing-Over Notes, Warri Division—G. S. Hughes (D.O.) to A. C. C. Swayne (A.D.O.) 26 April 1927, p. 6.
3 Ughelle Papers, File S.D. 41/1928, Annual Report, Ase Sub-District, 1927.

movement which developed as a result of the new policy, was started by the 'Young Jekri Party' whose chief spokesman was one Eda Otuẹdọn, a professional letter writer. This 'Party' was also the anti-Dọghọ party and it has been suggested that their opposition to taxation stemmed from the fact that Dọghọ had given his support to the measure.[1] Otuẹdọn was believed to have been in touch with the Democratic Party in Lagos, led by the late Herbert Macauley, which encouraged him in his agitation against the introduction of direct taxation. Otuẹdọn succeeded in winning over the bulk of the Itsẹkiri and then proceeded to canvass the support of the Urhobo, who hated the tax even more violently.

In the Urhobo country the anti-tax agitation was strengthened by the fact that the introduction of taxation coincided with a rumour, a false rumour as it turned out, that the plantation system was to be introduced in the palm oil industry—a rumour which filled the Urhobo with grave apprehension. As if that was not enough to make the Urhobo aggressive and unco-operative, they further learnt that the province was to become a 'licensed area' with regard to the trade in liquor and that even 'the paltry vendor of gin' would have to take out a licence.[2] It did not help matters that at the material time the cost of imported goods were rising while the prices for palm produce remained low. The Urhobo did not, therefore, require the goading of Otuẹdọn before making their feelings known and, in fact, before the joint meeting of the Itsẹkiri and Urhobo at Igbudu at the end of July 1927, the Isoko, who did not even attend that meeting, were already demonstrating their opposition by obstructing those sent out to compile the nominal rolls.[3]

Otuẹdọn found his Urhobo counterpart in one Oshue of Obodo, 'a man of no particular account but eloquent and inclined to be truculent on the factory beaches'.[4] Oshue would seem to have possessed all the qualities of an agitator. Fiery and eloquent, he had a gift for making people listen to his point of view. In fact, after a two-year prison sentence for his part in the anti-tax agitation, he

1 C.S.O. 26/2 File 11857 Vol. V, Annual Report, Warri Province, 1927, p. 6.
2 Ibid., p. 7.
3 Ughelle Papers, File S.D. 41/1928, Annual Report, Ase Sub-District, 1927, p. 1.
4 C.S.O. 26/2 File 11857 Vol. V, Annual Report, Warri Province, 1927, p. 6.

became the *Ọtota* of Udu,[1] a tribute to his eloquence and drive. With such a man spearheading the Urhobo agitation, it was possible to rally most of the Urhobo-speaking clans for the joint Itsẹkiri-Urhobo meeting at Igbudu in July 1927. At that meeting the Urhobo decided on a boycott of all trade with the Europeans; the stoppage of further production of palm oil; the closure of Native Courts and resistance to any arrests attempted either by the Native Courts or by the Police. The various clans were left to stipulate adequate punishments for any within their clans who contravened these decisions. A formal oath to be faithful to the above decisions marked the end of this memorable gathering.[2]

The joint Itsẹkiri-Urhobo meeting to protest against taxation was a public act of co-operation, the type of which was rare in the history of both peoples. It is significant that it was the Itsẹkiri and the Urhobo, and not either of these and any of the other peoples of the province, who decided to act together in opposition to the government. There had always been closer contact between the Itsẹkiri and the Urhobo than between either of them and any of their other neighbours, a phenomenon which also explains the fact that differences and conflicts between the Itsẹkiri and the Urhobo tend to receive more prominence, and to be fought with greater vehemence than similar conflicts between any of the other peoples of the province. As a matter of fact, the July meeting was about the only joint endeavour between the Itsẹkiri and the Urhobo with regard to taxation. Thereafter, there was little concerted effort or joint planning. The Itsẹkiri and the Urhobo left the meeting to act out their opposition in different ways and to differing lengths.

The agitation reached its greatest height during the months of August to October. In the Isoko and Urhobo areas, it took the form of hostility to the administrative officers; rescue of prisoners both from the hands of the police and from court messengers and native court hold-ups; destruction of the property of warrant chiefs, court scribes and messengers; and threat to, and sometimes attacks on, these persons, in addition to the boycott of trade and the closure of native courts. On 28 July, the Assistant District Officer, Ase,

---

1 C.S.O. 26 File 09098 Vol. X, Chief Commissioner's Inspection Notes, Warri Province, 1939, p. 17.
2 Ibid.

was threatened and mobbed at Uwherun; Mr. Swayne, Assistant District Officer, Warri, was similarly mobbed at Agbarho; at Ukhuokori on 27 September the car of Mr. de la Mothe (D.O. Kwalẹ) was damaged; rescue of prisoners took place at Oleh, Owe, Agbarho, Ughiẹnvwẹ.[1] Matters came to a head at Sapẹlẹ on 30 September. The Officer administering the Government was himself undertaking a tour of the area in connexion with the introduction of taxation. He addressed a large meeting at Sapẹlẹ on 30 September. During the meeting a man who attempted to create a disturbance was arrested by the police. The Urhobo people present at once set on the police in an attempt to rescue the arrested man. 'So determined and dangerous became the onslaught of the crowd' that the police had to open fire, killing one Urhobo and wounding two or three others.[2]

If the police thought that the show of force at Sapẹlẹ would deter the agitators, they were soon undeceived. The fury of the people was, in fact, directed less towards the administrative officers and the police than towards the local agents of the government: the warrant chiefs, court scribes, and messengers. It was this aspect of the agitation which made even more necessary the police patrols which visited the Urhobo areas in the months of November and December and finally, after a series of arrests and convictions, succeeded in quelling the unrest.[3]

The people's fury against the government's agents expressed itself in various forms. The closure of the courts and the determination of the *Ilẹtu* and *Evrawa* not to allow any court to be held was a demonstration against the warrant chiefs who were unpopular not only because of their high-handedness and corruption but also because they had apparently, without prior consultation with the people, accepted the imposition of the tax. In some places the chiefs

---

1 C.S.O. 26/2 File 11857 Vol. V, Annual Report, Warri Province, 1927, p. 8; Ughelle Papers, File S.D. 41/1928, Annual Report, Ase Sub-District, 1927, pp. 1–2.
2 C.S.O. 26/2 File 11857 Vol. V, Annual Report Warri Province 1927, p. 8. For some comparison between these riots and those which took place later in Eastern Nigeria see Obaro Ikime: 'Anti Tax Riots', p. 565; see also A. E. Afigbo: 'Revolution and Reaction in Eastern Nigeria: 1900–1929', *J.H.S.N.*, Vol. III, No. 3, December 1966, pp. 539–57.
3 Ibid., pp. 11–13.

and scribes were actually manhandled. At Owe the head warrant chief was beaten up in the presence of a policeman sent there to effect an arrest. The court messenger's house at Ozoro was broken into and the messenger himself assaulted. Indeed his life was saved only by the timely arrival the C.M.S. Superintendent who succeeded in rescuing him from the mob and escorting him away from the town. Similar incidents took place in various other places in Urhoboland. In Enwe clan the warrant chiefs were forced by the *Iletu* to pay a fine of £30 each for their past and current misdemeanours, and over £300 was collected in this way. When the head warrant chief, Okolosi, refused to pay the fine, the *Evrawa* were let loose on him, his house was damaged and his property confiscated. This act so terrified the other chiefs, that they either paid up quickly or ran out of the clan to the district headquarters at Ase for protection. The example of Enwe was quickly followed at Igbide, Oleh, Owe, Uwherun and some of the other Urhobo towns.[1] Despite this outburst of violence, it was remarkable that no attempt was made to destroy Government property. Court houses and rest houses were left intact.[2] This was a further indication that though it was the administration that imposed the tax, it was more against the warrant chiefs, the local agents of the government, that the people's anger was directed. No doubt this was because of the extortions and corrupt practices associated with these chiefs. In some respects, taxation was more the occasion than the real cause of the 1927 riots. In the general disorder that followed the agitation, Oshue became a 'national' hero and urged the people to resort to their ancient system of government and ignore the warrant chiefs. Everywhere the *Ekpako*, *Iletu* and *Evrawa* began to rule the towns and villages. The ensuing chaos was such that police patrols had to be sent into Urhoboland during the closing months of 1927.

The patrols in Urhoboland did not entail any bloodshed. By December the entire area had been 'pacified'. Most of the ringleaders were arrested, tried, and convicted; freed prisoners were re-arrested; the fines imposed on warrant chiefs were refunded and the Collective Punishment Ordinance was invoked against Enwe,

---

1 Ughelle Papers, File S.D. 41/1928, Annual Report, Ase Sub-District, 1927, p. 3.
2 C.S.O. 26/2 File 11857 Vol. V, Annual Report, Warri Province, 1927.

Evbreni, and Owe. Those sentenced to terms of imprisonment, ranging from three months to three years, numbered over a hundred.[1] The people discovered that do what they might, the government was determined to go ahead and collect the tax in 1928.

If the patrols were intended primarily to punish those responsible for the outrages of the period and restore law and order, as well as to convince the people to reopen trade, they also served the purpose of giving the administrative officers who accompanied them, an opportunity of finding out from the people what they really found obnoxious in the idea of taxation, apart from their natural reluctance to part with money. These investigations brought out interesting revelations. It was discovered that what the Urhobo man found most galling was the fact that he was forced to pay what to him seemed like an annual redemption fee.[2] This reminded him of the days of old when, having pawned his son, he had to redeem him or subject him to perpetual slavery. It was the realization that to insist on everyone paying a certain sum 'per head' was bound to create this feeling of revulsion, that led the government to adopt a system of lump sum assessment which the towns were left to pay in whatever way best accorded with their customs.

These investigations brought out even more forcefully the unpopularity of the warrant chiefs. In Agbarho Clan, the anti-tax agitators definitely refused to abandon their intransigence unless 'the existing warrant chiefs were swept away and others appointed, urging the present office holders were so corrupt that further submission to them was out of the question'.[3] At Ẹnwẹ, the *Iletu* accused the chiefs of retaining for their personal use, monies due to the townspeople for work done on rest houses, court houses and roads.[4] The warrant chiefs had so completely lost the confidence of their people, that the administration had to abandon their original

1 C.S.O. 26/2 File 11857 Vol. V, Annual Report, Warri Province, 1927, p. 12. Enwe was fined £200 and Evbreni and Owe each £100.
2 Ibid., p. 27. To this day the Urhobo equivalent for 'tax'—*osa unyovwi* (Osa-Uzou' in Isoko) literally means 'a fee paid on the head'—a redemption fee. One sees what havoc deficient interpretation could do in those days, for obviously the Urhobo equivalent is a faulty interpretation of 'per head'.
3 Ibid., p. 21.
4 Ughelle Papers, File S.D. 41/1928, Annual Report, Asẹ Sub-District, 1927, p. 4.

plan to make them collect the tax, for which service they were to have been paid ten per cent of the total sum collected. It became obvious that such a measure 'would be hotly resented by the people'. Indeed the Urhobo insisted on the District Officers collecting the tax rather than delegating the duty to the warrant chiefs.[1]

While the warrant chiefs were forcibly prevented from carrying out their duties, power fell into the hands of the *Iletu*, the traditional executive organs of the government of the people, and the *Evrawa*, the labour corps. These were the two age grades which spearheaded the anti-warrant chief movement. Their success indicated that they had the support of those *Ekpako* and titled men who had been excluded from power as a result of the régime of native courts. By the end of 1927 it was reported that village councils composed of Ekpako and titled men were ruling the towns. It thus became clear that the operation of the Native court system had not succeeded in destroying the indigenous political institutions. All that had happened was that the traditional authorities had been repressed and driven underground. The ease with which they revived showed a resilience which is not often credited to them. The anti-tax riots were therefore the most convincing indictment of the native court system as it had operated up to that time. In the prevailing circumstances, the government was forced not only to find a solution to the resultant *impasse* but to investigate, for the first time, the social organization of the people with a view to discovering where power ought really to lie.

The agitation in Itsẹkiriland receives but little attention in the administrative reports, for in Itsẹkiriland the agitation did not last as long as in Urhoboland not did it entail patrols. Very few Itsẹkiri men were prosecuted or convicted during the trials which followed the riots. The Resident, commenting on this fact, wrote, 'the astute Jekris were more careful to keep within the bounds of the law or more clever at covering up their illegalities than the less sophisticated Sobos'.[1] It was not, however, only in the astuteness and craftiness of the Itsẹkiri that the explanation for the extent of Itsẹkiri participation in the agitation was to be found. There were

1 C.S.O. 26/2 File 11857 Vol. V, Annual Report, Warri Province, 1927, p. 27.
2 Ibid., p. 9.

two other explanations. First, the Itsẹkiri were much nearer administrative headquarters than the Urhobo, and so were more within
the reach of the British political officers and the police, a fact which
undoubtedly affected the length to which they were prepared to
carry their agitation. Secondly, because the Itsẹkiri had become
accustomed to accepting some non-traditional authority since the
interregnum of 1848, the question of warrant chiefs was not such
an issue in Itsẹkiriland as it was in Urhoboland. Men like Dọghọ
and Chief Skin were too firmly in the saddle, and too much the
creatures of the government, to be easily or safely toppled by mob
action. Otuẹdọn, who was the leading Itsẹkiri figure at the beginning
of the agitation, only remained in Warri till the government began
to take firm action to combat the agitation. He then went off to the
Gold Coast on the pretext of recruiting counsel to prosecute the
police for the Sapẹlẹ shooting. He did not return to the fight.[1]
Deprived of its leader, and faced with government determination to
restore law and order, the agitation soon lost its fire and collapsed.

Taxation was only one aspect of a broader policy, that of the
introduction of 'Native Administration'. The essential features of
the policy were indigenous authorities with power to rule over their
people, and 'native treasuries' into which was to be paid 50 per cent
of the tax money and the court fees in the respective localities, for
use in paying the salaries of the ruling authorities and their staff,
and for the carrying out of local public works. It had become obvious
to the administration by the end of 1927, that the 'native authorities'
as they then existed were not the traditional authorities, and that
before the new system could be effectively worked, the right authorities would have to be discovered and enthroned. Yet before these
authorities were established, 'Native Administration came into
being'—by official declaration in October 1927.[2] In practice this
meant that the administrative officers began discussing with the
people the theory of the system, and emphasizing the benefits
to be derived therefrom. It also meant the setting up of 'native
treasuries' into which the tax which was to be collected the following
year could be paid. As a matter of fact, when these 'native treasuries'

---

1 Ibid., p. 9.
2 War. Prof. 3/9 File 201/27, Annual Report, Warri Division, 1927, p. 2.

were eventually established, they were more under the control of the District Officers than the 'native authorities'.

It has been suggested that it was the above introduction of Native Administration which set the Itsẹkiri thinking seriously about installing an Olu and thereby finding a more traditional figure around whom to rally as a united people.[1] With the Urhobo there could be no question of seeking to find a 'national' ruler. Yet even among them, despite their clannishness, the introduction of the system produced unprecedented co-operation in opposition. As the Resident remarked, 'the gathering of the fourteen clans of Sobos to oppose taxation showed an unexpected tribal consciousness and unity',[2] which he hoped could be turned into good administrative use. The 1930s were further to enhance this tendency towards unity among the Itsẹkiri on the one hand, and the Urhobo on the other—a development which was to have its own consequences for Itsẹkiri-Urhobo relations.

While the next few years were being used for the purpose of inquiring into the traditional social, political and judicial institutions of the people of the province, with a view to discovering, among other things, who should be the proper 'native authorities', the broader principles of Native Administration were being enunciated and implemented. Because the people were definitely interested, for a variety of reasons, in the new system, it was necessary to demonstrate at an early stage the differences between the new and the old systems. The warrant chiefs had been the victims of the furore of 1927: during those troubled months their unpopularity and impotence in the face of a spontaneous revival of traditional authority were clearly revealed. It was decided therefore that if the District Officers were not themselves to collect the tax, the only alternative was to ask the elders of the people to do so, using their customary agencies. Hence even before the intelligence reports had been compiled, and reorganization formally approved, the council of elders in the villages was being used for collecting the tax.[3] The shift of authority from warrant chiefs to the traditional authorities had already begun.

1 C.S.O. 26/2 File 11857, Annual Report, Warri Province, 1927, p. 25.
2 Ibid.
3 C.S.O. 26/2 File 11857 Vol. VI, Annual Report, Warri Province, 1928, p. 22.

Where in the pre-1927 era it had been illegal for the elders to meet to settle disputes among their people, they were now encouraged to arbitrate in cases of dowry, debt and other non-criminal causes. The warrant chiefs were warned not to molest the elders for thus resuming a duty which, it was now argued, naturally and properly belonged to them.[1] Despite the fact that this was only an administrative decision without the backing of law, and despite the fact that the village councils which were now beginning to function after a lapse of over thirty years had no legal power to enforce their judgements, it was reported that the people, nevertheless, took their cases to them and accepted their verdicts.[2] This was a useful way of preparing the *Ekpako* for the duties and responsibilities which reorganization was to restore to them.

Meanwhile, the legal native courts and 'native authorities' of the pre-1927 era continued to function. But adjustments were being constantly made. It was realized that a number of warrant chiefs had no right to be on the courts by virtue of any positions which they held in accordance with custom and tradition in their communities. Such members began to be gradually weeded. Until village and clan councils were legally reorganized as the 'native authorities', these courts were to continue to function, though attempts were now made to distinguish between the judicial work of the courts and their executive duties. So far as the latter were concerned, those members who did not possess such titles or other qualifications that would have entitled them to sit on village or clan councils were not to be consulted, and the village councils were to be encouraged to undertake executive work.[3] As the investigations into traditional organization progressed, it became understood that the major fault with the old system was not necessarily that the wrong people were appointed to the native courts (though there was always this factor). Rather it was that the delegatory nature of the members was lost, as the District Officers used the warrant chiefs as local agents of the government in the villages, and held them responsible for seeing that the orders of the government were carried out even when these entailed executive action, thereby transforming mere delegates into effective rulers.[1] What reorganization was to imply, therefore, was not a wholesale removal of current court members, but a gradual displacement of unqualified members and the appointment of new members until the courts became, in personnel, the same as the village councils, to which executive and judicial duties could then be entrusted in accordance with custom. In these circumstances, the clash between the warrant chiefs and the *Ekpako* was, in practice, less than anticipated. Indeed, the warrant chiefs were on the whole quick to realize the need to adjust themselves to the new policy. From Sapẹlẹ District it was reported in 1929 that there was no fear (at least among the Urhobo of the district) that the warrant chiefs would usurp executive functions: 'their reluctance to venture any private opinion on public matters without prior reference to their elders is remarkable.'[2]

In order further to ease the transition from the native court to the Native Administration system, a number of other administrative decisions were taken. The title 'Warrant Chief' was abolished in 1928, and in its place 'Court member' was substituted, and thereafter attempts were made to persuade some *Ekpako* to become court members in an attempt to lessen the cleavage between the village council and the native courts. The practice whereby District Officers recommended people's application for warrants was also discontinued and the Resident warned that there should be no question of anyone applying for a warrant; rather, the administrative officer was expected to know when a town was due for representation, and carry out inquiries about the right person to be appointed: 'such ideas as rewarding a man for good work done by appointing him to be a court member are things of the past.'[3]

As the membership of the courts needed reshuffling, so did the relations of the court clerks and messengers to the court members require re-examination. If the system of Native Administration was to enhance the prestige of the traditional rulers before their people, then the clerks and messengers had to be taught to regard themselves

---

1 C.S.O. 26/2 File 11957 Vol. VI, Annual Report, Warri Province, 1928, p. 19.
2 C.S.O. 26/2, File 11857, Vol. VIII, Annual Report, Warri Province, 1929, p. 60.
3 C.S.O. 26/2, File 11857, Vol. VI, Annual Report, Warri Province, 1928, pp. 25, 39.

as servants rather than masters as many of them thought they were. As one of the ways of achieving this objective, it was decided that the District Officer should have his own messengers as distinct from the court messengers: 'Administrative Officers should not be forced to give orders to Native court messengers. The Native Court and the Native Authority alone should do so.'[1] In this way it was hoped that the court messengers would be made to see themselves in the proper light.

A Native Administration, made up of local authorities of the type envisaged, necessarily implied placing emphasis on ethnic considerations. Therefore it was out of the question, in the implementation of the new policy, to have Itsẹkiri chiefs in Urhobo courts or vice versa. Similarly, it would be more difficult for a court clerk who was a stranger to the area in which he was placed to put up with the self-effacement which the new policy demanded and to enter fully into its spirit. The future development of the new system, as shall be seen, insisted on court members and scribes being citizens of their respective clans or community.

During the two years which followed on the anti-tax riots, the traditional organization of the Urhobo had been sufficiently investigated for it to be known that the vital organ of local government was the village council, with the clan council constituting a possible superior body.

For the Itsẹkiri, it was easy to discover that the traditional order was an Olu and his council, wielding authority over all Itsẹkiriland. But although there was some interest shown with regard to the election of an Olu, the old rivalry between the Ode-Itsẹkiri and Benin River factions presented a difficulty. A meeting held in December 1928 only succeeded in agreeing that an *Olotu*, the traditional regent and priest, should be appointed.[2] Another obstacle to the appointment of an Olu and the re-organization of the Itsẹkiri was the position of Chief Dọghọ. During the discussions in 1928 it became clear that his position constituted a bar to re-organization along the traditional lines:

1 Ughelle Papers, File 64/1928, Warri Division—Political and Administrative Report for Quarter ending 30 September 1929, p. 8.
2 C.S.O. 26/2 File 11857, Vol. VI, Annual Report, Warri Province, 1928, p. 17.

The net result of the year's inquiries would indicate that an Olu cannot be appointed in Dore's life time because Dore's position . . . has been too long established for the revival of the Oluship to be regarded in any other light than that of a reverse to the Ologbotsere faction which for half a century dominated Jekri politics.[1]

The best that could be expected was for the two factions to sink their differences, so that on the death of Dogho they could together elect an Olu who would be recognized by all the Itsekiri people. The position taken by the administration in this instance was in sharp contrast to that in Urhoboland, where the powers of the former warrant chiefs, irrespective of length of tenure of office, were being systematically reduced in preparation for full reorganization. Dogho had become too powerful to be treated like other warrant chiefs. All that the government felt able to do was to suggest to him that he should consider withdrawing from active participation in Native Administration affairs, and that if he so withdrew, the government would consider increasing his emolument from the Itsekiri 'native treasury'[2]—in other words grant him a pension. But Dogho was not prepared for that kind of self-effacement.

By 1930 enough progress had been made in the inquiries started in 1927 to enable the Resident to submit a broad scheme for the reorganization of the province. This scheme provided for the setting up of village and clan councils as the local authorities for the Urhobo; the establishment of a central council and village-group councils for the Itsekiri; the grouping of these local administrations into Native Administrations; and the recasting of the province into Divisions in line with the new Native Administrations. These new divisions were to coincide with the ethnic groupings of the province: people of the same ethnic group were to be placed within the same unit of Native Administration.[3] In December, the Lieutenant-

1 Ibid., p. 16.
2 Ibid., p. 17.
3 C.S.O. 26, File 26767, A Broad Scheme for the Reorganization of Warri Province on tribal lines. See also C.S.O. 26/2, File 11857, Vol. VIII, Annual Report Warri Province 1930. This scheme was based on the reports of the various District Officers who compiled 'Intelligence Reports' during the years 1929–32 in which they analysed the traditional set-up and suggested proposals for the future. These reports were really only useful in so far as the setting up of local administrations were concerned. The Resident was

Governor approved the scheme, and the years 1931–2 were spent setting up new 'native authorities'.

In Urhoboland these authorities were based on the clan. As much as possible they were made up of those who traditionally sat on the village and clan councils, though the *Ekpako* and the titled men were encouraged to seek the co-operation of the younger educated elements in their communities. As by 1931 no Olu had yet been appointed, Itsẹkiri reorganization took the form of 'a subtribal council' composed of the heads of the leading families and such other notables as the village groups and settlements desired. The *Olotu* (Chief Omagbemi was so appointed) and Chief Dọghọ were *ex-officio* members; the former was to preside at executive meetings and the latter at judicial meetings.[1]

There was one exception to the general rule of reorganization along ethnic groupings. The Resident proposed that there was to be a 'Jekri-Sobo' Native Administration, made up of all the Itsẹkiri and five Urhobo clans territorially close to Itsẹkiriland. His argument was that the Itsẹkiri were a dying race, and that intermarriage between them and the Urhobo clans he proposed to associate with them was so widespread, that it was possible to envisage a complete fusion and the emergence of a 'Jekri-Sobo subtribe'.[2] He realized that in the meantime, the two peoples though socially intermixed were politically distinct. He hoped to preserve, out of respect for the feelings of the people and in keeping with the fundamentals of the new policy, a measure of this political distinctness, by giving the Urhobo separate local administrations while bringing them together with the Itsẹkiri under a common Native Administration. In this way the two peoples would learn to co-operate in various activities and eventually develop into a single 'sub-tribe'. To some extent one can sympathize with the considerations which led the Resident into thinking in terms of a 'Jekri-Sobo subtribe'. Social and commercial intercourse between the Itsẹkiri and the Urhobo had led to a considerable inter-mingling between both peoples;

---

responsible for the scheme of Native Administration and the breaking up of the province into Divisions.

1 C.S.O. 26/2, File 11857, Vol. IX, Annual Report, Warri Province, 1931, p. 16.
2 C.S.O. 26, File 26767, A Broad Scheme for the Reorganization of Warri Province on tribal lines.

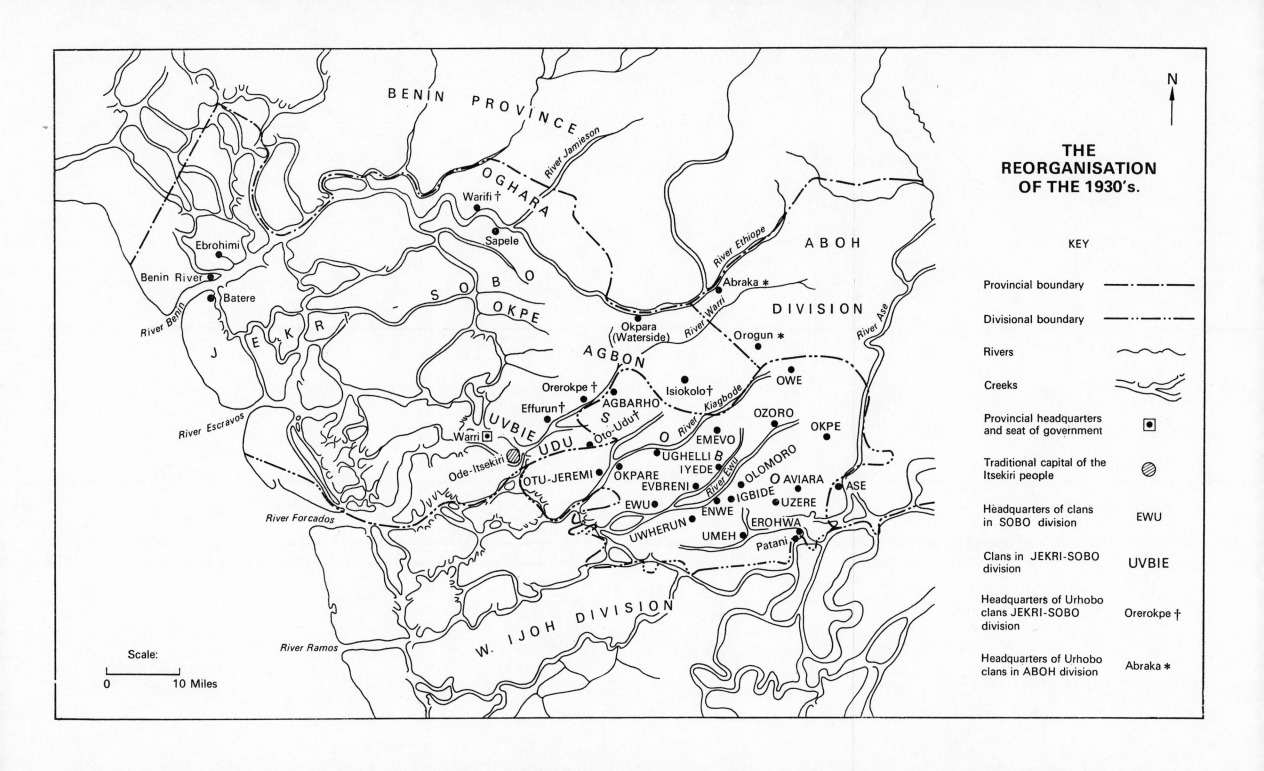

N

THE
REORGANISATION
OF THE 1930's.

BENIN PROVINCE

River Jamieson

OGHARA

Warifi †

Sapele

Ebrohimi

River Ethiope

ABOH

Benin River

Abraka *

S O B O

OKPE

DIVISION

Batere

River Benin

Okpara
(Waterside)

River Warri

Orogun *

River Ase

J E K R I

J

AGBON

River Escravos

Orerokpe †

Isiokolo †

OWE

Kiagbode

Effurun †

AGBARHO

OZORO

S

OKPE

Oto-Udu †

River

UVBIE

EMEVO

Warri ▣

UDU

UGHELLI B

OLOMORO

Ode-Itsekiri

IYEDE

River Ewu

AVIARA

O

OTU-JEREMI

OKPARE

OLOMORO

ASE

EVBRENI

IGBIDE

UZERE

EWU

ENWE

EROHWA

River Forcados

UWHERUN

UMEH

Patani

W. IJOH DIVISION

River Ramos

Scale:

0   10 Miles

KEY

Provincial boundary

Divisional boundary

Rivers

Creeks

Provincial headquarters
and seat of government   ▣

Traditional capital of the
Itsekiri people

Headquarters of clans
in SOBO division   EWU

Clans in JEKRI-SOBO
division   UVBIE

Headquarters of Urhobo
clans JEKRI-SOBO
division   Orerokpe †

Headquarters of Urhobo
clans in ABOH division   Abraka *

the linguistic barrier was considerably reduced as many Itsẹkiri understood and spoke the Urhobo language and vice versa; the customs of both peoples had become, to some extent, mixed and similar. It was easy for the Resident to envisage a fusion of both peoples or, at least, a fusion of the Itsẹkiri and those Urhobo clans nearest to them. But there were certain obstacles to such fusion. First, the Itsẹkiri were not a dying race as they were portrayed by the Resident; inter-marriage with the Urhobo had not led to a loss of their identity as a separate and distinct people. Secondly, the history of the years immediately preceding the introduction of Native Administration made the possibility of the type of fusion envisaged by the Resident remote. Since about 1920 the Urhobo had constantly protested against being forced into the same political and judicial institutions with their Itsẹkiri neighbours. The clans which had been foremost in this protest, Uvbiẹ, Agbọn, Udu and Okpẹ, were among those which were now proposed to be included in the 'Jekri-Sobo' Native Administration. Thirdly, the Resident was fully aware that the Itsẹkiri regarded themselves as superior to their Urhobo neighbours, and that the Urhobo resented this attitude.[1] So long as the Itsẹkiri attitude remained unchanged and the Urhobo resentment unassuaged, it was unlikely that the political matrimony into which the Resident sought to bring them would be a happy or lasting affair. In 1932 there was evidence that both peoples had not changed their respective attitudes one to the other. As the Resident himself wrote, 'The Jekris desire such a Native Administration but upon the old basis of Itsẹkiri predominance. The Sobos at present do not.'[2] The clash of interest and aspirations was there, but it was ignored in a pious hope that the pressure of administrative, commercial and other requirements would resolve this major clash. At any rate, it was scarcely wise to force the Urhobo into such a Native Administration when once it became clear that they did not desire to be in it, and when the advantages to be derived from the projected union were far from obvious. The creation of the

---

1 C.S.O. 26, File 26767, A Broad Scheme for the Reorganization of Warri Province on tribal lines.
2 C.S.O. 26, File 26767, Report on Proposed New Jekri-Sobo Division— Enclosure in Secretary Southern Provinces to Chief Secretary to the Government, No. 6925/238 of 10 February 1932.

'Jekri-Sobo' Division, incorporating the proposed Native Administration, was to be a major factor leading to a worsening of relations
between the two peoples.

By 1930 the Urhobo were intensely suspicious of their Itsẹkiri
neighbours, as a result of their experience during the native court era.
Consequently they were happy to take advantage of reorganization
to develop along their own lines. Knowing that they would be judged
by how quickly they settled down to the new system, the Urhobo
seemed to have lost little time in grasping the essentials of the new
policy. At this point the British administrative officers did not make
Itsẹkiri-Urhobo relations any easier by using the Urhobo as a
kind of political catalyst to quicken the Itsẹkiri reaction to reorganization, a reaction which, in the view of the administration,
was rather slow. At a meeting with the Itsẹkiri chiefs during a visit
by the Lieutenant-Governor in March 1931, the Resident harangued
the chiefs for their factiousness at council meetings and their
inability to work together and maintain a firm hold over their people.
He warned them:

> It is largely by their own efforts that the Sobos have come forward,
> and the Jekris must realise that being in the minority they cannot
> hope to take the lead in a combined Jekri-Sobo Native Administration
> except on the score of merit.[1]

The Lieutenant-Governor took up the same tale: 'In the old days
the Sobos were very 'bush' . . . Now times have changed and the
Sobos have come forward. However hard it is to realize, the Jekris
must understand that the Sobos cannot be kept back.'[2] Here in evidence once more was the point made earlier that Itsẹkiri-Urhobo
relations were such that it was between them that comparisons and contrasts were being constantly drawn: the British administrative officers
did not draw the attention of the Itsẹkiri to the progress being made
by the Ijọ or Kwalẹ but to that being made by the Urhobo, not
because the other people were not making any progress, but because
of the close social and other connexions between the Itsẹkiri and
the Urhobo. By so doing, however, the British were inadvertently

---

1 Ughelle Papers, File 35/1931, Interview between Jekri Notables and His
Honour the Lieutenant-Governor, Southern Provinces, at the Resident's
Office, Warri, on 31 March 1931.　　　　　　　　　　2 Ibid.

emphasizing that Itsẹkiri-Urhobo rivalry which was fast becoming a much more noticeable feature of the relations between the two peoples than it had been at any earlier period; they were also emphasizing the conflicting aspirations of the two peoples. Even more important was the fact that the administrative officers' harangues (however well meant) constituted a challenge to the Itsẹkiri. The natural reaction of the Itsẹkiri was a determination to demonstrate that they were still a vigorous, progressive, dominant people by putting up exaggerated claims to past glories, claims which almost invariably involved an assertion of dominion over the Urhobo in times past. The result was a deterioration in Itsẹkiri-Urhobo relations which the creation of a 'Jekri-Sobo' Division did little to assuage.

It was not till 1934 that reorganization among the Urhobo was completed and the new policy formally inaugurated. On 1 April 1932, the old 'District treasuries' were closed and 'Divisional treasuries' established, to serve the new divisions that were proposed. These divisions were formally approved in 1934. This meant that Ase ceased to be the headquarters of a sub-district, as the Isoko clans were merged with the Urhobo clans not in the 'Jekri-Sobo' Division to form the new 'Sobo' Division with headquarters at Ughelle.[1] As it finally emerged, reorganization implied recognizing the village and clan councils as the proper and legal 'native authorities' and, in keeping with custom, these councils also constituted the new native courts. According to their size and capability, the village councils were granted judicial powers of 'D' or 'C' grade. The clan councils were 'C' or 'B' courts according to the same criteria.[2] These councils were charged with the responsibility for ruling their people according to custom under the supervision of the District Officer. Their great duty was the collection of tax by

---

1 C.S.O. 26/2 File 11857 Vol. X, Annual Report, Warri Province, 1932, p. 35. Also C.S.O. 26/2 File 11857 Vol. XII, Annual Report, Warri Province, 1934, p. 1. Ughelle Papers: Annual Report, Warri Division, 1932, p. 11.

2 War. Prof. 3/15 File 48/1932, Quarterly Reports, Warri Division March 1932. Although the courts were usually graded B, C, or D, there were no hard rules governing these gradations. The power of each native court was usually 'set forth in its warrant'. Clause I Native Courts Ordinance, 1914. There were no courts of 'A' Grade in the Warri Province, these being mainly the Alkali courts of Northern Nigeria.

which they were often judged. One factor which made the administration satisfied with Urhobo progress during the years 1928–36 was that the elders were always prompt in collecting and 'taking in' the tax. This convinced the administrative officers that the machinery for local government was vigorous and was being well handled.

It was regarded as a matter of the utmost importance that the village and clan councils which made up what were described as the local administrations, should be taught to handle some of the money which they collected. Thus 60 per cent of the tax collected was given back to the local administration of the area from which it had been collected, as well as 40 per cent of native court process fees, for use in paying executive and judicial salaries to those who sat in the councils and to the council's staff, as well as for use in financing purely local public works. The actual distribution and appropriation of this money was left in the hands of the councils, to be done according to custom. This was seen as a useful way of inculcating financial responsibility.[1]

In 1934 therefore, Native Administration in the Urhobo area consisted very much of local administrations. It was hoped that after a number of years the local administrations would see the need for a larger unit within which to operate and would, on their own initiative, ask for a superior 'Sub-tribal native authority' that is, a superior council made up of representatives of all the clans in the 'Sobo' Division. In 1934 and 1935 there was no such superior authority. What existed was a Finance Committee made up of delegates from the clans as well as educated elements chosen by the District Officer and approved by the local administrations. These delegates could be changed from meeting to meeting. The main duty of this committee was to assist the District Officer in drawing up estimates for the Native Administration. For in the absence of a superior authority, it was left to the District Officer, after consultation with this Committee, to draw up estimates and plan public works like the building of roads, bridges, wells and market stalls, which were a striking feature of the years of reorganization. The aim behind associating the Committee with the District Officer in this work of drawing up estimates and planning development

---

1 C.S.O. 26/2 File 11857 Vol. IX, Annual Report, Warri Province, 1931, pp. 29–30.

schemes was that the Committee should form the nucleus of an Urhobo Council which could, in later years, take over from the District Officer, and act as a superior authority.[1] It was thus this Committee that planned the expenditure of that proportion of the tax, court fees, and court fines that was allocated to the Native Administration. In the first three years of its existence, the Committee was reported to be learning slowly but surely, and in 1936 a 'Sobo-Isoko Executive Council' came into being.[2] Although great emphasis was placed on a 'native treasury', such a treasury had not actually come into being by 1936, as there was as yet no superior 'native authority' to supervise the treasury, and it was felt that it would be inadvisable to set up a 'native treasury' for each clan. Consequently, what did exist was a 'Divisional treasury' in Ughelle, under the control of the District Officer, advised by the Finance Committee and later the Executive Council.

The 'native courts' of the reorganization era were, as has been said, the same bodies as the village and clan councils. As every village cried out for and obtained its own council, there was a multiplicity of 'courts'—many with very limited powers, and incapable of keeping proper records of proceedings. Although from the point of view of efficiency the administration regarded these 'courts' as unsatisfactory, it nevertheless decided to tolerate them for the first few years of reorganization, because the Urhobo were so enthusiastic about reorganization and Native Administration, that it was considered expedient, as a means of retaining that enthusiasm and ensuring their continued co-operation, to give every village at this initial stage an opportunity to manage its affairs through its *Ekpako*, titled men and age grades. It was hoped that the villages themselves would discover that it was in their interests to federate and form larger units in the interest of efficiency and general development. This hope began to be fulfilled when in 1937 the Ughienvwe Clan which originally had thirty-three courts decided to group most of these together and so form only four such

1 C.S.O. 26/2 File 11857 Vol. X, Annual Report, Warri Province, 1932, p. 18. Also War. Prof. 3/15 File 48/1932, Quarterly Reports, Warri Division, March 1932.
2 C.S.O. 26/2 File 11857 Vol. XIV, Annual Report, Warri Province, 1936, p. 9. See also War. Prof. 3/15 File 48/1932 as above.

courts.[1] Future reorganization in the other clans was to follow along similar lines.

When in 1932 Chief Dǫghǫ died, the Warri Native Court of Appeal was conveniently closed; the Isoko Appeal Court at Ase was closed in the same year. Until 1936 no Appeal Court for the 'Sobo' Division had been established though the pressing need for such a court was recognized. For some time the idea of making clan councils act as appeal courts to which cases from the village courts could be taken was considered, and indeed some such clan appeal courts were set up. While these courts were of some service, it was felt that a superior tribunal was necessary, as on the clan council sat a number of men who had already heard the cases which were brought up on appeal from the village councils. Up to 1936 this need was met by people being allowed to appeal to the District Officer to whom was reserved the right to hear the appeal or refer it back to the clan council if he saw fit. In the years after 1936 an Urhobo-Isoko Appeal Court was to be constituted—a court which was to be peripatetic, sitting at Ughelle and at Oleh in rotation, out of respect for the feelings of the Isoko, who objected to having to travel to Ughelle every time, and in recognition of the reluctance with which the Isoko had agreed to have a joint appeal court with the other Urhobo.[2]

For the Urhobo, reorganization was much more significant than it was for the Itsękiri. The anti-tax riots of 1927 were much more furious in Urhoboland than elsewhere in the province, because of the deep disgust which was felt by the people for the warrant chiefs. They disliked the native court system for other reasons as well. For some five years before the introduction of taxation, the Urhobo had become increasingly restive under a system which allowed Itsękiri chiefs to sit on their courts and spy on them; which made it obligatory for some of them to attend native courts in which the preponderance of Itsękiri chiefs gave no guarantee of fair trial or

---

1 Ughelle Papers, Ughelle Dist. 3 File 591, Annual Report, Sobo Division, 1937.
2 Ibid. See also Ughelle Papers, File 107/1931, Current Matters, Warri Division (4 March 1932). The A.D.O., Ase, reported that the Isoko insisted 'that they would press for a separate Isoko Appeal Court. After discussion, it was agreed that a separate Isoko Native Treasury would be popular and that a Sobo Native Treasury would be accepted but not popular.'

equitable judgement; which made it necessary for them to take their appeals to a court permanently presided over by an Itsẹkiri.[1] Their protests while significant as proof of their dissatisfaction with the system, and as a sign of their desire for separation from their Itsẹkiri neighbours, did not produce entirely satisfactory results. In reorganization they saw the answer to these problems which had exercized their minds for some years. They saw more than this. There was the attraction of the 'novelty' of the new system after over thirty years of rule by the warrant chiefs. For those clans which had had to travel to other clans to attend court, the new system was a happy event, relieving them of this burden and emphasizing their independence as distinct units. Where before a few warrant chiefs held sway, under the new system many more people were to be actively involved in the running of affairs. On the more material side, there was the hope that a large number of people would be paid huge salaries, as against the handful of warrant chiefs who had been the only beneficiaries from the old system. Finally, the people, disgruntled and disappointed with the warrant chiefs, evinced confidence in the capacity of the village and clan courts to dispense justice according to traditional ideas.[2]

The measuring rod for the success of the organs set up as a result of reorganization was ability to collect the tax, and in this all the Urhobo clans excelled. The years up to 1936 were too few to enable a full picture to be given about how reorganization worked out in other respects. That enthusiasm which tends to accompany every change had not had time to wear itself out, and the reports in the years 1930–6 recorded great interest in the idea of Native Administration, with the councils doing their best to give satisfaction. It was pointed out, however, that interest was focused essentially on the Clan rather than Division, and it was hoped that time would cure this dangerous clannishness, as indeed it was to do in certain respects. The criticism against the councils in their judicial capacity was that the large number of people involved tended to make a court sitting rather rowdy; had the result of enabling virtually every litigant to have a relation sitting on the court; and made

---

1 See Chapter 5, pp. 204–5 and 209–13.
2 Ughelle Papers, File S.D. 12/1931, Quarterly Reports, Ase Sub-District, September, 1931, p. 4.

unanimous verdicts well nigh impossible. Despite these weaknesses, it was reported:

> For the most part the elders perform their duties conscientiously and if the size of the bench militates against unanimous decisions, local public opinion counteracts tendencies to biased judgements.[1]

When the novelty of it all had had time to wear off, more faults and weaknesses of the system were to be noticed, and the need for further reorganization seen.

One factor which was of great moral and psychological significance to the Urhobo was the establishment, for the first time, of a divisional headquarters in their territory.[2] Until this development, the Urhobo country had been ruled from Warri, and, especially since the time of Dọghọ's ascendancy, Warri had become closely associated with Itsẹkiri predominance. Besides, it is common knowledge that people who live at, or near, administrative headquarters tend to arrogate to themselves superior airs. The old Appeal Court had been sited at Warri because it was the headquarters of the administration, and that court had had a majority of Itsẹkiri chiefs partly because these men were near to headquarters, and therefore better able to influence the administrative officers in their favour. From 1933 on it was possible for the administrative officers, now resident in Ughelle, to seek to know the Urhobo as they really were. Hitherto, occasional visits to native court centres was all that could be attempted. With routine office work to attend to, and with road transport still poor the District Officers were largely out of touch with the Urhobo people and their aspirations. Not only could they not go to meet the people, but the people could not, likewise because of poor communications and long distances, get in touch with their political officers. In these circumstances, the problems of Urhoboland could not be easily understood or sympathetically considered. The outcome was that the Urhobo were seen largely through the spectacles of the Itsẹkiri, and labelled with a stereotype—'bush', 'uncivilized', 'backward'. Reorganization and the establishment of a separate

---

1 C.S.O. 26/2 File 11857 Vol. XIV, Annual Report, Warri Province, 1939, p. 9. See Chapter 1, p. 28, where the point was made that the reaction of the people to the various aspects of the case was taken into consideration when the verdict was given.

2 Infra, p. 237.

divisional headquarters in Urhoboland enabled the administrative officers to see the Urhobo character and aspirations in their proper perspective. It was not for nothing that the Urhobo in the 'Jekri-Sobo' Division were to ask for a separate native administration headquarters sited in their own territory.

Although reorganization was directed towards reviving the ancient system of government, it had to be recognized that the problems which even village government had to tackle in 1936 were different, sometimes vastly different, from the problems which had confronted the village in the closing years of the last century. Therefore, from the very beginning of reorganization, the *Ekpako* were encouraged to seek the co-operation, and utilize the services, of the educated elements in their respective communities, as these latter were thought to be more conversant with some of the more modern developments and the changing needs of the society. Though this was not always acceptable to the *Ekpako* who tended to look on the educated elements with suspicion, these educated young men were, nevertheless, brought into the framework of the newly developing Native Administrations. Indeed, partly as a result of the services which the educated element could render in this respect, there was an increased demand for schools to be opened in the Urhobo country during this period.

Until 1927, Warri and Sapẹlẹ were the centres of education for the Itsẹkiri and Urhobo. In the earlier years, the Itsẹkiri provided the majority of the pupils for the Warri and Sapẹlẹ schools. As the years passed, however, the Urhobo began to show greater interest and to catch up (at least at the elementary school level) with their Itsẹkiri neighbours, until by 1936, at the Government School, Warri, both peoples stood nicely balanced, the Urhobo supplying 157 and the Itsẹkiri 155 of the total of 389 pupils.[1] The greater interest which the Urhobo took in education during these years was in itself important for Itsẹkiri-Urhobo relations, as it had the ultimate result of removing one of the inequalities that had existed between the two peoples—an inequality which had, to some extent, conditioned the British attitude to the Itsẹkiri on the one hand, and the Urhobo on the other.[2]

---

1 C.S.O. 26, File 09098, Vol. X, Chief Commissioner's Inspection Notes, Warri Province, 1936, p. 9.　　　2 See Chapter 5, pp. 203-4.

Until 1927 the Urhobo had to travel to Sapẹlẹ or Warri to receive education. The years after 1927 saw the establishment of schools in Urhoboland proper, and therefore made education more easily available. The Church Missionary Society (C.M.S.) which had started to penetrate the Urhobo area in 1912 was the prime mover in this respect. Up to 1927 a dearth of teachers had made the C.M.S. confine its educational programme to sporadic teaching by itinerant teachers who scarcely ever stayed longer than one month in any one place. In 1928, however, a regular school was opened at Ọzọrọ and in 1929 schools were opened at Uzere and Uwherun, though the Uzere school was closed in 1930 to enable the mission to concentrate more on the Ozọrọ and Uwherun schools. The Ọzọrọ school read up to Standard IV and the Uwherun to Standard VI.[1] In 1930 the Rev. J. W. Welch, the C.M.S. Supervisor of Schools, drew up a scheme of education for the above two schools, as well as for sixteen others reading up to Standard II. It placed emphasis not only on acquiring the ability to read and write, but also on gardening and handiwork.[2] This scheme, which was approved by the government and towards the operation of which the Ase sub-district made a contribution of £100 in 1931, was nearly completed by 1933, and laid the foundation of education in Isokoland. In 1934 the Rev. Welch was said to have started to extend his scheme to the other Urhobo clans.[3] Other missions, like the Roman Catholic Mission which already had schools at Ase, Uzere and Ozọrọ in 1928, and the African Church which had various schools in Urhoboland in 1935,[4] were to

---

1 Ughelli Papers, File 118/1930: Proposed Scheme of Education C.M.S. Isoko District. Up to today the C.M.S. remains the one single body that has done the most to spread education in Isokoland. The discussion of the development of education in the Isoko and Urhobo country which follows might appear to be somewhat of a digression. But it is vital for a full understanding of the factors that were shaping the attitudes of the Urhobo-Isoko people in these years.   2 Ibid.
3 C.S.O. 26/2 File 11857 Vol. XII, Annual Report, Warri Province, 1934, p. 23.
4 Ughelle Papers, File S.D. 42/1929, Annual Report, Ase Sub-District, 1929. The Catholic Mission did not begin to operate in the Warri Province till 1913 when Father George Ollier settled at Forcados to minister to the spiritual needs of Catholics in the sea ports of Burutu and Forcados. In 1914 an out-station was opened at Warri. It was not till 1917 that Warri became a principal Catholic station to which Father Louis Cavagnera, the pioneer Catholic missioner among the Urhobo and Itsẹkiri, was posted. See Martin J. Bane: *Catholic Pioneers in West Africa*, Dublin 1956, pp. 166–7.

follow the example of the C.M.S. Lack of suitably qualified teachers was a constant problem in forwarding the various schemes of education. To help solve this problem, the Native Administrations of the Province joined in establishing a Teacher Training College at Warri in the closing months of 1929.[1]

The opening of the above training college gave impetus to the demand for Native Administration Schools which had been made earlier, and in 1931 such a school was opened at Uzere, followed by another at Ughelle in 1933 and two at Agbarho and Ughiẹnvwe respectively in 1934, with a plan to establish two more of such schools.[2] By 1936 the Urhobo local administrations were crying for a secondary school to which their children could go when they left the Native Administration schools. The importance of this educational upsurge for this work is that it provided the personnel that could handle the native courts and work in the Native Administration offices. The 'Sobo' Division started off with a staff which was all Urhobo, and it was essential that this should be maintained.[3] The need which had earlier existed for using Itsẹkiri, Ibo and Bini clerks in Urhobo courts was thus eventually removed, and the Urhobo could enter into a period when they could supply all the personnel required by their Native Administration.

In the last chapter, it was pointed out that Itsẹkiri clerks were appointed to Urhobo courts during the operation of the Native Court system. Re-organization and the spread of education removed this necessity. It was part of the new policy that court clerks and messengers should be seen as the servants of the courts, and since these courts were the same as the village and clan councils, as the servants of the Elders-in-council. In order to make this reorientation of the position of the court clerks and messengers possible, it was decided, on the inauguration of clan courts, to terminate after due

---

1 C.S.O. 26/2 File 11857 Vol. VII, Annual Report, Warri Province, 1929, p. 65.
2 Ughelle Papers, Ughelle Dist. 3 File 445, Annual Report, Sobo Division, 1935. These were the famous 'N.A. schools' that one heard so much about in the 1940s.
3 Ughelle Papers, Ughelle Dist. 8/1/6, Handing-Over Notes, 'Sobo' Division —Chadwick (D.O.) to Miller (D.O.) 18 November 1932. The staff consisted of W. E. Otobo (now *Qtota* of Uzere) as N.A. Office clerk; E. A. A. Eghujovwe, Treasury clerk; and F. U. Jarikre, 'Office Boy'.

notice, and compensation where necessary, the appointments of all court clerks.[1] The new courts were then given a free hand to appoint their own scribes. It was laid down as a matter of principle that clan courts should appoint only scribes who were citizens of the clans concerned. Hence although former court clerks could be reappointed if they belonged to the clans to the court of which they were being appointed, they could not be so reappointed if they were total strangers. Urhobo clans could appoint a scribe who was Urhobo but not a clansman if the need arose. The court messengers were not eligible for reappointment in the Urhobo clans, as the councils were requested to use the traditional *Ikọ* for the duties of court messengers.[2]

In order to prepare for the new system, it was decided in 1930 that the various clans should nominate 'boys' to be trained as clerks at headquarters and then sent back to work in their clans of origin.[3] S. O. Omu of Igbide, and G. T. Bọkwẹre ('Bequery') of Uwherun were among the first 'boys' so trained.[4] Every effort was made to get the new scribes to understand their position *vis-à-vis* the *Ekpako*. Thus the Assistant District Officer, Ase, opposed the stationing of the clerks at headquarters and their 'descent from the "capital" ' every day the court was to sit, as calculated to enhance the prestige of the scribes.[5] Rather, they were to be resident in the clans and summonable at the wish of the council. At the beginning, and with the low standard of education of the scribes, the new policy produced badly-kept records, but as Captain Pender (D.O. 'Jekri-Sobo' Division) argued, it was 'better to have indifferently kept records than to have the court members completely dominated by more efficient clerks'.[6]

---

1 Ughelle Papers, File 59/1930, Quarterly Reports, Warri Division, September Quarter, 1930, p. 4.
2 Ibid.
3 Ughelle Papers, File 119/1930, A.D.O., Ase to Resident, Warri Province, Memo No. A.N.A. 21/1930/5 of 5 November 1930.
4 Ibid., A.D.O., Ase to Resident, Warri Province, Memo No. A.N.A. 21/1930/18 of 12 February 1931.
5 Ughelle Papers, File 69/1930, A.D.O., Ase to Resident Warri Province, Memo No. A.N.A. 16/1930/7 of 13 January 1931.
6 Ughelle Papers, Ughelle Dist. 8/1/8, Handing-Over Notes—Jekri-Sobo Division: Pender (D.O.) to Lambert (D.O.) 24 February 1936.

The reorganization of the Itsẹkiri took longer than their homo-geneity would have suggested and even by 1933 it had not become really complete as the Olu was not installed till 1936. The main reason for the slow progress of reorganization was the factions which existed among the Itsẹkiri to which reference was made earlier. In 1929 an *Olotu*, the traditional high priest and regent, was appointed in the person of Chief Omagbemi.[1] At first it was hoped that it would be possible to get an Olu installed soon after, but as has been indicated, the factions and the position of Chief Dọghọ made such an appointment extremely difficult. A spontaneous sinking of differences caused by the hearing of the Agbassah land case towards the end of 1929 proved to be merely temporary.[2] In the absence of an Olu, the Resident had to set up an Itsẹkiri Native Council in February 1930, a body which included some of 'the young intelligentsia'. At one of the meetings of this Council Chief Dọghọ was proposed as an Olu, but though the voting was said to be eighteen for and thirteen against, the opposition pointed to the fact that Dọghọ was only descended from the female line of the royal family and that this disqualified him from becoming an Olu. Dọghọ himself apparently dissociated himself from the movement.[3] The death of Chief Dọghọ on 24 September 1932[4] helped to create a situation in which it was possible for the Itsẹkiri to sink their differences. Between that date and 1934 the Council displayed more efficiency, though the collection and 'taking in' of the tax continued to be late.[5] At any rate, by 1934 the Itsẹkiri people were sufficiently reorganized for the 'Jekri-Sobo' Division to be approved along with the others.

It was unfortunate from the point of view of Itsẹkiri-Urhobo relations that the Itsẹkiri efforts to get an Olu installed attracted the

---

1 C.S.O. 26 File 09098 Vol. VIII, Lieut. Governor's Inspection Notes, Warri Province, 1935, p. 4.
2 Ughelle Papers, File 98/1929, Annual General Report, Warri Division, 1929. The Agbassah people again went to court in 1929. See Chapter 5, pp. 235–6.
3 Ughelle Papers, File 59/1930, Quarterly Reports, Warri Division, June Quarter, 1930, p. 3.
4 C.S.O. 26/2 File 11857 Vol. X, Annual Report, Warri Province, 1932, p. 19. In a short tribute to Dọghọ the Resident wrote, 'His services were valuable and his loyalty conspicuous.'
5 War. Prof. 3/15 File 48/1932, Quarterly Report, Warri Division, June 1932.

attention of the newspapers. On 13 June 1934, there appeared a newspaper article which discussed 'rumours' that an 'Olu of Jekriland' was about to be installed. This article contained a number of statements which the Urhobo, who were convinced that the article was inspired and probably written by an Itsẹkiri agency, regarded as objectionable and defamatory. One of these statements referred to Chief Dọghọ who was said to have been 'the recognized Ruler of the Itsẹkiris and Sobos'. In another passage the author argued that within the borders of Itsẹkiriland 'lived the Sobos, a hardy people, who served for several years in the capacity of slaves to their Itsẹkiri and Benin Masters'. The article concluded by pointing out that the Urhobo, 'within a comparatively few years of their emancipation', had worked so hard that they were a factor to be reckoned with in the affairs of the country, and had gained prominence in commercial circles as well as affairs of Native Administration.[1] It was hinted in the article that it was the progress achieved by the Urhobo which had forced the Itsẹkiri to think of reviving the office of Olu.

However well-meaning the newspaper correspondent might have been, the Urhobo resented the implications of his statements. A reply appeared in the same paper on 19 June. Writing under the name 'Pro Patria', an Urhobo challenged the validity of the statements contained in the article referred to above. While admitting that the Urhobo sold slaves to the Itsẹkiri, he pointed out that at no time were the Urhobo as a people the slaves of the Itsẹkiri in the sense in which 'the children of Israel' had been slaves in Egypt. Dọghọ was not a ruler over the Urhobo though the powers granted him by the British made him look like a 'sun' among 'stars'.[2] At any rate by 1924, when it appeared to the Urhobo that Dọghọ was overstepping his bounds, the former had begun a protest move against the latter's powers.[3] Meanwhile, in Urhoboland the five clans which were included in the 'Jekri-Sobo' Division met at Orerokpẹ on 17 July to protest against the article, and threatened to take action against the author and the newspaper. The Resident

---

1 *Nigerian Daily Times*, 13 June 1934, p. 7.
2 Ibid., 19 June 1934, p. 9.
3 Ibid. 'Pro Patria's' arguments were reinforced by similar arguments adduced by one Uyota in the issue of the same paper on 22 June 1934, p. 10.

Chief Yamu Numa, Member for Western Urhobo in the West Regional House of Assembly (1951).

Mr. J. G. Ako, Member for Central Urhobo in the West Regional House of Assembly (1951).

Mr. P. K. Tabiowo (l.), Member for Central Urhobo in the West Regional House of Assembly (1951).

James Ekprẹ Otobo, Member for Urhobo East (Isoko) in the West Regional House of Assembly (1951).

Some Urhobo political leaders in the 1950's

Chief Arthur E. Prest (l.), Member for Warri Division in the West Regional House of Assembly (1951) and First Central Minister of Communications. Mr. (later Chief) Festus Sam Edah (later Okotie-Eboh), died 1966, Member for Warri Division in the West Regional House of Assembly (1951).

Chief Reece Edukugho, Member for Warri Division in the West Regional House of Assembly (1956).

Some Itsẹkiri political leaders in the 1950's

While this was a definite problem it was not, as the future was to show, insurmountable.

The Urhobo demand for separation grew more insistent and bitter with the years. In 1935 the Resident reported:

> There has been no advance, during the year towards better relations between the Sobos and the Jekris. . . . The Sobos are growing more insistent in their requests for control of their own funds, and for the establishment of a native treasury on *their own land*.[1]

It was vain to point out to the Urhobo that the accounts were kept separately and the monies utilized for public works in the areas from which they were collected. There was more in it than that. The Urhobo saw in their continued association with the Itsẹkiri, despite repeated protests since 1930 when the plan was first mooted, an attempt to subject them to a people whose claims to superiority they had been fighting since the 1920s. The question of having their own headquarters actually situated on their own land was to them a vital issue. The selection by the Itsẹkiri of an Olu-elect in 1935 further determined the Urhobo to press for separation. This determination was not the result of any 'fantastic ideas of what would occur once the Olu was installed',[2] but rather a facing of realities. Once an Olu was installed, he would be the single, central rallying-point for the Itsẹkiri, and if unity and self-determination were good enough for the Itsẹkiri to have engaged their attention and to have been impressed on them by the British administration since 1928, these same attributes could hardly be denied the Urhobo, some of whom were already thinking of a central authority comprising all the Urhobo clans.

In July 1935 the acting Lieutenant-Governor, W. E. Hunt, a former Resident of the Province, visited it on a tour of inspection. He held a meeting with the Itsẹkiri council and chiefs, and raised the issue of a separate Native Administration for the Itsẹkiri, without the five Urhobo clans associated with them in the 'Jekri-Sobo' Division. According to the Lieutenant-Governor, the Okpẹ people had sent him a petition demanding such a separation. But

1 C.S.O. 26/2, File 11857, Vol. XIII, Annual Report, Warri Province, 1935, p. 5 (author's italics).
2 Ughelle Papers, File 10/27, Handing-Over Notes, Sobo Division—Mackenzie (D.O.) to Matthews (D.O.), 22 February 1936, p. 7.

the Itsẹkiri refused to countenance any such separation. Mr. Hunt commented:

> The objection is more sentimental than anything else as the two sub tribes are to nearly all intents and purposes separate already. But the Jekris seem still to entertain the idea that with the appointment of an Olu they will regain such suzerainty over the Sobo as they claim to have exercised and did I feel sure exercise over many of the Sobos on the river banks in the halcyon days of Benin supremacy some 50 years ago.[1]

The Itsẹkiri objection to separation was decidedly more than sentimental. For them the matter had become one of very real practical politics. Various developments consequent on the British penetration of the Urhobo hinterland had already begun to undermine that predominance which they had enjoyed during an earlier period. Reorganization had brought about a considerable dwindling of their area of activity. The Urhobo agitation for the break up of the 'Jekri-Sobo' Division threatened to further reduce their sphere of activity.

During the same visit, the Lieutenant-Governor visited Orerokpẹ and held a meeting with the Okpẹ people. Naturally, they raised the issue which he had already discussed with the Itsẹkiri. The Lieutenant-Governor told them he had 'no objection in principle' to separation, but wished to see a scheme worked out which would be acceptable to the two sides concerned. He went on to assure the Urhobo that their independence would not be affected by the installation of an Itsẹkiri Olu.[2] The real point at issue, however, was not that the Olu was likely to establish his rule over the Urhobo, but that the insistence of the administration on associating the Urhobo with the Itsẹkiri might give the impression that the Urhobo concerned were not mature enough to look after their own affairs.

On 7 February 1936, after an interregnum of nearly eighty-eight years, Ẹmiko, great grandson of Akẹngbuwa, was installed Olu with the reigning title, Ginuwa II.[3] For both the Itsẹkiri and Urhobo

---

1 C.S.O. 26, File 09098, Vol. VIII, Lieutenant-Governor's Inspection Notes, Warri Province, 1935, p. 7.
2 Ibid., p. 10.
3 C.S.O. 26/2 File 11857, Vol. XIV, Annual Report, Warri Province, 1936.

this was a most momentous event. The installation of an Olu, after many years of factional strife among themselves, was a sign that the Itsẹkiri had closed the breach which had threatened to undermine their traditional political structure: in the Olu the Itsẹkiri found a symbol of national unity. For the Urhobo this was a challenge to make up their own differences since unity or centralized institutions were seen as evidence of 'a higher degree of development'.[1]

The installation of the Olu had the effect of worsening Itsẹkiri-Urhobo relations. First, the reinstitution of the 'Oluship' after nearly one century of interregnum would seem to have filled the Itsẹkiri with an exaggerated conception of the importance of their ruler. Thus it began to be claimed that the Olu had full powers of rule over the Urhobo and Ijọ.[2] The Olu himself was reported to have claimed that he recognized no boundaries except that with the Ọba of Benin,[3] disregarding thereby the existence of the Urhobo, his immediate neighbours. The Urhobo naturally resented the Itsẹkiri claims. The Resident of the Province reported that there was 'increased bitterness' between the Itsẹkiri and the Urhobo, so much so that 'at one time the situation looked threatening'.[4] Secondly, the Itsẹkiri demand that their ruler be styled Olu of Warri instead of Olu of Itsẹkiri as hitherto provoked bitter controversy. The Urhobo argued that Warri was the name of the entire province and that to associate that name with the Olu's title would create the impression that all the people of the province were subject to the rule of the Olu. Mr. W. E. Hunt, the Chief Commissioner, Southern Provinces, thought little of the Urhobo argument. He pointed out, for example, that the fact that Abeokuta was the name of a province, and that in that province there lived both Egba and Ilaro, did not prevent the Alake being styled Alake of Abeokuta.[5]

---

1 War. Prof. Papers, File 48/1932, Quarterly Reports, Warri Division, March 1932.
2 See for example C.S.O. 26, File 54176, Edema Arubi to His Excellency Sir Bernard Bourdillon, No. D248/5/20 of 10 March 1936, p. 1. and another petition No. D248/6/21 of 12 March 1936 by the same author.
3 C.S.O. 26/2 File 11857 Vol. XIV, Annual Report, Warri Province, 1936, pp. 6–7.   4 Ibid.
5 C.S.O. 26 File 09098 Vol. X, Chief Commissioner's Inspection Notes, Warri Province, 1936.

But the Chief Commissioner's argument was scarcely tenable, as the two cases were not really analogous. In the first place the powers the Alake then enjoyed were of recent creation and were not strictly traditional.[1] Secondly, the Alake did not claim to exercise any original jurisdiction over the Ilaro in the province. Besides, although there are differences between the Ilaro and the Egba, both groups were Yoruba. In the case of the Warri Province, the Itsẹkiri, the Urhobo, the Kwalẹ and the Ijọ each regarded itself as a distinct political and ethnic group.

Thirdly, and perhaps most important of all, was the fact that the title Olu of Warri immediately raised the issue of the ownership of Warri land. The Urhobo felt that the Itsẹkiri demand was calculated to buttress their claim that Warri land belonged to them. For years the issue of the ownership of Warri land had been a bone of contention between the Itsẹkiri and the Urhobo. Although all the legal decisions up till 1936 had favoured the Itsẹkiri, the Urhobo had not accepted the legal verdicts as just. They therefore cried out against any administrative and political measures which would confirm the legal decision in favour of the Itsẹkiri.[2]

The question of the ownership of Warri land is one of the most vexed issues in Itsẹkiri-Urhobo relations. It is an issue which deserves a full and special study in itself. Here only a few comments can be made. Warri, the name of the modern township, is clearly a corruption of the name Iwere which the Itsẹkiri sometimes use to refer to themselves and their capital, Ode-Itsẹkiri, which is some five miles removed from the township. The name appeared for the first time in the records in the nineteenth century when both the Itsẹkiri capital and the trading station which later developed into Warri township were called Warri (sometimes Wari). An 1891 map shows the two places differently.[3] The identity of name, therefore, cannot be used as conclusive argument about origins. Nor can geographical proximity, for Obodo is just as near to Warri as is Ode-Itsẹkiri and yet is unquestionably Urhobo.

No detailed study has yet been made of the origins of Warri

---

1 S. O. Biobaku: *The Egba and Their Neighbours*, London 1957, pp. 4, 7, 52.
2 C.S.O. 26 File 54176, Secretary, Southern Provinces, to Chief Secretary to the Government, No. S.P. 11328/213 of 14 May 1936.
3 See map, p. 102.

township. The Agbassah have always claimed that at the time they settled in their own section of the present township, there were no other occupants there, and they did not therefore have to pay rent to anyone. In this regard it may be mentioned that the Agbassah have never attempted to claim any other area of land other than that on which they are actually settled. In 1933 a group of Ijọ people petitioned the Resident, claiming that the land now known as 'Ogbe-Ijọ' in Warri township belonged to their fathers. They stated that some time after the fall of Nana the then Provincial Commissioner, Seton James, requested the Ijọ to move out of that land because government desired to acquire it. This the Ijọ did and so lost all control over the land. They now demanded that that piece of land be returned to them or that they be enabled to benefit from the rents accruing therefrom. To substantiate the claim that the land originally belonged to the Ijọ they enclosed copy of a notice signed by P. E. Crawford and dated 21 October 1895, which stated that the British had decided to take Ogbe-Ijọ under their protection, 'the headman of Ogbe-Ejor having specially asked to be placed under such protection'.[1] No official notice was paid to this petition, yet it is of historical significance as indicating how the township of Warri probably developed.

As for the Itsẹkiri, the likelihood is that they began to move into the area of the present township in the nineteenth century as the European traders moved away from Ode-Itsẹkiri to the site where the vice-consulate was built. It seems reasonable, in the present state of our knowledge, to conclude that what grew into the present Warri township was probably in pre-British days, a collection of independent Ijọ, Urhobo and Itsẹkiri settlements, separated from each other by stretches of unoccupied land. The coming of the British and their formal acquisition of land for government and other purposes raised, for the first time, the question of the title to the land. The fact that it was Dọghọ, an Itsẹkiri, who signed the legal documents which conveyed the land to government has remained a key factor favouring the Itsẹkiri claim in the celebrated Warri land case. But to bring the issue of the controversy over the Olu's title to an end, the British government sympathized with the

---

1 Ughelle Papers, File S.240, Jiebideh, Yobogha and Oloye to the D.O., Warri, 13 January 1933.

Urhobo objection and refused to grant the Itsẹkiri demand. The whole controversy, however, was further evidence of that acute sensitivity in Itsẹkiri-Urhobo relations to which attention has already been drawn.

The controversy over the Olu's title merely served to intensify Urhobo agitation for separation. Whereas before 1936 the agitation had been confined to the Urhobo clans in the 'Jekri-Sobo' Division, from that year all the Urhobo clans joined the crusade for complete separation.[1] the Resident commented:

> Imbued with a national spirit as strong as that of the Jekris, the Sobos regard separation as the outward and visible sign of complete freedom from Jekri influence.[2]

Consequently, during the Chief Commissioner's tour of 1936, the Urhobo clans in the 'Jekri-Sobo' Division addressed a petition to him in which they set out their case fully. They began by stating that their demand was but 'the natural desire of a people to make themselves clear and distinct from their adjacent tribes'.[3] Close social connexions did not, in the view of the Urhobo, constitute sufficient reason for a fusion of peoples. It was highly unsatisfactory from their point of view to associate them with the Itsẹkiri, who had not only told 'fantastic tales' about them but proceeded to treat them with contempt. How could the Government claim that it was not aiding and abetting the Itsẹkiri claims, if it removed them, Urhobo people, from among their brothers in the 'Sobo' Division, and placed them in the same division and under the same Native Administration as a people who were essaying to establish a claim of past dominion over them? They recalled that it was the advent of 'the white man' that had enabled the Itsẹkiri to play some of the leading roles they had played in Urhoboland; and had also had the result of bringing the two people into closer contact. But greater intercourse had so far produced, not increased harmony, but greater strife in certain respects. The petition challenged the Itsẹkiri to name any

---

1 C.S.O. 26 File 09098 Vol. X, Chief Commissioner's Inspection Notes, Warri Province, 1936, p. 19.

2 C.S.O. 26/2 File 11857 Vol. XIV, Annual Report, Warri Province, 1936, p. 8.

3 C.S.O. 26 File 51642 III, Progress Report on the Jekri Subtribe and the Sobo clans in the Jekri-Sobo Division with special reference to the separation of the Native Treasury.

single Urhobo clan which Nana, Itsẹkiriland's greatest and most powerful man ever, had succeeded in bringing under political subjection ('what Urhobo clan was he able to dominate?'); it challenged the Itsẹkiri to name any Olu in their history who had set up his dominion over the Urhobo.[1]

One of the arguments advanced by the Itsẹkiri for not wanting separation was that separation would involve litigation over land. In their petition the Urhobo gave a pledge that they would not disturb those Itsẹkiri who were then settled on their land, and that if disputes arose over such land they could be settled by the normal processes of law. As for the particular case of Sapẹlẹ land, the Urhobo stated that that land was only a little fraction of the total area of Urhoboland and therefore it was unfair to refuse their request until that dispute was settled; the whole must always be greater than the part.[2]

On the question of the treasury the petition stated that the Urhobo could not, while they shared a common treasury, be certain that their money was not being used for paying the Olu and financing Itsẹkiri projects. They did not want a common ledger with one side used for the Itsẹkiri and the other for the Urhobo: 'we want a separate ledger—a separate Native Treasury in which all the clerks and office boys will be purely Urhobo.'[3] Finally the Urhobo argued that since reorganization, the government had encouraged the different peoples in the province to unite. The Itsẹkiri were already united under an Olu. The Urhobo sought no more than to be united on their own. The government, they argued, would be failing in its duties if it stood in the way of this unity out of respect for the feelings of the Itsẹkiri people.[4]

Faced with the Urhobo demand and the Itsẹkiri opposition, the government had to take some decision. The Chief Commissioner had maintained since 1935 that he had no objection in principle to the Urhobo demand. All he wanted as a prerequisite to their demands being met was a 'concrete scheme' which would set out lines which separation was to take. During this tour, he observed that despite much intermarriage and daily intercourse of a friendly nature between individuals among the two groups, 'there had been a growing sense

1 Ibid., pp. 5, 7. 2 Ibid., p. 6.
3 Ibid., p. 7. 4 Ibid.

of grievance on the part of Sobos at enforced union'. The Itsẹkiri
for their part were afraid of 'losing prestige by a Sobo schism',
and were apparently dropping their superior airs and professing to
look on the Urhobo as their brothers, a volte-face which had obviously come rather late. The Chief Commissioner thought, therefore, that in the circumstances, it was better to allow separation in
the hope that 'such a measure would probably lead later to better
relations, of which in existing conditions there seemed little hope'.[1]
The Urhobo were therefore asked to submit their plan for separation.

This plan was worked out in 1937. The five Urhobo clans concerned asked to be given a common treasury to be sited at Orerokpẹ.
Suggestions by the District Officer that to begin with it might be
wiser for each clan to have a separate treasury were categorically
rejected, on the grounds that the Urhobo clans desired unity. Each
clan was to delegate two 'chiefs' to form a Financial Council which
would discuss estimates with the District Officer. This Council
was to have custody of part of the money in the 'Native Treasury'
and to be responsible for giving an account of such money.[2] The
Itsẹkiri were to have their own 'Native Treasury' but the District
Officer recommended that control of the funds of this treasury be
vested in the District Officer, not the Itsẹkiri Council.[3] Apparently,
the District Officer did not consider that the Itsẹkiri had, since
1928, shown enough sense of responsibility to be entrusted with
control of part of their own revenue.

The proposals were sent up for formal approval in June 1937.
The Chief Commissioner, Southern Provinces, approved the scheme
with only one modification, namely, that the Itsẹkiri should be
entrusted with the same degree of financial responsibility as the
Urhobo.[4] It should be noted that the 'Jekri-Sobo' Division did
not cease to exist as a result of this development. All that happened

1 C.S.O. 26 File 09098 Vol. X, Chief Commissioner's Inspection Notes, Warri
Province, 1936, pp. 14, 15.
2 C.S.O. 26 File 51642 XII, Progress Report on the Jekri Sub-tribe and the
Sobo clans in the Jekri-Sobo Division, pp. 7, 13.
3 Ibid., p. 13.
4 C.S.O. 26 File 51642 III, Secretary, Southern Provinces, to Chief Secretary
to the Government, No. S.P. 12951/34 of 6 July 1937; Chief Secretary to the
Government to the Secretary, Southern Provinces, No. 26767/237 of 31
July 1937.

was that two distinct Native Administrations—the Itsẹkiri Native Administration, and the Western Urhobo Native Administration—existed within the old 'Jekri-Sobo' Division as from 1 April 1938.[1] Once again there was a departure from the strict policy of making the divisions coincide with ethnic groups, a legal fiction of Itsẹkiri-Urhobo association was kept alive in the name of the division. The consequences of this act for the future fall outside the scope of this work, but in it one sees a certain preoccupation with the desire to promote Itsẹkiri-Urhobo co-operation, the achievement of which was rendered difficult by the events of the 1930s.

The introduction of taxation and the reorganization which followed it therefore had extremely important consequences for Itsẹkiri-Urhobo relations. Although reorganization among the Urhobo was based on the clan as the highest unit for political organization, the emphasis laid by the British administrative officers on the need for some central authority, even if purely advisory, to tackle matters of finance, and plan works of public utility which cut across clan boundaries and interests, helped to promote 'national' consciousness among the Urhobo. The more they met together to discuss various matters of common concern, the stronger the feeling of unity grew.[2] A similar development took place among the Itsẹkiri. From the time when it became necessary to organize an Itsẹkiri Council in 1928, as distinct from the native courts which had operated in the past, interest was focused on 'national' unity. It was the desire to foster and encourage this unity that had eventually resulted in the election and installation of an Olu in 1936, with the consequences already described.

Reorganization had other results. It has been pointed out that a feature of the period was the insistence on each Native Administration appointing to its various offices men who belonged to the ethnic group which made up that administration. This, in a way, removed a possible source of grievance: no Native Administration could henceforth complain of its courts and their offices being staffed

---

1 C.S.O. 26/2 11857 Vol. XV, Annual Report, Warri Province, 1938, p. 5.
2 This unity was in 1936 still incomplete. The Isoko for instance, would have preferred to have their own appeal court. But it is significant that despite their reluctance they, nevertheless, agreed at least for the time being to have common institutions with the other Urhobo.

by people from outside it. One avenue through which the Itsękiri could make an inroad into Urhobo territory was thus closed— thanks not only to the new policy but the spread of education which provided the personnel the Urhobo needed.

As was pointed out in the last chapter, the British administration had recognized by about 1925 that 'it was a mistake' to let Itsękiri warrant chiefs sit on Urhobo courts. Reorganization provided the opportunity for rectifying this mistake. It was impossible, in a system which sought to leave executive and judicial powers in the hands of the traditional authorities, to allow Itsękiri chiefs to sit on Urhobo courts or vice versa. Thus as the Itsękiri court clerks were being removed from Urhobo courts, Itsękiri warrant chiefs were also losing their seats on Urhobo courts. Another source of Urhobo grievance was removed. However necessary or logical this policy was, the Itsękiri, both chiefs and clerks, must have felt that the administration was merely bowing to Urhobo clamour.

In addition to all that has been said, reorganization had its more practical side. During the years of reorganization, a great deal of emphasis was placed on 'public works' as a means of bringing home to the people the advantages to be derived from the new system of Native Administration. It was necessary to demonstrate to the tax-payers in clear and practical ways that their money was being sensibly and profitably used. The building of roads and bridges, wells and permanent market stalls featured prominently among the various works undertaken by the different clan councils.[1] The most important of these were undoubtedly roads and bridges. The road-building programme begun during the years of penetration was more assiduously pursued. A network of tracks and roads sprang up and connected not only clan to clan within Urhobo country, but also connected the Urhobo country to the government centres at Warri and Sapęlę. By 1932 the road system was sufficiently developed for light motor-traffic to use the Ughelli-Obetim, and Obetim-Warri roads, as well as the Okpare-Emevǫ road. In the same year a beginning was made in the building of the Ughelli-Warri motor road.[2]

---

1 Ughelle Papers, File 64/1928, Quarterly Report, Warri Division, June Quarter, 1929, p. 2. Ughelle Papers, File S.D. 12/1931, Quarterly Report, Ase Sub-District, June Quarter, 1931, p. 16.
2 War. Prof., File 48/1932. Quarterly Report, Warri Division, March 1932.

Contemporaneous with and perhaps partly resulting from the development of road transport, was the increased interest which the European firms took in the trade of the Urhobo country. In the pre-1914 period there was a Niger Company factory at Ivọrọgbọ, and Messrs John Holt and Co. were established at Okpare.[1] Okpare rapidly grew into the largest commercial centre in Urhobo-land, chiefly because of its position at the confluence of the Kiagbodo river and the Kakpamrẹ creek. By 1926 both the African and Eastern Trading Corporation and the Niger Company were starting factories at Okpare; about the same time the Dekage Trading Company (a German firm) was establishing at Ukan in Agbarho clan.[2] After the upheavals of the anti-tax agitation of 1927, these firms settled down to tap the palm produce trade of the Urhobo country. Long-established factories at Frukama and Ganagana were enabled, as a result of the road network, to serve the Urhobo country more effectively, while those at Ase and Patani continued to tap the trade of the Isoko country.

The improvement of the road transport system and the greater movement into the hinterland of the trading firms (by-products of the era of reorganization) had important consequences for Itsẹkiri-Urhobo relations. It was as middlemen traders that the Itsẹkiri had made their name. Their wealth and power, both during the slave trade period and that of 'legitimate commerce' which followed it, were based on their carrying trade. The superior culture and higher intellect with which they were credited by Europeans were, partly at least, the result of their commercial activities. Until about the close of the first decade of this century the Itsẹkiri remained largely unchallenged as the leading traders of this part of the Delta. By the 1930s, however, the advantages conferred on the Itsẹkiri as a result of their geographical location were already greatly under-mined by the building of roads in the hinterland and the elimination of highwaymen and pirates. Already the abolition of slavery had dealt a crippling blow to Itsẹkiri commercial organization. Now the development of more efficient land communication further weakened the commercial position of the Itsẹkiri as the Urhobo increasingly carried their produce directly not only to the branch factories

1 See Chapter 4, pp. 154–5.
2 Ughelle Papers, File 112/26, Annual Report, Warri Division, 1926.

within their territory, but also to the main centres where the various firms were established. The situation that developed in the 1930s was well summarized by the Resident:—

> So long as the canoe remained the universal vehicle the Jekri and Ijǫ controlled the waterways, but the steamer, the launch and the lorry have enabled the Sobo producer to compete on level terms, and by virtue of the natural resources at his disposal and of his greater inclination to labour to begin to take the lead.[1]

Thus at the same time as the political reorganization was dealing some hard blows at Itsękiri self-esteem and undermining the pre-eminent position which British policy had tended to create for him in the pre-taxation period, the developments described above were forcing him to lose his place as the leading trader of this part of the Delta. It was not easy for the Itsękiri to adapt himself to such a combination of adverse circumstances. Itsękiri reaction to reorganization and all its concomitants must not be seen as the reaction of a proud people unwilling to look hard facts in the face, but as the natural reluctance of a people accustomed to look on themselves (whether rightly or wrongly is immaterial) as the leading, and almost privileged group, to accept with equanimity a series of changes which robbed them of their predominant position. Many a people in their situation would have reacted in the same manner.

Despite the innovations which accompanied reorganization and which seemed to remove sources of Urhobo discontent, no final solution had, by the end of 1936, been found to the growing tension between the Urhobo and Itsękiri. Every innovation, however necessary, tends to have the effect of displeasing a section of the community. In this case, the displaced Itsękiri clerks and chiefs who found themselves removed from positions of influence and power obviously felt disgruntled. More important, however, was the fact that at the end of the period covered by this work, the Itsękiri and the Urhobo stood face to face in two organized blocs each extremely touchy about its 'ancient' rights, and competing with each other in the achievement of progress. It stood to reason that there might be strains in their relationship as each group worked out the new system and made, or failed to make, the progress by which it would be

1 C.S.O. 26/2 File 11857 Vol. VIII, Annual Report, Warri Province, 1930, p. 2.

judged by the British administration. Yet such a clash or strained relationship was bound to take time to come out in the open, for in 1936, there were many internal problems arising out of the new policy which had not been tackled and which demanded immediate attention.

At the end of the period, therefore, there was a lull in the tension which had arisen between the two peoples in the years 1932-6. The Itsękiri, having reluctantly accepted separation from their Urhobo counterparts in the division, settled down to their own internal problems. The Urhobo did likewise. The pattern of future relations could not, after the separation of 1938, be accurately forecast. But there were reasons for expecting future tensions, including the feelings generated by the agitation which preceded the separation. Would the Itsękiri for ever accept the implications of the separation which they had done their utmost to prevent, or would they, given a suitable opportunity, seek to establish those claims which had been disallowed in 1936-7? Would the Urhobo, flushed with the victory of separation, be content with the new *status quo*, or would they seek to carry their self-assertion to lengths which would provoke their Itsękiri neighbours? These were some of the questions the answers to which lay in the future.

Epilogue

The years immediately after 1936 were spent by both the Urhobo and the Itsẹkiri in working the new Native Administration system. As this policy was separative in effect, areas of contact between the two groups were reduced, but not totally eliminated. In these years the issues which decided Itsẹkiri-Urhobo relations were the Sapẹlẹ land case, the question of Itsẹkiri enclaves in Urhobo territory and vice-versa, the efforts made by the British administration to bring the different native authorities together at the provincial level, and the old issue of the title by which the Itsẹkiri ruler was to be known.

In 1908, as pointed out in Chapter 5, the British acquired 510 acres of land in Sapẹlẹ. The lease which conveyed this piece of land to the Government was signed by Dọghọ, then British Political Agent. The annual rent period for the land was £100. Of this Dọghọ received £40, the remaining £60 being paid to the Sapẹlẹ elders. Until the early thirties nothing happened to raise the issue of the legal ownership of Sapẹlẹ land. Shortly before his death in 1932, however, Dọghọ is said to have instructed the Itsẹkiri resident in Sapẹlẹ not to pay rent to their Urhobo landlords, arguing that Sapẹlẹ land belonged to the Olu of Itsẹkiri and that he, Dọghọ, merely represented the Olu. The Urhobo questioned both the claim that the land was Itsẹkiri and Dọghọ's right to stop the Itsẹkiri from paying rent to their Urhobo landlords. The issue of Sapẹlẹ land was fought with considerable acrimony on both sides. The British Administrative Officers stepped in to prevent a showdown but their success was only temporary. In 1941 the Urhobo decided to settle the matter once and for all by recourse to the law courts.

From what transpired at the hearing of the case, the issue turned on whether when Chief Dọghọ signed the lease in 1908, he was acting as an intermediary for the Urhobo elders of Sapẹlẹ or as an agent of the Itsẹkiri. The Urhobo maintained that they saw Dọghọ as British Political Agent and used him in that capacity to act as the intermediary between them and the government. It was, they argued, in appreciation of the services rendered by Dọghọ as intermediary

264

that they allowed him to take £40 of the annual rent. They called evidence to prove their historical claim to the land, arguing that when the various European firms operating in Sapẹlẹ first arrived there, it was with them and not with the Olu or Dọghọ or any other Itsẹkiri that they negotiated for purchase of land for buildings. The Urhobo stressed the personal nature of the £40 which they allowed Dọghọ to receive from the rent paid on the land every year, and challenged the validity of government action in transferring that sum of money to the Olu since the latter's installation in 1936. By that action, the Urhobo argued, the Government was buttressing the claim by the Itsẹkiri that they had some right of ownership over Sapẹlẹ land.

In his statement of defence, His Highness Ginuwa II, the then Olu, claimed 'that the late Chief Dore Numa leased the Sapele Township land in this own authority as the representative of the Olu of Itsẹkiri who has ever been the rightful owner of the land for the Itsẹkiri people.' The share of the rent given to the Urhobo people was, according to the Olu, 'an act of grace'.

The Urhobo won the case. In his judgement the trial judge noted that while the Urhobo elders of Sapẹlẹ were able to produce evidence of their dealings with European traders who sought land on which to build their 'factories', the evidence of the Itsẹkiri was surprisingly silent on the issue. He pointed out that 'no tittle of evidence' was advanced to back up 'the bombastic claim to royal privilege and overlordship'. He felt satisfied that Dọghọ signed the lease 'on the authority of the chiefs and people of Sapele' and not as a representative of the Olu. The Itsẹkiri appealed to the West African court of Appeal but lost their appeal in 1943.[1] The tension generated by the court action continued to linger even after 1943.

One of the outstanding features of reorganization was Urhobo unwillingness to remain in the same Native Administration with the Itsẹkiri. In recognition of this the Government had allowed separation in 1938. Separation did not, however, mean that the 'Jekiri-Sobo' Division legally ceased to exist. The new Western Urhobo Native Administration existed within a 'Jekiri-Sobo'

---

1 Records of the High Court of Warri, Suit No. W/37/1941. See also Obaro Ikime: 'Chief Dogho: The Lugardian system in Warri, 1917–1932', in *J.H.S.N.*, Vol. III, No. 2, December 1965, pp. 331–2.

Division. In 1949, however, that Native Administration was transferred to the Urhobo Division and what was left of the 'Jekiri-Sobo' Division became known as the Warri Division, now made up of only the Itsẹkiri Native Administration. All of these developments did not, however, remove the question of enclaves. In the Western Urhobo Native Administration area were Itsẹkiri enclaves in Okpẹ Ogharefe and Agbọn clans. In the Itsẹkiri Native Administration area the Agbassa in Warri constituted an Urhobo enclave. While relations at the personal level did not create any real problems for these enclaves, the question of taxation did. The Agbassa in Warri paid their tax to the Itsẹkiri Native Authority.[1] The Itsẹkiri in the Urhobo areas, however, continued to pay their tax to the Itsẹkiri Native Authority.[2] The Urhobo protested in vain against this arrangement. In 1949 the Agbassa of Warri requested that they be transferred to the Western Urhobo Native Authority so they could pay their tax to that authority. The demand was rejected.[3] Both the Agbassa and the Western Urhobo Native Authority resented the inconsistency in government action over this matter and this resentment did little to improve Itsẹkiri-Urhobo relations. Indeed the year 1949, for this and for other reasons which will be presently discussed, ended with increased tension between the Itsẹkiri and the Urhobo.

Whatever the virtues of Native Administration, the need to bring together all the peoples of the province for purposes of consultation and joint planning of certain common services was felt from the very beginning of the introduction of the Native Administration system. It was not until 1948, however, that the system of Provincial Native Authorities conference was inaugurated to meet this need. The details of the work undertaken by this conference are not yet available. But in one respect the functions of the conference had the result of worsening Itsẹkiri-Urhobo relations. The introduction of the Richards constitution in 1946 necessitated the appointment of a provincial member to represent the Warri Province in the Western House of Assembly. In 1946 Mukoro Mowoe, then President General of the Urhobo Progress Union, was appointed to

---

1 C.S.O. 26/2, file 11857 Vol. XVIII, Annual Report, Warri Province, 1949.
2 Ibid.   3 Ibid.

represent the province.[1] Whatever the personal merits of Mukoro Mowoe—and these were freely admitted on all sides—the Itsẹkiri felt that the Urhobo were beginning to have things too much their own way. Since the beginning of reorganization in 1930 the Urhobo seemed to have got all they wanted except with regard to the enclaves problem. Now an Urhobo was to represent the province in the regional legislature. Mukoro Mowoe died suddenly in 1948 the year the Provincial Conference was inaugurated. One of the things that conference had to do was to fill the place left vacant by Mowoe's death. The man chosen was another Urhobo, Jessa Ogboru from Abraka.[2] If Mukoro Mowoe's personal qualities took the edge off Itsẹkiri bitterness in 1946, there was nothing, from their point of view, to explain Ogboru's appointment apart from Urhobo numerical strength. The resident reported that as a result of the appointment there was a noticeable deterioration in Itsẹkiri-Urhobo relations.

In 1949 the whole country was faced with the problem of revising the Richards constitution. Each province was invited to discuss the constitution and indicate lines along which it should be revised. The Provincial Conference of Native Authorities was seen as the body best qualified to tackle the question of constitutional reform. Consequently, in May 1949, a meeting of the conference was summoned. Mr. Arthur Prest, an Itsẹkiri lawyer who had become a member of the Itsẹkiri Native Authority Council the previous year, and had been reported very active in interesting educated Itsẹkiri young men in Native Administration, was elected Chairman of the conference. The administrative officers were not particularly impressed by the deliberations of the conference.[3] Apparently the members of the conference did not grasp the technicalities of constitution-making and so could contribute very little that was worthwhile. This need not surprise anyone, because the large majority of these who made up this conference were either illiterate or semi-literate. Even the literate members, with a few exceptions like Arthur Prest himself, had had no previous experience of constitution-making. It was difficult for men whose participation

---

1 C.S.O. 26/2 File 11857, Vol. XVII, Annual Report, Warri Province, 1946.
2 Ibid., Annual Report, Warri Province, 1948.
3 C.S.O. 26/2, File 11857, Vol. XVIII, Annual Report, Warri Province, 1949.

in the political development of their country had been limited to clan and village affairs to apply themselves effectively to national issues as complex as the drawing up of a new constitution. In the circumstances, it is easy to understand why the lawyer, Arthur Prest, should have felt dissatisfied with the general report emanating from the conference and why he sent forward a minority report.[1] But his action was seen, especially by the Urhobo, as an act of pride and was resented as such. But what made 1949 a near-crisis year was not so much Arthur Prest's stand, as the election of W. E. Mowarin, an Urhobo from Agbarho clan, as the second member for Warri Province in the Western House of Assembly, the province having been granted an additional seat in 1949.[2] Mr. Mowarin's election meant that the two members for the province were both Urhobo. Apparently the fact that the Urhobo had two Native Authorities which sent delegates to the conference, and the fact that representatives at the conference was based on the population of the Native Authority areas concerned gave them a numerical superiority which they exploited to their advantage. The Itsekiri were so incensed at the result of the election that they threatened to withdraw from all provincial bodies. The Resident reported that there was a frightening, 'recrudescence of ill-feeling and bitterness between the Itsekiri and Urhobo'. Thus although the Native Authority system had to some extent removed the sources of conflict between the Itsekiri and the Urhobo, their participation in provincial and national affairs was producing new sources of conflict.

The ill-feelings generated by the events of 1949 were surpassed in intensity by those of 1952 which centred round the change in the official title of the ruler of the Itsekiri. It will be recalled that in 1936 the Urhobo had successfully protested against the ruler of the Itsekiri being styled Olu of Warri. Although the Itsekiri had accepted their defeat on that score at the time, they had not really given up the fight. In 1944 the Itsekiri reopened the matter in a petition to the Chief Commissioner, Western Provinces. After examining the historical background of the title and the political implications of a change at the time, the commissioner replied to the effect that the government would be prepared to change the title to

1 Ibid.   2 Ibid.

'Olu of Iwere' (Iwere being a name sometimes used for the Itsẹkiri) but not 'Olu of Warri' as the latter title was likely to lead to political upheaval in the province.[1] The Itsẹkiri were deeply hurt by government attitude on this matter. A meeting of the Itsẹkiri Native Authority Council of February 1945 resolved to style the Itsẹkiri ruler 'Olu of Warri' arguing that their ruler had been so styled 'from time immemorial'. The resolution challenged anyone who objected to the title 'Olu of Warri' to take legal action against the Itsẹkiri 'nation'.[2] Despite the resolution, however, the Itsẹkiri ruler did not officially style himself 'Olu of Warri' as from that date. In March 1946, Mr. Edema Arubi, the prolific letter writer whose influence over the Olu had irritated not only the British Administrative Officers but also his fellow Itsẹkiri, addressed a petition to the British Secretary of States for the colonies on the issue. No new arguments were adduced in the petition. Edema Arubi accused the British political officers of 'showing favour to the Urhobo' by refusing to allow the title 'Olu of Warri' and insisting on 'Olu of Itsẹkiri'[3] The petition was sent to the Governor in Lagos for his comments. The Governor recounted the history of the agitation for a change of the title, indicating why the government considered it impolitic to accede to the Itsẹkiri demand. The Secretary of State thereupon replied to the petition to the effect that the proposed change of title could not be sanctioned.[4] The agitation for a change in the Olu's title was thereupon dropped until 1952.

In 1951 the first elections under the Macpherson constitution were held throughout the country. The six successful Urhobo candidates belonged to the National Council of Nigeria and the Cameroons (N.C.N.C.) as it was then known. Of the two Itsẹkiri representatives one, Chief Arthur Prest, declared for the Action Group (A.G.) and the other Chief Festus Sam Edah (later known as

1 War. Prof., File W.P. 86, Vol. I. See H.F. Marshal, Acting Secretary, Western Provinces to the Senior Resident, Warri Province, No. 1132–343 of 9 October 1944.
2 C.S.O. 26 File 54176, Extracts from minutes of Itsẹkiri Native Authority, Ode Itsẹkiri, 2 February 1945.
3 Ibid., Edema Arubi to Secretary of State for the Colonies, No. P55/32/ D28, 25 March 1946.
4 Ibid., Secretary of State for the colonies to the Officer Administering the Government of Nigeria, 4 September 1946.

Chief Festus Okotie Ẹboh) for the N.C.N.C.[1] Eventually the Action Group succeeded in forming the government of the Western Region as it then was. The Itsẹkiri were thus represented in the Government Party while the Urhobo were not. What is more, Chief Arthur Prest was elected to the central legislature by the Western House of Assembly and became the central Minister of Communications. Since 1946 the Urhobo had, both at the provincial and at the regional level, appeared to be on the ascendance. Now in 1952 although they had, as a result of their numbers, three times the number of Itsẹkiri representatives in the Western House of Assembly, they possessed no single minister at either the regional or the national level. This was, of course, merely one of the regular hazards of party politics. But it was nevertheless a matter of grave importance for Itsẹkiri-Urhobo relations that now the Itsẹkiri had, in Arthur Prest, a minister of state while the Urhobo had not. Urhobo successes since 1936 had thus been arrested.

In 1952 came the crisis. The Itsẹkiri once again took up the question of the title of their Olu. The Western Regional Minister of Local Government, Chief Ọbafẹmi Awolọwọ, who was also leader of the Action Group, visited Warri some time after the Itsẹkiri request was made. The Urhobo protested to the Minister on the same old grounds that the title Olu of Warri 'would give a universal impression that the Olu was paramount chief of the province.' The Urhobo did not fail to mention their view that the renewed demand for a change in title was put forward because the Itsẹkiri felt that they had some influence in the party in power. Despite the Urhobo protest, however, the government of the day granted the Itsẹkiri request in May 1952: the Olu became known as Olu of Warri.[2]

The Urhobo reaction to the government decision was at first not violent. It was apparently hoped that by proceeding through constitutional means the government might be made to reconsider its decision. The members for Urhobo and Isoko in the Western House of Assembly suggested to the government that the temper of their constituents might be placated by changing the name of the province from Warri—the name now associated with the Olu—to Delta.

1 C.S.O. 26/2 File 11857, Vol. XVIII, Annual Report, Warri Province, 1951.
2 C.S.O. 26/2, File 11857/S.1, Annual Report, Delta Province, 1952.

This was ultimately done, but by the time government took that step, the Urhobo were already too angry to be placated by such action. Matters actually came to a head in September. The central Minister of Communications Chief Arthur Prest, proposed to visit Warri on the eighth. The minister, as the only Itsẹkiri Action Group member of the Western House of Assembly, was naturally regarded as being largely responsible for government action in granting the Itsẹkiri request. The Urhobo therefore determined to prevent his entry into Warri. The Itsẹkiri for the same reason were determined to give the minister an enthusiastic welcome. The stage was thus set for what turned out to be a major civil disturbance first in the township of Warri and then in the environs. The minister himself was saved from getting involved in the fracas by the post-ponement of his visit on the advice of the Resident of the province. But tempers had risen so high that even the postponement of the visit failed to prevent that clash between the Itsẹkiri and the Urhobo for which both sides seemed poised since the announce-ment of the minister's visit. The signal for the civil disturbance was an Urhobo attack on an Itsẹkiri procession of welcome. Very quickly the whole town was engulfed in one of the most severe riots that it has ever known. The riots spread to Sapẹlẹ and a few other places. Itsẹkiri settlements in Urhobo country were sacked and many Itsẹkiri men who had lived for many years in such settlements lost a vast amount of property. No lives were lost, thanks to the brisk action of the police, but there were severe injuries and extensive damage to property. The Urhobo boycotted the Warri market and forbade their people selling food to the Itsẹkiri.[1] So inflamed did the Urhobo become that they forced their assemblymen to withdraw their proposal that the name of the province be changed to Delta.[2] Various Urhobo groups including a member of the Western House of Assembly demanded a com-mission of inquiry into the right of the Itsẹkiri to the title now

---

1 Ibid.
2 C.S.O. 26 File 54176, Telegram Addressed to Governor, Lagos, by Mowarin Obahor, Okene and Sido. Also telegram to Lieut. Gov., Western Provinces by Ako, Agidee, Tabiowo, Otobo, Oki, Oweh, Numa (the non-Itsẹkiri members from Warri Province in the Western House of Assembly) with-drawing their earlier proposal for a change in the name of the province.

accorded to their ruler.[1] The government refused to set up such a commission and stood its grounds with regard to the title. Despite the withdrawal of the proposal about a new name for the province, the government went ahead and gazetted the new name, Delta Province, in October 1952. By the end of the year the police had succeeded in restoring law and order.[2] But the bitterness arising out of the events of 1952 continued to linger on.

The situation as it emerged at the end of 1952 was an uneasy one. Urhobo successes since 1936 had been virtually neutralized by the events of 1952. Both sides now possessed a new crop of leaders operating on a plane wider than that of their respective Native Authority. Where before Itsẹkiri-Urhobo relations had been determined by British Administrative policy and by Native Administration affairs, the future lay in the hands of party politicians who have not, since that date, had any scruples about feeding the fire of tribal strife by references to real or imagined grievances of past generations. The emergence of the late Chief Festus Okotie Ẹboh since 1956 as a figure of great importance in Nigerian national politics did little to assuage Itsẹkiri-Urhobo tension as he was often seen as using his position to fight for the development of the Itsẹkiri and to prevent the emergence of responsible leadership among the Urhobo by ensuring that only his lackeys won elections in the province. It remains to be seen whether the events and experience of the military régime will help to ease Itsẹkiri-Urhobo relations in the general drive to break down ethnic loyalties and forge national unity.

As the phenomenon of 'ethnic nationalism' or tribalism is one of Nigeria's major problems at the time of writing, one may be permitted to pose the question, what has been responsible for the tensions and conflicts discussed in this work. It is easy to see the conflicts as arising from British colonial policies. While this is largely true, it is to be stressed that British colonial policy was not deliberately formulated to produce tensions and conflicts. The tensions and conflicts arose mainly out of the bringing together of different peoples who had been accustomed to an independent existence. In a sense, therefore, the issue can be seen as one of the

1 Ibid. Telegram to colonial Secretary by Yamu Numa.
2 C.S.O. 26/2, File 11857/S.1., Annual Report, Delta Province, 1952.

problems of adjustment to a new political and social order imposed by the colonial power. It will be instructive to see how the pattern which emerges from this study compares with the pattern in other areas—both in Nigeria and outside it—where a foreign administration, seeking to create a new political order, has brought together in new ways peoples who, before the colonial period, had been independent of one another. The other determining factor in Itsẹkiri-Urhobo relations was clearly the conflict in interests and levels of development between a coastal people on the one hand and a hinterland people on the other. The theme of coast versus hinterland in Nigerian history may well furnish some explanation of the conflicts between different groups in the country and so deepen our understanding of a phenomenon which has so profoundly influenced Nigeria in modern times.

Appendix I
Traditional justice in Urhoboland:
A list of some offences
and punishments

MURDER:
Death by hanging as a general rule. There usually was a special tree in 'Egborahọ' (forbidden bush) from which the hanging was done. Hanging took place after formal trial and was carried out by the Iletu or Ikọ. In some places the family of the murdered man did the hanging (cf. Udu, Ewu). This satisfied the debtor-creditor relationship. If the murderer was caught in the act he could be dispatched by the relatives of the victim provided the latter could call witnesses to testify to the fact of a murder having been committed. In the Agbọn clan there were special executioners known as Ikọrikpokpo who came from the more elderly ones among the Evrawa. Their method was to beat the murderer to death with sticks.

MANSLAUGHTER:
To the Urhobo this meant murder by accident. The penalty was hanging or compensation. The family of the murdered man had a say in whether it was to be hanging or compensation. If the family of the 'murderer' were quick enough to send emissaries to the victim's family to plead for the life of their relation, they might get away with paying compensation in the form of giving a daughter of their family to the victim's family, the idea being that this daughter would replenish her new family through her issue. In addition the family of the offender had to meet part of the burial expenses. If the family of the victim insisted on hanging the Council would give in if they were satisfied that there was evident carelessness leading to the accident.

THEFT:
Stealing, burglary and robbing were all classified together as one

offence and the usual penalty was a fine which varied in amount according to the gravity of the offence. In some clans (e.g. Owe) stealing farm produce was regarded as particularly odious and such a thief might be sold into slavery or even killed. Persistent offenders were sold into slavery. In Ọzọrọ thieves were often blinded by having boiling oil poured into their eyes. In Agbọn clan habitual rogues were killed and were lucky if sold into slavery. Of the fine imposed, part went to the injured party as compensation, and part was retained by the Council. Where a robber injured the man whose property he robbed, he had to pay the doctor's fee as well as pay a fine for assault in addition to whatever fine was imposed for the theft. On the whole theft was regarded as a particularly heinous offence and many families preferred that any thief in their midst should be sold into slavery rather than that he should for ever soil the name of the family.

ARSON:

Arson was regarded as a very serious offence, as it could easily lead to death. It was a rare crime for which the penalty was for the offender to pay the cost of rebuilding the house and the value of all property destroyed. In addition, he was liable to a fine as this, like theft, was an offence against the community as a whole. Where it could be proved that the burning of the house was accidental, there was no fine. All that was needed was for the offender to assist the owner of the house in rebuilding it.

ADULTERY:

Adultery was only committed when a man had sexual relations with a married woman. If a married man had sexual connexions with an unmarried woman, this was no offence, unless the female concerned was under the age of puberty in which event the man was charged with rape, punishable by a fine and compensation to the girl's father. The penalty for adultery was a fine, compensation to the husband, and propitiation of the ancestors of the clan against whom the offence was also regarded as having been committed. It was not always that cases of adultery were reported to the elders. The husband of the woman involved or any of his relations could, soon after the offence, take vengeance by committing adultery with a wife of the family from which the original offender came (provided he could find such a wife!). In such a situation it would appear that the elders were prepared to ignore the facts even if these came to their notice. Such a situation did not, however, arise frequently as it was difficult to find a woman who could allow herself to be the tool of vengeance against the family into which she was married. The compensation paid was heavier if the woman was pregnant at the time of the offence, or as a result of it. Any child born as a result of a man committing adultery with a married woman belonged to the man. The husband could, of course, get rid of the woman and claim all his expenses on her marriage from the adulterer.

Adultery was further regarded as a grave personal insult to the husband of the woman. Indeed, before the trial, the husband's family could destroy with impunity property belonging to the offender. Should they destroy property other than that belonging to the offender, the latter was bound to pay the value of all property so destroyed. In some cases the Ehọnvwọnren would plant their staffs of office outside the door of the offender. This was the signal for destruction of property as described above and a warning to the adulterer to send emissaries to the offended party to plead for an early settlement. Where the adulterer came from an entirely different clan, inter-clan war could very easily result.

INCEST:

This was a most uncommon offence and the punishment was a fine on the male and propitiation of the ancestors by both parties.

ASSAULT:

This was punished by a fine and compensation or occasionally by allowing the offended party to damage the offender's property. If during the affray the offender had bitten the other man, additional compensation was levied. Cases of assault were not frequent as the assaulted party usually fought back at once and the matter ended there. But where the village issued a proclamation against fighting, cases of assault came up more frequently.

DEFAMATION:

The most serious manifestation of the offence was for one free man to call another a slave. This was a very grave offence for which the offender paid an extremely heavy fine and compensation. Where other forms of defamation occurred the victim was expected to indulge in cross abuse.

PERJURY:
This was extremely rare as any suspicion of it led to trial by ordeal. Where it was otherwise proved a fine was levied.

NOTE: Habitual offenders, whatever their offences, were usually sold into slavery, as they were regarded as bringing disgrace on their family, and ultimately on the community as a whole.

It will be clear from the above that deprivation of liberty in the form of imprisonment was unknown. That punishment was the consequence of the introduction of British rule.

Appendix II
Agreement between Consul John Beecroft and Diare (Governor) and other Itsẹkiri Chiefs 4th April, 1851

At a conference held this day, the 4th of April 1851, on board Her Majesty's Steamer 'Jackal', present John Beecroft Esqr Her Britannic Majesty's consul for the Bights of Benin and Biafra, Lieut. Commander Bedinfeld, Her Majesty's Steamer, 'Jackal', Lieutenant Lombard . . ., Mr. Pendlebery, Agent for Messrs. Horsfall and Sons, W. Day, Harrison and Co., W. Stowe, Reuben Hemmingway Esqr, and Mr. Briden Demean Gibb, Jerry of Jacqua, the chief duly elected, with Jubuffaa and the principals of their town, Odessa of Yellow Town, Offalicoo of Fish Town and Tomah of Ullibah, the following laws and regulations were made and enacted.

ARTICLE 1st

That the Chief of the River Benin with the chiefs and people of the above mentioned Towns, pledge themselves that no British subject from this date shall be detained on shore or molested in any way under any pretence whatever, and if they (the chiefs and people as above mentioned) do so they will incurr the displeasure of Her Majesty, the Queen of England, and be declared enemies of Great Britain, and on such a complaint being made a Man of War will immediately come to Benin River and protect British Subjects and Property.

ARTICLE 2nd

That in case of any misunderstanding between the Resident Agents Super-cargoes and Masters of any of the vessels and the chief and people of the River Benin all and every such Resident, Agent, Super-cargoes and Masters of the British Vessel shall be at full liberty to
278

go on shore free of molestation, and will with the chief and Gentlemen of the River Benin peacefully settle any dispute between the Parties.

ARTICLE 3rd

That upon the arrival of any British merchant vessel off or in this River for the purpose of trading therein, the Agent or Super-cargoes of such vessels shall upon the sending of five Pawns per register tonnage to the Chief or person authorized to receive such custom, or comey, be allowed the privilege of trading without further molestation, the comey or custom to consist of a fair assortment of the goods usually brought out for Trade viz Guns, Powder, Cloth, Cowries, Rum, Tobacco, Salt, Beads, Caps, Knives, Iron Bars, Earthenware, etc.

ARTICLE 4th

The Comey or Custom, to be tendered on the ship's arrival, or as soon as convenient, and if not accepted by the Chief such vessel shall be at liberty to commence trade. This however does not exempt such ships from paying the usual custom or comey if subsequently demanded.

ARTICLE 5th

That if at any time any Agents or Supercargoes of any ship or vessel (after having paid or tendered the usual comey or customs for the Privileges of Trading) can prove that the trade of his ship has been stopped whether directly or indirectly upon any pretence whatever the Chief is to be held responsible for such stoppage and pay one Puncheon of Saleable Palm Oil per diem per 100 tons Register to said ship as compensation for the loss incurred, the said oil to be paid within 7 days, after such stoppage shall have been made and continue to pay the same as long as the trade of any such ship is stopped.

ARTICLE 6th

That after the custom or comey has been paid, or tendered, to the Chief every Trader shall be allowed to trade in his own name, and neither the Chief nor any other trader is entitled to extact other customs, comey or pay whatever.

ARTICLE 7th

That the Chief shall not, nor shall he permit any of his principals or chiefs or rather Tribes of the different towns or villages to demand or enforce any trust from any of the Resident Agents or Supercargoes of any ship or ships upon any pretence whatever.

ARTICLE 8th

Whereas several boats have been plundered, and lives sacrificed, it is deemed just and right, that all such aggressions, and depredations, committed upon British Subjects and Property crossing the Bar or otherwise within the limits of the Chief of the River Benin dominions shall be satisfactorily adjusted by the said Chief.

ARTICLE 9th

And further be it enacted that any breach of any article of this Treaty shall be punished by the party or parties being guilty of the same, paying ten puncheons of saleable Palm Oil.

ARTICLE 10th

Should any person take any trust from any Resident Agent or Supercargo of any vessel and be unable to pay his debt his house and property to be forfeited and sold by orders of the Chief of the River Benin. The proceeds of the sale to go to the liquidation of the debt and that he be no longer allowed to trade. The Agent or Supercargo of any vessel trading with him after his name has been published by the Crier to be liable to the penalty of Five Puncheons of Palm Oil. After the debtor has paid his debt he shall again be allowed to trade.

Given under our hands on board HM Steamer 'Jackal' River Benin 4th day of April, 1851.

(Signed)   John Beecroft, Her Britannic Majesty's Consul of
                        Bights of Benin and Biafra.
             Lt. Commander Bedinfeld, HM Steamer 'Jackal'
             Mr. Pendlebery, Agent for Messrs Horsfalls and Sons
             Jerry (Diare)   his
                                        ×
                                        mark

Jubuffaa (Idibofun)   his
×
mark

Alluma (Olomu)   his
×
mark

(and 31 other Itsękiri traders)

Appendix III
Treaty with Chiefs of
Itsẹkiriland, 1884

Her Majesty the Queen of the United Kingdom of Great Britain and Ireland, Empress of India, & c., and the Chiefs of Jakri being desirous of maintaining and strengthening the relations of peace and friendship which have for so long existed between them;

Her Britannic Majesty has named and appointed E. H. Hewett, Esq., Her Consul for the Bights of Benin and Biafra, to conclude a Treaty for this purpose.

The said E. H. Hewett, Esq., and the said Chiefs of Jakri have agreed upon and concluded the following Articles:—

ARTICLE I
Her Majesty the Queen of Great Britain and Ireland, & c, in compliance with the request of the Chiefs, and people of Jakri, hereby undertakes to extend to them, and to the territory under their authority and jurisdiction, Her gracious favour and protection.

ARTICLE II
The Chiefs of Jakri agree and promise to refrain from entering into any correspondence, Agreement, or Treaty with any foreign nation or Power, except with the knowledge and sanction of Her Britannic Majesty's Government.

ARTICLE III
It is agreed that full and exclusive jurisdiction, civil and criminal, over British subjects and their property in the territory of Jakri is reserved to Her Britannic Majesty, to be exercised by such Consular or other officers as Her Majesty shall appoint for that purpose.

The same jurisdiction is likewise reserved to Her Majesty in the said territory of Jakri over foreign subjects enjoying British protection, who shall be deemed to be included in the expression 'British Subject' throughout this Treaty.

ARTICLE IV

All disputes between the Chiefs of Jakri, or between them and British or foreign traders, or between the aforesaid Kings and Chiefs and neighbouring tribes, which cannot be settled amicably between the two parties, shall be submitted to the British Consular or other officers appointed by Her Britannic Majesty to exercise jurisdiction in Jakri territories for arbitration and decision, or for arrangement.

ARTICLE V

The Chiefs of Jakri hereby engage to assist the British Consular or other officers in the execution of such duties as may be assigned to them; and, further, to act upon their advice in matters relating to the administration of justice, the development of the resources of the country, the interests of commerce, or in any other matter in relation to peace, order, and good government, and the general progress of civilization.

ARTICLE VI

The subjects and citizens of all countries may freely carry on trade in every part of the territories of the Kings and Chiefs parties hereto, and may have houses and factories therein.

ARTICLE VII

All ministers of the Christian religion shall be permitted to reside and exercise their calling within the territories of the aforesaid Kings and Chiefs, who hereby guarantee to them full protection.

All forms of religious worship and religious ordinances may be exercised within the territories of the aforesaid Kings and Chiefs, and no hindrance shall be offered thereto.

ARTICLE VIII

If any vessels should be wrecked within the Jakri territories, the Chiefs will give them all the assistance in their power, will secure them from plunder, and also recover and deliver to the owners or agents all the property which can be saved.

If there are no such owners or agents on the spot, then the said property shall be delivered to the British Consular or other officer.

The Chiefs further engage to do all in their power to protect the persons and property of the officers, crew, and others on board such wrecked vessels.

All claims for salvage dues in such cases shall, if disputed, be referred to the British Consular or other officer for arbitration and decision.

ARTICLE IX

This Treaty shall come into operation, so far as may be practicable, from the date of its signature, except as regards Articles VI and VII which are to be left for negotiation on a future occasion.

Done in duplicate on board H.B. M.S. 'Flirt' anchored in Benin River this sixteenth day of July, 1884.

(Signed) Edward Hyde Hewett.

Nana	His × mark Governor	Chanomie	his × mark
Dudu	his × mark	Numa	his × mark
Ogree	his × mark	Fragonie	his × mark
Nafomie	his × mark	Etchie	his × mark
Mudwa	his × mark	Brigby	his × mark
Awalla	his × mark	Peggy	his × mark

Witness to above signatures:

(Signed) Theo. Hilliard
Chairman of Court of Equity.

Bibliography

In order to avoid the confusion sometimes posed by breaking up the sources into primary and secondary, it has been decided to divide this bibliography into two parts—Contemporary Sources, and Later Works. While the second part is in fact almost exclusively secondary sources, the first part cannot be said to be completely primary.

I. CONTEMPORARY SOURCES
A. ARCHIVAL MATERIAL

1. *Nigerian National Archives, Ibadan*

Cal. Prof. Papers: These are the records of the Oil Rivers, later Niger Coast, Protectorate with headquarters at Calabar. They include dispatches from the consuls to the British Foreign Office for the period 1885–99. More important than the dispatches, however, are reports dealing with specific districts or subjects. The particular heads to which reference has been made in this work are Cal. Prof. 6 to Cal. Prof. 10. Each of these is made up of a number of volumes.

C.S.O. Papers: These are records which have been collected from what used to be the office of the Chief Secretary to the Nigeria Government, Lagos and Enugu, and cover a large number of subjects. The bulk of the material is in files, not bound volumes. As can be seen from the body of the work a great deal of reference has been made to C.S.O. 26, a head which includes Annual Reports, Intelligence Reports, Tour Reports, Inspection Notes, Petitions and a host of other subjects. Reference has also been made to C.S.O. 1 and C.S.O. 12.

Kwalę Papers: Records collected from the District Office, Kwalę Division.

Warri Papers (War. Prof.): Records of the provincial administration with headquarters in Warri. The unfortunate destruction by fire in 1944 of the offices of the Resident of Warri has reduced very much both the size and the utility of this group of papers.

Ughelle Papers: These are records of the District Office, Ughelle. This group consists of hundreds of files numbered as they were opened each year. Included in this group are Annual Reports on the Warri Division, Ase sub-district, 'Jekri-Sobo' Division, 'Sobo' Division; Administrative officers' Handing Over Notes, Memoranda from District Officers to the Resident and other senior officers and vice-versa. This group constitutes an indispensable source of material for a study of the history of the Delta Province, especially since 1914.

2. *Public Records Office, London*

F.O. 84: *Slave Trade* (Vols 1002–2195): Correspondence to and from consular officials of the Oil Rivers Protectorate in the period 1856–92.

F.O. 2: *General Correspondence*: *African*: Niger Coast Protectorate Drafts and Dispatches for the years 1893–99.

F.O. 93: Protocols of Treaties, West Africa.

F.O. 403: Confidential Prints.

C.O. 520: Southern Nigeria Dispatches.

C.O. 588: Proclamations and Ordinances.

C.O. 591: Government Gazettes.

C.O. 592: Sessional Papers.

3. *C.M.S. Archives*

(Salisbury Square, London) Only the Niger Mission Papers were consulted.

4. *John Holt Papers*

Records of the firm of John Holt and Co Ltd., housed at the firms headquarters in Liverpool. Material on the Western section of the Niger Delta is extemely scanty. The files are arranged in 'Boxes' Box 1/6 and Box 7/14 are the only ones I found useful for this work.

B. PRINTED BOOKS

ADAMS, (CAPT.) JOHN. *Remarks on the Country Extending from Cape Palmas to the Congo*, London 1823.

BARBOT, JEAN. *A Description of the Coast of North and South Guinea*, London 1732.

BINDLOSS, H. *In the Niger Country*, London and Edinburgh 1898.

BLAKE, J. W. *European Beginnings In West Africa 1458–1578*, London 1937.

BOISRAGON, ALAN. *The Benin Massacre*, London 1703.

BOSMAN. *A New and Accurate Description of the Coast of Guinea*, London 1703.

GEARY, WILLIAM, N. M. *Nigeria Under British Rule*, London 1927.

JOHNSTON, SIR HARRY. *The Story of My Life*, New York 1923.

KINGSLEY, MARY H. *West African Studies*, London 1899.

LEONARD, A. G. *The Lower Niger And Its Tribes*, London 1906.

MOCKLER-FERRYMAN, A. F. *British Nigeria*, London 1902; *Up the Niger*, London 1892.

MOORE, WILLIAM. *A History of Itsekiri*, Stockwell 1936.

MOREL, E. D. *Nigeria : Its Peoples And Its Problems*, London 1911.

OWEN, W. F. N. *Narrative of Voyages to Explore the Shores of Africa, Arabia and Madagascar*, London 1833.

PEREIRA, DUARTE PACHECO. *Esmeraldo De Situ Orbis*, c. 1505 (H. T. Kimbles Translation—Hakluyt Society, Series II, Vol. LXXIX, London 1937)

PINNOCK, J. *Benin Concerning the Country, Inhabitants and Trade*, Liverpool 1897.

TALBOT, P. AMAURY. *The Peoples of Southern Nigeria*, Vol. I, London 1926.

THOMAS, M. W. *Anthropological Report on the Edo Speaking Peoples of Southern Nigeria* (2 vols.), London 1910.

C. ARTICLES

ALLEN, H. A. 'The Jekries, a Tough Race', *West African Review*, Vol. XXX, 1949.

COPLAND-CRAWFORD, W. E. B. 'Nigeria' *Manchester Geographical Society Journal*, Vol. XXXI, 1915.

GALLWEY, H. L. 'Nigeria in the Nineties', *Journal of the Royal African Society*, Vol. XXIV, 1930. 'Pioneering in Nigeria', *Proceedings of the Royal Geographical Society (Australasia)*, Vols. XVI–XVIII, 1914.

GRANVILLE, R. K. AND ROTH, F. N. 'Notes on the Jekris, Sobos and Ijos of the Warri District of the Nigeria Coast Protectorate', *Journal of the Royal Anthropological Society*, Vol. XXVIII, 1898.

HASTINGS, A. C. G. 'The Real Nigeria', *The National Review*, July 1927.

HICKLEY, LIEUT, J. D. 'An Account of the operations on the Benin River in August and September, 1894, *British United Services Journal*, Vol. XXXIX, 1894.

HUBBARD, J. W. 'The Isoko Country, S. Nigeria', *Journal of the Royal Geographical Society*, Vol. LXXVII, 1931.

NEVILLE, G. W. 'Nana Oloma of Benin', *Journal of the Royal African Society*, Vol. XIV, 1915.

THOMAS, W. M. 'On the Oil Rivers of West Africa', *Journal of the Royal Geographical Society*, Vol. XVII, 1872-3.

THOMSON, SIR GRAEME. 'Some Problems of Administration and Development in Nigeria', *Journal of the Royal African Society* Vol. XXVI 1926-7.

WELCH, J. W. 'Witchcraft and Christianity in the Niger Delta', *Church Overseas*, Vol. IV, 1931; 'An African Tribe In Transition', *International Review of Missions*, Vol. XX, 1931.

OFFICIAL PUBLICATIONS

British Parliamentary Papers: Various 'Command' Papers containing Annual Reports of the Niger Coast Protectorate and Southern Nigeria during the years 1898-1913.

NEWSPAPERS

Only *The Liverpool Review* (1887) and *The Nigerian Daily Times* (1932 and 1934) are cited in the work.

II. *LATER WORKS*

A. ORAL TRADITIONS

In the course of preparing this work, the author spent a total of some nine months in the field. Field work was only undertaken after the author had become reasonably acquainted with what documentary matter there is available. This line of action was adopted in order partly to familiarize him with the main events, and partly to enable him to draw up a list of the families which had been particularly involved in the history of the period. It was found useful to know this beforehand. Interviews were held both privately with individuals and publicly with the elders-in-council. Both types of interview were equally profitable. The author took rough notes at each interview. These notes were written out in full the night after while the memory was still fresh. Details of these interviews as well as of methodology can be found in Appendix I of the author's thesis (Itṣẹkiri-Urhobo Relations And The Establishment of British Rule, 1884–1936), deposited in the Library of the University of Ibadan.

B. BOOKS

ANENE, J. C. *Southern Nigeria In Transition* 1886–1906, Cambridge University Press 1966.

AJAYI, J. F. A. *Christian Missions In Nigeria 1841–1891*, Longmans 1965.

AYANDELE, E. A. *The Missionery Impact on Modern Nigeria 1842–1914*, Longmans 1966.

BANE, MARTIN J. *Catholic Pioneer In West Africa*, Dublin 1956.

BIOBAKU, S. O. *The Egba and Their Neighbours*, London 1957.

BRADBURY, R. E. AND LLOYD P. C. *The Benin Kingdom and Edo speaking Peoples of South Western Nigeria*, London 1957.

BURNS, A. C. *History of Nigeria*, London 1955.

COOK, A. N. *British Enterprise in Nigeria*, University of Pennsylvania Press 1943.

CROWDER, MICHAEL. *The Story of Nigeria*, London 1962.

DARYLL FORD AND G. I. JONES. *The Ibo and Ibibio Speaking Peoples of South-Eastern Nigeria*, London 1962.

DIKE, K. O. *Trade and Politics In the Niger Delta*, London 1956.

EGHAREVBA, JACOB. *A Short History of Benin*, Ibadan University Press 1960.

FLINT, J. E. *Sir George Goldie and the making of Nigeria*, London 1960.

FORTES M. AND EVANS PRITCHARD, E. E. *African Political Systems*, London 1961.

HUBBARD, J. W. *The Sobo of the Niger Delta*, Zaria 1951.

JONES, G. I. *The Trading States of the Oil Rivers*, London 1963.

OLIVER, R. *Sir Harry Johnston And The Scramble for Africa*, London 1959.

OMONEUKARIN, C. O. *Itsekiri Law And Custom*, Lagos 1942.

C. ARTICLES

ADERIBIGBE, A. B. 'The Ijebu Expedition, 1892: An Episode in the British Penetration of Nigeria Reconsidered', *Historians in Tropical Africa* (*Leverhume conference Proceedings*), September 1960.

AFIGBO, A. E. 'The Warrant Chief System in Eastern Nigeria: Direct or Indirect Rule?', *J.H.S.N.*, Vol. III, No 4, June 1967.

BIOBAKU, S. O. 'An Historical Sketch of the Peoples of Western Nigeria', *Odu*, No. 6, 1958.

LLOYD, P. C. 'The Portuguese in Warri', *Odu* No. 4, 1956; 'Captain Landolphe and the Compagnie D'OWhere et de Benin', *Odu*, No 5, 1957;
'Tribalism in Warri', *West African Institute of Social and Economic Research* (*Proceedings*), 1956;
'Nana Olomu, Governor of the River', *West Africa*, June 29, 1967;
'The Itsekiri In the Nineteenth Century', *Journal of African History*, Vol. IV, No 2, 1963.

RYDER, A. F. C. 'An Early Portuguese Voyage to the Forcados River', *J.H.S.N.*, Vol. I, No 4, 1959;
'Missionary Activity in the Kingdom of Warri to the Early Nineteenth Century', *J.H.S.N.*, Vol. II, No. 1, 1960;
'The Benin Missions', *J.H.S.N.*, Vol. II, No. 2, 1961.

SALUBI, A. 'The Establishment of British Rule in the Urhobo Country', *J.H.S.N.*, Vol. I, No. 3, 1958;
'The Origins of Sapele', *J.H.S.N.*, Vol. II, No. 1, 1960.

D. UNPUBLISHED THESES

AFIGBO, A. E. *The Warrant Chief System in Eastern Nigeria* (Ph.D., University of Ibadan 1964)

TAMUNO S. M. (now T. N.) *The Development and Consolidation of Imperial Government in Southern Nigeria, 1891–1914.* (Ph.D., University of London 1962)

Index

Index

Index

Kiagbodo, River, 2, 261
Kirk, Sir John, 135
Koko, 123
Kokori, 136
Kwalẹ, 139, 236, 356; and Eni ordeal, 38, 148; expedition, 151; Itsẹkiri disputes, 156; and palm oil trade, 66
Kwalẹ Appeal Court, 212, 218

Lagos, 115, 118, 120, 149, 185, 269
Landọlphe, Captain, 50, 55–6, 61
Lecky, Hugh, 108, 139–40
Leonard, Major, 4, 30
Liverpool Chamber of Commerce, 101
Lloyd, Dr. P. C., 48, 49, 56, 66, 69, 98, 100
Locke, A. F., 110, 113, 141
Louch and Co., Messrs. J. H., 76
Louis XVI, 55
Lugard, Sir Frederick, administration under, 185, 189, 195; and 'indirect' rule, 192, 193; Native Court system under, 189–90, 191, 197

Macauley, Herbert, 222
Macdonald, Sir Claude, establishment of Government posts by, 96, 127, 130; and import duties, 101, 127; and judicial system, 167; and Nana, 93, 95, 96, 100, 104, 121; official positions of, 4–5; penetration of Urhoboland under 92, 99, 133; and slavery, 95–6, 97; and Urhobo, 5
McLeod, Consul, 71
Macpherson constitution, 269
McTaggart, 142
Maddocks, H., 211
Madubi, 85
Mahins, 11
Matolo, 9–10
Maxwell, Mr. Justice, 215
Memese, 73
Memiafo, 209
Mendenez, Mr. Justice, 174
Minor Courts, 171–2, 173, see also Native Courts
Mockler-Ferryman A. F., 4–5
Mogba, 72, 73, 123, 170, 178
Monteleone, 54, 56
Moor, Sir Ralph, and Dọghọ, 188; and European traders, 99–100; and Native Courts, 166, 167, 183; and Royal Niger Company, 134–6, 137; penetration of Urhoboland under, 136, 147;

and rule through chiefs, 193; see also Nana
Moore, William, 11, 39, 186, 214
Mowarin, W. E., 268
Mowoe, Mukoro, 266–7
Mufeme, 69
Murphy, Mr., 195, 196

Nana, Chief, abilities of, 86, 88–9, 98, 104; and Abraka war, 89–90; allegations against, 94, 108, 110, 117, 118, 122; antedecents of, 69, 73; behaviour of 'boys' of, 88, 106, 111, 121, 124; blockade against, 113, 115; death of, 124; deportation of, 112, 117, 122–3; difficulties of, 110, 111; effect of old feuds on, 70, 78, 81, 118–19, 196; and Ẹku war, 81; escape of, 118; expansion of trade by, 85, 86, 103; fall of, 79; and 'free trade', 83–4, 104, 108, 110–11, 118; as Governor of the River, 81, 84, 90; home-coming of, 123–4; inheritance of, 81; loyalty to, 114, 115; and Macdonald mission, 94–5; and market disputes, 82, 118; mistrust of British by, 94, 107, 110, 112; opinions about, 80, 82, 86, 97, 98, 103, 104; power of, 87–8, 90, 92, 97, 99, 103–4, 107, 164; and rejection of Company rule, 95; and slavery, 88, 89, 90, 95, 105; and social reform, 95, 96, 100–1; and 'stoppages', 91–2, 104, 109, 111–12; surrender of, 118; and trade organisation, 87, 104, 124; and treaties, 42, 82–3, 90, 113, 122; trial of, 121–2; Urhobo disputes with, 89
Nana, Chief Newton Celleone, 85, 88
Nana town, 123
Napoma, 152
National Courts Proclamations, 168, 173, 174
Native Authorities, adjustments made to, 230; Dọghọ as, 193, 194, 195; establishment of, 228, 234; function of, 232, 234; and Native Administration, 221; Native Courts as, 193–4; recognised chiefs as, 193; and the Urhobo, 195, 196
Native Administration, and Dọghọ, 233; establishment of, 259; ethnic grouping within, 237–9, 259–60; local administration within, 237–9, 259–60; Native Courts as, 231; policy of, 228; proposed Jekri-Sobo Administration,

296

Index

Index

The Ibadan History Series

General Editor K. O. DIKE PH.D.

CHRISTIAN MISSIONS IN NIGERIA 1841–1891
The Making of a New Élite
by J. F. A. AJAYI, Professor of History, University of Ibadan

The first major study of Christian missionary activity in Nigeria, which also touches on Sierra Leone, Ghana and Dahomey. In discussing every aspect of the missions' work and its effects, the author stresses the emergence of a new élite as their most crucial contribution to Nigerian history.

Contents: Christianity and Civilisation; The Return of the Exiles; Missionaries, Traders, and Consuls; The Mission and the State; Civilisation around the Mission House; Towards Selfgovernment in Church and State; Bishop Crowther, 1864–77; The Turning of the Tide. Appendix. Bibliography. Index.

Demy 8vo   xvi + 317 pages   Maps, Plates   Cased $6.50

THE ZULU AFTERMATH
A Nineteenth-Century Revolution in Bantu Africa
by J. D. OMER-COOPER, Professor of History, University of Zambia

A detailed study of the factors involved in the emergence of the militaristic Zulu Kingdom and its far-reaching consequences in early nineteenth-century central and southern Africa.

Contents: Bantu South Africa before the Mfecane; The Zulu Kingdom; The Birth of the Swazi Nation; Soshangane and the Empire of Gaza; The Ngoni Invasion of East Central Africa; The Invasion of the Highveld by Mpangazita and Matiwane; Moshesh and the Basuto Nation; The Career of Sebetwane and the History of the Kololo; Mzilikazi and the Ndebele; The Devastation of Natal and the Flight to the South; The History of the Fingo People;

The Mfecane in the History of South and East Central Africa.
Bibliography. Index.

Demy 8vo   xiv + 208 pages   Map, Plates   Cased $5.95

*The two titles above are published by Northwestern University Press,
1735 Benson Avenue, Evanston, Illinois 60201*

THE MISSIONARY IMPACT ON MODERN NIGERIA
1842–1914
A Political and Social Analysis
by E. A. AYANDELE, Department of History, University of Ibadan

*The emphasis in this work is on the reactions of various sections of
the African community—chiefs, educated Africans, ordinary people
and slaves—to missionary activity and also to other agencies linked
with it, in particular the colonial administration.*

Contents: The Beginnings, 1842–1875; Missionary Enterprise
and the Pacification of Yoruba-land, 1875–1900; The Missions and
'Southern' Nigerian Politics and Society, 1875–1900; The Triumph
of Gin; The Missionary Impact on Society. Bibliography. Index.

Demy 8vo   xx + 393 pages   Maps, Plates   Cased $7.50

THE SOKOTO CALIPHATE
by MURRAY LAST, Northern History Research Scheme, Ahmadu
  Bello University, Zaria

*An account, based largely on nineteenth-century Arabic documents
from Sokoto, of the origins and history of the caliphate until the coming
of the British in 1903. It includes, in particular, a study of the rôle of
the vizierate in maintaining the administrative and the spiritual
position of the caliphate.*

Contents: The Establishment of Dār al Islām in Sokoto 1754–
1817: 1168–1232 (The Community; The Jihad; The Early Caliphate); The Maintenance of Dār al Islām in Sokoto 1817–1903:
1232–1320 (The Consolidation of the Caliphate 1817–1859: 1232–
1276; The Composition of the Caliphate; The Period of Security

and Settlement 1859–1903: 1276–1320); The Vizierate in Sokoto 1804–1903: 1218–1320 (The Viziers, The work of the Viziers); Concluding Remarks. Bibliography. Index. Genealogies.

Demy 8vo   lxxxii + 280 pages   Maps, Plates   Cased $8.50

BRITAIN AND THE CONGO QUESTION 1885–1913
by S. J. S. COOKEY, Department of History, The University, Nsukka

Beginning from the emergence of the Congo Free State under the private rule of Leopold II of Belgium, this book examines Belgian interests and the consequences for the Congolese. The origins, motives and organisation of the Congo Reform movement in Britain are revealed for the first time, and its influence on British and Belgian diplomacy.

Contents: Early Evidence on Congo Maladministration; Origins of British Intervention; The Casement Inquiry and its Aftermath; The Congo Commission of Inquiry and the Royal Manifesto; International Reactions on the Eve of Annexation; the Belgian Solution; Non-Recognition; Recognition. Appendices. Bibliography. Index.

Demy 8vo   xvi + 340 pages   Map   Cased $6.75

BENIN AND THE EUROPEANS 1485–1897
by A. F. C. Ryder, Professor of History, University of Ibadan

A study in depth of European relationships with a West African kingdom, to which, in the course of four hundred years, most of the commercial and colonial powers of Europe turned their attention. The author's research has embraced oral tradition, art and artifacts as well as documentary material in Portuguese, Italian, Dutch and British archives.

Contents: The Benin Kingdom—Historical Perspective; Era of Portuguese Monopoly; English and Dutch Beginnings; the Capuchin Missions; The Dutch at Ughoton; The Slave-Trade Era; British Encroachment. Appendices. Bibliography. Index.

Demy 8vo   Maps, Plates   Cased $8.50

In Preparation

THE INTERNATIONAL BOUNDARIES OF NIGERIA
1885–1960
The Framework of an Emergent African Nation
by J. C. ANENE, Professor of History in the University, Nsukka

A pioneer work in its field. The author has studied, from field-work, oral tradition and primary documentary sources the types of indigenous frontiers—not necessarily stable—which existed before European boundary intervention, and objectively assesses the results of that intervention and its consequences for modern Nigeria.

Contents: Introduction; The Atlantic Littoral and the Problems of the Hinterland; The Eastern Boundary—I; The Eastern Boundary—II; The Western Boundary—I; The Western Boundary—II; The Northern Boundary; Conclusion. Bibliography, Index.

Demy 8vo   xi + 300 pages   Maps   Cased

POWER AND DIPLOMACY IN NORTHERN NIGERIA
1800–1906
The Sokoto Caliphate and its Enemies
by R. A. ADELEYE, Department of History, University of Ibadan

An analysis, based upon an exhaustive study of Arabic and English manuscript material, of the internal and external factors which led to the fall of Sokoto and the final destruction of the Caliphate.

Contents: Establishment and Consolidation of the Caliphate 1804–1880; Elements of Stability and Instability 1880–1900; Era of Trade and Treaties 1879–1894; Encirclement, Diplomacy and Hostility 1894–1899; Fall of Southern Emirates and the Invasion of Bauchi and Gombe 1900–1902; Fall of Sokoto; Final Destruction of Caliphate. Appendices. Sources. Bibliography. Index.

Demy 8vo   Maps   Cased